THE SOCIAL CONSTRUCTION O
1870–1990

The Social Construction of Democracy, 1870–1990

Edited by

George Reid Andrews
Professor of History and UCIS Research
Professor of International Studies
University of Pittsburgh

and

Herrick Chapman
Associate Professor of History and French Civilization
New York University

 NEW YORK UNIVERSITY PRESS
Washington Square, New York

First published in the U.S.A. in 1995 by
NEW YORK UNIVERSITY PRESS
Washington Square
New York, N.Y. 10003

Library of Congress Cataloging-in-Publication Data
The social construction of democracy, 1870–1990 / edited by George
Reid Andrews and Herrick Chapman.
p.   cm.
Papers presented at a conference held at Carnegie Mellon
University and the University of Pittsburgh on May 3–4, 1992.
Includes index.
ISBN 0–8147–1508–7
1. Democracy—History—Congresses. 2.   Social history—19th
century—Congresses. 3. Social history—20th century—Congresses.
I. Andrews, George Reid, 1951– . II. Chapman, Herrick.
JC421.S559   1995
321.8—dc20   94–47398
                                                          CIP

Printed in Great Britain

Contents

Acknowledgements

This volume had its beginnings in the Pittsburgh Center for Social History's Working Group on State and Society. Originally coordinated by W. Andrew Achenbaum and George Reid Andrews, and after 1987 by Andrews and Herrick Chapman, the group brought together historians, sociologists, political scientists, and other scholars to discuss possible intersections and points of contact between political and social history. By 1990 the group had decided to organize a conference on this theme, focusing on the problematic of twentieth-century democracy.

The event was held on May 3–4, 1992, on the campuses of Carnegie Mellon University and the University of Pittsburgh. A number of people were instrumental in its realization. We are grateful to Peter Karsten and Peter N. Stearns, at that time the co-directors of the Center for Social History, and to Burkhart Holzner, director of the University of Pittsburgh's Center for International Studies, for their support and encouragement throughout the project. Efficient and cheerful logistical assistance was provided by Glenna Burke, Gina Hames, Judy Kane, Judy Lamonde, and Mary Ann Varhola. Financial support was provided by the Departments of History at Carnegie Mellon University and the University of Pittsburgh, by Duquesne University, by the Center for International Studies at the University of Pittsburgh, and within the Center for International Studies, by the Asian Studies Program, the Center for Latin American Studies, the Russian and East European Studies Program, and the West European Studies Program.

In addition to the individuals represented in this volume, a number of scholars took part in the sessions. They include Seymour Drescher, Maurine Greenwald, Van Beck Hall, Donna Harsch, Eiko Ikegami, Katherine Lynch, John Markoff, Paul Mason, Holly Mayer, John Modell, Alberta Sbragia, and Peter Stearns. Their comments and insights contributed greatly to the success of the event, as did those of the audience. It was a most rewarding and stimulating two days, and we hope that at least some of the energy and excitement of the discussions is captured in the following essays.

Notes on the Contributors

Gary D. Allinson is Ellen Bayard Weedon Professor of History at the University of Virginia, and author of *Japanese Urbanism* (1975) and *Suburban Tokyo* (1979).

George Reid Andrews is Professor of History at the University of Pittsburgh, and author of *The Afro-Argentines of Buenos Aires, 1800–1900* (1980) and *Blacks and Whites in São Paulo, Brazil, 1888–1988* (1991).

Herrick Chapman is Associate Professor of History and French Civilization at New York University, and author of *State Capitalism and Working-Class Radicalism in the French Aircraft Industry* (1990) and with Peter N. Stearns of *European Society in Upheaval: Social History Since 1700*, 3rd edn (1992).

Diane E. Davis is Associate Professor of Sociology and Historical Studies at the New School for Social Research, and author of *Urban Leviathan: Mexico City in the Twentieth Century* (1994).

Geoff Eley is Professor of History at the University of Michigan, and author of *Reshaping the German Right: Radical Nationalism and Political Change after Bismarck* (1980), *Peculiarities of German History* (with David G. Blackbourn; 1980), and *From Unification to Nazism: Reinterpreting the German Past* (1986).

Daniel James is Associate Professor of History at Duke University, and author of *Resistance and Integration: Peronism and the Argentine Working Class* (1986).

Samuel P. Hays is Distinguished Service Professor Emeritus of History at the University of Pittsburgh, and author of *Response to Industrialism, 1885–1914* (1957), *Conservation and the Gospel of Efficiency: The Progressive Conservation Movement, 1890–1920* (1957), *American Political History as Social Analysis* (1979), and *Beauty, Health and Permanence: Environmental Politics in the United States, 1955–1985* (1987).

Earl Lewis is Associate Professor of History and Afro-American Studies at the University of Michigan, and author of *In Their Own Interests: Race, Class, and Power in Twentieth-Century Norfolk, Virginia* (1991).

Robert G. Moeller is Professor of History at the University of California-Irvine, and author of *German Peasants and Agrarian Politics, 1914–1924* (1986) and *Protecting Motherhood: Women and the Family in the Politics of Postwar West Germany* (1993).

Philip Nord is Associate Professor of History at Princeton Univerity, and author of *Paris Shopkeepers and the Politics of Resentment* (1986).

Richard Oestreicher is Associate Professor of History at the University of Pittsburgh, and author of *Solidarity and Fragmentation: Working People and Class Consciousness in Detroit, 1875–1900* (1986).

Richard J. Smethurst is Professor of History at the University of Pittsburgh, and author of *A Social Basis for Prewar Japanese Militarism: The Army and the Rural Community* (1974) and *Agricultural Development and Tenancy Disputes in Japan, 1870–1940* (1986).

Gale Stokes is Professor of History at Rice University, and author of *Legitimacy through Liberalism: Vladimir Jovanović and the Transformation of Serbian Politics* (1975), *Politics as Development: The Emergence of Political Parties in Nineteenth-Century Serbia* (1990), and *The Walls Came Tumbling Down: The Collapse of Communism in Eastern Europe* (1993).

Charles Tilly is University Distinguished Professor of Sociology and Historical Studies, and Director of the Center for Studies of Social Change, at the New School for Social Research. His many publications include *The Vendée* (1974), *As Sociology Meets History* (1981), *Big Structures, Large Processes, Huge Comparisons* (1985), *The Contentious French* (1986), *Coercion, Capital and European States* (1990), and *European Revolutions, 1492–1992* (1993).

Barbara Weinstein is Associate Professor of History at the State University of New York-Stony Brook, and author of *The Amazon Rubber Boom, 1850–1920* (1983).

The Social Construction of Democracy, 1870–1990: An Introduction

George Reid Andrews and Herrick Chapman

The decade of the 1980s was ushered in by two seemingly unrelated events in two small, relatively obscure countries. In August 1980, Polish workers, organized under the banner of the Solidarity movement, launched a general strike demanding the creation of trade unions independent of the Communist regime. Three months later, in Uruguay, voters overwhelmingly rejected a draft constitution which would have formalized the military regime in power in that country since 1973.

Both events represented defiance of well entrenched authoritarian governments by thoroughly repressed and dominated societies. As such, they were almost entirely unexpected. Even more surprising were their outcomes: in both countries, gradual transition over the course of the 1980s from authoritarian regimes to electoral democracy. During that decade, however, surprises became the norm: between 1980 and 1990 dictatorships of the right and left were replaced by elected civilian governments in most of Eastern Europe, the Soviet Union, much of Latin America, and in Pakistan and the Philippines. Longstanding dictatorships in sub-Saharan Africa faced increasing internal opposition, and the white-controlled government of South Africa began to prepare for a transition to majority rule. By 1990, among major world powers, only China had succeeded in repressing its citizens' demands for democracy.

The 1980s thus witnessed a dramatic world-wide wave of democratization. But it was not the first such wave. At the turn of the century, a series of electoral reforms had greatly expanded male suffrage in Europe and had begun to admit women to the polls as well. Increases in suffrage were more modest in Latin America; still, property restrictions on voting were struck down in Brazil and Chile, and universal male suffrage put into effect in Argentina and Uruguay. Mexico's failure to respond to popular demands for electoral reform was the immediate catalyst for the revolution of 1910, and one of the motives for the writing of a new constitution in 1917. Perhaps the boldest experiment in electoral rule took place, not in

1

the West, but in Japan, where the Constitution of 1889 instituted restricted male suffrage and a national parliament where neither had existed before.

A second wave of democratization occurred in the years immediately following the Second World War. Civilian democracy was restored in the defeated Axis nations and in such major Latin American countries as Argentina and Brazil. Democratic governance was further expanded by the creation of parliamentary regimes in newly independent countries in Asia and, in the 1950s and 1960s, in Africa. While most of the nation-states created at that time subsequently succumbed to authoritarianism, the most important of them, India, remains today the world's largest electoral regime.

Political participation has thus expanded dramatically over the course of the twentieth century. And that expansion has taken place under conditions which have shown some marked similarities across countries. Industrial development and urban growth enlarged the ranks of working- and middle-class groups demanding a greater role in politics. Women made similar demands, which were strengthened by their increasing participation in national economic life. These calls for expanded participation were asserted against state structures which almost everywhere were growing in size and importance as bureaucracies expanded and administrative functions proliferated. And since 1945 those nation-states, and the populations which they govern, have been tied ever more tightly into an international division of labor and, until the late 1980s, a bipolarization of international politics.

Despite these commonalities, neither the pace nor the manner nor the outcomes of democratization have been uniform from country to country. While some countries have maintained relatively stable democratic institutions over the course of the century, others have experienced one or more episodes of authoritarian rule. Some nations have expanded the terms of participation through parliamentary and legislative channels; others have had to undergo wrenching civil wars or revolutions; still others have had democratic reforms imposed on them by external forces. And of course the specific terms of participation, and the institutions through which it is channeled, have varied enormously from country to country.

How have national democracies formed and developed over the course of the twentieth century? How have political mobilization and popular demands "from below" interacted with institutional reforms and policies "from above" to produce the expansion, or contraction, of popular political participation over time? In what ways have the institutions and programs of given democratic regimes determined the forms and avenues of such participation? And ultimately, what patterns of interaction between state institutions and social groups seem to favor, or impede, the strengthening and expanding of democratic governance?

The goal of this volume is to explore these questions in a number of national settings, in an effort to construct comparative explanations of how and why political participation has changed as it has from the late nineteenth century to the present. Our initial inspiration for such an inquiry is Barrington Moore's classic text, *Social Origins of Dictatorship and Democracy*.[1] Beginning with the establishment of representative political institutions in seventeenth-century Britain, and proceeding through a series of comparative cases in Europe, North America, and Asia, Moore argued that the creation (or absence) of democratic institutions in each country was largely determined by the interactions among landowning nobilities, urban bourgeoisies, and peasantries, and how those social classes negotiated the transition from a subsistence-oriented agrarian society to a commercialized, market economy. This present volume of essays employs a similarly class-based approach, though modified in three ways.

First, we intend to look, not at the origins of democracy in previous centuries, but rather at democracy's travails from the 1870s through the present. For all of the countries which we will be examining, this was a period of intensifying international flows of investment, commerce, and ideas, and, partly as a result of those flows, of rapid industrial and urban growth. This period requires both a close attention to international influences on the development of national democracies, and a broadening of Moore's analytical focus on lords, peasants, and capitalist bourgeoisies to include new social classes: rural proletarians, urban workers, and urban and rural middle classes.

Second, in examining those classes and their evolving interactions over time, we want to use the findings and insights of social history to move beyond Moore's macro-level, structural style of inquiry. In recent years social historians have suggested a number of ways in which class analysis, and the analysis of political change, can be expanded and enriched. Gender, ethnic, and racial divisions introduce further complexities into the class structure of societies, and into those societies' struggles for expanded political participation. Popular culture, mentalities, and national and religious symbols helped define the terms of struggles for popular sovereignty, and were themselves affected by the outcomes of those struggles.

Third, some of the best work in social history has focused on the reciprocal interactions between national states and social groups. Most of this research and writing is based on local-level case studies; a handful of more ambitious studies synthesize extensive primary and secondary research to explain events and developments at the national level.[2] Whether it looks at nation-states or at localities, this work suggests the multiple ways in which communities, families, classes, and other social groups have been affected in different times and places by political ideologies, state policies, and the structure and character of political regimes. And it also makes clear how the actions and behavior of those groups have had direct and powerful consequences for the political systems in which they live – as evidenced most recently by the democratic movements of the 1980s, and the startling collapse of the European, Asian, and Latin American dictatorships.

These efforts to combine political and social history by "fusing history from above with history from below" suggest ways for realizing an analytic goal which in recent years has been often invoked, but rarely achieved: to focus intensively on the ongoing interplay between states and social groups over time.[3] During the 1980s, and partly in response to the rise of social history, historians, political scientists and sociologists argued for more state-centered modes of analysis, that is, approaches which take seriously the role of state structures, legal systems, and government actors in shaping society.[4] This healthy corrective to society-centered views of historical change runs the danger, however, of producing a return to the narrow forms of institutional determinism against which social history was itself a reaction. Clearly what is required is a "greater theoretical [and, we might add, empirical] integration of the two obviously non-autonomous spheres: state and society."[5] To achieve this integration, historians must not only examine the interaction between political regimes and social movements; they must also investigate conflicts within state institutions, and within social groups, and then explore how all three types of interaction – between state and society and within both domains – led to evolving forms of political action and new forms of political participation. Only such a trifocal approach can capture the dynamics of the creation, transformation, and at times the destruction of democratic regimes since the late nineteenth century. Moreover, historians must also track these interactions over relatively lengthy periods of time in order to see how social groups shaped policies and how the implementation of policies in turn forced groups to modify their goals, strategies, and internal structures.

With these several modifications of Barrington Moore's approach – the shift in historical period, the linking of macro- and micro- level analysis, and the close attention to state–society interaction – we hope to explain the historical process by which state institutions and social groups and movements interacted to create political systems based on the principle of popular sovereignty. We have chosen to call this process the social construction of democracy.

It is important to make clear what we mean by both terms: "social construction" and "democracy." For the latter, our starting point is the essential formal features of a democratic regime: broad-based suffrage, free and open elections, freedom of speech and assembly, the rule of law, government accountability to parliament, and an independent judiciary. It is the effort to construct full-fledged formal democracy – and the failure to do so in many countries through much of the twentieth century – that the essays of this volume seek to explain. In doing so, however, the essays go behind the struggles to build formal democratic institutions to investigate less formal changes in people's political thought and action. Theorists of democracy have long made the distinction between formal and substantive democracy, that is, between constitutions and institutions, on the one hand, and genuine habits of political participation, on the other.[6] Several essays stress how informal practices at the grassroots – the organizational life of religious fraternities in France, for example, or of the Solidarity movement in Poland – later influenced the way politicians and parties structured new democratic regimes. Other essays stress the reverse – how innovations in formal democratic institutions reshaped the character of political participation at the grassroots.

In both cases, democracy implies continuous interaction between formal institutions and ever-evolving practices of popular participation. Democracy also means struggle and disagreement over the very meaning of the word. The definition of democracy itself has been contested over time, and historians must pay careful attention to what different actors at different times had in mind when they invoked the term.[7] To activists in the American civil rights movement of the 1960s, democracy connoted racial equality in a way that it had not to Jacksonian democrats a century and a quarter before. Dissidents in Eastern Europe in the 1980s associated democracy with a market economy much more readily than did left-wing radicals in Western European resistance movements during the Second World War who questioned the very compatibility of capitalism and democracy, and for whom political democracy and social democracy went hand in hand.

Meanings, understandings, language, and values are thus an inescapable part of democratic theory and practice. Politics and state-building are inherently cultural activities, collective processes of conferring authority. Constructing democracy requires nurturing a particular kind of political culture, a complex web of symbolic actions and understandings, even misunderstandings, that give meaning and justification to the otherwise highly abstract notions of "popular sovereignty," "popular participation," and "democratic representation." As Edmund Morgan reminds us in his studies of the English and American revolutions, all these notions are to some extent fictions.[8] Nowhere do citizens truly enjoy conditions of political equality, nor do representatives speak fully on behalf of their constituents. Few elections completely escape subtle (or not so subtle) forms of manipulation. Yet in most stable democratic regimes enough people come to believe in the fiction of popular sovereignty, or find the fiction close enough to reality, to endow the state with the mantle of "democratic" legitimacy. A democratic constitution, in short, important as it has been to the stability of many democratic states, has never been enough. Democracy requires a host of cultural practices – habits of mind, rituals of participation, forms of dialogue between ruler and ruled – that make large numbers of people across generations believe in the meaningfulness of basic democratic principles.

Still, by "social construction of democracy" we mean something different and distinct from the "cultural construction of democracy." Without denying the power of words and symbols to inspire human actions, we wish to keep our central focus on people in the past as complex social actors, people who are more than mere agents of particular cultural values or material interests. A cultural approach in the narrow sense places too much emphasis on the invention and diffusion of ideas and discourses, and too little on the social and political processes that explain *why* democratic ideas and institutions take hold (or lose hold) when they do. We also question the notion that democracy requires the creation of one particular kind of political culture, a unitary system of values with a logic of its own. Real existing democracy in the twentieth century has taken a wide variety of forms, especially in terms of political culture. Voting, for example, acquired different kinds of significance and became associated with different kinds of local custom in one-party Mexico than in multi-party France and Italy. If in Japan the emperor retained an important role in legitimizing the state, and in Fifth Republic France the presidency acquired a monarchical aura, the "imperial presidency" became an epithet in the United States. The construction of democracy, in short, has involved many kinds of cultural practices which have taken a variety of forms in particular societies at different times. By focusing on the social, we seek to look carefully at how specific actors – individuals, groups, organizations – create and sustain these cultural practices within and outside the state.

THE ESSAYS

The volume consists of fifteen essays organized into five sections. All of the essays save two – Gale Stokes's examination of Eastern Europe since the Second World War, and Charles Tilly's comparative essay – examine individual countries. Four nations – Brazil, France, Germany, and Japan – receive the attention of two authors each; one, the United States, is the subject of three essays; two – Argentina and Mexico – are the subject of individual essays. Four of the five sections deal with specific periods and themes; Tilly's essay stands alone in a fifth and final section.

Part One: Industrialization, Urbanization, and Nation-Building from the 1870s to the Great Depression

By 1900 Western Europe and the United States were in the grip of the second industrial revolution, Japan had embarked on a program of national economic development, and processing and light consumer industries were in place in Mexico and southern South America. The rise of industry was directly linked to rapid urban growth, and the expansion of urban working and middle classes. This in turn raised crucial questions concerning the terms on which these new urban classes were to be admitted to political participation.

Philip Nord focuses on urban professionals, tradespeople and shopkeepers in nineteenth-century France and their struggles from the 1850s through the 1880s to reduce state control of their corporate associations: lay religious organizations, the bar, chambers of commerce, and universities. These struggles cemented the urban middle class's commitment to a "civic culture" which provided the ideological and symbolic underpinnings of the Third Republic (1870–1940). And as republican activists gradually won control of their civic organizations, those entities provided an institutional base from which to organize a broader campaign for power within the state. As a result, the dominance of the conservative elites who had shaped French politics and public life during the first half of the century declined sharply during the Third Republic – which helps explain those elites' embrace of Pétainist authoritarianism in 1940.

Liberal reforms had a similarly alienating effect on conservative elites in Argentina. Daniel James examines the effects of the Sáenz Peña law of 1912, which guaranteed universal male suffrage and the secret ballot. Conservatives agreed to the reform because of their fear of working- and middle-class mobilization, which was taking place outside the formal political system and asserting itself in the form of strikes and civil violence. They were also confident of their ability to mobilize a mass-based conservative movement. Such confidence proved misplaced. Instead, the new system of voting promptly brought the opposition Radical Party to power and during the 1920s produced a new cadre of professional politicians who began to displace the "gentlemen" politicians of the landowning oligarchy. Frustrated by their inability to compete effectively under these conditions, conservatives supported the military coup of 1930, which ushered in a half-century (1930–1983) of oscillation between authoritarian and elected regimes.

Conservative elites – in this case, dissident warlords who overthrew the Tokugawa Shogunate and established the Meiji regime in 1868 – played an even more activist role in Japan, as Richard Smethurst shows. Seeking to promote political and economic modernization, the Meiji oligarchs instituted a system of elected local and regional assemblies and, in 1889, a national parliament. The goal of the oligarchs was to retain power in their own hands; but during the early decades of the 1900s, party competition and social mobilization sparked by economic growth and development exerted increasing pressure on the oligarchs to open the political system yet further. By 1925 this pressure culminated in the enactment of universal male suffrage; and had it not been for the economic crisis of the Great Depression, Smethurst argues, electoral democracy might very well have survived in Japan through the 1930s. As it was, the experience of pre-war democracy greatly facilitated the work of the Allied occupation, providing a base of both personnel and experience on which to construct a post-war electoral regime.

Geoff Eley presents a similar argument for Germany. That nation's descent into Nazism during the 1930s has tended to blind historians to the vigor of its parliamentary institutions during the Wilhelmine period, as measured in terms of electoral participation, party competition, and the increasing acceptance by all classes of the efficacy and legitimacy of the parliamentary process. As in Argentina and France, conservative elites were weakest in their adherence to democratic norms, while members of the urban middle and working classes were strongest. But those elites made no effort during this period to undercut the constitutional arrangements of the *Kaiserreich*, with the result that the turn-of-the-century flourishing of competitive electoral politics which one sees in Argentina, France, and Japan was evident in Germany as well. Democracy fell in the 1930s, not because of the weakness of a parliamentary tradition, but because of the political consequences of the First World War and the Depression.

The only one of our national cases in which popular participation was not expanding during this period, it seems, was the United States. The golden age of American democracy is to be found, argues Richard Oestreicher, not in the 1890s and early 1900s, but rather during the first half of the 1800s, when an ideology and practice of universal white male suffrage enjoyed unquestioned hegemony in national politics. By the end of the century, urban electoral reforms aimed at reducing the voting weight of the immigrant population, and the disfranchisement of blacks and poor whites in the South, had substantially reduced national rates of electoral participation. Local and state governments also imposed a series of restrictions on public meetings and demonstrations, while state and federal courts severely limited the workers' right to strike.

The experience of the United States contrasts strikingly with that of the other cases, in two ways. First, while parliamentary systems took stronger hold and suffrage expanded in Europe, Latin America, and Japan, political participation suffered severe inroads in the United States, which were only partially compensated for by the inclusion of women in the polity. Second, unlike the European, Latin American, and Asian cases considered here, the United States' electoral regime managed to survive the world-wide epidemic of right-wing authoritarianism in the 1930s. Even France, a relatively stable democracy in the midst of the Depression, succumbed to authoritarian rule after the defeat of 1940. We will return to these contrasts below. In the meantime, this part demonstrates both how widespread, and at the same time how tenuous, the growth of democracy proved to be during this period.

Part Two: Creating Single-Party Dominance 1930–1960

Multi-party electoral competition is not the only form through which political participation can take place. One-party states offering varying levels of political rights and liberties, and more competitive systems nevertheless dominated by a single party, offer possible alternatives to multi-party regimes. This part examines two such cases in the years immediately preceding and following the Second World War: "guardian democracy" in Japan, and "uncommon democracy" in Mexico.

Gary Allinson agrees with Smethurst that Japan's experience of pre-war democracy provided a base on which to build a new electoral regime after 1945. He argues, in fact, that the tendency of scholars to divide Japanese history into pre- and post-1945 periods, and to see the latter as shaped mainly by the Allied occupation, has led them to neglect the strong continuities between pre- and post-war social and political structures. Allinson focuses on several such features which contributed directly to the Liberal Democratic Party's domination of the post-war Japanese state. These include: the close ties between Japan's business and bureaucratic elites; the weakness both of organized labor and of the urban middle class; the continuing strength of the farm lobby; and a hegemonic ideology of communal solidarity, expressed in terms of the village and the family. All of these factors, when combined with the economic growth of the post-war period, formed the basis for conservative hegemony and a "guardian democracy" which ruled uncontested until the electoral upset of 1993.

Diane Davis's essay on Mexico finds the roots of one-party rule, not in longstanding historical continuities, but rather in specific interactions and negotiations between the ruling revolutionary party, army officers, and civic organizations representing the urban middle class. Under President Lázaro Cárdenas (1934–1940), the party (founded in 1929 and reorganized in 1938 as the Partido de la Revolución Mexicana, or PRM) based its popular support on concessions and appeals to peasants and organized labor. This badly alienated members of the middle class and the military; and following the elections of 1940, the conservative Avila Camacho administration negotiated the entry of both groups into the party, granting them institutional weight equal to that of the PRM's peasant and worker wings. This integrated the urban middle class and the military into a ruling populist coalition in a way that no other Latin American nation ever achieved. Thus while middle classes elsewhere in the region acquiesced in military coups and the overturning of civilian democracies in the 1960s and 1970s, Mexico has remained a stable electoral regime to the present.

Part Three: Democratic Movements 1945–1990

Since the Second World War, democratic movements have flourished, if sometimes only fleetingly, across the globe. In well established constitutional democracies, such as the United States or France, marginalized groups have sought to win a more meaningful voice for themselves in the polity; in authoritarian states from Poland to the Philippines, people have struggled to create democratic regimes; and in one-party democracies, reformers have tried to establish the political space for alternative parties. At first glance, it would seem easier to create a social movement to expand an existing democracy than to tackle the awesome challenge of toppling an authoritarian regime. But neither effort is easy, and indeed it can even be argued that democratic institutions have often formed unexpected obstacles to grassroots mobilization, while authoritarianism has provided unexpected stimuli or openings for democratic movements.

The difficulties involved in building a democratic movement, and the ingenuity required to surmount them, come through clearly in all three essays in this section. Earl Lewis examines how African Americans drew on the political and cultural tradition of American democracy, and on their own experiences of racial subordination, to create the civil rights movement of the post-war era. Each of the major initiatives in the civil rights struggle – the suits brought by the legal division of the NAACP, the consumer boycotts against segregation in the South, the battle for voting rights – manifested a vision, widely shared by African Americans, that the basic principles and institutions of American democracy could be used to overcome the injustice of racial oppression and in so doing be redeemed. Lewis pays considerable attention to the cultural dynamics of the movement – how the "double-voiced" qualities of civil rights songs, for example, expressed clearer meanings to African Americans than to whites who heard them "on the outside." These texts illustrate how much the social construction of both democracy and race go hand in hand in America.

George Reid Andrews explores the role of racial politics in democratic state-building in another context, Brazil in the 1970s and 1980s. During the period of gradual transition from military dictatorship to civilian democracy (1974–1985), Afro-Brazilian activists succeeded in undermining the semi-official ideology of "racial democracy," which portrays Brazil as a nation free of racial oppression or inequality. But they failed in their efforts to mobilize the black poor and working class, in whose name they claimed to speak. Middle-class activists remained too remote from their mass constituents, and the patron–client relations on which the poor and working class had long depended remained too entrenched, to make an autonomous black mass movement feasible in the 1980s. If by the end of the 1980s the black movement had succeeding in placing the issue of racial equality on the public agenda, it had not provoked the government to take major steps to address the issue nor enlarged the scope of Brazilian democracy through the creation of an independent black electorate.

Gale Stokes also emphasizes the limited social reach of recent democratic movements in his article on the revolutions in Eastern Europe in 1989. He argues that, with the notable exception of Poland, the opposition movements that stepped in to occupy the space created by the collapse of Soviet hegemony lacked "organizational thickness" and strong roots in society. Not that the socialist regimes of the eastern bloc had a popular following by the 1980s. On the contrary, as Stokes describes, after the failed reform efforts of the late 1960s and the destruction of the Prague Spring, these regimes hollowed out with "utter moral rot" and turned into "empty husks ready to be blown away with the first strong winds." But because these regimes remained both repressive and resistant to reform, dissidents were forced into a form of opposition which was explicitly anti-political and anti-organizational in character. They turned their backs on political life and tried to live a life of individual integrity in an inchoate civil society.

Only in Poland did the anti-politics of the 1970s evolve into a social movement, Solidarity. Elsewhere in Eastern Europe few people had much experience with autonomous participation in public life; thus the social construction of democracy began only during and after the revolutions of 1989. Democracy in these countries remains a fragile experiment, threatened by economic dislocation and the passions of ethnic nationalism.

Part Four: Democracy and the Welfare State 1930–1990

The welfare state need not be a harbinger of democracy. Autocratic governments feel pressure to sustain social security systems, fund hospitals and schools, and make credible claims to be caring for the public welfare. And the longevity of non-democratic socialist states rested in large part on their provision of pensions, medical services, and other social benefits to all citizens. Yet there is no gainsaying the importance of the welfare state in consolidating many a democratic regime. The expansion of social insurance programs, welfare services, and publicly financed medical care have given workers, farmers, and the middle classes a greater sense of investment in the political system. Since 1945 political elites in Western Europe and North America, including most conservatives, have endorsed the notion that political democracy in wealthy capitalist societies brings with it a healthy dose of social democracy as well. Even with the conservative backlash against welfare spending in the 1980s, all but the most diehard laissez-faire liberals accepted some degree of public management of social security and public welfare as part and parcel of modern democracy.

Why this close association developed between democracy and welfare provisioning, and what the expansion of state functions has done to democratic political cultures, is the subject of the essays in this section. In his analysis of American democracy and the welfare state, Samuel Hays presents the vast expansion of government-sponsored social services since the New Deal as largely a middle-class triumph rather than a victory for lower classes. It was mainly the "mass middle class," says Hays, who benefitted from social security, federal mortgage financing, the GI Bill, and many of the policy innovations of the 1960s and 1970s, such as Medicare, student loans, and federal and state subsidies for the arts and culture. Although the poor did win some benefits, such as food stamps, Medicaid and the expansion of aid to dependent children, these gains constituted "a relatively small part" of the total program of social services. The United States welfare state, therefore, served to perpetuate economic inequality rather than reduce it.

Hays takes the argument one important step further by arguing that the construction of the social security state also deepened political inequality.

Not only did the mass middle class reap greater material benefits from government social services; its members also became better equipped than the poor to participate in political life. The expansion of state functions had the counter-democratic consequence of making government more bureaucratic and more subject to the influence of highly specialized interest group lobbies. Citizens became more remote from government, more passive, less able to devote the time and energy necessary to participate in the increasingly technical deliberations in legislatures, courts and executive agencies that preside over policy. Participation, then, has narrowed. Only the mass middle class (and upper class) has the resources to participate, and even it participates largely through its tenuous connections to specialized lobbies.

Herrick Chapman finds some similar trends in the rise of the welfare state in France. As the French created a national system of social insurance – in 1930, 1945, and more gradually during the 1960s and 1970s – they did so in a way that reflected the strength of large employers and middle-class interest groups. What emerged by 1980 was a welfare state at once both immense in size – France ranked first in Europe in the proportion of public expenditures allocated to social security programs – and conservative in character. The French social security system remains regressive in its financing and non-redistributive in its income effects. Unlike Hays, Chapman stresses the essential role left-wing parties and unions played in propelling the growth of the welfare state. But in the end right-wing politicians, large employers, and middle-class groups proved decisive in shaping the programs that the left had initially put on the national agenda. Likewise, Chapman argues, as does Hays, that by the mid and late twentieth century state administrators and technical experts became the key initiators of policy, in contrast to earlier in the century when spokesmen for societal groups often played such roles. Thus in both countries, state expansion in the realm of social policy has had the effect of strengthening middle-class (and to a lesser extent working-class) investment in the democratic political regime, even as it has enhanced the power and autonomy of state officials.

Barbara Weinstein presents a contrasting case in which the growth of the welfare state did as much to undermine as to consolidate a democratic regime. Weinstein traces the evolution of social welfare functions linked to industry, especially vocational education, through two eras in Brazil's political history: the provisional government and dictatorship of Getúlio Vargas (1930–1945) and the democratic Second Republic (1946–1964). In both periods, she finds, industrialists controlled those programs, with the state doing little more than collect funds for services planned and managed by private elites. Rather than serving as arenas for cross-class alliances and new sites of democratic participation, as happened in the United States and France, welfare programs in Brazil became a means for employers to enhance their authority in the workplace. As a result, the labor movement remained weak at the factory level and looked mainly to the state and national politics as its avenue of redress. By the early 1960s working-class political mobilization had brought enough electoral success and governmental accommodation to the unions to lead many industrialists to call for military rule, which began in 1964 and lasted until 1985.

If class conflicts and cross-class alliances helped to shape welfare states differently from one country to another, gender politics did as well. Chapman explores this dimension of state building in his discussion of family allowances as a central feature of the French welfare state. Robert Moeller investigates the realm of gender relations even further in his essay on citizenship rights and social policy in post-war West Germany. Such policy reinforced traditional gender roles: family allowances were designed to encourage reproduction and keep mothers out of the work-force, and women's "social citizenship" was defined mainly "in terms of their status as wives and mothers." Similar tendencies had emerged in other post-war democracies; but Moeller shows how the particular conditions of post-war West Germany made the democratic welfare state there unusually biased toward anchoring women in the private domain of the home. The traumas of wartime and post-war family dislocations, the strength of Catholic values as promoted by the Christian Democratic Party, an investment in reprivatizing the family after the Nazis had tried to make childrearing a duty to the state, and a Cold War anti-communist aversion to gender equality shared as much by the Social Democratic left as by the right (an aversion made all the more poignant by rivalry with East Germany) all served to reinforce support for a narrow conception of women's roles as mothers that was "ultimately incompatible with equality and full rights of democratic political participation."

Part Five: Comparative Perspectives

When we organized the conference that gave rise to the essays published in this volume, we asked historical sociologist Charles Tilly to attend the meetings as critic and rapporteur and then write an essay that offered a comparative perspective on some of the major themes the conference explored. In "Democracy is a Lake," Tilly develops a conceptual framework for thinking about democracy that not only responds to the central theme of our project, "social construction," but also reflects upon a larger body of recent literature on the transition to democratic regimes.

Tilly notes that in studying the recent re-emergence of democracy, most theorists have emphasized the crucial role of elites in regime transitions, rather than broadly based social movements. They have also stressed state-craft and interest-group bargaining in the short term more than long-term historical transformations. Whereas Barrington Moore's historical perspective presented democracy as the metaphorical equivalent of an oilfield – long in the making, and readily tapped in only a handful of sites around the globe – these theorists view democracies as gardens which, with the proper cultivation, can grow in a host of places under widely varying conditions.

Tilly responds to these debates by first offering a conceptualization of democracy based in equal parts on Robert Dahl and Max Weber, and defined in terms of the breadth (inclusiveness) and equality of citizenship, of the level of consultation between government and citizens, and of the protection of citizens from arbitrary state actions. He considers the historical circumstances capable of producing these conditions, and proposes an alternative metaphor: democracy as a lake, which can be constructed and maintained through long-term geological processes, through short-term natural events, such as earthquakes or landslides, or even by human action (the construction of dams, for example). Democracies can arise under a similar variety of circumstances: through "geological," long-term political development, through short-term social and political "earthquakes" (wars, revolutions), or through purposeful social and political engineering.

In a large number of cases, Tilly argues, two conditions have played an especially prominent role – military mobilization and proletarianization. Since the eighteenth century, governments throughout much of the world have built sizeable standing armies and mobilized their countries for war. In doing so they have had to bargain with social groups, raise taxes, enlarge the reach and meaning of citizenship, and sometimes concede new forms of democratic participation. In countries where the expansion of the state's military capacity has also involved the subordination of military elites to civilian authority, the prospects for stable democracy have been good. Where the military has remained autonomous and powerful, as in much of Latin America, democratic transitions have been late in coming and difficult to secure.

Tilly also highlights the role working classes played in forging democracy. When pressured by economic change to defend themselves more effectively through the polity, workers provided the critical momentum behind efforts to enlarge citizens' rights and make political regimes more democratic. Middle-class or elite support often proved essential to the success of these efforts. But Tilly endorses the recent work of Dietrich Reuschemeyer, Evelyne Huber Stephens, and John D. Stephens in emphasizing the primacy of working-class mobilization as a condition for democratization.[9]

PATTERNS AND COMPARISON

Tilly's observations, and Rueschemeyer, Stephens, and Stephens's major comparative study of twentieth-century democratization, provide a useful starting point from which to consider some of the comparative conclusions yielded by the volume's essays.[10] As indicated at the outset, these essays draw much of their inspiration from recent work in social history. Given that subdiscipline's focus on subordinate social groups – workers, peasants, women, slaves – and the background of many of our authors in labor history, one would expect to find ample evidence of the centrality of workers and organized labor in struggles for democracy. And indeed, the essays do suggest some general conclusions concerning the role of workers and organized labor in twentieth-century democratization.[11]

Turn-of-the-century unionization was uniformly met with state repression. Oestreicher argues that such repression was most extreme in the United States, where white elites felt justified in using violence to control an "alien," immigrant and non-white workforce. Coercion and violence took place in all of the countries explored in this volume, however, and formed a prominent feature of state labor policy through the 1930s.

By mid-century, state policy toward workers and their movements, and the role of those movements in national governance, had changed dramatically. Argentina, Brazil, and Mexico had created state-sponsored national union movements; in France, Germany, and the United States, organized labor remained free of overt state intervention but formed an integral part of electoral and administrative politics. As a result, the size and political weight of the labor movement had increased enormously; and as its political importance increased, its militance tended to decline in every case considered except for Argentina and Brazil. Post-war purges of the German and Japanese unions, and the tight rein exercised by Mexico's revolutionary party over the national labor federation, are examples of how state policy contributed to this process. But particularly in the developed countries, reduced union militance was primarily the result of post-war economic growth, which reduced class tensions and the conflicts inherent in electoral competition conducted along class lines.

Labor militance at the beginning of the century widened and deepened democratic participation; labor moderation since mid-century further reinforced and strengthened democratic regimes.[12] Such moderation was a product both of the process of inclusion itself and of the increasing ability of growing industrial economies to meet workers' demands. The consequences of its absence can be seen in Argentina and Brazil, where low rates of growth (Argentina), or acutely unequal distribution of the benefits of growth (Brazil), caused union militance to continue unabated into the 1950s and 1960s. In both countries electoral democracy provided a highly effective vehicle for the expression of worker demands; precisely for this reason, conservative elites and members of the middle class found electoral competition increasingly threatening and unacceptable. By the 1960s both groups were ready to close down democracy and support military dictatorships encharged with "disciplining" organized labor.

Workers and their movements were thus central in the story of twentieth-century democratization. But most of the essays in this volume place particular emphasis on the middle class as a pivotal force behind the expansion or reduction of mass-based political participation.[13] Middle-class movements played this role not because of any innately prodemocratic orientation on their part. To the contrary: a number of the essays show how such movements sought to reduce the scope of political or social democracy in France, the United States, Mexico, and Brazil. Rather, the reason for their prominence in these essays is that, in class and political struggles among workers, employers, and the national state, urban middle classes occupy a uniquely strategic position.[14] Their higher levels of education and earning power, as compared to urban and rural workers, and their geographic concentration in urban areas, endow them with a political weight disproportionate to their numbers. And economic elites have tended to view members of the middle class as important potential allies in their confrontations with workers, for several reasons. First, many of the small entrepreneurs and businesspeople who comprise that class are themselves employers, or hope someday to be. Second, the middle class includes the executives and administrators whose skills are essential in the management and control of labor forces. Third, businesspeople, managers, professionals, and white-collar employees tend to be motivated by a frank and unconcealed desire for upward mobility and for putting as much distance as possible between themselves and the world of manual labor. Alliance with powerful elites can be helpful in realizing such ambitions, both individually and collectively.

Nevertheless, middle-class responses to the possibility of such alliances are often ambivalent. Political movements based in the middle class can view elites as potential allies against working-class radicalism; but they can also see elites as arrogant, self-interested oppressors. Workers and their organizations are perceived in a similarly ambiguous light. Middle-class movements struggling to open up restrictive, elite-dominated political systems to broader participation are often receptive to the idea of cross-class alliances with organized labor. But once the political system has been opened to free electoral competition, labor-based parties and movements based on constituencies which outnumber the middle class, and which pursue political agendas at odds to middle-class interests and concerns, no longer form such appealing allies.

These ambiguities and ambivalences set the stage for a broad range of possible alliances and conflicts across classes. Which of those possibilities become real depends, not on abstract laws of historical causation, but rather on the specific conditions in effect in given historical settings. The cases covered by the essays suggest four national variants in middle-class participation in democratization. The first, vividly described in Gale Stokes's essay on Eastern Europe, is that of utter domination of civil society by authoritarian states, and the resulting inability of any group or groups in that society to form effective oppositional movements. A second variant, exemplified by Japan, Mexico, and Brazil in the 1960s and 1970s, is that of relatively weak middle-class movements being co-opted by conservative, elite-dominated regimes. A third, represented by turn-of-the-century Argentina and by Poland and Brazil in the 1980s, is that of tense, uneasy alliances between middle- and working-class movements in opposition to conservative authoritarianism. And a fourth variant, most visible in France, Germany, and the United States, is that of highly mobilized middle classes competing successfully for political power, sometimes in alliance with, sometimes in opposition to, elites and working classes. This last variant is the one which comes closest to exemplifying classical "bourgeois" democracy.

None of these variants is fixed or immutable. As several of the papers suggest, national politics can move from one variant to another over time. The conflict between middle and working classes described by Oestreicher for the turn-of-the-century United States had been reduced considerably by mid-century, as the "mass middle class" described by Hays incorporated much of organized labor into its ranks. The alliance of Argentine working- and middle-class movements analyzed by James broke down later in the century as the labor movement grew stronger and overpowered the Radical Party in electoral weight. The Radicals responded by joining forces with the military in an anti-labor coalition, thus moving Argentina from the third variant to the second. In Mexico, by contrast, incorporation of middle-class organizations into the ruling party, followed by forty years of strong economic growth, greatly strengthened the role of that class in national politics. This could be seen both within the party, where middle-class concerns became increasingly central to policymaking, and outside the party, in the rise during the 1980s of revitalized opposition movements calling for open elections and other features of "bourgeois democracy." And even in Japan, which Allinson suggests has displayed perhaps the greatest continuity of political structures over time, by the early 1990s economic growth had strengthened the urban middle class to the point where it was questioning the continued hegemony of the Liberal Democratic Party. Thus both Japan and Mexico may be poised to move from the second variant to the fourth.

The essays make clear the multiple forms of mobilization and organization adopted by middle classes in different countries. Oestreicher and Hays discuss the parties, reform movements, and citizen lobbies through which the "mass middle class" has dominated national and local-level politics in the United States. Nord shows how the nineteenth-century struggle for middle-class control over French business, professional, and religious associations provided the institutional base both for a "civic culture" of republicanism and for the participation of middle-class politicians and movements in national affairs of state. The impacts of that participation are then visible in the policies of social provision enacted in France over the last sixty years, which, as Chapman shows, favor middle-class interests.

Even in Latin America, where the middle classes are not usually viewed as political actors of central importance, middle-class mobilization has had major impacts on the character of national democratization.[15] In Mexico, middle-class civic associations forced the ruling party to take seriously a social class which was vastly outnumbered both by peasants and by urban workers, and to concede its representatives equal status in the party structure. And in Argentina, the Radical Party proved unexpectedly successful at mobilizing and channeling middle-class and working-class votes to remove conservative elites from power. In the process they transformed politics itself from a "gentlemanly" elite calling to a new, quintessentially middle-class profession.

In Argentina, elites responded to this rise in middle-class assertiveness by suspending electoral politics in 1930; nor were they alone in doing so. Conservative elites in Brazil, Germany, and Japan also agreed to the dissolution of democracy during the 1930s. French elites seemingly had little choice in 1940; but as Nord suggests, they too saw their interests poorly served by middle- and working-class republicanism, and were by no means opposed to Pétain's rule.

The essays thus tend to confirm Rueschemeyer, Stephens, and Stephens's identification of elite classes, both agrarian and industrial, as the principle social obstacles to twentieth-century democratization.[16] Elite struggles against increased popular participation were fought on various fronts, depending on the resources available to them. One of the most subtle and least understood of those fronts was that of culture and ideology. Here too we note several national variants which correspond fairly closely to the variations in middle-class mobilization discussed above.

The first such variant is that of post-war Eastern Europe, where Communist regimes prevented the formation of a political opposition partly through repression but partly through imposing a totalizing political discourse which pre-empted the necessary ideological space for such opposition. The response of those regimes' opponents was to try to create a completely new such space, in the form of an "anti-politics" based on individual ethics and morality. In Poland this strategy formed the basis for a coalition of workers and middle-class intellectuals who eventually succeeded in bringing the regime down; but with the partial exception of Czechoslovakia, "anti-politics" failed to generate any comparable movements elsewhere. This deprived the recent democratization of Eastern Europe of any discernible social base, argues Stokes, and renders the construction of democracy in the region in the 1990s highly problematic.

The second variant is larger and more internally varied. It consists of states and societies characterized by a powerful tension between liberal doctrines of civic equality and broad-based participation, and "organic statist" ideologies based on limited or tightly controlled participation, an acceptance of social hierarchy and inequality, and a tradition of state autocracy.[17] As Nord's essay suggests, the adoption of liberal constitutional arrangements in Argentina (1853), France (1875), and Mexico (1857, 1917) was both the product, in part, of previous middle-class activism and demands, and the spur to further such mobilization. Liberal constitutions in Brazil (1824, 1891) and Japan (1889) were the product of elite deliberations rather than middle-class agitation; nevertheless, they had a similar stimulating effect on popular demands for further expansion of political rights. Such mobilization had to contend, however, with conservative upper classes (Argentina, Brazil, and France), with modernizing state elites (Mexico), or with both (Germany and Japan). Those elites portrayed the nation-state as a harmonious, integrated community in which competing class interests could be reconciled and smoothed away by enlightened elders ruling with the best interests of the society at heart. A variety of symbols was used to express this concept: racial democracy in Brazil, the emperor and the agrarian village in Japan, and, in almost every case considered, the symbol of the family.

The effect – and, we would argue, the purpose – of such rhetoric was to undercut the liberal ideal of broad-based political participation, or, failing that, to channel such participation in ways acceptable to ruling elites. Nowhere was this clearer than in the political discourse on gender and the family. A feminist – or even gender-blind – reading of liberalism argued persuasively for the admission of women to the franchise and to full political participation. Calls for female suffrage provoked passionate invocations of women's role in the national family as the guardians of civic virtue and the nurturers of future citizens. The consequence of such rhetoric was to bar the majority of the population from direct political participation and to confine it to a secondary role in the "private" sphere.

The clearest triumphs of the organic statist model were in Mexico and Japan, two cases of "revolution from above" in which modernizing elites constructed regimes which combined liberal rhetoric and institutions with a strong statist orientation. In both countries the tension between these two components was visible in the political turmoil of the 1920s and 1930s; but by 1950 both countries, following different routes, had successfully incorporated all major social groups into conservative, one-party systems.

Lacking the revolutionary transformations which took place in Japan and Mexico, Argentina and Brazil have displayed less stability and more volatile oscillations between the two ideological poles. Between 1890 and 1930 both societies struggled to accommodate republican institutions and rhetoric to the political conservatism espoused by powerful agrarian elites. In Brazil this was achieved through a tightly restricted franchise; in Argentina elites sought to appease a larger and more assertive urban middle class by agreeing to enforce universal male suffrage and gambling on their ability to attract a mass-based conservative following. By 1930 both systems had been repudiated by the landowners, ushering in a sixty-year period in which the two nations moved repeatedly from open electoral regimes to right-wing military authoritarianism and back again.

In both France and Germany, liberal republicanism eventually prevailed over statist traditions, though by a different path in each case. In France, a well developed civil society succeeded in counterbalancing the power of conservative elites and state institutions over the course of the Third Republic. In Germany, landowning and industrial elites were too powerful, and middle classes too conservative in their orientation, for democratic ideologies to triumph. In this case international factors tipped the balance: defeat in the First and Second World Wars, which led to the revamping of political institutions, the creation of electoral democracies, and, by 1945, the discrediting of statist ideologies. We shall return to this point in the concluding section of this chapter.

A third and final variant of ideological struggle is represented by the United States, where, as Oestreicher notes, no tradition or practice of organic statism existed to impede "militantly democratic egalitarian republic[anism]." During the second half of the nineteenth century, however, this commitment to free and open political participation generated its own ideological contradiction as two new social groups – recently freed African Americans and newly arrived European immigrants – sought to make good on its claims and exercise their franchise. The response was a campaign of ethnic and racial exclusion – municipal electoral reform in the North, and black disfranchisement in the South – carried out in the name of progressive, liberal reform.

In the multiracial United States, racism played much the same role in limiting the scope and promise of liberal democracy that organic statism did in other countries. As in other countries, the tension between democratic and anti-democratic ideologies was tense and dynamic; and African Americans were able to use liberalism's critique of racism as a weapon in their struggle to win inclusion in the polity. But the "two souls" of American liberalism remain very much with us, contributing to the climate of racial tension and misapprehension we live with today.

Nowhere, then, did democratic values and ideals take hold and prevail easily and automatically; and in some cases they did not prevail at all. Nor, once established, should their permanence be assumed. There is nothing whiggish about the history of democracy.

AN INTERNATIONAL HISTORY OF DEMOCRACY

The previous section sought to compare several national experiences of class conflict, state-building, and ideological contestation. We would like to conclude by placing those national experiences within the context of a global political economy that, over the course of the twentieth century, impinged on all the world's regions more directly than ever before.

Our story begins with the explosive economic growth of the 1870–1914 period, based on the massive expansion of manufacturing in the advanced capitalist countries and agricultural and primary-commodity production in the Americas, Russia and Eastern Europe, Africa and Asia. Economic growth fueled demographic change in the form of accelerated urbanization and major migrations, especially from Southern and Eastern Europe to North and South America and the industrial centers of the European northwest. These trends in the international economy help explain why, despite unique national histories, so many countries in Europe and the Americas, along with Japan, became sites for intense political struggles to democratize regimes. These struggles took different forms in each country. But behind them all lay similar patterns of urban growth, working- and middle-class formation, and in many cases major migrations that challenged elite control of political institutions.

This period culminated in the outbreak of the First World War. As Tilly argues in his essay, wars have often been occasions for major political transformations, as the need to mobilize people and resources forces governments to renegotiate the rights of citizenship. War also alters military–civilian relations, in some cases strengthening the generals, in others the civilians. Victory and defeat in war can strengthen or destroy governments of either democratic or authoritarian hue.

All these effects were visible in the First World War and its aftermath. Mass mobilization and total war forced governments in all the belligerent countries to grant concessions to labor, which in turn strengthened movements for democracy in Germany, Japan, and Eastern Europe. Victory, costly though it was for France and Britain, certainly strengthened democratic regimes in these countries and weakened the potential appeal of fascist parties in the inter-war years. And wartime service made it easier for women in Britain, the United States, and Germany to make compelling moral and political claims to suffrage.[18]

At the same time the war and its aftermath had profoundly undemocratic consequences. Left-wing resurgence in 1918 and 1919 triggered a powerful, transnational wave of right-wing reaction – from the Palmer raids in the United States to the Semana Trágica in Argentina to the abortive Kapp putsch in a young Weimar Germany – as conservatives rallied to check what they saw as an international red tide. European fascist movements, and the regimes they inspired in Latin America and Asia in the 1930s and 1940s, had important roots in the experience of the war. Many a fascist militant idealized combat as the most authentic form of political action and viewed the war as proof of the failure of liberal and democratic values.

That failure seemed to be further confirmed by the Great Depression of the 1930s. The collapse of trade and prices, staggering unemployment, and epidemic bank failures proved catastrophic for democratic rule, particularly in countries such as Argentina, Germany, and Japan, which had only recently made headway in expanding political participation. Fascism and military authoritarianism in Europe, East and West, militarism and imperialism in Japan, the collapse of electoral republics in

Argentina and Brazil – all these changes fed on fear and the search for new social and economic certainties. Economic depression weakened labor movements and the left-wing parties they supported, and made frightened middle-class groups more susceptible to authoritarian appeals and open to renewing alliances with landed elites.

Democracy did not collapse everywhere, however. Electoral regimes survived the Depression in France, Mexico, and the United States, in large part because landed elites had lost their power in those countries and had little to offer potential middle-class allies. In France and the United States middle-class groups had also acquired sufficient confidence in their ability to use the party system to defend their interests that they remained loyal to the electoral regime. Recognizing the importance of such support, Mexico's revolutionary party incorporated middle-class organizations during the early 1940s, cementing the stability of its own electoral regime.

If the First World War left a complex legacy, strengthening democracy in some countries while giving rise to anti-democratic movements elsewhere, the Second World War proved to be a more decisive turning point in the international history of democratic regimes. Allied victory over Nazi Germany, fascist Italy and imperialist Japan, along with the Holocaust and other brutal atrocities committed by those regimes, discredited the fascist model the world over. The language of democracy became hegemonic in both the capitalist West and socialist East, even as the meanings of "democracy" varied enormously. The Second World War also proved pivotal in promoting anti-colonial movements in Africa and Asia which, even if they later failed to create democratic regimes, nonetheless adopted many of the basic premises of popular sovereignty and democratic participation in propagating a nationalist ideology. Finally, Allied victory created conditions for building enduring democratic institutions and practices in Germany and Japan. As Moeller and Allinson show, democracy was not simply imposed by Allied occupation. It took hold in no small part through domestic conflict and innovation. Still, external support proved crucial in stabilizing democracy in both countries, and in Western Europe more generally.

In the decades since the war, trends in the international political economy have had more ambiguous consequences for democracy. Economic growth from 1945 through the mid-1970s helped consolidate democracy in France, Japan, and West Germany, as well as Mexico's one-party system. Relative prosperity and high levels of employment helped fuel movements to expand social democracy in Western Europe and overcome racial exclusion in the United States. Transitions to democracy in Spain, Portugal, and Greece in the 1970s were built in part on the effects of European-wide economic growth in previous decades.

Growth in the international economy did not produce democratic transition in Latin America, however, to say nothing of most of Asia and Africa. As Andrews, Davis, and Weinstein make clear, this was due primarily to internal patterns of class conflict and alliance in those countries. A significant contributing factor, however, was the international balance of power: the political dimension of the international political economy.

Since the Second World War, two transnational political phenomena have shaped the international history of democracy: decolonization, and the Cold War. The latter has particular relevance for the cases in this volume. Great-power rivalry between the United States and the Soviet Union had profoundly chilling effects on any tendencies toward democracy in the front-line states of Eastern Europe. That rivalry had an opposite impact on the Western front-line states – France, West Germany, Japan – tending to fortify democracy there. In the West, the anti-democratic impact of the Cold War was felt most strongly in the rear echelons, most notably in Latin America, where US support for rightist coups in the 1960s and 1970s contributed to the demise of democracy in much of the region. Social democratic parties and trade unions, the very organizations that had proven essential to democratization in Western Europe, were anathema to American cold warriors. Only in the late 1970s and 1980s did the United States begin to support democratic transitions away from authoritarian rule – and even during this period Cold War strategy and deep-seated anti-communist ideology continued to dominate US policy in Central America and Africa. Despite the continuing rhetorical power of the Wilsonian vision of an American policy making the world safe for democracy, the Cold War served to strengthen democracy only in the advanced capitalist West, while impeding its development in much of the rest of the world.

The ending of the Cold War in the late 1980s therefore seemed to open stunning new possibilities for the expansion of democracy, not just in the former Soviet bloc, but in other parts of the globe no longer oppressed by bipolar confrontation. As we write, in the opening months of 1994, those possibilities no longer look so promising. In much of Eastern Europe and the former Soviet Union, nationalism, ethnic warfare, overdeveloped militaries, economic deprivation, and the weak development of an autonomous civil society pose formidable obstacles to the consolidation of fragile democratic institutions and habits of mind. Newly re-established civilian democracies face only slightly less daunting obstacles in Latin America, where the international debt crisis of the 1980s produced a "lost decade" of economic stagnation and decline comparable in its destructiveness to the Great Depression of the 1930s. Not coincidentally, the siren song of fascism can now be heard in full voice both in Eastern Europe and in Latin America.[19]

The transnational influences which have shaped the history of democracy during the past hundred years will be even more in force in the years to come. Countries in the late twentieth century are more deeply embedded than ever before in a world polity, a globalized economy, and dense international networks of images, information, and ideas. Global capital markets, the continued growth and proliferation of multinational firms, the swelling transnational flows of people, goods, and services which took place in the 1980s and 1990s – these will have even more powerful impacts on national struggles over issues of political participation than was the case in the 1890s, the 1930s, or the 1970s.

As in previous decades, however, these transnational influences will continue to interact with specific national configurations of class structure, state institutions and ideology, and civic culture. These configurations can and do cluster in variants of the sort that we identified earlier in this chapter; but ultimately each is unique, the product of a concrete historical experience which cannot be replicated by any other society. An understanding of the future of democracy, whether in specific nations or in transnational perspective, therefore requires careful attention to that historical experience and to the present-day conditions to which it has given rise. It is to that task that we now turn.

NOTES

1. Barrington Moore, Jr., *Social Origins of Dictatorship and Democracy: Lord and Peasant in the Making of the Modern World* (Boston, 1966).

2. For examples of the former, see Lizabeth Cohen, *Making a New Deal: Industrial Workers in Chicago, 1919–1939* (Cambridge and New York, 1990); Iver Bernstein, *The New York City Draft Riots: Their Significance in American Society and Politics in the Age of the Civil War* (New York, 1990); William Beik, *Absolutism and Society in Seventeenth-Century France: State Power and Provincial Aristocracy in Languedoc* (Cambridge and New York, 1985); William J. Chase, *Workers, Society, and the Soviet State: Labor and Life in Moscow, 1918–1929* (Urbana, 1987); Steve J. Stern, *Peru's Indian Peoples and the Challenge of Spanish Conquest: Huamanga to 1640* (Madison, 1982); Peter Winn, *Weavers of Revolution: The Yarur Workers and Chile's Road to Socialism* (New York, 1986). For examples of the latter, see Eric Foner, *Reconstruction: America's Unfinished Revolution, 1863–1877* (New York, 1987); Alan Knight, *The Mexican Revolution* (Cambridge and New York, 1986).

3. Phrase from Winn, *Weavers of Revolution*, 8.

4. Most notably, Peter B. Evans, Dietrich Rueschemeyer, and Theda Skocpol, eds., *Bringing the State Back In* (Cambridge and New York, 1985). See also essays by William T. Rowe, William B. Taylor, and Charles Tilly in Olivier Zunz, ed., *Reliving the Past: The Worlds of Social History* (Chapel Hill, 1985).

5. Alfred Stepan, *The State and Society: Peru in Comparative Perspective* (Princeton, 1978), 7.

6. For classic statements of this argument, see Alexis de Tocqueville, *Democracy in America* (New York, 1956); Gabriel A. Almond and Sidney Verba, *The Civic Culture: Political Attitudes and Democracy in Five Nations* (Princeton, 1963); Robert A. Dahl, *Polyarchy: Participation and Opposition* (New Haven, 1971), 124–88. For a more recent treatment, see Robert Putnam, *Making Democracy Work: Civic Traditions in Modern Italy* (Princeton, 1993).

7. This point was made in John Markoff's useful comment at the conference; see his forthcoming *The Great Wave of Democracy in Historical Perspective*.

8. Edmund Morgan, *Inventing the People: The Rise of Popular Sovereignty in England and America* (New York, 1988).

9. Dietrich Rueschemeyer, Evelyne Huber Stephens, and John D. Stephens, *Capitalist Development and Democracy* (Chicago, 1992).

10. Like the present volume, Rueschemeyer, Stephens, and Stephens use Barrington Moore's *Social Origins* as a starting point, endorsing his emphasis on class analysis while proposing to modify his approach in several ways. Like us, they shift the time frame to the nineteenth and twentieth centuries and stress the importance of state formation and international factors. Unlike us, they examine a large number of national cases – almost fifty, by our count – only a few of which are examined in detail; and, except for Australia and New Zealand, all of their cases are drawn from Western Europe or the Americas, with no representation from Eastern Europe or Asia. This volume, then, shares Rueschemeyer *et al.*'s thematic interests, but tends to follows Moore's principles of sample selection (fewer cases, with broader global coverage, examined in depth).

11. For comparative examinations of the relationship between organized labor and democracy, see Charles Bergquist, *Labor in Latin America: Comparative Essays on Argentina, Chile, Colombia, and Venezuela* (Stanford, 1986); Ruth Berins Collier and David Collier, *Shaping the Political Arena: Critical Junctures, the Labor Movement, and Regime Dynamics in Latin America* (Princeton, 1991); Ira Katznelson and Aristide R. Zolberg, eds., *Working-Class Formation: Nineteenth-Century Patterns in Western Europe and the United States* (Princeton, 1986); Adolph Sturmthal, *Unity and Diversity in European Labor* (Glencoe, Ill., 1953) and *Left of Center: European Labor since World War II* (Urbana, 1983). On Japan, which is seldom included in comparative analyses, see Andrew Gordon, *Labor and Imperial Democracy in Prewar Japan* (Berkeley, 1991).

12. "The optimal configuration of working-class organization for the development of democracy would be one in which the class was well organized, both in unions and a party, but that [sic] these organizations

were not radical. Indeed, it would be most optimal if they raised no substantive demands at all other than those for democracy itself ..." Rueschemeyer *et al.*, *Capitalist Development and Democracy*, 143.

13. This emphasis converges in an interesting way with the Rueschemeyer volume, the theoretical chapters of which repeatedly assert the centrality of the working class in constructing democracy. The book's empirical chapters, however, make clear the equal or greater importance of middle classes in democratizing France (89–90), Denmark (91), Sweden (94), Spain (120–1), virtually all of South America (167, 181, 282), and the Caribbean (244). In Switzerland, the United States, and Canada, agrarian smallholders and family farmers played a similar role.

14. See, for example, Luc Boltanski, *The Making of a Class: Cadres in French Society* (New York, 1987); Jürgen Kocka, *White Collar Workers in America, 1890–1940* (Beverly Hills, 1980); Jürgen Kocka and Allen Mitchell, eds., *Bourgeois Society in Nineteenth-Century Europe* (Oxford, 1993); C. Wright Mills's classic *White Collar: The American Middle Classes* (New York, 1951); Steven M. Zbatny, *The Politics of Survival: Artisans in Twentieth-Century France* (New York, 1990).

15. Again our authors' findings converge with those of Rueschemeyer, Stephens, and Stephens. In Latin America, "the middle classes emerge as the crucial forces behind the alliances effecting initial breakthroughs to restricted democracy and, in collaboration with the working class, to full democracy. It was in the middle classes that the parties or movements mobilizing and exerting pressures for democracy had their main base." *Capitalist Development and Democracy*, 181; see also 282.

16. On this point Rueschemeyer, Stephens, and Stephens differ sharply from Barrington Moore, who saw capitalist bourgeoisies as "an indispensable element in the growth of parliamentary democracy. No bourgeois, no democracy." Moore, *Social Origins*, 418. Rueschemeyer *et al.* find that bourgeois classes are "generally supportive of the installation of constitutional and representative government, but opposed to extending political inclusion to the lower classes . . . [C]apitalists and the parties they primarily supported rarely if ever pressed for the introduction of full democracy." *Capitalist Development and Democracy*, 8, 271.

17. On organic statism see Stepan, *State and Society*, 26–45.

18. This was not the case in France, where feminists were surprised to find their war efforts unrewarded. Stephen C. Hause, "More Minerva than Mars: The French Women's Rights Campaign and the First World War," in Margaret Randolph Higonnet *et al.*, eds., *Behind the Lines: Gender and the Two World Wars* (New Haven, 1987), 112–13.

19. Paul Hackenos, *Free to Hate: The Rise of the Right in Post-Communist Eastern Europe* (New York, 1993); "Region's military see threat ahead, not from revived Left, but from the Right," *Latin America Weekly Report* (28 October, 1993).

Part One
Industrialization, Urbanization, and Nation-Building from the 1870s to the Great Depression

1 The Origins of the Third Republic in France, 1860-1885[1]
Philip Nord

France became a republic in the 1870s, a parliamentary democracy endowed with the most generous franchise – universal manhood suffrage – in great-power Europe. The fact itself is not so remarkable. The nation had experimented twice before with republican government in 1792 and again in 1848. But these regimes had collapsed in short order whereas the Third Republic was destined to a seventy-year life span, a feat of longevity unmatched by any other post-revolutionary French regime. Why then did democratic institutions take root in France in the 1870s? Explanations of the phenomenon come in at least three varieties.

The first is centered on problems of ideology, and in this domain the research of François Furet has been pioncering. The Second Republic had been snuffed out by Louis-Napoléon Bonaparte's putsch in 1851. Driven underground or abroad by the coup, veteran *quarante-huitards* began to rethink the republican project. Furet has fastened attention on the figure of Edgar Quinet, a historian and lifelong republican who, in 1865 from exile in Switzerland, penned a forceful critique of the Revolution of 1789 and of the Jacobin episode in particular. Quinet interpreted the terrorist practices of the First Republic as a throwback to the despotic ways of the old regime. His message to fellow republicans was quite clear: repudiate now a violent revolutionism or forever be condemned to repeat the self-destructive failures of the Jacobins of yesteryear. A rising generation – young lawyers like Jules Ferry and Léon Gambetta – took Quinet's counsels to heart, eschewing the romantic posturing of bygone days in favor of a more sober, pragmatic approach to the science of politics. It was this "positivist generation" that shepherded the Third Republic into existence.[2]

The issue of how they assembled a working majority for the Republic, a social coalition to underpin the regime, has prompted explanations of a second order, focused less on ideas than on alliance-building. The problem has been approached from multiple angles. Stanley Hoffmann, who experienced first hand the Republic's dismal decline in the 1930s, was inclined to stress the brittleness of what he called "the republican synthesis." Ferry, Gambetta, and other republican leaders were spokesmen for a new middle class (Gambetta himself preferred the term "new social stratum") of businessmen and professionals. It was men such as these who in the 1870s rallied rural France to the Republic. They wooed a countryside populated by small-owning peasants with a specific and welcome promise: material and moral improvement within the confines of a socio-economic order anchored in the family enterprise. At base, then, the republican synthesis was conservative in orientation, wedded to a property regime that sustained attitudes – for example, an intense preoccupation with preservation across generations of a family patrimony – inimical to the advance of an entrepreneurial industrialism. The end result was a "stalemate society," resistant to change even when, as in the interwar years, change was the price of survival.[3] Eugen Weber has placed a more positive gloss on the republicanization of the countryside, understood by him as the dissemination, via the seductions of the market and the impositions of the state, of urban modes of thinking across a peasant society hitherto backward in material terms and fatalist in outlook. For Marxists, like Sanford Elwitt, the entire operation has the look of a bourgeois scam. The republican elite, it is argued, had the interests of property at heart first and foremost. Its democratic and reforming project, such as it was, was intended less to advance high-minded principle than to breed a citizenry respectful of the new governing class and prepared to serve it in the military.[4] But whether the accent is placed on stalemate, urbanity, or manipulation, the conclusion remains the same: the Republic rested on a social compact between a middle-class governing elite, on the one hand, and a rural and small-town mass, on the other, who might be counted upon to produce the requisite electoral majorities.

But what, it is asked, became of France's old governing elite, of the so-called *notables* who had managed public affairs to a greater or lesser degree in the half-century preceding the Republic's advent? This question has prompted elaboration of a third species of explanation, which places principal emphasis on the notion of compromise. New elites struck a bargain with old, with the landlords and grands bourgeois of yesteryear. The compliance of France's still powerful notability, so necessary to the stabilization of a new and democratic order of things, was not of course obtained without cost, although how high the cost is a matter of some debate. On Furet's accounting, it was minimal. Republicans shucked off the Jacobin legacy bequeathed by the Great Revolution. Established elites steeped in a liberalism that counted Tocqueville and Guizot among its progenitors were reassured, made common cause with the likes of Ferry and Gambetta, and from such union was born a new democratic parliamentarism. Christophe Charle tells a similar tale of compromise but paints the outcome in less cheerful colors.[5] The coming of the Republic delivered a setback to the administrative elites of yore. The new regime purged politically unreliable old-timers and pledged itself to the meritocratic recruitment of civil servants. But such changes, Charle points out, left business elites in the corporate sector intact. And old families contrived to find ways to re-enter public administration, acquiring through private education the exam-taking skills necessary to a successful civil service career. For a period, *la haute fonction publique* took on a more democratic cast, but over time, in social profile and to a lesser degree in political orientation, it reverted to type. A republicanized elite ruled in the Chamber and Senate, in the prefectoral corps, in the University, but the business world and, over the long term, the senior civil service escaped its reforming grasp. Furet's happy compromise is recast here into a veiled competition for place, the state apparatus itself being the object of contention. The uneasy division of spoils worked out between new and old takes on a more sinister look when politics is added to the mix. The Republic's new men were in the main democrats, but much less so the big business and civil service establishments who were annoyed with the dithering of parliamentary politicians and pinned hopes for France's future on the administrative capacities of a competent few. They tolerated the new regime as the best option at present but did not embrace it, constituting a node of potential disloyalty at the Republic's very heart.

For all that they differ in tone and focus, such accounts of the Republic's origins agree on one point: new elites are assigned a critical, catalytic role in the fashioning of democratic institutions. It is they who devise novel intellectual strategies; who maneuver to line up popular support; who negotiate deals with still powerful old-timers. But where did such new men come from? The question is all the more compelling when placed in a comparative perspective.

The French, of course, held no monopoly on the democratizing impulse at mid-century. Mazzinians and Garibaldians dreamt of an Italy that would be not just unified but republican. In England, radical Dissent agitated for Church disestablishment, school reform, and an extension of the franchise. And in Germany, partisans of a genuine constitutionalism like Eugen Richter or the veteran '48er Rudolf Virchow rallied to the banner of an oppositional progressivism, distancing themselves from Liberals who had with a disconcerting facility come to terms with Bismarck's blood-and-iron authoritarianism. But in all such instances, democratizing thrusts were blunted or absorbed. Garibaldi and Mazzini, in the interests of national unity, subordinated themselves to Piedmontese policy, to the canny maneuverings of Count Cavour who may have been a liberal monarchist but was no democrat. In England, a Liberal Party recast in the Gladstonian mold welcomed Dissent into its ranks, exacting in return Dissent's submission to a party leadership in no small part composed of Whig grandees and Peelite administrators. German Progressives retained a measure of independence but found themselves in a squeeze that reduced them to ineffectuality. The gathering momentum of a socialist and working-class left tempered the Progressives' democratic commitments and induced them to consider making peace with a Liberalism they had once judged too compromised.

In France, however, it was different. Here, in the 1870s, the democratic movement broke through, giving birth to a new republican order. The monarchy and all its paraphernalia were banished. The restricted franchise so characteristic of aristocratic polities in the nineteenth century gave way to universal manhood suffrage. Cabinets were populated, not by noblemen or landed gentry, but by bourgeois. It is not that the institutions of the Republic were unmarked by compromise, far from it. But the terms were set by new men, not the old. Democratic elites did not have to bend themselves to the rules of a political order still dominated by notables, but the other way around (although how far the notables were obliged to bend remains to be seen).

The problem under consideration here may then be reformulated as follows. At issue is not just the origins of France's democratizing elites but the peculiar zeal they manifested, their capacity both to overcome resistance and, once in power, to make democratic institutions work and last. How is such exceptionalism to be accounted for? Democratic theory and an expanding social science literature on democratic transitions suggest where an answer might be looked for.

THEORIES OF DEMOCRATIC TRANSITION

Theories of democratic transition fall into two principal categories. The first, rooted in Cold War battles against communism, accents the structural preconditions of participatory government. Robert Dahl, Samuel Huntington, and others have worked this ground to exhaustion, identifying a wide range of variables said to be conducive to the consolidation of representative institutions: a high level of economic development, general literacy, a variegated social structure with a heavy middle-class ballast, and so on.[6] The policy implications of this line of argument are straightforward: fund growth and education, foster a native bourgeoisie, and democratic institutions will stabilize, enough so at least to withstand communist encroachments. But the international climate has changed in recent years, and a new angle of approach has been elaborated in response. The mid-1970s collapse of Iberian authoritarianism, the multiplying failures of military dictatorship in Latin America, and the "velvet" revolutions of 1989 in the Eastern bloc have inspired a rethinking of the issue of democratic transition. A new literature has taken shape that is centered less on structures than on voluntary action, on the dynamics by which democratic institutions can be made to sprout on the seemingly inhospitable ground of authoritarian rule.

Two distinct, but not contradictory, lines of inquiry have been pursued along these lines. The first, much influenced by Latin American examples, hones in on elite behavior. Prospects of a democratic transition brighten, the argument goes, when elites, old and new, have learned from violent past experience to eschew confrontation. Bloody memories of former repressions can have a sobering effect on incumbent authorities. When faced with a new democratic challenge, the landlords, generals, and bureaucrats who hold power may well hesitate to embark on yet one more round of violence. Opposition elites too may have mulled over the lessons of the past.[7]

The experience of exile, prison, or enforced silence can work as a powerful solvent, eating away at the maximalist rigidity of former years in favor of a more flexible and reassuring pragmatism. In such circumstances, a bargain becomes possible: the opposition is conceded the commanding heights of the state in exchange for refraining from serious retaliation against erstwhile authorities; the outgoing elite, while obliged to abandon the political high ground, continues to exercise critical material power thanks to its still extensive property holdings as well as critical (albeit reduced) political power thanks to ongoing control of certain institutional redoubts, such as the army. To students of the Third Republic's origins, such a scenario, focused as it is on problems of political learning and pact-making, is bound to have the ring of familiarity. But whether it is France in the 1870s or Argentina in the 1980s, the question still remains: whence comes the democratic challenge that enables elites to demonstrate the lessons they have learned in restraint and negotiation?

Transition theorists who have addressed this problem have edged away from the study of high politics toward a discussion of what they call "civil society," of the social and institutional settings in which new elites get their start. This avenue of inquiry, so promising in the present context, has a venerable pedigree that reaches back to the early 1960s: to Gabriel

Almond and Sidney Verba's work on "the civic culture," and to Jürgen Habermas's speculations on the rise and fall of the "public sphere."[8] To be sure, Almond and Verba, on the one hand, and Habermas, on the other, came to the problem from quite different perspectives. Almond and Verba, Anglo-American social scientists in the liberal mold, touted a democratic political culture as the surest antidote to the temptations of totalitarianism. Habermas, as a student of critical theory, worried less about fascist or communist threats than about the corrosive effects of an expansive consumer capitalism on the possibilities of free and rational discourse. But for all that they differ in point of departure, the civic culture school and Habermasians see eye to eye on one critical proposition: a resilient public sphere is the *sine qua non* of a functioning democracy. There is agreement as well as to what may be counted as the building blocks of a vibrant civil society: first, dense networks of communication and sociability (Habermas is more inclined to stress the importance of a critical-minded print culture, Almond and Verba of a lively associational life); and second, an informed public, neither deferential nor defiant to excess, that is committed to making the institutions of public life work.

But missing in the work of Almond and Verba and Habermas is an account of origins: how does a democratic citizenry with all the requisite skills and attitudes come into being in the first place? Almond and Verba take a well-developed civic culture as a given and never inquire into its historical genealogy. Habermas does offer a sketch of origins: the public sphere first took shape in the eighteenth century, expanded and democratized in the nineteenth, and now has begun to wither. But few states, even in the great-power Europe from which Habermas's evidence is drawn, have ever followed a trajectory so smooth. Sharp alternations between moments of revolutionary possibility and more extended periods – post-1815, post-1848, post-1918 – of reactionary closure, such is the more common experience. The apposite question for continental Europe (and for Third Republic France in particular) is how this cycle of revolution and reaction was broken, how empires and monarchies were made to metamorphose into democratic states without subsequent backsliding.

It is on the issue of origins that society-centered transition theorists have struck out in new directions. Given, *pace* Almond, Verba, Habermas, that an articulated civil society is the bedrock of democracy, how does such a civil society come to be? How was it built on and out of the debris of authoritarian government? The beginnings of an answer are to be found in the destabilizing consequences of economic transformation. Dictatorships believe that they want growth but make a serious mistake in fostering it. For development favors the "expansion of [the] educated middle classes;"

it engenders a "pluralistic infrastructure," a ramifying civil society ever more difficult to manage from the top down.[9] Whether in response to pressures building within civil society or for tactical reasons of its own, the authoritarian state may opt at this juncture to relax its grip on public life. The decision is a fatal one for into the openings created by liberalization pour accumulated discontents which, now articulated, more and more take on the character of outright opposition.

The hardening of opposition takes place at particular sites, certain institutional locales that enjoy or succeed in laying claim to a measure of autonomous activity. Autonomy may be an institutional tradition dating back to a non-authoritarian moment in the past as in the case of churches, bar associations or even trade unions. Or it may be a goal aspired to by newcomers: by organizations of businessmen, journalists or human rights activists determined to shake off the tutelage of an overweening state. Such institutions and organizations are important, not only as "free zones" in which an independent public opinion begins to formulate itself, but also as arenas of democratic experiment and education. Here might be practiced and learned the electoral arts which in the wider polity have been tampered with and falsified.[10]

To the extent that such battles for autonomy are won, to the extent that the state is driven out of a reawakening civil society, a new sphere of activity, a public sphere, begins to form. Communication is all important to the process. The various institutions, leagues, and clubs that constitute the component parts of a public opinion in formation make contact through informal networks of sociability, the printed media, and, as the hold of dictatorship loosens, demonstrations out of doors. By such means, multiplying but hitherto localized conflicts are woven into a widening movement of opposition.

Such a "resurrection of civil society," as it has been called,[11] presents dictatorships with a stark choice between repression or withdrawal. The decision might well be to cut a deal, opening the way to new elites and a new regime. But will the new democratic order survive? That depends in part on the kind of deal that has been cut. In much of the transition literature, there is a deep-seated anxiety that democratization not go too far. Oppositional elites who, on inheriting power, bear down on an outgoing authoritarian establishment, invite a reactionary backlash. Better, therefore, that the new men not be too strong, that they treat the outgoing authorities with a gentle hand, sparing them extensive purges, reprisals, and the like.[12] It helps too that incoming elites know how to use the institutional apparatus bequeathed to them. At issue here is not just constitution-making, but the deployment of state power to legislate and police a civic order in which habits of citizenship may be learned and exercised.[13] Movement culture can in this way be transformed into official culture, acquiring a solidity that will make it all the more difficult to dislodge, whether by revolutionaries of the right or left. But that civic order, however much the state may work to elaborate and entrench it, cannot be legislated *de novo*. It must be in place prior to the advent of democracy, having been worked out on the battlefield, so to speak, in the process and as part of the political struggle against dictatorship. The conclusion of such a line of argument, though not always stated, is evident: what makes possible a democratic transition is the prior elaboration, while dictatorship is still in place, of a counter-elite anchored in autonomous institutions and buoyed by an alternative political culture. The more articulated and coherent that culture and the institutional frame on which it sits, the more powerful in the short term the thrust toward democratization and, in the long, the likelier a democratic transition will endure.

THE REAWAKENING OF CIVIL SOCIETY

What bearing does such a schema have on the problem at hand: France's precocious and, at least by national standards, longlived transition to democracy in the mid-nineteenth century? It does not contradict existing interpretations that emphasize the political skills and determination of a new republican elite. But it does suggest that the analysis be pushed further, that the republican elite be situated in the organizational and cultural web that first gave it life and strength. And it prescribes as well a place to begin such an analysis: with the character and structures of institutional life in the decades prior to the founding of the Third Republic.[14]

France's national elite at mid-century, a mixture of landed, mercantile, and industrial interests, was not a reactionary elite. The so-called *notables* were not hostile to industrialization or the French Revolution *per se*. But they had been shaken and weakened by repeated bouts of popular upheaval and were determined to bring the revolutionary era to a close. To this end, over the course of the nineteenth century, they had entrenched themselves in a network of state and para-statal institutions. The Institute and the University may be cited as examples.

The Institute consisted of four state-chartered academies: the Académie française, des Beaux-Arts, des Inscriptions et belles lettres, and des Sciences. A fifth was added in 1834, the Académie des Sciences morales et politiques, the brainchild of Orleanist notable François Guizot. The academies were conceived as ancillaries to the state. The Academy of

Moral and Political Sciences, for example, functioned as a proto-policy institute, furnishing public officials with useful statistics and survey reports on issues of the day. The Academy of Fine Arts, in collaboration with the Ministry of Fine Arts, mounted the biannual and later annual *salon des arts*, until late in the century France's premier arts exhibition. The academies, while connected to the state by charter and function, enjoyed a critical measure of autonomy in that they were self-selecting bodies with a co-opted membership.

The University (which in France encompasses public secondary as well as higher education) stood in a similar relationship to the state. Its constitution was dictated by the state; its most senior official, the Grand Master, was a state appointee who answered on matters of high policy to the minister of public instruction. For all that, the institution conceived itself as an "independent corporation," attached but not subservient to public authority.[15] The minister and Grand Master were not the sole administrators of University affairs. They worked in tandem with a Council of Public Instruction which was in the majority an elective body composed of representatives of the University's multiple faculties.

In the days of the July Monarchy, in the 1830s and 1840s, relations between the central state apparatus and such para-statal institutions were cordial. Guizot, prime minister from 1840 to 1848, was himself a historian who counted numerous friends on the University faculty. He saw to it that the Academy of Moral and Political Sciences, his particular creation, was well stocked with men of enlightened views much like himself. In 1840, Guizot appointed a fellow-*universitaire*, the philosopher and academician Victor Cousin, minister of public instruction. Cousin, an able and well-connected administrator, schemed with considerable success to pack the University with teachers and professors who shared the same eclectic philosophy as did he. The upper reaches of the state administration and of allied institutions, like the Institute and University, were staffed then by a narrow elite of accomplished, but like-minded, men. They used the accumulated and quite considerable institutional powers at their disposal to administer and, if need be, to discipline an unruly civil society in the name of order, reason, and progress.

The coming of the Second Empire tightened institutional controls to an extraordinary degree. The right of association was curtailed and press censorship stiffened. The Imperial regime blanketed civil society, annexing to itself and breaking to its will all institutions that might breed independence of mind or action. Bonaparte for a moment had considered outright abolition of the University but contented himself with appointment of a tough-minded minister of public instruction, Hippolyte Fortoul, who in turn loaded the once autonomous Council of Public Instruction with more pliable, appointed members. In like manner, the Emperor had debated suppressing the Masonic Grand Orient de France but ended by placing it under the tutelage of an appointee and near relative Prince Lucien Murat. The Paris Bar had in years preceding elected its governing council and presiding officer (*bâtonnier*) by direct and universal suffrage. The Emperor maneuvered to reduce the *bâtonnier*'s authority by tinkering with the electoral process. From 1852, it was the council and not the run of Bar members who picked the *bâtonnier*, and they were obliged to choose one amongst themselves. The Paris Chamber of Commerce which had a formal right to advise the government on matters of economic policy was an elective body. In 1848, the suffrage had been extended to all businessmen who met certain requirements of residence and honorability. The Emperor cut back the electorate to a mere two thousand *notables-commerçants* and made admission to the ranks of the commercial notability contingent on the blessing of a watchful prefect of the Seine.

Since the first Napoléon, France's minority religions – Protestant and Jewish – had been organized in consistories, constituted bodies invested with a double mandate: to represent *vis-à-vis* the state the interests of the faithful and to perform *vis-à-vis* the faithful a variety of policing functions. Consistorial boards were composed in the main of lay representatives elected in the Jewish case by universal suffrage, in the Protestant by a more restricted franchise. Louis-Napoléon subjected both consistories to an institutional overhaul. The political motive was the same in both instances: to strengthen the hand of religious currents deemed well disposed to the regime or at least to weaken potential opponents. In the case of the Jewish consistory, such a policy translated into backing for its Rothschild-led, liberal-minded (in religious matters) and beleaguered governing elite who communicated a willingness to deal with the Empire in exchange for the regime's assistance against a menacing orthodox majority. Bonaparte responded positively to such overtures, imposing new restrictions on the consistorial suffrage in 1860, which in effect excluded from participation the poorest and often most orthodox sections of the Jewish community. From the Empire's point of view, the Reformed Church's governing elite represented a problem of a different sort. The Church was run by a close-knit network of select families; its religious orientation was evangelical; and its dominant lay personality was none other than François Guizot, an Orleanist loyalist and determined enemy of the Empire. The challenge in this instance was not to strengthen but to subvert elite authority. Louis-Napoléon, accordingly, curried favor with liberal, anti-evangelical currents in the Reformed Church. He at the same time imposed universal suffrage in consistorial elections in the hopes of inciting a liberal Protestant groundswell that might unseat the Guizot faction.[16]

On the whole, the abrasive institutional interventions of the Imperial state irritated established elites accustomed, at least since the days of the July Monarchy, to an easy-going partnership with officialdom. The favored position of the Jewish consistorial elite may be counted an exception to the pattern. Notables dug in their heels and sealed off as best they could institutions like the Institute or the Paris Bar from Bonapartist interference. The Académie française snubbed the regime time and again, rejecting candidates with Imperial connections in favor of scions of the Orleanist notability.[17] The Paris Bar in the 1850s elected governing councils of an oppositional complexion, who in turn elected a series of anti-regime *bâtonniers* from Berryer on the Legitimist right to Bethmont and Liouville on the republican left. What remained then in the wake of official efforts to close down public life was an extensive state apparatus, dominated by Bonapartists but, at strategic sites, colonized by notables who, in the majority, were cool to the new regime.

Bonaparte's rollback of the public sphere might have stabilized had it not coincided with a sustained economic boom. Economic growth, spurred on by the Imperial regime itself, fed the expansion of a new middle class of businessmen and professionals. The institutional carapace Bonaparte had clamped on civil society proved too tight-fitting to absorb these "new social strata," as Gambetta referred to them in later years. They chafed against franchise arrangements that excluded them, against enforced silences, and against arbitrary impositions from above. And the ferment which began under the Empire persisted well beyond the regime's collapse. Louis-Napoléon departed the scene in 1870, but he was succeeded by the centrist Thiers administration (1871–1873) and then by the so-called regime of Moral Order (1873–1877) which was authoritarian and clerical-minded in its policies.[18] Under the circumstances, middle-class discontent did not flag but even, in certain instances, intensified.

University students heckled deans and faculty deemed too subservient to established authority. Student disturbances forced the closing of the Ecole normale in 1867 and of the Ecole de Médecine in 1874. Dissenting Masons called for the ouster of Murat, indeed for the suppression altogether of the office of Grand Master, which they condemned as an "autocratic" and "quasi-royal" imposition incompatible with the Order's democratic essence.[19] In 1858, export-oriented Paris businessmen formed an Union nationale du commerce et de l'industrie(UNCI) which mounted a widening campaign on behalf of free trade and a democratization of the Chamber of Commerce franchise.

There was vocal discontent in the Jewish and Protestant communities as well. In the former, a dissident minority accused the Rothschild-dominated Paris consistory of defending Jewish interests with insufficient zeal and publicity. Discontent took institutional form with the creation of the Alliance israélite universelle in 1860. The Alliance is best remembered for the network of schools it sponsored across the Mediterranean basin intended for the regeneration of a "benighted" Oriental Jewry. But the AIU had an impact in France as well. It allowed no anti-Semitic slur to go unanswered; it shook up the consistory too, running candidates in consistorial elections who with increasing success displaced incumbent elites. Protestant consistorial elections were disputed with yet greater vigor. Liberal Protestants, unhappy with what they judged to be the sectarian dogmatism of Guizot's evangelical clique, formed a lay association, the Union protestante libérale, which conducted itself as a kind of opposition party within the Reformed Church. It ran slates of accredited candidates, collected funds, held public meetings, but its efforts fell just short. The evangelical faction won election after election, even if by the smallest of margins, and in the mid-1870s, with assistance from the regime of Moral Order, took its revenge, driving the UPL out of the Church.

Elections to the Paris Bar's council of discipline were by contrast peaceful affairs. The council in fact took steps in the early 1860s to dampen incipient efforts at politicking. Traditional decorum was maintained in so far as the Bar's internal proceedings were concerned, but the legal profession's stance *vis-à-vis* the state was far from a model of good behavior. In 1864 and again in 1868 lawyers of outspoken republican views were elected *bâtonnier*. In 1864, the regime indicted a band of young lawyers on charges of violating laws restricting political association. The Bar intervened as a corporate entity, making known its solidarity with the defendants' cause. In the late 1860s, journalists repeatedly challenged the Empire's press laws. The stars of the Paris Bar, young and old alike, competed for the privilege of representing the accused in court.

Nor was the Institute spared agitation. A rising generation of artists – Manet, the Impressionists, and others – via the arts press, petition campaigns, and private exhibitions, challenged the Académie des Beaux-Arts, its philosophy and institutional prerogatives. At stake was the constitution of the salon system: how juries were to be constituted, whether by the suffrage of all artists as the dissidents demanded or by the state/academy nexus as was established practice.

The institutional battles of the 1860s and 1870s shaped in decisive fashion the middle-class politics of the era. In every instance the demands and modus operandi were the same. Dissidents staked out a claim to institutional autonomy. Masons, *universitaires*, and artists had a right to self-government. Self-government in turn was conceived as the rule of an informed opinion, constituted in public debate and expressed through the exercise of universal suffrage. Such demands invariably met with resistance, whether from an unbudging Imperial state or from entrenched notable elites. But militants pressed on, petitioning constituted authority, campaigning for office or wooing institutional electorates.

If not at the outset, then over time, such battles took on an oppositional character. In every case, republican minorities were involved, who maneuvered to turn the conflict to political advantage. Given the structure and terms of the battles, the task was an easy one. On the one side stood the state or constituted elites, accused of dogmatism, exclusivity, and an imperious high-handedness, on the other an aroused opinion that embraced the principles of publicity, universal suffrage, and self-government. What might have begun as a localized squabble over the office of Grand Master ended as a political confrontation between partisans of democracy, indeed, of the Republic on the one hand and of regime loyalists on the other. And these divers institutional struggles were by no means isolated phenomena. They intersected and overlapped, recruiting from a common pool of militants. They were bound together by a common democratic rhetoric, the ensemble constituting the infrastructure of an awakening republican movement.

Institutional conflicts channeled a mobilized middle-class into a regenerated republican movement. The particular genesis of the movement left a permanent stamp on its program and aspirations. What republicans sought above all was the emancipation of civil society from the stranglehold of a massive and invasive state apparatus. To this task, the republican movement came well equipped. Its multiple battles had trained a democratic counter-elite practiced in the methods of electoral politics. Well in advance of the movement's accession to political power, moreover, it had begun to anchor itself in certain organizations (Freemasonry and the University), in certain milieux (France's religious minorities above all), and in certain associational constituencies (for example, the UNCI and AIU). It had erected an institutional scaffolding that assured the solidity of the democratic edifice that was to be built over it in subsequent years.

POLITICAL CULTURE

In the 1860s, a republican movement began to crystallize within the interstices of the Imperial order. But the movement confronted a tactical problem: how to expand the range of its activities, how to reach and give shape to a broader public beyond the boundaries of its various institutional constituencies. Although the Empire (apart from a brief liberalizing thaw in 1869–1870) and, after it, the government of Moral Order allowed a minimum of space for public activity, republicans managed to devise stratagems to roll back existing restrictions, to expand the limits of public life. By such means, they won converts to the cause, but more than that: they began reconstruction of a public sphere fractured by decades of authoritarian rule, and in the process they gave shape to a new and democratic political culture.

The political silence imposed on France in the 1850s was broken in the ensuing decade. Political issues, as we have seen, were discussed in veiled form within the confines of quasi-private bodies: masonic lodges, businessmen's associations, Protestant lay organizations. Overt debate was possible only beyond France's borders: in Belgium, where radical students gathered in 1865; in Switzerland, where peace activists convened for international conferences in 1868, 1869, and 1870; and in Guernsey, where Victor Hugo maintained a safe haven for republican exiles of all persuasions. From such bases, at home and abroad, the republican movement mounted its campaign.

In periods of repression, it was difficult to make headway by means of the spoken word. In the 1860s, Paris-based republicans organized public lecture series. Speakers contrived to inject political debate into presentations ostensibly confined to non-political matters: art, literature, history. Officialdom intervened to terminate discussions deemed dangerous to public order, but they had a more difficult time controlling the written word. Republicans launched newspaper after newspaper, creating a student press, a *presse d'opinion*, even a mass press (the *Petit Journal* was founded in 1863) which kept up critical pressure on Imperial authorities.[20] A publishing network, too, was created. Pagnerre and Paulin, militants of long-standing, were joined at mid-century by a new generation of republican *éditeurs*: Flammarion, Reinwald, Hetzel, Armand Le Chevalier, Charpentier. The new men published a new literature – science texts and science fiction, realist novels, and popular tracts intended to reach a mass audience. So that such useful books might be accessible to an expanding public, associations like the Ligue de l'Enseignement, which was republican in orientation, and the Société Franklin, which was less so, worked to create a network of well-stocked public libraries.

The republican movement, however, did not conduct operations by word alone. Militants adeptly exploited symbolic occasions to arouse and shape a still inchoate republican political consciousness. They publicized civil marriage ceremonies, turning private celebrations into public events that dramatized secularist values. The same tactic was applied to funeral rites. Civil burial societies multiplied in the 1870s expressly organized in defiance of the pro-Church policies of the government of Moral Order. And indeed, in the formative decades of the new republican order, funerals provided repeated occasion for the crystallization of popular sentiment. That sentiment might be insurrectionary, as in the case of the Victor Noir funeral in 1870. (Noir was a radical journalist who had been murdered by a relative of Louis-Napoléon.) Or it might be commemorative, as in the case of the magnificent official rites organized in Victor Hugo's honor in 1885.

Republicans, in fact, made a cult of the commemorative ceremony, not only of the funeral rite, but also, and perhaps above all, of the anniversary and the centennial. Such occasions might be used to mobilize public opinion. In 1868, the republican press opened a subscription to erect a monument in memory of Dr. Baudin, a republican deputy killed in 1851 resisting Louis-Napoléon's *coup d'état*. The enthusiastic public response prompted authorities to bring the journalists involved to trial. In December of that year, a tumultuous demonstration was held at Baudin's grave site on the anniversary of his death. Once again, the authorities responded with repression. But commemorative events provided an opportunity not just to inflame opinion but also to shape the public memory. 1878 marked the centennial of the deaths of both Voltaire and Rousseau. Moderate republicans organized ceremonials to honor Voltaire, radicals to honor Rousseau. But both camps joined to celebrate the first *quatorze juillet* in 1880, a polyvalent occasion which enshrined a double memory, one of revolutionary ardor (the fall of the Bastille in 1789) and the other of political reconciliation (the *Fête de la Fédération* of 1790).

Republican militants appealed to public opinion and shaped it through ritual events – weddings, funerals, centennials, and festivals.[21] The making of a republican citizenry involved a concentration of public affect around particular symbols and occasions. And through demonstrations and celebrations, militants laid claim to public space, investing particular places and moments with republican meaning. By such means, notable and Bonapartist domination was undermined; by such means, an alternative civic order was set in place.

The practical and symbolic efforts of republicans to mobilize and create a citizen body bore fruit in a series of electoral victories. The elections of 1869 confirmed the republican movement's conquest of urban France, 1877 its conquest of a national majority. *Ad hoc* committees organized the campaigns, endorsed candidates and sponsored public meetings. The republican press exhorted citizens to go to the polls. And a phalanx of voluntary associations – leagues, lodges, business groups – bore down on the hesitant and turned them out to vote.

The republican struggle to defeat a succession of authoritarian regimes, to expand the boundaries of public life, and to capture elected office involved the elaboration of a new political culture. To be a republican entailed more than simple loyalty to a set of political institutions. It meant also reading a particular literature and press; it meant belonging to a league, a lodge, a library association, an electoral committee; it meant taking part in certain public rituals; it meant responding to certain public symbols. What needs to be underlined is the extent to which a republican political culture had been worked out and begun to take root even before the republican movement's electoral victories of the late 1870s. If France's republican middle class won office, if it managed to create durable political institutions, it owed its triumphs in large part to its prior success in the elaboration and dissemination of a democratic political culture.

POLITICS AND PRIVATE LIFE

Republicans were committed to the construction of a new civic order. They understood that a democratic citizenry was necessary to uphold such an order and that the making of citizens implied not just a reordering of political mores but of private life as well. This, indeed, had been one of the lessons learned from the failures of the Second Republic. That regime had faltered because France as yet lacked the moral underpinnings necessary to sustain republican institutions. For a future Republic to survive, it was imperative first that private life be redesigned, that the French learn the domestic virtues conducive to a democratic public life.

Republicans were in the main partisans of the free market, for reasons of material interest of course, but also because they believed the operation of the market taught moral lessons: the principle of reciprocity, the value of a manly independence, and so on. Laissez-faire, to be sure, was not without its pitfalls. The strong were not generous to the weak in the economic struggle for life. But there was a corrective to excessive competition. Through voluntary association (cooperatives, mutual aid societies, trade unions), the disadvantaged might defend themselves, and in the process, they too might learn necessary moral lessons, of cooperation and of self-reliance. The workings of the free market, tempered by association, helped make all Frenchmen, propertied and unpropertied alike, into better citizens, independent but at the same time capable of group solidarity.

Similar motives inspired republican advocacy of family reform. The Civil Code enshrined patriarchy; state-tolerated prostitution legitimated the double standard; and a Church-dominated pedagogy reduced women to an ignorant submissiveness. A family configuration based on patriarchy sanctioned infidelity, and obscurantism bred monarchical attitudes. Republicans envisioned a new kind of marriage, based on mutual respect, a loving intimacy, and cooperation. Republican feminists, who were never more than a minority current within the movement, were prepared to advocate full sexual equality within the marriage bond; a few went so far as to advocate the enfranchisement of women. But most republicans had no intention of elevating women to full citizenship. What they wanted was to fashion a moral environment in the home that would help make citizens of men and teach civic virtues to male children.[22]

The molding of children into citizens was, of course, a primary preoccupation of mid-century republicans. One of the constituent organizations of the republican revival, Jean Macé's Ligue de l'Enseignement, focused its considerable energies on the creation of a system of secular, primary education.[23] The moral education of the child began in the home; it was carried forward by the school; and literature too had a role to play in the process. Macé wrote pedagogical novels for children; along with publisher P.-J. Hetzel, he edited France's first illustrated children's magazine, *Le Magasin d'éducation et de récréation.* And the magazine laid claim to an uncontested popularity through serial publication of a half-dozen Jules Verne novels. Republicans did not practice a dry-as-dust pedagogy but set about packaging lessons of science and morality in *contes* and adventure stories of immediate appeal to children.

The pedagogical ambitions of republicans extended as well into the domain of aesthetics. A shameless Mammonism, mid-century republicans lamented, had corrupted public taste. What better proof than the vacuity of *l'art pompier*, the pretentiousness of crinoline fashions, the chaotic eclecticism of furniture styles? But republicans differed as to how best to redeem a wayward public. The more moderate, a Charles Blanc or Juliette Adam, stood by the classical ideal: an idealizing art modelled on that of the ancients, (relative) sobriety of dress, solidly designed furniture framed in well-ordered home interiors. A return to the discipline of classical tradition, however, did not appeal to all republicans. A minority of radicals, Zola and Manet for example, were determined to elaborate a new aesthetic of modern life. Realism, they argued, not an imitative idealism, ought to be a new art's guiding principle. Modishness was not of itself a sign of moral decay. It was possible to be fashionable and still sincere. And in matters of interior design, modernists touted self-expression and hygiene over the values of solidity and good order. Whatever the stylistic differences separating classicizers and modernists, however, they agreed that aesthetics had a shaping impact on public life. The creation of a democratic public, in a word, required the education of taste.

To reconstruct the state, republicans recognized, it was necessary at the same time to reorder the private sphere. The market, the family, education, literature, art, all might be put to good use in the cultivation of a new, republican man. And a remarkable being he would be too: manly, cooperative, respectful, loving, high-minded, sincere, and modern. Men such as these were suitable material with which to build a republic.

THE REPUBLIC OF THE REPUBLICANS

When republicans assumed office in the late 1870s, they did not hesitate to deploy state power to enact the project they had worked out in movement days.[24] A series of localized and economical purges eliminated unreliable officials from the prefectoral corps, Council of State, and senior judiciary. In the domain of civil liberties, a new press law and law on associations were voted in 1881, and trade unions were legalized in 1884. A secular primary school system was created in the 1880s. By 1905, Church and state had been separated and both the Protestant and Jewish consistories disestablished. In 1879, France was endowed with a new national anthem, the Marseillaise, and in 1880, with a new national holiday, Bastille Day. The regime undertook, once again in 1880, to inscribe the device "Liberty, Equality, Fraternity" on the front of all public buildings. It acted as well in the domain of family law: children's rights were extended and, in 1884, divorce re-established. Provision was made for the secondary education of women; and by 1901, the state-tolerated system of prostitution had been cleaned up (but not eliminated). In the 1870s, official efforts to regulate Freemasonry were abandoned; in 1880, the Ministry of Fine Arts handed over the organization of annual salons to a syndicate of artists; in the 1880s and 1890s, the University was overhauled; and in 1908, the state ceased to play a role in the constitution of Chambers of Commerce.

The republican achievement was remarkable, indeed, unparalleled in Europe, but it was not without its limitations. The regime's record on accident, health, and old-age insurance, for example, did not shine when compared to states elsewhere on the continent. But was not such a failure built into the republican project from the very beginning? Republicans wanted first and foremost to rebuild the state. Social reform, save in the domain of family legislation, was not high on its agenda. Nor did a strong labor movement exist to force the regime to rethink its priorities. The industrial sector was too small, and the disarray in labor circles too great in the repressive aftermath of the Commune, to generate the sustained pressure necessary to persuade the regime to budge. And yet, the Republic did recognize labor's right to organize. In 1901, it created a network of labor councils with a portion of seats set aside for elected trade-union representatives. While the Republic did not pioneer in the domain of social legislation, it did create avenues of access through which workers might exert pressure on the state to make good its promises to serve all the people. Much the same could be said of the regime's record on the women question. Republicans acknowledged women had a role to play in the education of a democratic citizenry, but as wives, mothers, and teachers, not as citizens themselves. A *manly* independence after all was deemed the prerequisite of full citizenship. Republicans, as anti-clericals, worried too about what they believed to be the peculiar susceptibility of women to priestly influence. Give women the vote, it was feared, and they would cast ballots for a religious and anti-republican right. The republican project then countenanced such reforms as might better fit women to the pedagogic role assigned them, but not much more. Accordingly, much of the old Civil Code survived the coming of the Republic intact, as did state-sanctioned prostitution. All the same, a feminist strain persisted within the republican movement, pressuring it always to extend the bounds of citizenship, exploiting to advantage such opportunities as the regime had opened (to daughters of the middle class in the main) to make a career in the professions or in public service.

For workers and for women, certain exclusions (albeit neither total nor irreversible) were built into the republican project from the outset. Was the Republic as exclusive in its treatment of old elites? Up to a point, yes. Notables, discredited by ties to bygone regimes, were driven out of the administration. Efforts were made, through the imposition of a state examination system, to make bureaucratic service a more meritocratic affair. But the new regime had at the same time made compromises with old elites, conceding them more or less uncontested a huge swath of institutional terrain. The army and diplomatic corps remained quite aristocratic in recruitment, although less so than elsewhere in Europe. The Académie française continued in its hidebound ways, settling into a stodginess that bordered on reaction. As for the Catholic hierarchy, which retained an institutional connection to the Republic through 1905, it never brought itself to a wholehearted reconciliation with the new political order.

Important fractions of the private sector, too, maintained a certain distance *vis-à-vis* the new regime: the Lille textile patriciate, the ironmasters of the Nord, the great landlords of the Parisian basin. And over time, they made their influence felt in the corridors of power through a powerful interest-group network that included the Comité des forges and Société des agriculteurs.

Of equal importance, there were critical sections of the republican establishment itself, who were prepared to listen to the entreaties of yesterday's powerful. The Ecole libre des sciences politiques had been founded to train a new elite with the requisite moral vigor and administrative skill to elevate the nation out of the slough into which it had been plunged by the defeat of 1870–1871. The project was launched by liberal Protestants like the Siegfried brothers, but over time it attracted the patronage of social Catholics as well, partisans of a conservative, religiously inspired reform. The school's project was liberal-conservative in orientation, a mix of new and old both in terms of the curriculum it purveyed and the clientele it appealed to.[25] Its graduates went on to employment in the senior civil service which, indeed, they came in time to dominate. The men who staffed the upper echelons of the Republic's bureaucracy then were not so much purebred democrats as an amalgamated elite, willing to serve the present regime but not of necessity married to it. In the business world, too, there were pressures toward amalgamation. The onset of the Great Depression in the 1880s and the rekindling of socialist militancy in the ensuing decade fueled a *ralliement* of business opinion in the interests of protectionism and social defense. The enterprise attracted the backing of iron magnates and gentlemen farmers, and of portions of the Paris commercial community as well, who had in former years been so staunch in their republican loyalties. A new conservative coalition was in the making which included old elites but which operated under the political aegis of men like Jules Méline, a republican of long standing who as an up-and-coming lawyer had militated at the Paris Bar against the Empire.[26]

The Third Republic, as aggressive as it was in pursuit of institutional democratization, left old elites ample room for maneuver. The latter accommodated themselves to the new regime, turned it to advantage as circumstances permitted, and courted alliance with the more conservative fractions of the new political class. This did not mean, however, that they had become sincere democrats, and the point is an important one. For when the Republic experienced crushing defeat in 1940, it was abandoned with unseemly haste by men of influence who ought by rights to have stood by it: by senior civil servants, military men, *agriculteurs* and corporate executives who had never been *républicains de coeur*. Not only did such elites abandon democracy without a backward glance, but they proved all too willing to enlist in Maréchal Pétain's National Revolution.

A deal was struck with France's old notability in the 1870s, which expedited the consolidation of the new Republic. It looked like a good bargain at the time, but not from the perspective of *l'étrange défaite* and the first years of Vichy.

CONCLUSION

To return then to the question posed at the outset: how is the Republic's peculiar longevity to be accounted for? The Revolution bequeathed to France the republican idea, a notion of what institutional configurations and ritual practices were constitutive of a democratic polity. Well prior to the period discussed here, 1860–1885, a republican party had existed. Indeed, in 1848, it had had occasion to attempt an application of its vision. The experiment ended in failure, which prompted a reappraisal of the republican project. Republican institutions had collapsed for want of a democratic citizenry to invigorate them. Such a citizenry was not a given in France but had to be made, to be formed by experience: in voluntary activity, at home and school, in *foro publico*.

Such critical reflection coincided with a particular social, institutional and political conjuncture. An expanding middle class, born of the mid-century economic boom, found itself compressed in an institutional strait-jacket, in part inherited from the past, in part imposed from above by the Imperial state. Local battles exploded on a number of institutional fronts, and republican discourse proved itself tailor-made for articulating the grievances involved. It prescribed at the same time a modus operandi that placed principal accent on the efficacy and virtue of democratic procedures. These various local conflagrations were woven into a more encompassing movement to construct and consolidate, not just a democratic civil society, but a democratic polity.

That movement derived critical strength from the institutional battles that fed into it. Still under the Empire, it had begun to penetrate, even to capture, institutional outworks of the state. Over the course of the movement's "slow march through the institutions," a republican counter-elite had been formed, ready and equipped to take office when the occasion presented itself. When that moment arrived, they came to the task armed with a set of practices and beliefs that were, because themselves the product of democratic contestation, suited to making the institutions of a democratic polity work. It is true that the republican movement, on accession to formal office, deployed state power with considerable skill to consolidate its institutional gains and to convert the nation to its vision. How republicans used office explains in part the comparative longevity of the regime they founded. The argument outlined here, however, sets greater store by what republicans accomplished in advance of taking power. The first and best indicator of how a fresh-minted democracy will conduct itself is to be found in the character and composition of the movement that gave birth to it. The more aggressive and ramified the movement, the greater its chances of success, not just at winning office, but at keeping it.

The preceding summation prompts three critical observations about current accounts of democratic transitions. As the fate of France's Third Republic suggests, democratic movements, however well prepared, can fail to take full advantage of victory, allowing old elites excessive room for maneuver. For all that certain political scientists exhort newborn democracies to restraint toward ousted authoritarians, it may be wiser policy in the long term to run them out when the running is good.

A second observation touches on the role of the middle classes in the construction of democratic institutions. It was a commonplace assumption not so long ago that the stronger the bourgeoisie in a given setting the better the prospects for democracy. This connection has come under withering fire in much recent work. Historians of modern Germany have been at pains to demonstrate that a numerous and organized middle class may embrace a variety of political positions, liberal or illiberal, democratic or statist. Nor can the middle classes claim a monopoly on democratic sentiment. Stable representative institutions, it has been pointed out time and again, are born of a social compromise. The middle classes may well be a party to such a bargain, but they do not bargain alone. Workers and peasants have a crucial role to play in the negotiations, and, indeed, in much recent literature, the democratic potentialities of "ordinary folk" have been placed center stage. The account presented here acknowledges the contingency of middle-class democratic commitment and the negotiated character of democratic transitions, but it insists on the centrality of an awakened middle class to a successful outcome.

There is last of all the troublesome question of just how democratic the much touted "public sphere" actually is. There is more than one critic prepared to label such democratic pretensions a confidence trick and for good reason. For the bulk of the nineteenth century after all, the heyday of Habermasian *Öffentlichkeit*, women were disenfranchised altogether, and working class access to public life restricted at best. In France, the "resurrection of civil society" that culminated in the Third Republic's founding turned out in large part to be a male and middle-class affair. And the Republic's founding fathers, on accession to office, did much to institutionalize the class and gender biases they brought with them.[27] But the

Republic's record, it has been suggested here, was not so dismal as all that. It opened spaces for labor and women's activism which, turning republican rhetoric against itself, bore down on the regime to abide by its promises of equal citizenship for all. The idea of the public sphere in practice proves not quite the promised land of legend, but neither is it just a fraud. It is an ambivalent notion, distorted by biases of all kinds in its first constructions, yet at the same time creating opportunities and secreting rhetorics by which such biases over the long term may be overcome.

NOTES

1. I owe a special debt to Nancy Bermeo and Peter Hall who offered critical guidance and commentary in the preparation of this essay.
2. Furet, *La Gauche et la révolution au milieu du XIXe siècle, Edgar Quinet et la question du Jacobinisme 1865–1870* (Paris, 1986), 7–97; and *La Révolution, de Turgot à Ferry, 1770–1880* (Paris, 1988), 499–507; John Eros, "The Positivist Generation of French Republicanism," *Sociological Review*, 3, no. 2 (December 1955): 255–73.
3. Hoffmann, "Paradoxes of the French Political Community," in Stanley Hoffmann *et al.*, *In Search of France* (New York, 1965), 1–117. See also: David Landes, "French Entrepreneurship and Industrial Growth in the Nineteenth Century," *Journal of Economic History*, 9, no. 1 (May 1949), 45–61; Michel Crozier, *La Société bloquée* (Paris, 1970).
4. Elwitt, *The Making of the Third Republic: Class and Politics in France, 1868–1884* (Baton Rouge, 1975); Weber, *Peasants into Frenchmen: The Modernization of Rural France, 1870–1914* (Stanford, 1976).
5. Charle, *Les Elites de la République 1880–1900* (Paris, 1987).
6. Dahl, *Polyarchy: Participation and Opposition* (New Haven, Conn., 1971); Huntington, "Will More Countries Become Democratic?" *Political Science Quarterly*, 99, no. 2 (Summer 1984): 193–218; Dankwart A. Rustow, "Transitions to Democracy: Toward a Dynamic Model," *Comparative Politics*, 2, no. 3 (April 1970): 337–63.
7. Nancy Bermeo, "Democracy and the Lessons of Dictatorship," *Comparative Politics*, 24, no. 3 (April 1992): 273–91.
8. Almond and Verba, *The Civic Culture: Political Attitudes and Democracy in Five European Nations* (Princeton, 1963); Habermas, *Strukturwandel der Öffentlichkeit, Untersuchungen zu einer Kategorie der bürgerlichen Gesellschaft* (Darmstadt, 1986 [first published 1962]).
9. Larry Diamond, "Persistence, Erosion, Breakdown, and Renewal," in Diamond, Juan Linz, and Seymour Martin Lipset, *Democracy in Developing Countries* (Boulder, Colo., 1989), III: 1–52; Diamond and Linz, "Politics, Society, and Democracy in Latin America," in the same work, IV: 1–58; Alfred Stepan, "State Power and the Strength of Civil Society in the

Southern Cone of Latin America," in Peter Evans, Dietrich Rueschemeyer, and Theda Skocpol, eds., *Bringing the State Back In* (New York, 1985), 317–43. A flavor of how such processes worked themselves out in the Eastern bloc may be gotten from: Vaclav Havel, *Disturbing the Peace* (New York, 1990); and Boris Kagarlitsky, *The Thinking Reed: Intellectuals and the Soviet State from 1917 to the Present* (London, 1988).

10.   Bermeo, "Democracy and the Lessons of Dictatorship," *passim*.

11.   Guillermo O'Donnell and Philippe C. Schmitter, "Tentative Conclusions about Uncertain Democracies," in O'Donnell, Schmitter, and Laurence Whitehead, eds., *Transitions from Authoritarian Rule* (Baltimore, 1986), 16–56.

12.   See Huntington, "Will More Countries Become Democratic?" 212; O'Donnell and Schmitter, "Tentative Conclusions," 61–4.

13.   The issue of how states may act to determine the content of political culture is addressed in Skocpol, "Bringing the State Back In: Strategies of Analysis in Current Research," in Evans, Rueschemeyer, and Skocpol, eds., *Bringing the State Back In*, 3–37.

14.   On the general usefulness of an institutional focus to historical research, see Patrick Fridenson's programmatic statement, "Les organisations, un nouvel objet," *Annales ESC*, 44, no. 6 (November–December 1989): 1461–77.

15.   Georges Weisz, "Le corps professoral de l'enseignement supérieur et l'idéologie de la réforme universitaire en France, 1860–1885," *Revue française de sociologie*, 28, no. 2 (April–June 1977), 203.

16.   The majority of French Protestants belonged to the Reformed Church. The Protestant community included as well an important Lutheran minority and a number of smaller sects, which are not discussed here.

17.   In 1869, the Empire embarked on a short-lived experiment in liberalization, which led to a warming of relations between the Academy and the regime.

18.   There was a republican interlude between Bonaparte's fall and Thiers' installation, but it lasted a brief six months, from September 1870 to February 1871.

19.   See Nord, "Republicanism and Utopian Vision: French Freemasonry in the 1860s and 1870s," *Journal of Modern History*, 63, no. 2 (June 1991), 216.

20.   On the republican press in the 1870s, see Pierre Albert, *Histoire de la presse politique nationale au début de la Troisième République (1871–1879)*, 2 vols. (Paris, 1980).

21.   The fashioning of a republican political culture has been the subject of much recent research. The seminal work was done by Maurice Agulhon: "La 'statuomanie' et l'histoire," *Ethnologie française*, 8, no. 1 (1978): 145–72; *Marianne Into Battle, Republican Imagery and Symbolism in France, 1789–1880* (New York, 1981); *Marianne au pouvoir, l'imagerie et la symbolique républicaines de 1880 à 1914* (Paris, 1989). See also the splendid volume edited by Pierre Nora, *Les Lieux de mémoire*, I: *La République* (Paris, 1984).

22.   See the relevant passages in Claire Goldberg Moses, *French Feminism in the Nineteenth Century* (Albany, 1984); and Françoise Mayeur, *L'Enseignement secondaire des jeunes filles sous la Troisième République* (Paris, 1977).

23. On the Ligue de l'Enseignement, see Katherine Auspitz, *The Radical Bourgeoisie: The Ligue de l'Enseignement and the Origins of the Third Republic 1866–1885* (New York, 1982).

24. The new regime's achievements are argued for with greatest force by Charles Seignobos, *L'Evolution de la 3e République (1875–1914)* (Paris, 1921).

25. Pierre Favre, *Naissances de la science politique en France, 1870–1914* (Paris, 1989).

26. Herman Lebovics, *The Alliance of Iron and Wheat in the Third Republic 1860–1914: Origins of the New Conservatism* (Baton Rouge, 1988).

27. This is more or less the same charge Joan Landes levels against Habermas in *Women and the Public Sphere in the Age of the French Revolution* (Ithaca, NY, 1988). Almond and Verba's notion of "the civic culture" has been criticized on similar grounds by Carole Pateman: *Participation and Democratic Theory* (Cambridge, 1970); and "The Civic Culture: A Philosophic Critique," in Almond and Verba, eds., *The Civic Culture Revisited* (Boston, 1980), 57–102.

2 Uncertain Legitimacy: The Social and Political Restraints Underlying the Emergence of Democracy in Argentina, 1890-1930

Daniel James

"The problem of democracy," and the failure of democratic political institutions to take root in a consistent fashion in Argentina, has exercised the minds of statesmen and political philosophers in that country since the early years of the century. Argentina was blessed with many of the resources and conditions deemed necessary for the installation and development of a viable democracy. It enjoyed – at least until recent decades – high levels of economic growth and relatively high comparative income levels. It possessed a social structure dominated by urban groups with relatively high levels of social mobility reflected in the presence of numerically significant middle sectors. There was, moreover, no semi-feudal rural society with its corresponding political systems of clientelism and patrimonialism. From the beginning of the century it had been characterized by a relative cultural and ethnic homogeneity due primarily to the lack of large-scale sedentary indigenous populations in the core areas of the country and to the particular profile of European immigration, which reached its height in the 1890–1930 period. Finally it enjoyed, from early in the century, comparatively high public cultural levels as measured by such indices as literacy and extension of public education.

Argentina's failure to democratize has contradicted the promise apparent in these social, economic, and cultural resources. The toll taken by this failure is clearly evidenced in a certain underlying cynicism in Argentine popular culture concerning political institutions and actors and democratic possibilities. Much of the academic literature devoted to analyzing the democratic failure has been dominated by the metaphors of the riddle, the conundrum, and more generally by what Alvin Gouldner called in a rather different context "the pathos of pessimism."[1] Some authors see the roots of this failure in the structures and habits formed in the colonial era. More commonly, other analysts and politicians have questioned the content of popular and working-class political culture and have sought there the seeds of both a passive acquiescence in, and a more active support of, authoritarian political regimes.

The most common focus of such a search has been the Peronist era of 1943–1955. The case constructed against populism has varied from discourse analysis of the authoritarian structure of Peronist rhetoric to more general deductions derived from assumptions about working-class political culture and allegiances. Yet the more astute authors have also recognized that Peronism in some basic sense responded to, and sought to repair, an already existing fundamental disjuncture in Argentine society and polity: a disjuncture between a political system created by a dominant economic and social elite and the demands placed on that system by the emergence of increasingly mobilized masses onto the national scene.[2]

If Peronism was in fact a response to existing failings and inadequacies, this clearly justifies pushing the search for the historical antecedents of Argentina's democratic travails back to the founding period of Argentine democracy, between 1890 and 1930. This chapter attempts to sketch some of the basic constraints on the construction and operation of a democratic politics in this period and in particular to examine the issue of the legitimacy granted to the system or withheld from it by both the lower classes and the elites.

THE CONSERVATIVE REPUBLIC AND THE POLITICAL OPENING OF 1912

The political system which characterized the Conservative Republic (1880–1916) was created by and served the interests of the rural elite of stock breeders and grain producers who were the principal beneficiaries of Argentina's incorporation into the world market. Taking direct control of the state in 1880, they fashioned a political system which reflected their social, economic, and cultural domination and which guaranteed them access to and unimpeded control of the organs of public policy. This political control was engineered and maintained at election time through the activities of the Partido Autonomista Nacional (PAN), the only effective nationwide political party. The PAN articulated a complex set of local and regional alliances by which the support, and votes, of local *caudillos* were negotiated. Elections in this system were openly fraudulent and participation rates were low, averaging some 9 percent of the electorate.

Oppositional forces were effectively excluded from access to political participation. Most significant decisions were taken by informal agreements among crucial figures of the political elite and Congress had correspondingly little effective decisionmaking or consultative powers.

The effectiveness of the regime was ultimately assured by its control of the national army and, more crucially, by the legitimacy bequeathed to it by the success of its economic project and the political stability it succeeded in fostering. The generation of 1880 seemed to have solved the basic dilemma confronted by the Argentine political and intellectual elite since independence: how to combine the prerequisites of a representative political system as defined by liberal political theory with the requirements of economic progress in a country whose citizens, in the eyes of this elite, lacked the minimal civic culture necessary for such a venture. The post-1880 solution was an appropriately *sui generis* form of political liberalism which guaranteed the institutions of representative government together with an array of basic civic rights while effectively marginalizing the exercise of suffrage rights as a meaningful channel through which the relations between political elite and the governed were conducted.[3]

As Argentina was integrated into the world economy in the last decades of the nineteenth century and the first decades of the twentieth, it underwent a number of profound economic and social changes. By the outbreak of the First World War Argentina was the world's largest producer of corn and linseed, the third largest exporter of wheat and ranked third in the raising of cattle. The value of its foreign trade far exceeded that of other Latin American nations and its per capita income equalled or surpassed that of many West European countries. Mass immigration sponsored by the state had transformed the demographic make-up of the society. Between 1871 and 1914 almost six million immigrants entered the country and slightly more than half of them stayed, concentrated in the rapidly expanding urban centers. By 1914 53 percent of the population lived in urban areas. The city of Buenos Aires saw its population increase almost tenfold in the same period, to over a million and a half inhabitants. The immigrants were also heavily concentrated in certain areas of the economy; in the city of Buenos Aires, for example, they accounted for 70 percent of those employed in industry and commerce.[4]

At the same time, the process of economic expansion led to a marked increase in the middle sectors associated with the urban economy, the state administrative apparatus, and the service sector tied to the rural economy. These middle sectors were broadly divided into two groups: small entrepreneurs, shopkeepers and tradesmen, who tended to be overwhelmingly immigrants, and another group of white-collar employees in state administration and the professions, who were typically first-generation Argentines. By 1914 these middle sectors constituted about a third of the economically active population, and of the total urban population of Buenos Aires.[5]

A number of social and political tensions associated with these developments emerged in the years following 1890. These tensions gradually undermined the credibility of the traditional political system, not least in the eyes of crucial figures within the political class. Two factors in particular placed the viablity of traditional political arrangements in question. First, the economic expansion had created a growing urban proletariat made up of largely immigrant workers employed in the service sector of the export economy and in an emerging industrial sector centered around food processing and light manufacturing industries. By 1914 the urban working class of Buenos Aires numbered some 400,000. While wage levels were relatively high in comparative international terms, urban workers faced acute problems of inadequate housing, poor health, intense labor exploitation, and unstable employment. The years from 1900 to 1910 saw a wave of strikes which pitted an emerging labor movement against both employers and the state and which did much to undermine the confidence of the elite in its ability to ensure social control and civic peace.

The militant leadership behind this growing wave of social conflict was made up principally of anarcho-syndicalists who preached a gospel of direct action in the confrontation between capital and labor and a radical hostility toward any dealings with the state and the political system. Their message found a clear response among an immigrant working class which was marginalized socially, politically, and culturally. Between 1901 and 1910 there were six general strikes led by the anarchist labor movement. This agitation culminated in the assassination of the Buenos Aires police chief in 1909 and the bloody suppression of a general strike called to coincide with the official celebrations of the centennial of Argentine independence in 1910. The Argentine ruling class responded to this social upheaval with a series of repressive measures ranging from the Residence Law of 1902, which facilitated the expulsion of non-Argentine labor militants, to the Law of Social Defense, passed after the events of 1910, which extended government powers over a wide array of labor and working-class political organizations and suspended a number of legal rights for those accused of "disturbing social peace." While in the short term the repression of 1910 disrupted the labor and anarchist movements, the more far-sighted members of the elite were convinced of the need to find a more effective long-term strategy to defuse social conflict and to recast the bonds of authority between the state and at least some sectors of the working class.[6]

The second factor operating in these years was the emergence of two coherent opposition parties which represented increasingly vocal sections of the new social groups tied to the expansion of the export economy. One was the Unión Cívica Radical (UCR). Though the Radical party's leadership was drawn overwhelmingly from the landowning elite, and its constituency drew from a wide spectrum of dissident local elites and other "out-groups" excluded by the regime's political monopoly, by 1912 it had succeeded in establishing itself as a major presence among the rural and urban middle sectors of the export-oriented Littoral provinces (Buenos Aires, Santa Fé, and Entre Ríos). Under the leadership of Hipólito Yrigoyen the party had adopted an intransigent refusal to participate in the corrupt and fraudulent politics of what it referred to as "the Regime." With a political program which consisted primarily of a call for free elections and which had about it much of the tone of a moral crusade, the Radicals succeeded in tapping into the growing political aspirations of middle sectors frustrated by their exclusion from effective political participation even as they experienced significant upward social mobility. Their attempted insurrections in 1890, 1893, and 1905 proved their ability to harass the regime.

The other political party which had emerged on the scene was the Socialist Party, which drew its strength from certain working-class and lower-middle-class sectors in the city of Buenos Aires. It succeeded in electing the first socialist congressman in Latin America in 1904, and advocated a program of social reform legislation tied to the gradual acquisition of parliamentary power.[7]

The pressures posed by these parties, as well as by the anarchist labor movement, were sufficiently great to provoke elite response. In 1912 the Argentine Congress passed a group of measures, known collectively as the Sáenz Peña Law, which effectively instituted universal suffrage for Argentine males over the age of twenty-one. While universal male suffrage had been formally enshrined in the Argentine constitution since 1853, the Sáenz Peña Law for the first time provided the institutional and legal means for its effective implementation. Provisions were made to guarantee effective secrecy in balloting and the army was given responsibility for the care of the ballot boxes after voting. In addition the voting system adopted guaranteed a certain degree of minority representation in Congress. Finally, voting was made obligatory for all eligible Argentine males.

Faced with middle-class demands for political participation and representation, and with what they perceived as a growing threat of social rebellion by an immigrant working class, the elite had responded with a strategy of democratization and a controlled opening of the political system. Their calculations in doing so were clear: they hoped to co-opt certain social groups and defuse the threat posed by others. The Sáenz Peña reforms left the immigrant working class disenfranchised and politically isolated while simultaneously incorporating into the political system the native middle sectors and certain sectors of the native working class. This was carried out through universal male suffrage – the minimum demand of the Radicals to abandon their abstention and enter the system. Yet this was a price that the leading figures of the elite were willing to pay, convinced as they were of their capacity to transform their traditional political apparatus into a modern, mass-based conservative party. In their writings and in the debates over the Sáenz Peña Law, they invoked the names of Peel and Disraeli as the founders of a modern, popular conservative movement, and cast the Radicals, and to a lesser extent the Socialists, in the role of the loyal opposition – hence the provision for minority representation.

Continued restrictions on Argentine democracy were a key component of this strategy. Women continued to be denied access to political rights.[8] And in a society in which immigrants made up between 50 and 70 percent of the adult males in the principal areas of economic activity and population density, limiting the right to vote to Argentine nationals had a clearly restrictive impact on the expansion of political participation. This impact was compounded by the fact that the percentage of immigrants who became naturalized citizens was extremely low throughout the period of mass immigration; by 1914, for example, only 1.4 percent had bothered to do so.

This was not a casual oversight on the part of the elite, but rather a vital part of their strategy of a controlled and limited opening of the system. Their explicit refusal to simplify the procedures of naturalization – an issue raised in the debates of 1911–1912 – is testimony of this. Thus the incorporation of new voters was offset by the exclusion of the immigrant masses from the political process. In 1910 the percentage of voters in relation to the total adult male population was 9 percent, a figure which rises to 20 percent if only native Argentine males are counted. In 1916 these figures were 30 and 64 percent, respectively, and in the presidential elections of 1928, 41 and 77 percent. In other words, even after the legislation of 1912 some two-thirds of the adult males in Argentina were excluded from the electoral process.[9]

DEMOCRATIZATION AND LEGITIMACY, 1912–1930

Despite these limitations on Argentine democracy, the period from 1912 to 1930 saw dramatic increases in popular participation and a genuine transformation of the political system. In the Federal Capital the number of registered voters grew from 123,936 in 1912 to 345,383 in 1930. Despite the obligatory voting provision in the Sáenz Peña Law, the numbers of actual voters in the capital dropped slightly during the 1910s, from an 84 percent turnout in 1912 to figures in the high 60s or low 70s in succeeding elections. But the last two elections of the period, in 1928 and 1930, saw a marked increase in participation, with turnouts of 91 and 86 percent respectively. National voting figures show a similar trend. In the 1912 elections, 640,852 Argentines voted, from a total of 935,001 registered voters – a 69 percent participation rate. Four years later, in the first presidential elections under the new system, 61 percent of 1,189,254 registered voters went to the polls. But by the 1928 presidential election, the number of registered voters had risen to 1,807,566, of whom 80 percent cast ballots.[10]

How could we characterize the wider social meaning of the democratic experience of the 1916–1930 period? Viewed from the vantage point of its ending, the military coup of September 1930 which overthrew Radical President Yrigoyen, it appears to represent a failed experiment. Yet in searching for reasons for this breakdown we need to look beyond short-term political conjunctures and re-examine the issue of the legitimacy of the regime established in 1912. This in turn raises the issue of the relationship between elites and popular sectors and between elites and the political system.

While the traditional elites had not foreseen the emergence of Radicalism as the dominant national political force after 1912, nor their own failure to establish a viable, hegemonic conservative party, the project to expand political participation and guarantee free elections had clearly been successful in creating an expanded base of support and consensus for the state. In this sense the strategy of co-optation underlying the Sáenz Peña Law succeeded. But more factors were at work here than the opening up of the political system. The construction of consensus, legitimacy, and hegemony is a complex, multi-faceted historical process. In Argentina between 1890 and 1930 the socioeconomic system showed a remarkable stability. In part this was due to the presence of a number of structural characteristics of Argentine society: the generation of economic resources which offered at least the prospect of social mobility and relatively high living standards for most of the population, the existence of broad-based urban and rural middle sectors, and the absence of profound agrarian social problems.

Other factors also have to be taken into account. One which has not been examined in sufficient depth was the changing role of the state, both national and local, which coincided roughly with the opening of the political system.[11] The socialization function of the state, as expressed in the growth and changing content of public education, was of particular importance. The state placed an increasing emphasis on primary education and, especially after 1908 under the leadership of José María Ramos Mejía, the National Council on Education sought to place "Argentinization" at the forefront of primary school curricula, mandating texts on Argentine history and culture and the increasing use of patriotic symbols and rituals within the classroom. This "patriotic education" in turn reached a growing number of future citizens and voters. Between 1900 and 1929 in the Federal Capital the proportion of children between the ages of six and fourteen who went through some form of public education increased from 66 percent to 88 percent; in absolute numbers this represented a fourfold increase in the numbers of children registered in those schools, reaching some 232,000 in the latter year.[12]

In a broader sense, too, the changing role of the state was crucial in re-establishing the terms of working-class subordination and the legitimacy of authority relations so disturbingly challenged between 1900 and 1910. The new terms of subordination included the continued use of state repression, as in the Semana Trágica of 1919 and the massacres in Patagonia in 1921, but they were also increasingly premised on elements of popular consent.

The opening of the political system offered one of the terrains on which this consent could be negotiated and constructed. In part this was achieved through the perception of the political process as a viable channel for expressing sectional interests *vis-à-vis* a state with greatly increased powers of intervention and arbitration. In part, too, it was expressed in the development of a set of political practices which flourished after 1912 and a popular political culture derived from them. Political activism in the Socialist and Radical ward committees, and participation in the social and cultural networks established by the same parties, attendance at election time at the meetings, conferences, and street rallies characteristic of this expanded public sphere all offered alternatives to the radical contestation and rejection of the earlier period.[13]

The growing legitimacy of the renovated political system for both the enfranchised middle and working classes is attested to by various sources. From leftist critics of bourgeois democracy came frequent complaints about the efficacy of its attractions for the working class. Anarchist papers lamented that their denunciation of electoralism was falling on deaf ears. Communist militants bemoaned the fact that even those who professed to hate politics, and even claimed to espouse anarchist ideas, usually ended up voting for Radical party *caudillos*. The middle class had perhaps an even more active involvement, especially with the Radical party. It has been estimated that there were some 70,000 affiliates in Buenos Aires and in the 1920s about 50,000 took part in internal party elections. Many more had some less activist involvement with the extensive network of ward and *barrio* committees.

The credibility and legitimacy of the political system was tempered to a certain extent by the exclusion of non-Argentines. As we have seen, the numbers excluded were large both in the working class and in the middle sectors, where the vast majority of commercial proprietors and industrial entrepreneurs were immigrants. In addition, the numbers of immigrants picked up dramatically after a hiatus during the First World War; the 1920s saw the second largest influx in the 1880–1930 period. Yet the impact of this exclusion seems to have been muted by several factors. The nature of immigrant culture and perceptions played an important part; political participation seems not to have been a priority among immigrants seeking to "*hacer América*" and uncertain of their permanence in the new land.[14] Moreover, a majority of them came from societies and social groups with little or no experience of democratic practice and political participation; indeed, this was one of the reasons for the appeal of anarchism's anti-political discourse. There were also other channels of participation open for immigrants to express their aspirations and to seek to organize their interests. Immigrant society was not an anomic, destructured social space. Rather it consisted of dense networks of social and cultural institutions which since the middle of the nineteenth century had offered an important alternative form of political participation.[15] Immigrant mutual aid and cultural societies achieved an influence in Argentine society far greater than their equivalents in North America. The emergence of the labor movement and its increasing willingness after 1910 to adopt a participatory stance *vis-à-vis* the state also provided a channel for both an experience of democratic practice and the articulation of needs and interests. Finally, it should be noted that non-Argentine residents enjoyed all other civic rights and the protections of the law regardless of the fact that they could not vote.

Underlying these changes in popular political practice and participation in the electoral system was not simply the presence of a democratic government after 1916 but other profound changes in society. While we have little sense as yet of the scope of these changes in the interior provinces, thanks to a new generation of Argentine historians we are now beginning to achieve an understanding of their character in the urban areas of the Littoral, especially Buenos Aires.[16] In the words of Luis Alberto Romero:

In a context characterized by the presence of a State with much greater capacity of control and a much more consolidated society than that at the end of the century, a vision began to emerge among the popular sectors of a much less contestatory world. The real process of social mobility and the even more exaggerated image of it, the image of an open society with opportunity for all, was creating attitudes of a distinctly reformist and integrative hue.[17]

The basic elements around which this transformation centered are clear: the emergence of suburban *barrios* of working- and middle-class homeowners and the consequent breaking up of the ghetto-like concentrations of the earlier period; the process of diffusion of a mass culture and the growth of leisure pursuits; the growing importance of *barrio*-centered institutions like the neighborhood improvement societies and popular libraries; the impact of state education policies, particularly on second-generation Argentines; and finally, a growing internal differentiation within the working class and the consolidation of certain strata of a "labor aristocracy." The political corollary of these changes was a predisposition to work within the political system, or at least to oppose it on the terrain it had chosen.

DELEGITIMATION AND THE BREAKDOWN OF DEMOCRACY

The result of the political democratization undertaken in 1912 and the profounder social changes which underlay it would seem therefore to constitute what in Gramscian language might be termed a successful process of "transformism," or at least its renewal after its crisis during the first decade of the century.[18] Ideologically this success could be said to be embodied in the failure of the Radical Party, despite its holding power continuously from 1916 to 1930, to elaborate even the minimum basis of an alternative ideology to that of the dominant liberalism of the traditional elite. In terms of public policy it was reflected in the maintenance of fundamental economic and social policies deemed necessary for the furtherance of the elite's interests.[19] And in leadership terms this transformism was personified by Radical leaders who at least initially were drawn from the same social strata and inhabited the same social clubs as their Conservative opponents.

Yet for all its apparent success as a strategy it seems clear that the democratic politics inaugurated in 1912 never achieved real legitimacy in the eyes of the Conservative elite. A number of explanations – or partial explanations – can be offered for this. In an influential essay published in the 1970s, Peter Smith drew attention to the political presuppositions behind the elite's co-optation strategy, or more precisely to what they understood by political democracy. Their commitment to democracy, he argued, was premised upon the respect by all legitimate political competitors of some basic rules of the game. A central tenet of this code was "that power would be shared among competing factions that would reach decisions by consensus," and that political disagreements would be resolved through "gentlemen's agreements" rather than "demagoguery." It was the breakdown of these assumptions in the late 1920s, Smith argues, which led the conservative elite to seek alternatives to the democratic system.[20]

Central to Smith's argument is the exclusion of the Conservative elite from access to political power, which became progressively worse after 1916 and which clearly made untenable the central assumption of power sharing. The Conservative forces never succeeded in creating a coherent national political organization and remained essentially a loose conglomeration of provincial groups less and less capable of competing with the Radicals on the terrain of an emerging modern party political system.[21] Thus the result of Argentina's first experiment with democracy was that powerful social and economic groups were excluded from direct access to political power at a national level.

Yet we may again ask why was this exclusion so crucial? If the economic structure of Argentine society remained unchallenged, and if the social and cultural power of the elite remained largely uncontested, why did their marginalization from formal political power matter? Or to put it another way, why was the breach of the code alluded to by Smith so significant? A possible approach to this question may be found in Pierre Bourdieu's concept of the political field. A field in Bourdieu's terms is one of many distinct spheres of practice in a society, "each involving specific forms and combinations of capital and value and specific institutions." The political field is "the site par excellence in which agents seek to form and transform their visions of the world and thereby the world itself . . . Through the production of slogans, programs agents [sic] in the political field are engaged in a labor of representation by which they seek to construct and impose a particular vision of the world."[22] It follows from this that two things are primarily at stake in the contest for the construction or re-elaboration of the political field in a society. First, there is the monopoly of the elaboration and diffusion of legitimate representations regarding the social world, its agents, its categories. The symbolic capital acquired in the achievement of such monopoly is crucial since it also bestows the capacity to mobilize groups whose support is the ultimate basis of power in the political field. Such a monopoly is most effectively attained in modern political fields through political parties and the professionals who run them.

The second issue at stake is, in Bourdieu's words, "the struggle to maintain or subvert the distribution over public powers (state administrations)."[23] The ability to monopolize the instruments of state power had a number of significant implications. First, the Argentine state had enormous influence within the society at large, especially in establishing the framework for elite-dominated economic development. The national army had played a crucial role in the creation of many of the large estates, and state fiscal and credit resources had been vital to the consolidation of the export economy. Second, a wide array of jobs, resources, and political patronage networks was attached to the state and to its budget. It was this aspect of the emerging Argentine political field that the Radical party had appropriated and which underlay the construction of their political machine. It enabled them, in Bourdieu's words, to "win positions capable of ensuring that they can wield power over those who grant power to them." There was an element of self-fulfilling prophecy in this, since the emergence of a modern political system placed a high premium on the ability of the Radicals to consolidate their constituency and to become increasingly, in Gramsci's phrase, "bankers of men in a monopoly system."[24]

The Conservative elite thus rejected democracy in large part because of their exclusion from "the public power." Equally important, however, was Bourdieu's first element: control over the production and diffusion of "legitimate" representations of the social world. The elite's fear of losing that control, I believe, was at the root of their uneasiness over the changing social composition of the Radical leadership, increasingly composed by the late 1920s of professional politicians drawn from the middle classes. Professionals of this sort not only violated the traditional code of what a politician should be, expressed in dismissive Conservative references to the collapse of good manners and language with the advent of the "Radical scum." Conservatives also feared professional politicians' potential ability to monopolize the symbolic representation of the contours of an emerging Argentine society and the production of ideological discourse within that society.

This concern formed part of the general preoccupation of the Argentine elite, expressed with varying intensity throughout the period 1890–1930, about how to construct their profile of an ideal Argentina, about who was or was not fit for citizenship in such an entity, and what the cultural and institutional parameters of this new nation would be. These concerns were played out in a shifting struggle in the cultural and intellectual fields which were reflected in such features as the emergence of a certain hispanicizing nationalism among sectors of the traditional elite. Argentina was in this period still very much a society in construction and many of the elements of its "imagined community" still awaited representation and legitimation, subject to the results of struggles in many fields including the political. The parameters of the public sphere in Argentina were, in the course of this period, beginning to be remapped in gender, class, and ethnic terms. This inevitably produced tensions and anxieties among the dominant elite as they viewed the unfolding of some of the unintended consequences of the economic model to which they owed their status and success.[25]

It was, indeed, a recognition that more was at stake in their marginalization within democratic politics than simple electoral calculus that fatally flawed the democratic experiment in the eyes of the Conservative elite. The collapse of Argentina's first democratic experience in 1930 was, therefore, due not to some putative lack of an adequate "democratic" civic culture on the part of Argentina's working and middle classes. It was rather the elites who ultimately found mass participation unacceptable and withdrew their support from the regime.

NOTES

1. Alvin Gouldner, "Metaphysical Pathos and the Theory of Bureaucracy," in L.A. Coser and B. Rosenburg, eds., *Sociological Theory* (New York, 1964).
2. Gino Germani, the doyen of Argentine sociologists, argued for example, in the language of the modernization sociology in vogue in the 1950s and 1960s, that Peronism both arose from and responded to the gap between the intense social mobilization of the modernization process and the inadequate institutions and mechanisms of political and social integration present in Argentine society in the 1930s and 1940s. See his *Política y sociedad en una época de transición* (Buenos Aires, 1962).
3. See Natalio Botana, *El orden conservador: La política argentina entre 1880 y 1916* (Buenos Aires, 1977).
4. See David Rock, *Argentina, 1516–1987: From Spanish Colonization to Alfonsín* (Berkeley, 1987), 172.
5. See David Rock, *Politics in Argentina, 1890–1930: The Rise and Fall of Radicalism* (Cambridge, 1975), 18–24.
6. See Juan Suriano, *Trabajadores, anarquismo y estado represor: De la Ley de Residencia a la Ley de Defensa Social (1902–1910)* (Buenos Aires, 1988); Ronaldo Munck, *Argentina from Anarchism to Peronism: Workers, Unions and Politics* (London, 1987).
7. On the Socialist party, see Richard J. Walter, *The Socialist Party of Argentina, 1890–1930* (Austin, 1977). On the Radical Party see Rock, *Politics in Argentina*.

8. On women's struggle for the vote in this period, see Marifran Carlson, *Feminismo! The Women's Movement in Argentina from its Beginnings to Eva Perón* (Chicago, 1988).

9. Atilio Borón, "El estudio de la mobilización política en América Latina," *Desarrollo Económico*, 12, no. 46 (July–September 1972): 211–45.

10. Walter, *Socialist Party of Argentina*

11. On the role of the state in Argentina in this period, see Jorge Sábato, *La clase dominante en la Argentina moderna: Formación y características* (Buenos Aires, 1988), 163–75. For a study of the ideological forms underlying changing notions of state involvement in issues such as social reform, public health and immigration policy, see Eduardo Zimmerman, "Racial Ideas and Social Reform: Argentina, 1890–1916," *Hispanic American Historical Review*, 72, no. 1 (February 1992): 23–47.

12. On education in Argentina, see Carlos Escudé, *El fracaso del proyecto argentino: Educación e ideología* (Buenos Aires, 1990); Hobart Spalding, "Education in Argentina, 1880–1914: The Limits of Oligarchical Reform," *Journal of Interdisciplinary History*, 3, no. 1 (1972): 31–61; James Scobie, *Buenos Aires: From Plaza to Suburb, 1870–1910* (New York, 1974), 240–4.

13. On the emerging political practices associated with the new democratic political system, see Aníbal Vigueira, "Participación electoral y prácticas políticas en los sectores populares en Buenos Aires, 1912–1922," *Entrepasados*, 1, 1 (1991).

14. This relative absence of political concern is evident in the correspondence of the Sola family. See Samuel L. Baily and Franco Ramella, eds., *One Family, Two Worlds: An Italian Family's Correspondence across the Atlantic, 1901–1922* (New Brunswick, 1988).

15. See Hilda Sábato, "Citizenship, Political Participation and the Formation of the Public Sphere in Buenos Aires, 1850s to 1880s," *Past and Present*, no. 136 (August 1992): 139–63.

16. Though this is beginning to change. See, for example, Nicholas Biddle, "Oil and Democracy in Argentina, 1916–1930" (Ph.D. diss., Duke University, 1991). Biddle's work is a salutary reminder of the dangers of generalizing from the experience of Buenos Aires. He points out that in Salta the scope of the democratic innovations was soon limited by the local oligarchy, who continued to use both force and fraud to enforce their political and social control of the province. Even the Radical practice of federal intervention, much favored by Yrigoyen as a device to break the hold of traditional elite practices, had little practical effect in democratizing Salta.

17. Luis Alberto Romero, "Sectores populares, participación y democracia: El caso de Buenos Aires," *Pensamiento Iberoamericano*, 7 (1985). See also Diego Armus, ed., *Mundo urbano y cultura popular* (Buenos Aires, 1990).

18. On "transformism" as a concept, see Antonio Gramsci, *Selections from the Prison Notebooks* (London, 1971), 587. Gramsci uses the concept to refer to the process by which oppositional groups and social classes are absorbed into the status quo and transformed into politically harmless elements. It is closely linked to his notion of "passive revolution."

19. David Rock details the ways in which the elite's economic interests were safeguarded by Radical governments who demonstrated a constant willingness to accommodate the fundamental economic and social claims of both

Argentine elites and international investors. This did not necessarily mean, however, that popular sectors could not at times see in Radicalism both a discourse and a vehicle capable of contesting certain elements of the status quo. See for example the use of petroleum nationalism by Yrigoyen in the late 1920s. Biddle, "Oil and Democracy."

20. Peter H. Smith, "The Breakdown of Democracy in Argentina, 1916–1930," in Juan Linz and Alfred Stepan, eds., *The Breakdown of Democratic Regimes: Latin America* (Baltimore, 1978).

21. See Ana María Mustapic, *El Partido Conservador de la Provincia de Buenos Aires ante la intervención federal y la competencia democrática: 1917–1928* (Buenos Aires, 1987); Richard J. Walter, *The Province of Buenos Aires and Argentine Politics, 1912–1943* (New York, 1985).

22. Pierre Bourdieu, *Language and Symbolic Power* (Cambridge, Mass., 1991), 26.

23. Bourdieu, *Language and Symbolic Power*, 181. This aspect of the construction of the political field has been the one generally emphasized in the literature on Argentina in the 1916–1930 era, above all in David Rock's influential work, *Politics in Argentina*.

24. Antonio Gramsci, *Selections from Political Writings, 1921–1926* (London, 1978), 17–18.

25. See Sandra McGee Deutsch, *Counter-Revolution in Argentina, 1900–1932: The Argentine Patriotic League* (Lincoln, 1986). Deutsch emphasizes the importance of elite reaction to what they perceived as a threat to gender hierarchies, and the efforts of the Argentine Patriotic League to speak to this gender anxiety. For an analysis of the impact of such tensions and uncertainties within the intellectual and literary fields, see Beatriz Sarlo, *Una modernidad periférica: Buenos Aires, 1920–1930* (Buenos Aires, 1988). See also Donna J.Guy, *Sex and Danger in Buenos Aires: Prostitution, Family and Nation in Argentina* (Lincoln, 1991).

3 Japan's First Experiment with Democracy, 1868–1940

Richard J. Smethurst

On July 18, 1993, the *New York Times* published an editorial on the Japanese elections of the previous day. Entitled "The Dawn of a Democratic Japan," the editorial observed that finally in the summer of 1993 Japanese voters "face real choices ... Affluent, educated and well traveled, Japanese society was revealed as more complex and sophisticated than even some of its professional interpreters imagined ... This election is likely to mark only the first stage of a long transition between the one-party politics of the past and a more democratic future."[1] In fact, the *Times* editorial writers were three-quarters of a century late. The "dawn" of democracy in Japan broke, not in 1993, but in the first third of the twentieth century when Japan had already developed a workable two-party system.

As a working definition, I consider a democratic society to be one in which the populace, usually through their right to vote, govern. In practical terms, voters elect representatives to local and national assemblies who represent the interests of those who elect them.[2] At the same time, the rights of the losers in the electoral process and of various religious, ethnic, political, and ideological minorities are guaranteed basic protections from the arbitrary actions of the majority and its elected representatives.

One should view democratic and non-democratic regimes not in absolute terms – unlike pregnancy, it is possible to be a little bit democratic – but on a continuum. Democracy and totalitarianism are the two extremes of this continuum and all existing polities fall somewhere in between. Between 1868, when the modernizing Meiji government came to power, and 1932, when the democratic trend was reversed, Japan's political system moved steadily away from the non-democratic and toward the democratic pole of this continuum. The period from 1924 until 1932, during which the Seiyūkai (Friends of Constitutional Government Party) and the Minseitō (Constitutional Government Party), Japan's two major parties, alternately provided prime ministers, and the rights of all but the most radical opponents of the polity were protected, marked the high water point of pre-war Japanese democracy. During these eight years,

71

Japan's political system was not remarkably different from those of the democratic regimes of Europe and North America. In this light, we should not see the reforms of the Allied occupation of Japan after the Second World War as turning an authoritarian, fascist Japan into a potential democracy. Rather, we should view the occupation authorities as rebuilding Japan on a foundation of pre-existing democratizing institutions which unfortunately had been eclipsed in the 1930s.[3]

THE ORIGINS OF DEMOCRATIZATION

Industrialization and modernization began in Japan in the late 1860s because of an "aristocratic revolution."[4] The revolutionaries were not landowners. Rather, they were young, landless members of feudal samurai warrior elites who had lost power during the 1600s and 1700s to the central authorities of the Tokugawa shogunate. By the 1860s the weakness of the Tokugawa regime, painfully symbolized by the incursion of American and European naval forces, had led to its removal by these youthful, often low-ranking warriors, who now faced the challenge of creating a new regime dedicated to two goals. Internally, the fledgling oligarchs wanted to keep others from usurping their newly won power. Externally, they wanted to protect Japan from the threat of European and American imperialism, a very real danger in the second half of the nineteenth century. The new rulers thus set out to make Japan rich and strong, goals enunciated in their borrowed Chinese motto, *fukoku kyōhei*, "rich country, strong army."

Although the new leaders did not have a clear blueprint for the remaking of Japan, they were committed for the most part to using Western technology, institutions, and ideas as the basis for their new Japan – they thought they could best expel the barbarians by using the enemy's own tools. Thus, over the last third of the nineteenth century, the state, using the skills of Western advisors and of Japanese who studied abroad, built itself a modern infrastructure. By the turn of the century, Japan had schools, universities, banks, an army and navy using up-to-date equipment and techniques, modern communications, railroads, factories, and most important for our discussion here, new political guidelines, all based on the latest European and North American models. The government's goal was no longer to expel the imperialists, but to join them.

The Meiji political system was based at the local level on a structure that combined a degree of local autonomy with centralized control, and at the national level on a constitution that placed severe limits on the possibility of popular sovereignty. The local governmental system was created in the 1880s by Home Minister Yamagata Aritomo, one of the most powerful (and before the Meiji era, lowest ranking) of the ex-samurai oligarchs. The country was divided into 47 prefectures, to which the Home Minister appointed governors. Prefectures were in turn divided into cities and counties, and counties were further subdivided into towns and villages. Some major cities, such as Tokyo, had mayors appointed by the national government; but other cities, and all towns and villages, elected their own mayors. Local administrative units also elected assemblies, and particularly at the town and village level these assemblies wielded considerable power. Electoral districts within villages and towns tended to coincide with the small, co-residential villages that had existed in late feudal times and thus reinforced the importance of these tiny hamlets as the building blocks of rural society. During the formative years of the new Japan in the late nineteenth and early twentieth centuries, powerful landowners, who had not been part of the national political elite before 1868, controlled hamlet and village political life, as Yamagata had intended. However, as we shall see, in the era of most rapid democratization and even afterward, smallholders and even tenant farmers replaced landlords as village leaders.

Another of the founding oligarchs, Itō Hirobumi, took primary responsibility for the Meiji Constitution of 1889. Itō and his fellow oligarchs decided that Japan needed a written constitution based on Western models, not only because they wanted to legitimize and formalize the *ad hoc* government that they had run during the first two decades of modern rule, but also because by the 1880s one of their primary goals was treaty revision, that is, ridding Japan of the unequal treaties imposed on it in the 1850s and 1860s by the imperialist powers.[5] Negotiating the end of these treaties required proving that Japan had become "civilized." Accordingly, Itō went abroad to study foreign constitutions, decided that the conservative Prussian model was best for Japan, and conferred in Berlin with some of the most prominent German constitutional lawyers of the time. One of these men, Herman Roessler, came to Japan and worked with Itō and a small group of his colleagues to write the new constitution.[6]

The new constitution, promulgated in 1889, posited imperial sovereignty and was presented to the Japanese people as a gift of their emperor. In other words, Itō, Yamagata, and the other oligarchs who dominated the government wrote a constitution that would allow them to maintain a great deal, if not all, of their power. But these men were not political Neanderthals. They realized that they could best maintain power by not monopolizing it. Thus, the new constitution established a bicameral legislature with a lower house elected by the voters and an upper house dominated by a peerage appointed by the very men who had written the constitution. The oligarchs decided to divide their opposition by sharing power with some of its members – rich landlords, new industrialists, local and lower-ranking national officials, and high-ranking members of the old samurai elite – while excluding others – mostly former samurai, including some ex-oligarchs, and prosperous farmers. This system of co-optation, repeated over and over again for larger and larger circles of people, would allow Japan to become increasingly democratic between 1890 and 1932.

Still, for those interested in creating a democratic Japan, the Meiji Constitution was not a congenial document. Not only could the largely appointed upper house slow or even prevent the passage of legislation passed by the House of Representatives, but the constitution included several other provisions which stood between Japan and real democracy. The document gave the army's and navy's general staffs the "right of supreme command," that is, the right under certain circumstances to report directly to the emperor and thus to operate independently of the prime minister. Citizens received the rights of free speech, assembly, religion, etc., but these rights were subject to the needs of the government. Treaties with foreign countries were ratified by the Privy Council, another appointed body, and not by the popularly elected legislature.

Several extra-constitutional regulations, promulgated in the early years of constitutional government, also inhibited the efforts of those Japanese interested in creating a more democratic polity. The cabinet announced that voters for and members of the new House of Representatives had to be substantial taxpayers, which limited the electorate for the first national election in 1890 to only slightly more than one percent of the total population. The army and navy ministers could be chosen only from among officers holding the top two ranks of generals and admirals; together with the constitutional "right of supreme command," this severely limited civilian control of the military. The government promulgated a variety of police regulations, culminating in the Peace Preservation Law of 1925 and its 1928 revision, which together with the absence of absolute constitutional guarantees of the various freedoms allowed the government to suppress political opposition deemed dangerous. Finally, the oligarchs created an orthodox ideology that established the emperor as the sacred national father figure. Pictures of this *arahitogami* or "living man god" and his empress were placed in every elementary school in Japan, and he became the center of a cult of Japanese nationalism that limited criticism of and opposition to the state.

The constitution and its surrounding regulations gave proponents of democracy only one powerful weapon: the House of Representatives had the power to approve or disapprove the government's annual budget. Even this power was limited. The constitution stated that if the lower house did not approve a budget, that of the preceding year automatically went into effect. But the political parties that arose in the next two decades used budget politics skillfully to increase their power. In an era of gradual, and then during and after the First World War rapid, inflation, and of rising military expenditures as Japan competed with the Western imperialist powers to build its empire, previous years' budgets did not suffice for long.

Given the extent of these legal and institutional constraints, one has to be amazed by how far Japan moved toward democracy in the early twentieth century. Many Japanese and some Western scholars have written that the "emperor system" described above, a system supported not only by the government's constitution, regulations, ideology, and higher civil servants, but also by its natural allies – industrialists, landlords, and military officers – precluded the possibility of significant democracy in Japan.[7] They overstate their case. Certainly the system created by the Meiji oligarchs inhibited the growth of democracy between 1890 and 1924, and certainly its constitutional framework helped in the demise of democracy in the 1930s. But it did not preclude democracy altogether. It is important to remember that the Meiji regime contained within it a number of political and social tensions and faultlines which, when exploited by bourgeois political parties and other potentially democratic forces, created real opportunities for expanding democratic governance and participation. Indeed, one reason that Japan did not have the revolution in the 1920s that so many activists hoped for was that during the preceding half-century the country had evolved in a democratic direction.

One force stimulating such democratization was the oligarchy itself. Proponents of the "emperor system" approach to understanding the prewar Japanese state would reject this idea as preposterous, but Western scholars such as George Akita have argued that men like Yamagata and especially Itō were not as conservative as they have often been portrayed.[8] While they clearly did not envisage a Japan where all men and women, regardless of wealth and education, should be allowed to vote, there is no doubt that they knew that they had to broaden the base of government for two reasons: first, the oligarchs would not live forever and they wanted to co-opt trustworthy outsiders to ensure that Japan would be in good hands after they were gone; and second, as the oligarchs' policies raised the standards of living and education of more and more Japanese, the leaders realized that they could not successfully monopolize power indefinitely. We shall return to this point shortly.

Another reason that has been advanced for the growth of democracy in early twentieth-century Japan was competition among the oligarchs themselves. While the oligarchs as a group held substantial political power, no single member of the group, hard as he might try, could dominate the government. Each member devised different strategies to advance his own interests, and party politicians used these divisions to expand the role of the parties in Meiji-Taishō governance.[9]

The rivalry between Yamagata and Itō was particularly important in this context. Field Marshal Yamagata was highly skilled on the interpersonal level but lacked mass appeal. He was able to create several cliques of followers to carry on his work, both in the army and the home ministry, but he could not attract a popular following.[10] Itō , on the other hand, was less skilled than Yamagata at attracting personal followers, but much better able to make mass appeals (though under the Meiji constitution, the only "masses" who enjoyed the right to vote were substantial taxpayers). In an effort to counter Yamagata's efforts at bureaucratic coalition-building, Itō founded the Seiyūkai political party at the turn of the century, based on landlords and small-scale regional businessmen disaffected over rising taxes.[11] His party, later led by the last of the oligarchs, Prince Saionji Kimmochi, and then by the first "commoner" prime minister, Hara Kei, became one of the two major parties of "Taishō democracy."[12]

The parties and their politicians were another force impelling Japan toward democracy. Many of the men elected to the first session of the House of Representatives in 1890 organized themselves into parties, and the two largest of these groupings held a majority of the seats in the Diet's first six sessions (1890–1894). In order to get their budgets passed, the oligarchs had no choice but to deal with these fledgling parties, usually through either "candy or the whip," the Japanese equivalent of the "carrot or the stick." The new parties alternately opposed or supported government initiatives and joined government or opposition coalitions, both on the basis of policy views and of government inducements or coercion.

Scholars have advanced two conflicting interpretations of the Meiji-Taishō party system. Some emphasize the shortcomings of the parties and thus see the system as a failure. Politicians had a rare opportunity to create a democratic Japan, but were much too willing to accept the government's inducements – e.g., cabinet posts, construction projects in their districts, and even bribes – or to give in to its coercion. The reasons for the failure of democracy, they argue, can be traced to the institutionalization of compromise, pork-barrel politics, and corruption twenty or thirty years earlier.[13]

Other scholars, however, have focused on the considerable skill with which politicans employed long-range vision and short-term tactics to guide their parties through the pitfalls of a repressive constitutional and legal order, and, eventually, to bring those parties to power. Hara Kei, a leader of the Seiyūkai party from its founding at the turn of the century, and prime minister from 1918 to 1921, exemplified those skills.[14] Hara, his Finance Minister Takahashi Korekiyo, and the Seiyūkai supported an expansionary economic program that proved highly effective both at stimulating economic growth and at building the party's electoral base through pork-barrel politics. As part of their program of railroad appropriations, for example, they favored the construction of new local rail lines over the improvement of the main trunk lines favored by bureaucrats in the Transportation Ministry. (In May 1920 Hara established a separate Railroad Ministry.) As one might expect, this spending and building not only stimulated economic growth but also helped the party because they took place in districts which had elected, or might elect, Seiyūkai representatives to the lower house.[15] Hara's vision and tactics played a major role in the institutionalization of parliamentary government, and his assassination in November 1921, on the eve of the Washington Disarmament Conference, was, I think, a major setback to the long-term success of democracy in pre-war Japan.[16]

ECONOMIC AND SOCIAL CHANGE AND THE BROADENING OF POLITICAL PARTICIPATION

The rise of the parties, and their ability to institutionalize their role in the political process, are indicators of Japan's evolution toward democracy. Part of the credit for this evolution must go to the politicians. Another part must go to the oligarchs' success in promoting Japan's economic and infrastructural development, which in turn created new economic and social conditions conducive to the expansion of democracy. Between 1890 and 1925, as these policies succeeded and as the government gradually lowered the tax requirement for voting, the social base of democracy widened. In 1890, only the wealthy elite voted and held office. In 1919, when the tax requirement was lowered to 3 yen (equivalent at the time to US $1.50), small farmers, businessmen, and the new urban middle class of white-collar workers won these powers. And in 1925, with the enactment of universal male suffrage, all social classes earned the right to participate in Japan's political system.

Industrialization and economic growth were the underlying causes of these changes. By the 1920s the development of a modern capitalist economy had brought all Japanese, many of whom had lived close to the margin of subsistence in the mid-nineteenth century, better living standards. Japanese not only became more prosperous, but also better educated, more cosmopolitan, and increasingly independent of their traditional overlords (in 1870, mostly landlords); thus, they expected more political power. Political and economic elites were forced to negotiate with and make concessions to these forces from below – forces that were nurtured by the very nation-building and modernizing policies of that same ruling elite.

Real per capita income, as Table 3.1 indicates, grew dramatically between the early Meiji period and the Second World War. So too did other economic indicators. Real manufacturing wages in 1925 were 2.3 times 1885 levels; agricultural productivity in the mid-1920s was more than 2.5 times higher than in 1879–80; and real personal consumption rose by almost three times in those same four decades. Per capita caloric consumption increased by 40 percent between 1870 and the 1920s – Japanese were now eating better than ever before in their country's history.[17]

Another indicator of rising standards of living is the widespread and increasing use of modern facilities. In 1905 in Yamanashi Prefecture, a small mountainous agricultural region about 100 miles west of Tokyo, there was no electricity, and even bicycles were almost non-existent. By the 1930s, all the prefecture's households had electricity, and half had bicycles. The average household now sent 5 packages, 8 telegrams, 333 letters, attended 12 motion pictures, and took 33 train trips per year. Between 1906 and the 1930s, the number of packages sent increased by over five times, the number of letters by over three times, the number of telegrams by four times, and the number of railroad passengers by almost five times.[18]

Table 3.1 Index of real gross national product per capita, 1881–1940

Year	Index	Year	Index
1881	100	1920	269
1890	122	1930	318
1900	168	1939	459
1910	195		

Source: Calculated from Kazushi Ohkawa and Miyohei Shinohara, *Patterns of Japanese Economic Development: A Quantitative Appraisal* (New Haven, 1979).

Medical care in Iwate Prefecture in the relatively impoverished north-east shows similar changes. In 1935, 546 doctors practiced in the prefecture, one for every 1,916 citizens – about the same level as Turkey and South Korea, above the level of the ASEAN countries, Pakistan, and India, and 2–5 times higher than most of Africa in the 1980s. In the two decades between 1915 and 1935, dentists increased in number by almost four times, pharmacists by almost three times, and midwives by almost two times. And Yamanashi and Iwate were not unique in these trends. When one compares real national per capita spending in 1935–1939 with 1879–1880, one finds an increase of almost five times for clothing, six times for medical treatment, 50 times for transportation, and seven times for recreation and education.[19] While one cannot ignore the existence of poverty in inter-war Japan, standards of living had clearly risen well above the margin of subsistence. Poorer Japanese no longer found it necessary to follow obediently and quietly their former social, political, and economic masters in order to stay alive.

The most dramatic changes of all took place in education and literacy. Although the government established compulsory education in the 1870s, in 1879 only 41 percent of eligible children – 58 percent of boys and 23 percent of girls – attended school. But as the nineteenth century progressed, attendance gradually increased until by 1903, 93 percent, and by 1912 98 percent, of eligible children went to school. A 1924 survey of 1,124 tenant union households in Okayama Prefecture in western Japan indicates how pervasive education had become among the rural poor. Altogether 99.6 percent of the boys and 99.4 percent of the girls between the ages of eight and fifteen attended school, and over 98 percent of men and 93 percent of women between the ages of 16 and 40 had studied in school. Although one hesitates to generalize about all of Japan from this Okayama evidence, it is probably safe to say that by 1924 more poor Japanese were better educated than ever before.

At the same time, Japanese became increasingly cosmopolitan. At the beginning of the modern era in 1868, over four-fifths of Japan's population lived in the countryside. Few of the rural poor had ever left their home districts or in many cases even their home villages. But increasingly from the 1880s, the army, factories, trains, buses, and bicycles drew villagers to other parts of their region and nation. The permanent population of Japan's ten largest cities tripled between 1887 and 1925 while the total population grew by only 50 percent. The number of temporary residents at army bases, factories, small businesses, etc., added thousands more to the urban scene.[20] Wider literacy strengthened this new cosmopolitanism because it allowed at least some of the newly educated in the inter-war decades to read the rapidly expanding number of newspapers, magazines, and books, many of which were written simply so that they could be easily understood by elementary school graduates.[21] In fact, the growth in the number of new journals, many of which appealed to specific segments of the population – farmers who raised silkworms, animal husbandmen, fruit tree cultivators, members of nationalistic organizations – must have come about because in the interwar decades far more people knew how to read. Few if any of these journals specifically advocated democratic government. Nevertheless, what they did do was to make large groups of people more and more independent of their traditional paternalistic leaders. When a Yamanashi Prefecture tenant farmer learned new techniques for growing mulberry or raising silkworms from reading the pages of *Yamanashi Silkworm and Mulberry News* rather than from one of his landlords, as he had in the late nineteenth century, he achieved a sense of economic independence and self-sufficiency. Why would that same farmer not claim a greater degree of political independence as well?

And in fact he did. As members of the rural and urban poor became better off and better educated between 1870 and 1930, they gradually came to play a greater role in governing their local communities. During the late feudal and early modern periods, no one had voted and few commoners participated in government; even after the establishment of local representative assemblies and a national parliament in the 1870–1890 years, only substantial taxpayers cast votes or held office. But in the twentieth century, the government extended suffrage to more and more people until, from 1925 on, all men over the age of 25 gained the right to vote.[22] The first local elections held after the enactment of universal male suffrage showed that the newly enfranchised Japanese were ready to take a larger share of political power. Tenant and owner-tenant farmers won 9,061 of 42,738 town and village assembly seats contested (21 percent) and took control of 340 assemblies (one-ninth). Eight years later they expanded their strength to 14,514 seats (26 percent) and took control of 634 assemblies (one-sixth). It is in part this dramatic increase in tenant-farmer power that led political scientist Masumi Junnosuke to view the interwar decades as an era in which smallholders and tenant farmers replaced their landlords as hamlet and village leaders.[23]

The political power of the rural and urban working class did not express itself only through electoral success. The labor and tenant-farmer movements were another manifestation of Japan's growing democracy. Urban workers formed unions and went on strike to improve their wages and working conditions. In 1924, 54,526 workers took part in 333 strikes; two years later, 67,234 workers participated in 495 strikes; and strikes even continued into the late 1930s after the last party government fell in 1932. Tenant farmers organized to lower rent and gain more control over the land they rented from their landlords. In 1927, the peak year of tenant union membership, 365,332 tenant farmers joined unions; in 1924, 110,920 tenants took part in 1,532 disputes; two years later, 151,061 tenants participated in 2,751 disputes. Such disputes continued even after the demise of party governments – in fact, 32,289 tenant farmers took part in 3,308 disputes in 1941, the year of Japan's attack on Pearl Harbor.[24]

There has been much lively debate over the causes and effects of these strikes, disputes, and movements. Did workers and farmers join unions and challenge their managers and landlords because conditions and incomes were deterioriating in the 1920s and 1930s, or because conditions were improving and workers and farmers saw activism as a way to improve their livelihoods even more? Were the strikes and disputes omens of an incipient revolution or were they social democratic efforts to reform the system from within? Were workers and farmers successful in their efforts to raise wages, lower rents, and improve working conditions, or did the "social movement" fail because of state repression?[25] Whatever the answers to these and other questions, one conclusion is unavoidable: workers and tenant farmers, that is, the urban and rural working classes in the 1920s and 1930s, were politically active through both their newly won right to vote and their participation in industrial and farm-village unions. Higher standards of living, education, literacy, and political and social activism were the hallmarks of a new kind of worker and farmer in interwar Japan. A greater role in determining the nature of his government – democracy, if you will – was both his demand and his reward.

THE DECLINE OF DEMOCRACY IN THE 1930s

Cabinets headed by the leader of one of the major political parties held office from September 1918 until June 1922, and again from June 1924 until May 15, 1932. For most of a decade and a half in the late Taishō and early Shōwa periods, Japan had a government toward the democratic end of the political continuum. But even in this era of "Taishō democracy," there were constraints on the power of the politicians to govern and on the freedom of the radical opposition to function freely in the political arena. I would like to discuss briefly six of these constraints, each of which contributed to the demise of Japanese democracy during the 1930s.

First, as discussed above, the Constitution of 1889 was not congenial to democracy. The emperor, not the people, was sovereign. The military was semi-independent. Civil rights were not absolute. While democratic government bloomed within this restrictive framework in the decade and a half after the First World War, the constitution also contained the seeds of democracy's downfall. Second, in the absence of constitutional guidance about how to choose prime ministers, an extra-constitutional system arose. Dominant Meiji oligarchs such as Yamagata, Itō, and Matsukata, and then their protégés like Prince Saionji and General Katsura Tarō, were (self-) selected as elder statesmen (*genrō*), and this group of men chose the next prime minister. By the mid-1920s, the last remaining *genrō* was Prince Saionji, who was one of the founders of the Seiyūkai Party and was committed to stable democratic government. Ironically, the succession of party governments between 1924 and 1932 was to some extent dependent on the goodwill of a man who held his position because of his earlier status as one of Japan's ruling oligarchs.

Third, the military did not sit idle while party prime ministers controlled Japan's foreign policy. Even during the nadir of their popularity in the 1920s, the army and navy were active as political pressure groups. They staked out policy positions in direct opposition to the party governments, and used the school system and semi-military organizations like the Imperial Army Reserve Association to build their own "electoral constituency" in rural and even urban Japan.[26] Fourth, parts of the bureaucracy actively opposed party rule and even the more liberal elements within the civil ministries urged progressive social and economic policies from a sense of *noblesse oblige* rather than from a sincere commitment to popular government.[27]

Fifth, the government, especially through the activities of the Justice Ministry's Special Higher Police (*tokkō*), forcibly suppressed its radical opposition. In 1925, when parliament enacted universal male suffrage, it also passed the Peace Preservation Law, which allowed the courts to convict people for a number of political offenses including attempting to overturn the *kokutai*, the emperor-centered political order. Since the newly founded Japan Communist Party advocated an end to Japan's monarchy, it was an obvious target for the police. During 1927 and 1928, the *tokkō* arrested 3,400 party members.[28] These mass arrests of the radical opponents of "imperial democracy" were certainly a blot on pre-war Japan's democratic record – and they were also an omen of worse to come as a civil bureaucratic/military alliance gradually replaced the party politicians at the helm of Japan's political order in the 1930s.[29] But one must bear in mind that, harsh as the government's treatment of political dissidents was in the late 1920s, it was not atypical of its times. The administration of Woodrow Wilson rounded up for deportation 3,000 alleged "alien radicals" in the Palmer Raids in 1919, and the McCarthy era in America was yet to come. Japanese democracy in the 1920s was flawed, but it was within the parameters of what was accepted elsewhere as democratic in the interwar decades.

Sixth, many of the party politicians themselves acted in ways that constrained the parliamentary system that gave them political power. Party politicians voted for the Peace Preservation Law in 1925. They consorted and made alliances with bureaucrats and military leaders who were not committed to democratic government. They pursued policies which might help their party seize power in the short run but which undermined the democratic foundations of party government in the long. The most famous example is the London Naval Disarmament Conference crisis of 1930. The leaders of the Minseitō Party, who were committed to a policy of cooperation with the Western powers, non-intervention in China, and fiscal prudence at home, negotiated a treaty which limited the size of the Japanese navy *vis-à-vis* those of the United States and Great Britain. The navy resisted ratification of the treaty, arguing that the government had violated the armed forces' right of "supreme command," their authority under certain circumstances to report directly to the emperor and thus to be free from control by the prime minister. The opposition Seiyūkai joined with the navy in calling for the rejection of the treaty. The party did have a history of advocating activist foreign and fiscal policies; but its opposition was owing at least in part to the immediate political objective of removing the Minseitō from power. Although the Privy Council rejected the navy/Seiyūkai position and ratified the treaty, the Seiyūkai leaders' support of the military against the very political system that brought them their power helped weaken that system and speed its demise.[30]

Party government ended on May 15, 1932, when a group of young military officers assassinated Prime Minister Inukai Tsuyoshi because of his attempt to tighten government control over the army after its seizure of Manchuria the previous year. Most political leaders at the time did not realize that Inukai's death also marked the end of party government; they expected that the formation of the "transcendental" cabinet of Admiral Saitō Makoto would mark only a temporary respite from party rule. And in fact, the parties and other popular movements displayed considerable vigor through the end of the decade. Party politicans continued to be elected to parliament and to exert some control over events through the House of Representative's budgetary authority. Tenant farmers continued to win a sizeable number of seats in village and town assemblies. The two major political parties continued to control Tokyo's prefectural assembly and city council. In 1936 and 1937, on the eve of Japan's invasion of

China, left-wing parties won 20 percent of the seats in the Tokyo prefectural assembly, 16 percent in the Tokyo City Council, and 9 percent (37 seats) in the House of Representatives.[31] And tenant farmers and factory workers continued to form unions and take part in disputes and strikes.

Democracy in Japan did not die with Inukai; nevertheless, its peak had been passed, and it finally expired in 1940 with the dissolution of the established political parties and the formation of the Imperial Rule Assistance Association, the government's war-time instrument of political control. There are many reasons for its demise: constitutional and extra-constitutional constraints, military and bureaucratic opposition, political intrigue, and governmental repression of radical opposition, all discussed above, are crucial. But these causes all existed in the 1920s without producing the breakdown of democracy. The immediate stimulus to the downfall of party government was the impact of the Great Depression. Like other countries, Japan suffered from reduced wages, industrial unemployment, rapidly falling prices for agricultural commodities, plunging demand for finished goods, excess industrial capacity, and virtually no demand for investment capital. As the world's industrial powers grappled with this unprecedented crisis, economic autarky replaced the relative internationalism and free trade environment of the 1920s. Herbert Hoover signed the infamous Smoot-Hawley Tariff Act into law on June 17, 1930, and within a year other nations were retaliating with tariffs of their own.[32] Protectionism and regional blocs became the order of the day.

Two other events of 1930–31 heightened the sense of crisis in Japan. First, Inoue Junnosuke, the Minseitō Finance Minister, took Japan back on the gold standard in January 1930, just as the Depression was devastating the price of Japan's primary export commodity, raw silk. In order to take Japan back to gold, Inoue had to appreciate the yen's value by 10–15 percent, intensifying the already severe deflationary effect of the Depression. Second, on the night of September 18, 1931, the Japanese army, without notifying the Minseitō prime minister, began the military conquest of Manchuria. The government tried to stop the invasion, but to no avail – the army simply ignored the civilian authorities in Tokyo. The Minseitō government fell in December 1931 and was replaced by a Seiyūkai cabinet headed by Inukai, Japan's last party prime minister until 1945.

While it is dangerous to oversimplify a complex process that took many years to unfold, I believe that the primary causes of the downfall of democratic government were the impact of the Depression, the resultant trend toward economic and political autarky and direct military action, and their effects. Those people who advocated international cooperation lost their audience to public figures who advocated solving problems through direct and independent action. Japan's military leaders, with their ideas of continental conquest, now became popular in an era when virtually all the world's leaders were advocating various forms of political and economic nationalism. Japan's party leaders had operated through compromise, negotiations, deal-making, and the pork barrel. The people who replaced them were more committed to the use of force – and they claimed to have purer, more patriotic motives.

The compromisers lost out to the actors, because in the crisis atmosphere of the early 1930s the actors won the public's support. One reason that the Minseitō government could not bring the army under control when it set out to conquer Manchuria was that the conquest was popular. Very few of Japan's political, bureaucratic, or intellectual leaders condemned the war. Major newspapers, including relatively liberal ones like the *Tokyo Asahi*, editorialized in support of the seizure. In an era when regional blocs like the American one in the Caribbean were becoming the order of the day, most Japanese believed that Manchuria was rightfully theirs. The Minseitō leaders who opposed the army's actions were easily discredited as unpatriotic. This sense of crisis and of the inability of party politicians to solve it, together with the image of strength and competence projected by the elite civil bureaucracy and the military, brought about the politicians' downfall.

Democracy still had shallow roots in Japan in 1932. It did not have a long history and it had to compete with the powerful authoritarian traditions promoted by hundreds of years of samurai rule and a half-century of patriotic education in Japan's elementary schools and elsewhere. At the time of the annual conscription examination in May–July 1930, the Education Ministry distributed a questionnaire to 8,561 young men in eleven communities all over Japan. Over 60 percent of the respondents were able to identify correctly such people, events, terms, and organizations as Japan's primary export, unemployment, London Naval Disarmament Conference, mortgage, League of Nations, *Chronicle of Ancient Matters*, land tax, and Army Day. Over half successfully answered questions about the Japan-centric scholar Motoori Norinaga, the Kamakura period government, Mussolini, the national budget, the organization that issued the one-yen note, the nation's primary product, and the nation that produced most of Japan's raw cotton. But only 21 percent of the respondents were able to define the term "democracy" correctly. The primary mistaken answers were "egoism" (16 percent) and "radicalism" (11 percent).[33] While one hesitates to generalize about an entire society from a small sample of 20-year-olds, it seems safe to conclude that many Japanese seem not to have had a firm understanding of the concept of democracy in the early 1930s – even while they wanted to play a larger role in governing themselves. Japan's short history of democratic government between 1918 and 1932, and the demise of that form of government between 1932 and 1940, are both a triumph and a tragedy – the same bourgeois and working-class people who brought Japan democracy let it slip away. But partly as a result of these earlier experiences, they were prepared to establish a sounder democracy when the chance came again in 1945.

While Japan's "imperial democracy" rested on a weaker constitutional, legal, and popular base than does Japan's post-war democracy, Japan's government in the 1920s was not unlike those of nations which all of us consider to have been democratic. After 1925, men of all economic classes voted for their local and national representatives. And these men were discriminating enough to split their vote: many of them voted for their own class in local elections – that is, for tenant farmers or urban union leaders – but for the representatives of bourgeois parties in national ones. Ultimately Japan's pre-war democracy failed because a cataclysmic crisis, the Great Depression, intervened in what were still the formative years of Japanese democracy. But even if democracy failed in the early 1930s and gave way to military authoritarianism in the 1940s, the post-war Allied occupation did not have to create a democratic Japan out of whole cloth. Japan's pre-war democratic experiment provided the basis for post-war democracy. The "dawn of a democratic Japan" came after the First World War, not in the summer of 1993.

NOTES

1.   *New York Times* (18 July 1993).
2.   Contrary to the view of the *New York Times*, a two-party system is not an essential ingredient of democracy. Otherwise we would have to conclude that Sweden, which has recently ended its half-century of social democratic rule, also falls into the newly democratic camp.
3.   Shidehara Kijūrō, the first prime minister to assume office in the post-war period, was foreign minister in the next-to-last pre-war party government. He and his government had actively opposed the military annexation of Manchuria in 1931.
4.   Thomas C. Smith, "Japan's Aristocratic Revolution," in *Native Sources of Japanese Industrialization, 1750–1920* (Berkeley, 1988), Chapter 5.
5.   The treaties limited tariffs on imports, institutionalized "extraterritoriality" (the right of foreigners to live in "treaty ports" such as Yokohama under the laws of their own countries and outside the jurisdiction of Japanese law),

and posited the "most favored nation clause," by which the Japanese government had to extend to all imperialist powers whatever concessions it negotiated with any one of them.

6. There are two ironies here. First, when Japan and Germany formed a wartime alliance in 1940, Japan's government operated under a constitution modeled after one that Germany had lost after the First World War. Second, Japan managed in a little over half a century to have both German- and American-style constitutions.

7. Junichirō Kisaka, "The 1930s: A Logical Outcome of Meiji Policy," in Harry Wray and Hilary Conroy, eds., *Japan Examined: Perspectives on Modern Japanese History* (Honolulu, 1983): 241–51; Herbert P. Bix, "Rethinking 'Emperor-System Fascism': Ruptures and Continuities in Modern Japanese History," *Bulletin of Concerned Asian Scholars*, 14, no. 2 (1982): 2–19.

8. George Akita, *Foundations of Constitutional Government in Modern Japan: 1868–1900* (Cambridge, Mass., 1967).

9. J. Mark Ramseyer and Frances McCall Rosenbluth, "The Politics of Oligarchy: Institutional Choice in Imperial Japan," unpublished book manuscript.

10. Yamagata served as army minister, home minister, and prime minister, and four of his followers – three retired generals and a former home ministry bureaucrat – later headed cabinets.

11. Oka Yoshitake, *Kindai Nihon no seijika* (Tokyo, 1979), translated into English by Andrew Fraser and Patricia Murray as *Five Political Leaders of Modern Japan* (Tokyo, 1986); *Yamagata Aritomo* (Tokyo, 1958).

12. Taishō democracy is a much used term in Japanese historical writing. The Taishō era refers to the years between 1912 and 1926, when the grandfather of the current emperor held the throne in Japan. Actually, the high point of pre-war democracy began in the Taishō period but continued into the reign of Hirohito, the Shōwa emperor. As a kind of shorthand, historians write of Meiji authoritarianism (1868–1912), Taishō democracy (1912–1926), and Shōwa militarism (1926–1945).

13. Robert A. Scalapino, *Democracy and the Party Movement in Prewar Japan: The Failure of the First Attempt* (Berkeley, 1962).

14. Tetsuo Najita, *Hara Kei in the Politics of Compromise, 1905–1915* (Cambridge, Mass., 1967).

15. Nakamura Takafusa, *Shōwashi* (A History of the Shōwa Period), vol. 1 (Tokyo, 1993), 31–7.

16. The actions of Hara's successor, Takahashi, underline this point. Takahashi, a brilliant economic thinker who introduced Keynesian counter-cyclical fiscal and monetary policies in Japan in 1931–32, lacked Hara's political skills. While serving as finance minister in Hara's cabinet at the end of the First World War, for example, Takahashi wrote an essay calling for the abolition of the army and navy general staffs, a proposal not likely to win him friends in the military. Although Hara shared Takahashi's view, he was far too astute a politician to antagonize a powerful political group needlessly. Takahashi succeeded Hara as prime minister in 1921; his cabinet lasted only six months.

17. Kazushi Ohkawa and Miyohei Shinohara, *Patterns of Japanese Economic Development: A Quantitative Appraisal* (New Haven, 1979); Alan H. Gleason, "Economic Growth and Consumption in Japan," in William W. Lockwood, ed., *The State and Economic Enterprise in Japan* (Princeton, 1965); Kazushi Ohkawa *et al.*, *Long-Term Economic Statistics in Japan: Prices*, vol. 8 (Tokyo, 1967); Umemura Mataji *et al.*, *Long-Term Economic Statistics of Japan: Agriculture and Forestry*, vol. 9 (Tokyo, 1966).

18. *Yamanashi-ken tōkeisho* (Yamanashi Prefecture Statistical Yearbook), 1905–1939. Iwate Prefecture, one of Japan's poorest regions in the pre-war decades, shows similar trends. See *Iwate-ken tōkeisho* (Iwate Prefecture Statistical Yearbook), 1897–1935.

19. *Iwate-ken tōkeisho*; *The Economist World Atlas and Almanac* (New York, 1989); Sōmuchō Tōkeikyoku, *Kokusai tōkei yōran* (A Summary of International Statistics) (Tokyo, 1993), 218–19.

20. Military leaders like General, Army Minister, and later Prime Minister Tanaka Giichi railed about the evils of urban life, but the army had all of its training bases for recruits in cities. Prior to the Second World War the army's conscription system brought 100,000 to 120,000 young men per year to urban areas.

21. 30.5 percent (343 of 1,124) of the households surveyed in the national tenant union's 1924 study of tenant union households in Okayama Prefecture subscribed to newspapers. If, as some scholars suggest, rural people circulated newspapers and magazines within their neighborhoods, more than one-third of Okayama tenant union households had members who read newspapers in the 1920s. Ōta Toshie, "Kosakunō kaikyūno keizaiteki shakaiteki jōtai (The Economic and Social Situation of the Tenant Farmer Class), *Sangyō Kumiai*, no. 261 (1927).

22. In May 1930, the House of Representatives passed a bill giving women the right to vote in local elections, but it died in committee in the House of Peers. During the Allied occupation, in December 1945, women finally won the right to vote in national and local elections.

23. Masumi Junnosuke, *Nihon seitōshiron* (A Theory of the History of Japanese Political Parties), vol. 5 (Tokyo, 1979), 342–51.

24. Nakamura Masanori, Rōdōsha to nōmin (Workers and Farmers), *Nihon no rekishi* (The History of Japan), vol. 29 (Tokyo, 1976), 215; Richard J. Smethurst, *Agricultural Development and Tenancy Disputes in Japan, 1870–1940* (Princeton, 1986), 321, 347.

25. See Andrew Gordon, *Labor and Imperial Democracy in Prewar Japan* (Berkeley, 1991), and Smethurst, *Agricultural Development*. See also Nakamura Masanori, "The Japanese Landlord System and Tenancy Disputes: A Reply to Richard Smethurst's Criticisms," *The Bulletin of Concerned Asian Scholars*, 20, no. 1 (1988): 36–50; Nishida Yoshiaki, "Growth of the Meiji Landlord System and Tenancy Disputes after World War I: A Critique of Richard Smethurst," *Journal of Japanese Studies*, 15, no. 2 (1989): 389–415; Smethurst, "Nihon ni okeru nōmin no hatten to kosaku sōgi: Nakamura Masanori-shi Nishida Yoshiaki-shi e no hanron" (Agricultural Development and Tenancy Disputes in Japan: A Reply to Nakamura Masanori and Nishida Yoshiaki), *Rekishigaku kenkyū* (Historical Studies), no. 653 (December 1993): 16–31.

26.   On rural mobilization, see Richard J. Smethurst, *A Social Basis for Prewar Japanese Militarism: The Army and the Rural Community* (Berkeley, 1974). On urban Japan, see Sally Hastings, *Neighborhood and Nation in Tokyo, 1905–1937* (Pittsburgh, forthcoming 1995). On the army's political pressure activities, see Smethurst, "The Social Basis for Japanese Militarism: The Case of the Imperial Military Reserve Association," (Ph.D. diss., University of Michigan, 1968), Chapter 6.

27.   Sheldon Garon, *The State and Labor in Modern Japan* (Berkeley, 1988).

28.   Richard H. Mitchell, *Janus-Faced Justice: Political Criminals in Imperial Japan* (Honolulu, 1992).

29.   See Gordon, *Labor and Imperial Democracy*, for use of the term "imperial democracy" to describe Japan's political system in the 1920s.

30.   James B. Crowley, *Japan's Quest for Autonomy: National Security and Foreign Policy, 1930–1938* (Princeton, 1966).

31.   Gordon, *Labor and Imperial Democracy*, 305.

32.   Charles P. Kindleberger, *The World in Depression, 1929–1939* (London, 1986), 123–30.

33.   Education Ministry, *Sōtei shisō chōsa* (A Survey of the Thinking of Draft-Age Young Men) (Tokyo, 1931), 107–10.

4 The Social Construction of Democracy in Germany, 1871–1933

Geoff Eley

GERMAN EXCEPTIONALISM

Elsewhere I have written extensively about the way in which assumptions about German history function in the comparative understanding of the social sciences.[1] "Germany" is a sign for the authoritarian as opposed to the democratic path of late nineteenth- and early twentieth-century political development – for "dictatorship" as opposed to "democracy" in Barrington Moore's famous typology, for misdevelopment and failed modernization, for illiberalism, for what went "wrong." This German syndrome – the *Sonderweg* or "special path," which makes German history different from the history of the "West," in the conventional view – is thought to involve a disjunction between economic modernity and political backwardness, the grand contradiction of a dynamic economy developing within an unreformed political framework, in which pre-industrial elites preserved their dominance against the rising forces of a modern society. Such a combination, involving the "unusually protracted retardation of democratization as against industrialization,"[2] defined the parameters of Germany's developmental history between 1871 and 1945, left the German polity prone to structural instability, encouraged the elites to fabricate and exploit political crises, and produced the strains and stresses that ultimately led to the catastrophe of 1933.

This view of German exceptionalism has been based on a combination of political and intellectual or cultural history linked to a social analysis of the primacy of pre-industrial elites, namely, the Junkers and their equivalents in the bureaucracy and army. It was the dominant Anglo-American reading of German history after 1945, which during the 1960s and 1970s then promised to become the prevailing historiographical wisdom in the German Federal Republic (FRG), and which during the more conservative 1980s and 1990s has remained the preferred approach to their past of most progressive Germans. This was also how German history was incorporated within the social sciences, as in Moore's aforementioned classic (1966), though interestingly without any systematic historical investigation (in some ways Germany provides the defining questions of Moore's book, while being denied a full-scale treatment of its own, being confined within a short concluding chapter).[3] Standing in for such historical investigation are the equally classic works of Alexander Gerschenkron and Hans Rosenberg. The approach can be traced further back to the early twentieth century and to left liberal and radical critiques of German society and politics expressed by Weber and Marx.[4]

The *locus classicus* in the immediate German literature is Ralf Dahrendorf's *Society and Democracy in Germany* (1968). Dahrendorf formulates the question very directly: What is it that prevented Germany from becoming a modern society in the liberal-democratic sense (that is, in the double sense of a "society of citizens," and a society "dominated by a confident bourgeoisie")?[5] Why is it that German society, which developed extraordinary economic dynamism between the late nineteenth century and 1914, failed to experience a liberal-democratic political modernization comparable to the processes of political development that had taken place in Britain and France? Why instead did it remain dominated by unreformed, semi- or pseudo-constitutional political arrangements, authoritarian political traditions, and an illiberal political culture? The question guiding these other questions, of course, was *the* big question of German history, namely, that of 1933. That is: Why did Germany alone, by contrast with the other developed capitalist societies of the West, produce a fascist political outcome to the world economic crisis after 1929?

The preferred answer was to conceptualize Germany as being not part of the West, as being different from the West; and the basis of that difference was taken to be German history's failure to demonstrate the progressive unity of socioeconomic and political modernization thought to have been characteristic of British and French development. Thus the key to Germany's vulnerability to Nazism was taken to be the persistence of pre-industrial and authoritarian traditions at the center of the state, linked to a powerful political bloc of dominant socioeconomic interests, which consistently obstructed the possibility of liberal-democratic modernizing reform. In Dahrendorf's book, this argument is further grounded in a deeper-lying claim about German social structure: "The social basis of German authoritarianism, thus of the resistance of German society to modernity and liberalism, consisted in a structural syndrome that held people to social ties in which they had found themselves without their doing and that prevented them from full participation."[6]

This gesturing toward a deep sociology of backwardness is the least adequately theorized or historicized part of the *Sonderweg* thesis, although it remains key to the basic scaffolding of Anglo-American historical interpretation, from Leonard Krieger's celebrated commentary on the nineteenth-century "German idea of freedom," through Mack Walker's study of "German home towns," to Fritz Stern's essay on "The Political Consequences of the Unpolitical German."[7] What exactly is being postulated here about the bases of German social life is somewhat elusive, and in different versions covers everything from childraising practices and family life, to cultures of provincialism, and what Stern calls "vulgar idealism," or the unpolitical veneration of *Kultur, Bildung*, and the cultivated life. Clearly there is some kind of argument about deep-rooted cultural traits at work in this tradition. There is some connection to a couple of equally vague and under-specified essays of Talcott Parsons, "Democracy and Social Structure in Pre-Nazi Germany" and "Some Sociological Aspects of Fascist Movements," written during the 1940s, which for obvious reasons were the founding period for this body of interpretation.[8]

The closest we get to a fully explicated argument about this deep sociology is in the extraordinarily influential essays of M. Rainer Lepsius, the doyen of historically inclined late twentieth-century German sociology. Lepsius locates the German difference in the abnormal persistence of crucial "elements of a pre-industrial social order" in a time of rapid industrialization and economic transformation. In this view, the possibility of democracy was impeded by the continuity of pre-industrial lines of affiliation, which structurally pre-empted the growth of liberal pluralism within representative institutions, and instead ensured the inadequate integration of hostile and mutually exclusive political subcultures in the life of the state. According to Lepsius, the German party system was to remain embedded within a field of identification and conflict that predated the foundation of the single German state in 1871 and that was highly resistant to "modern" political concerns like the "achievement of democratic institutions" and the "realization of claims on social equality." Political identities remained "fixed" around regional, local, confessional, and other particularistic interests rather than being reshaped and easing the integration of the emergent citizenry within a participant political culture comparable to those of the West. Lepsius calls the resulting situation a mutually reinforcing structure of self-sealing, culturally autonomous "social-moral milieus," each with its characteristic party formation. The German political system was organized around four milieus of this kind: the conservative ("Protestant, agrarian, regionally closed, and wedded to traditional paternalistic concepts"); the Catholic Center; the *Mittelstand*; and the socialist.

Together, Lepsius argues, these milieus endowed the entire period from 1871 to 1933 with an imposing stability and continuity. Increasingly, each entrenched itself behind a wall of defensive preoccupations, focusing on the integrity of its own particularistic interests rather than a more pluralist conception of the interest of the whole, and cemented by a carefully nurtured subcultural identity. Even the rise of the labor movement, which by 1912 had given the SPD 4.2 million voters, could not unlock this situation. Social democracy itself formed a highly organized and defensive subculture, while its growing strength simply deepened the others' attachment to "pre-industrial conceptions of value." This created and reproduced "a moral frontier between the bourgeois-confessional communities of sentiment and the labor movement," which militated against the "structural conditions of industrial society" and prevented any gradual democratization.[9] In other words, the juxtaposition already mentioned, between a modern industrializing economy and a backward unreformed state, is matched by another, between a strong authoritarian state and a weak, segmented society. '

While grounded in a social and cultural analysis of sorts, however, the argument that proceeds from the primacy of pre-industrial traditions has acquired most of its recent force from a particular analysis of German politics between Bismarck and the First World War, which was pioneered in the 1960s by historians such as Fritz Fischer and Hans-Ulrich Wehler. "Social imperialism" has been one of several key concepts through which this analysis has been presented. A diversionary model of economic growth and social containment, as Wehler conceives it, which satisfied social aspirations and defused social conflicts via an aggressive and economically driven program of foreign expansion, this idea formulates the contradiction between economic growth and political backwardness into an explicit policymaking syndrome. Beginning with Bismarck's colonial initiatives of the early 1880s, but acquiring more adventurist and dangerous form in the *Weltpolitik* and naval arms drive of the later 1890s under Bülow and Tirpitz, this social imperialist move (a "diversionary technique of rule") was undertaken at the expense of enormous long-term risk – escalating international tensions, perpetuating repressive systems of exclusion of subordinate classes from the polity, creating an over-stimulated right-wing radical-nationalist public pushing government policy even more aggressively in the same directions, and locking German government into a long-term strategy of foreign expansionism and militarist demagogy that culminated in the First World War and ultimately proved disastrously self-defeating.

Furthermore, this implies a manipulative model of political management and mobilization, in which the powerholders sought to stave off pressure for reform by using a variety of issues (nationalist foreign policy, naval arms drive, anti-clericalism and *Kulturkampf*, anti-Polish sentiments, anti-semitism, anti-socialism, etc.) to build popular support behind the status quo. In the absence of a mass political force of the radical right comparable to the Nazis, that is, the legitimacy and popular support for the undemocratic status quo was maintained by strategies of manipulative authoritarianism on the part of pre-industrial elites. Finally, the recurring slogan of this governmental conservatism was *Sammlungspolitik* (the "politics of rallying together"), a strategy of coalition-building within the property owning classes, which made an alliance of heavy-industrial and agrarian interests ("iron and rye") the fixed term of government politics between the late 1870s and 1918. In general, the polity of the Second Reich was a striking example of "secondary integration" – the counterpart to a society held together artificially by a mixture of repression and manipulation, rather than by the modern practices of democratic consensus.[10]

As I have argued elsewhere, this is where the bourgeoisie makes its collective entry into the story – that is, as the progressive political agency whose interests allegedly opened the way for liberal democratic change in the West, but in Germany failed to do so. There the bourgeoisie was fragmented, subordinated, "feudalized," and lacking in collective political will. The real absence in German history, therefore, was the absence of a self-confident and combative bourgeoisie, and the real origins of that absence were in the missing bourgeois revolution, the breakthrough to political modernity that Germany failed to have. The social and political origins of the German *Sonderweg* thus lay in this earlier period between 1789 and the 1860s, in what Wehler has recently called "the fatal pathogenesis of the German bourgeoisie."[11] Whether historiographically as a view of what supposedly happened successfully in British or French history, or conceptually as an explanation for the rise of liberal democracy, this model of bourgeois revolution is extremely problematic. For one thing, it attributes to the bourgeoisie a unified and coherent class-political agency which is theoretically and empirically highly questionable; for another, it proceeds from an assumed relationship between bourgeoisie as a social category or a postulated unity of economic interests and the historical possibility of liberal democracy as a set of political ideals and arrangements, so that if liberal democracy fails to materialize, the process of bourgeois class formation must *ipso facto* have been deformed. In this way of thinking, the possibility of liberal-democratic political development is thought to be inscribed in the structures and processes of capitalist economic growth; and the actor of this script, the bearer of liberal-democratic political values, the agency of progress, is the bourgeoisie. Accordingly, if one proceeds from this causally articulated model of economic growth, class agency, and political development, then to deal with the German historical experience a language of exceptionalism is almost necessarily entailed.

It is hard not to be impressed by the powerful teleology running through such an account. "Modernization" in this discourse is avowedly abstracted from present-day forms of pluralist democracy. As just indicated, it is thought to be built into the structures of economic growth, and to explain why German history diverges from this model until after 1945 German historians have logically been thrown back onto vocabularies of "wrong turnings," "failures," "blockages," and "misdevelopment." As Wehler baldly states: "any modern society attempting to be equal to the demands of constant social change" logically requires a constitutional framework of parliamentary democracy.[12] Conversely, the authoritarianism of the Imperial state becomes the constitutional expression of the "pre-industrial traditions" and their modernization-obstructing dominance in the pre-1914 political culture. Thus a radical disjunction is postulated between "wealth" and "power," between the "modern" basis of the industrial-capitalist economy and the "traditional" political arrangements which the bourgeoisie in Germany proved incapable of sweeping away. In the long run, stability could only be assured by the development of more "modern" institutional arrangements for containing social conflicts – that is, by "welfare-statist" and parliamentary democratic replacements for "the rule of an authoritarian leadership and of privileged social groups centering around the pre-industrial elites of the aristocracy."[13]

This approach constructs an extraordinarily powerful structural frame for interpreting the history of the *Kaiserreich*, a frame which severely restricts the latitude for analyzing particular problems or events within this fifty-year period of time. Moreover, this "permanent structural crisis" itself provides the framing for a larger story, the specifically German "master narrative" of the origins of Nazism, which are thought to be deeply inscribed in the flaws of the *Kaiserreich*:

> Modernization seems not to have been possible without a transformation of the social structure and the traditional power relationships, and without social and political emancipation, if the domestic and international peace was to be kept. The fatal consequences of the government policy through which the political predominance of the pre-industrial elites in the period of high industrialization was to be maintained were revealed quite clearly between 1914 and 1929, when these structures broke apart. By that time such a policy had helped create the conditions that smoothed the way for National Socialism.[14]

As many readers will know, this is the master narrative of German exceptionalism, of the German *Sonderweg*, which performed such an important function in the intellectual politics of the 1960s and early 1970s, and authorized many of the key historiographical breakthroughs of that time. The *Sonderweg* thesis also became the object of wide-ranging critical debate in the early 1980s, a discussion which the present author played some modest part in helping to begin. It would be inappropriate to replay that whole debate here, although its terms are necessarily presumed in the rest of my discussion which follows.[15]

ELECTIONS, PARLIAMENT AND THE PUBLIC SPHERE

Backwardness and traditionalism are found so easily in the political culture of the *Kaiserreich* partly because perceptions are guided so powerfully by the a priori assumption that Germany *was* different because of the retroactive light cast by the significance of 1933. The hold which 1933 exercises on the historical imagination is, in fact, extraordinarily strong. If Germany produced fascism and the other developed capitalist societies experiencing comparable conditions of economic crisis after 1929 (Britain, France, the USA) did not, for instance, then deep historical peculiarities must be the explanation. For Jürgen Kocka, turning a famous anti-capitalist aphorism of Max Horkheimer's on its head, "Whoever does not want to talk about pre-industrial, pre-capitalist, and pre-bourgeois traditions should keep quiet about fascism;" and for Heinrich August Winkler:

> The reasons why democracy was liquidated in Germany in the course of the world economic crisis and not in the other developed industrial societies have less to do with the course of the crisis itself than with the different pre-industrial histories of these countries. The conditions for the rise of fascism have at least as much to do with feudalism and absolutism as with capitalism.[16]

Thus, the commonest approach to the place of 1933 in German history now focuses on "historical handicaps from the time of the authoritarian state, without which the collapse of Weimar is impossible to understand." Such handicaps included not only the "authoritarian traditions" in the stricter sense, but also their manipulative adaptation – "that partial democratization of the authoritarian state that began with the introduction of universal equal suffrage [sic] by Bismarck."[17] The decisive influence on the outcome of the fascism-producing crisis of 1929–1933 was a complex of "traditional" factors rather than the dynamics of a capitalist crisis *per se*:

"Prussian militarism ... Junker cliques ... veneration of the state by clergy and professoriat ... preponderance of heavy industry in the political decision-making process." Fascism resulted from the pathology of an only partially "bourgeois" society. "In Germany there was no 'bourgeois dominance' based in successful industrial capitalism that tipped over into fascism, but a deficit of civility [*Bürgerlichkeit*], of bourgeois parliamentarism, and of firmly anchored bourgeois political culture that opened the way to the abyss."[18]

Clearly, it would be silly to deny the importance of deep historical perspectives for distinguishing the structural trajectories of particular societies in the nineteenth and twentieth centuries. There *is* a problem, however, with the normative teleology of "development" and "modernization," which constitutes some national histories as healthy and successful and others as backward and flawed, and which postulates an ultimate complementarity between economic growth and political democratization that in Germany (until the imposed settlement after 1945) was not to be. On the one hand, the causal primacy of "pre-industrial traditions" specifically displaces certain other approaches to the rise of Nazism, those which begin with the interior dynamics of the immediate fascism-producing crisis in 1929–1933. What is seen to be the driving contradiction of that crisis – the anti-democratic mentalities that left various social groups so receptive to the fascist appeal – is displaced from its own contemporary context onto a much deeper argument about the longer course of German history and its singularity. On the other hand, the same explanatory syndrome is replicated for the *Kaiserreich* too. Not only fascism/Nazism, therefore, but also the authoritarianism of Imperial Germany and the forms of pre-1914 right-wing politics are to be understood in terms of the legacies of a "feudal" or absolutist past rather than as the complex effects of the capitalist present (which, lest we forget, was the most dynamic and advanced capitalist present in Europe before 1914). What I would like to do in what follows is to step outside this framework of German exceptionalism and teleologically inflected normativity to consider certain features of German political history under the *Kaiserreich* whose significance tends to be effaced so long as we concentrate on the primacy of pre-industrial traditions as the unifying continuity of the whole period between 1871 and 1933.

A good place to begin is Stanley Suval's important analysis of Wilhelmine electoral politics. Drawing on the work of the cultural school of American electoral history, he argues that "religion, ethnicity, nationality, and race," together with the impact of a politically interventionist state, were more salient to the lines of political cleavage in Imperial

Germany than an approach based on the exclusive primacy of class can reveal. Accordingly, he finds four "social groupings" that broadly correspond with Lepsius's four "social-moral milieus," supplemented with two smaller ones based on the Jewish and Polish minorities; these were the Conservative/East Elbian rurals, the Center Party/German Catholics, the SPD/working class, and a fourth with a more fragmented party-political representation, based on the Protestant *Bürgertum* and *Mittelstand*. Suval then argues that the main effect of Wilhelmine elections was to assert and confirm the differences between these stable camps.[19]

At the same time, Suval marks some important distance from Lepsius in two ways. First, he presents the Wilhelmine electoral system in a far more positive light. He sees the Wilhelmine polity as being increasingly organized around a stable political culture articulated through the process of voting, which served to affirm people's basic allegiance and commitments in an integrative and thoroughly modern way. Indeed, so far from being a source of fragmentation and instability as Lepsius maintained, the lines of cleavage and voter affiliation were delivering the bases of political cohesion. As Suval shows, the Wilhelmine electoral process was not really susceptible to the authoritarian management and plebiscitary manipulation many historians have claimed to detect; and adult males exercised their citizenship at the polls remarkably unencumbered by corruption, paternalism, deference, and intimidation. On the contrary, the period after 1890 was marked by a continuous and constructive politicization of the electorate: "Turnout increased; dropoff decreased; local councils became politicized; the number of voters engaged in more intensive campaign activity rose enormously. This is the Wilhelmine system."[20] This electoral behavior led to the growth of a stable political culture, which was certainly comparable to contemporary electoral systems in conventionally recognized parliamentary polities: "Wilhelmines were voting for past, present, and future as embodied in continuing and durable social groupings. The Wilhelmine inheritance then was a series of stable commitments by a politicized electorate exercising its citizenship roles."[21] As Suval suggests in his conclusion, this has major implications for the question of continuity and our understanding of Weimar and its instabilities: rather than crippling Weimar democracy, the Wilhelmine legacy may have provided one of its positive foundations.

Secondly, Suval also discovers considerable flux and indeterminacy within Lepsius's four social-moral milieus, notably within that of the Protestant *Bürgertum* and *Mittelstand*, that undermines the force of the structural continuity Lepsius sees descending down from the 1860s and 1870s. Here Suval points to the effort at forming a new "social grouping" in the three decades before 1914 capable of replacing the liberal ascendancy of the unification decades – an anti-socialist and patriotic bloc based on the Protestant bourgeoisie and petty bourgeoisie, coordinated by the government for anti-democratic ends. The space for such a strategy was opened up by the breaking apart of liberal hegemonies in Protestant Germany during the politicization of the 1890s, which created the possibility of transforming the old liberal constituency into a new one more loyal to the government. While this change remained fairly amorphous in organizational terms before 1914, the aspiration lent much unity to the politics of the government and dominant classes, Suval argues, and corresponded to the never-quite-realized *Sammlungspolitik* that occupies such a central place in the historiography of the Wilhelmine years. In addition, in explaining the failure of this strategy to take hold, Suval also points to a "radical populist" version of the effort, taking various forms but ultimately moved by a fierce brand of nationalist ideology that threatened to outflank the government from the right.[22]

Suval's re-evaluation of the Wilhelmine polity is salutary. By freeing the years before 1914 from their usual place in the teleology of German exceptionalism, by considering the Wilhelmine era "in its own terms," and by simultaneously defining a more realistic basis for cross-national comparison, he casts Wilhelmine electoral behavior in a refreshingly new light. The issue of comparison is explicitly enjoined, and this "normalizing" of pre-1914 politics is the very opposite of the untheoretical neo-historicism with which such analysis is frequently tagged.[23] Moreover, by standing Lepsius on his head – that is, by seeing the various subcultures as training grounds for active citizenship and as the building blocks of an integrated political culture rather than as an entrenched obstruction – Suval supplies an alternative to the most patently misleading aspects of Lepsius's argument, namely, the idea that there was no significant realignment of political forces or popular allegiances between the founding period of unification in the 1860s and the outbreak of the First World War and even 1933. In fact, as I and others have argued, the 1890s constituted a major moment of flux, bringing precisely a basic shift in alignments and a striking upsurge of popular mobilization.[24] In this sense the decade was a vital moment of transition between two distinct electoral "systems," the Bismarckian and the Wilhelmine in Suval's terms. One configuration of dominant-class politics, in which the leading force was liberal, was replaced by another, in which a more complex and even more fragmented array of forces was taking shape.

Suval's analysis provides an excellent context for starting to think about the bases of change in the German polity before 1914 – changes, that is, whose logic tended towards a parliamentary normalization of political life that leaves Germany looking less different and more comparable to other national polities in Europe at that time. I have three points to make here, in deliberately summary form, which have been partly developed in my work elsewhere and which are offered here as a basis for discussion. The first concerns processes of generalized popular mobilization in the 1890s, whose transformative effects on the political system allow us to speak of a fundamental enlargement of the German public sphere. The second concerns an associated stabilization of public life within the given parameters of parliamentary governance. The third explores the converse of the second point, namely, the recession of conservative desires for an overturning of the parliamentary constitution, whether by restricting the franchise, or reducing the elements of parliamentary accountability, or some more radical attack on the liberal constitutional foundations of the Empire. Together these points seek to specify an argument about parliamentary normalization between the later 1890s and roughly 1908–1912, when renewed polarizations called the further unfolding of that process into question.

(1) The 1890s witnessed an unprecedented growth of popular participation in the German political process, measured most directly in the electoral analysis offered by Suval, including the expansion of the voting electorate, the proliferation of candidates in the constituencies and the rise in the numbers of contested elections, the growing numbers of second ballots, the escalating costs of campaigning, the general intensity of electioneering, and so on. This intensification of local electoral politics was linked to a concomitant transformation in the structure of parties and their relations with their supporters – from the informal dominance of local notables, whose political leadership was the "natural" emanation of local social relations of power and precedence (*Honoratiorenpolitik*, the politics of notables), to a new system of organized party politics, based in formal constitutions, procedural visibility, membership structures, continuous organization, and public competition for support. The transition to a new mode of party-political affiliation was not initiated by party leaderships themselves, but occurred through a difficult and uneven accommodation to popular mobilizations happening beyond their immediate control, which challenged the parties' established practices and legitimacy. Such popular mobilizations had a number of sources, the most salient of which included: (a) the lifting of the Anti-Socialist Law in 1890, which freed the SPD for less restricted public agitation and simultaneously facilitated the transition to mass trade unionism; (b) the structural crisis of German agriculture, which from the late 1880s was generating widespread peasant agitations in most parts of Germany, independently of the notable-controlled corporate

agrarian organizations that already existed; and (c) the growing importance of nationalist issues in German public life after the turn to *Weltpolitik* in the economic upswing of 1895–1896.

The existing parties varied greatly in the effectiveness of their response to this popular political challenge, with the creative adaptability of the Catholic Center Party at one end of the spectrum and the elitist ineffectuality of the National Liberals at the other, with the more complicated case of the Conservatives – whose politics were largely usurped by the new agrarian agitational organization, the *Bund der Landwirte* or Agrarian League, formed in 1893 – somewhere in between. But by the early 1900s the process of transformation was well under way. The point I wish to make here was that the popular mobilization occurred within the electoral arena and on the ground defined by the parliamentary constitution. This was even true of those agitations usually cited as examples of an anti-democratic, "plebiscitary," and "manipulative" politics – such as the radical-nationalist drive for colonies, a big navy, and a strengthening of Germany's power in the world, or the anti-socialist campaigning after 1903 under the auspices of the Imperial League against Social Democracy and its auxiliaries – because these were also practically and explicitly articulated within the given framework of electoral politics and parliamentary representation.

Now, it is true that after 1912 there was a renewed and intense speculation around forms of constitutional revision (taking the form of corporative representation) which promised to neutralize the effects of the democratic franchise, and some forms of right-wing extra-parliamentary agitation started taking an explicitly *anti*-parliamentary direction.[25] But between the late 1890s and 1912 it is hard to find any evidence of right-wing popular mobilization *against* the Reichstag, as opposed to agitation directed towards electing sympathetic deputies, pressuring a parliamentary majority for the passage of legislation, and so on. In the 1907 elections, for example, which saw an exceptionally concerted effort at building anti-socialist unity behind patriotic slogans, from the core parties of the old *Sammlungspolitik* (Conservatives, Free Conservatives, National Liberals) to the Left Liberals, the Anti-Semites, and the extra-parliamentary nationalist pressure groups, the action was wholly devoted to achieving a popular electoral victory and a majority in parliament.

Moreover, it is far from clear that this process can be dismissed as a "pseudo-democratization" in Rosenberg's well-known phrase,[26] simply because many of the right-wing politicians had an opportunistic or instrumental view of the democratic process. It is surely the surrounding context of pluralist competition – the underlying assumptions about how an effective politics needed to be conducted – that is the more important here. To take another example, one of the major monographs of the 1970s marshalled massive evidence to show the legal harassment of SPD and trade unions through policing and the courts after 1900. Yet read differently, the same evidence shows the legal system as the site of a constantly shifting guerrilla struggle, with the unions frequently securing favorable judgments only for the state and the employers to retreat to fresh ground and a different set of legal expedients.[27] In both cases – the electoral and parliamentary arena on the one hand, the arena of civil rights on the other – it is less the antipathy to labor *per se* than the ground of the struggle, the legal and constitutional context, and the political resources it provided, that mattered most.

(2) After the fall of Bismarck and his replacement by the new Chancellor Caprivi in 1890, there had been much speculation about a new liberal era under the new young Kaiser Wilhelm II, but by the time Caprivi had himself been forced out of office by an incipient right-wing coalition in 1894, such exaggerated hopes had been laid to rest. Most historians then represent the events of the following years culminating in the ministerial reconstruction of summer 1897 as the gradual reassertion of a solidly authoritarian neo-Bismarckian governing coalition, based on the alliance of heavy industry and big agriculture and a corresponding parliamentary front of the right (the *Sammlungspolitik* referred to earlier in this essay). This is true in different ways of John Röhl's pioneering book, *Germany without Bismarck*, and of the various works published in Germany in the late 1960s and early 1970s in the wake of the Fischer Controversy.[28]

By contrast, I would prefer to stress the party-political rather than the governmental dimension of this process, because in my view the 1890s see a resurgence of National Liberal parliamentary influence together with the simultaneous emergence of a Catholic Center from its former confessional ghetto. We can identify a series of successful and moderately liberal parliamentary fronts between the mid-1890s and 1902, which were generally organized along a National Liberal/Center Party axis.

(a) The new Code of Civil Law was finally passed in 1896, 25 years after the Empire had originally been proclaimed. This was regarded by the National Liberals as the completion of national unification, and was the first major example of constructive parliamentary cooperation between National Liberals and Center under the latter's new leader, the impeccably bourgeois parliamentarian, Ernst Lieber. (b) This constructive parliamentarism was then sealed by another major legislative achievement that appealed to the National Liberals' historic national sensibilities, and which likewise hinged on cooperation with the Center, namely, the passage of the two Navy Laws in 1898 and 1900. (c) Third, these two positive achievements were reinforced by an extremely important parliamentary defensive operation which effectively blocked successive attempts by the government to introduce new anti-socialist legislation seriously restricting civil liberties: the *Umsturzvorlage* (Revolution Bill) in 1895; the proposal for a new Prussian Law of Association (the so-called "little Anti-Socialist Law") in 1896–1897; and the *Zuchthausvorlage* (the Penitentiary or Hard Labor Bill to penalize picketing) in 1899. The key point about each of these measures, I would argue, is not the authoritarian intentions of the government that introduced them (the preferred interpretation of the existing literature), but the successful parliamentary opposition by which they were all *defeated*. (d) Finally, I would also cite the passage of the new tariff settlement of 1902, because although this represented a defeat for the Left Liberal and free trading opponents of higher tariffs, it was nonetheless a compromise settlement that fell way short of what the extreme agrarian movement was demanding, and once again depended on the parliamentary axis of National Liberal and Center initiative and support.

What this amounted to was a significant stabilization of political life within the established parliamentary constitutional forms, and as a result of that process the emergence of a National Liberal/Center parliamentary condominium. In effect, from around 1897, when the government's own oscillation between a politics of confrontation with the Reichstag and a strategy of negotiated cooperation became resolved, the legitimacy of the parliamentary framework *per se* became increasingly well established, so that in practice all parts of the party-political spectrum became reconciled to working through the given framework of elections and parliamentary majorities.

(3) The real test of this argument, perhaps, would be whether the government itself respected the integrity of parliamentary life, because the dignity of National Liberal and Center parliamentarians would be rendered somewhat nugatory if the government continued to behave in the old high-handed way. Judging the real weight of the Reichstag in the political system is a fraught and controversial business. From the 1890s there was definite growth in the Reichstag's legitimacy and prestige, with the symbolic validation of the new Reichstag building and the concession of deputies' allowances, and a shift of practical authority toward it and away from the Bundesrat, a development matched by the growing shift in fiscal, administrative, and legislative power from Prussia and the other states to the Reich. As David Blackbourn says, this could "be seen in the mounting volume of Reichstag business, especially in committee, the growing importance of

major party leaders and committee experts in influencing political decisionmaking, and the increasing readiness of successive chancellors to take such
figures into account."[29] But in some versions this argument can be down-
right tendentious. Certainly, to argue that there was a limited practical
stabilization of public life within the available forms of Wilhelmine
constitutionalism is not the same as arguing that the political system was
well on its way to a parliamentary democracy of the British variety.[30]

One more oblique way into this problem is to consider the question of
Staatsstreich or *coup d'état*, for the latter has been generalized into a
larger claim about the constraints on the very possibilities of liberalizing
reform within the Imperial political system, namely, the idea of the
Permanenz der Staatsstreichsdrohung or "permanence of the threat of
Staatsstreich," another of those immensely appealing phrases bequeathed
to us from the liberal revisionist historiography of the 1960s. The threat of
a *coup d'état*, it is argued, was wielded by Bismarck and his successors as
a constitutional damocletian sword, so that if a parliamentary majority
continued to oppose the government beyond a certain point (in a situation
comparable to the Prussian constitutional conflict of the 1860s), the government would simply suspend the Reichstag, impose a new and reactionary constitution, and ensure the election of a more compliant
legislature. In effect, this acted as a general authoritarian constraint on the
political culture, which leading parliamentarians (it is argued) tended to
internalize. That is, politicians would never press their liberalism very far,
because if they did a reactionary revision of the constitution might result.

The best evidence of such pressure towards conformity and compliance,
both as a calculation of government and as a factor in parliamentary
behavior, comes from 1878–1879, when Bismarck toyed with the idea to
assist his turn to the right via the Anti-Socialist Law and the high tariff settlement; from 1890, when Bismarck again dabbled in the possibility
during his conflict with Wilhelm II; from the mid-1890s, when the Kaiser
and Eulenburg incorporated threats and fantasies of *Staatsstreich* into their
repertoire of strategies for securing the Kaiser's "personal rule"; and from
1897, when a more generalized flirtation with a policy of extreme confrontation with the Reichstag was dramatized in two memoranda of Field-
Marshall Alfred Graf von Waldersee in January and February of that
year.[31] In none of these cases are we dealing with clearly formulated intentions of either government or a coherent grouping within the right-wing
parties. Instead, we are dealing with contingency speculation at a time of
acute government difficulties in the Ministry of State or the Reichstag,
much of which has been inferred on the basis of extremely fragmentary
evidence.

But whatever the reality of *Staatsstreich* threats before 1897 (my own view is that the evidence doesn't permit a firm conclusion), *after* that date such threats definitely recede. We can see this quite clearly in the deliberations that accompany the ministerial reconstruction of summer 1897. Basically, the choice for the government had become: *either* a continued confrontation with the Reichstag, to the point of repeated dissolutions and an overturn of the constitution; *or* a new parliamentary strategy based on a modus vivendi with moderate parliamentarians in the National Liberal Party and the Center. In the course of June and July 1897, the government opted explicitly for the latter, and this choice opened a period that lasted until 1912, in which political life settled down into a pattern set by the terms of the existing parliamentary constitution.

I would call this a practical stabilization of parliamentary forms, which rendered the operation of the political system, and the behavior of governments and parties, indistinguishable from a situation defined by a constitution that was officially more strongly parliamentary. To argue this doesn't mean accepting an evolutionary model of parliamentary development in the manner of some older interpretations of the *Kaiserreich*. The authoritarian provisions of the 1871 Constitution continued to exist and set limits to any process of putative parliamentarization. In this more modest sense, the real political configuration of the years 1897–1902 was *practically* a parliamentary one, which definitely ruled out most forms of the so-called "exceptional legislation." Here is the Chancellor Bülow, responding to a Conservative parliamentarian's demand for a new Anti-Socialist Law in the aftermath of the SPD's imposing successes in the 1903 elections:

Certainly, it is not excluded that a legislative intervention *vis-à-vis* Social Democracy can, with time, turn out to be necessary. However, as practical politicians we have to wish that such interventions only occur when the National Liberals and the Center also see the dire necessity of such an act, so that the measure against Social Democracy not be paralyzed by a fight of the bourgeois parties among themselves or by a conflict between the government and the bourgeois parties. Therefore … I see the need to shield the bourgeois parties from one thing – that if they do not hold together, the dilemma could arise: victory of the revolution, or *Staatsstreich* with absolutism. I have preached this cohesiveness of the bourgeois parties again and again … My view is that both the fight against Social Democracy and the fight in parliament should not be … left up to the government, but that it must be waged by the parties of order …[32]

What this meant, I think, is that politics now had to be conducted on a very particular terrain, that of the given parliamentary and constitutional framework. Most observers now accepted that the SPD had to be fought on its own terms – that is, by agitation and propaganda, and by the organized patriotic mobilization of workers, rather than by straightforward repression in the manner of the Bismarckian Anti-Socialist Law.

THINKING ABOUT DEMOCRACY

How does the retelling of this story affect our understanding of democracy in this German setting? In answering this question, I want to begin with a reflection on the grand historical assumptions around which most social science conceptions of democracy's origins tend to be ordered, which (as I've suggested earlier in this chapter) see the latter as being embedded either in the outcomes of the conflicts and coalitions among the class forces involved in the process of industrialization or in the logics of socioeconomic development *tout court*. The construction of the possibility of democracy, in this respect, is often misconceived via a series of conflations.

First, the understanding of democracy tends to be abstracted inappropriately from a particular historical form of democracy's realization, the strong forms of liberal democracy (including its welfare statism) in the late twentieth century, whose possibility is then projected quite unhistorically into very different situations a hundred years before, thereby producing an unnecessarily inflated standard of evaluation for German liberalism in particular. The more sensible context for judging German liberalism in the foundation years of the *Kaiserreich* – the Europeanwide conjuncture of constitutional revision, nation-forming, and state-making in the 1860s, together with the culture of progress and the general remaking of the social environment for capitalism, under circumstances where liberals accepted that specifically democratic aspirations had to be contained – gets confused.

Second, in such discussions there is an unfortunate conceptual slippage from dealing with the "bourgeoisie" as a social category to dealing with "liberalism" as a political tradition. The demonstrable affinities between a liberal political outlook and a specific configuration of bourgeois interests and aspirations at one particular time – in the middle third of the nineteenth century – are allowed to license harder assumptions about the conceptual unity of bourgeois and liberal identities in general, whereas really these are separable phenomena. Indeed, in Germany after the 1870s the language of bourgeois assertiveness and consolidation and the language of liberal constitutionalism began to diverge, so that the requirements of the one began to be uncoupled from the requirements of the other. Consequently, that most familiar of nineteenth-century conflations – "bourgeois liberalism" – seriously confuses the issue when judging the social and political coordinates of German government after 1871. As I argued elsewhere, there are two distinct problems mixed up in such an approach:

> On the one hand, there is the question of the conditions under which a bourgeois capitalist society could successfully reproduce itself, or to put it another way, the legal, political, and ideological conditions of existence for a successful German capitalism. Then on the other hand, there is the question of how a more liberal political system might have been achieved. *These are not the same question.*[33]

Third, the common equation of "liberalism" and "democracy" compounds the conceptual elision of "liberal" into "bourgeois" still further, making the connotative continuum of "bourgeoisie = liberalism = democracy" into an implied causal chain. A term like "bourgeois democracy" can be seriously misleading, as it implies a positive relationship between specifically democratic institutions and the achievements of political movements in which fractions of the bourgeoisie played the leading part. In fact, democratic advances have more often occurred against the resistance of such bourgeois fractions than with their support, with divisive consequences for the liberal movements in which both bourgeois elitists and democratically inclined working men had originally been joined. By any strict definition of democracy, the coupling of "liberalism" and "democracy" makes no sense for most of the nineteenth century, because liberals showed themselves consistently attached to highly restricted and exclusionary systems of political representation. When democratic reforms were introduced, they came through broad popular mobilizations outside the normal frameworks of liberal politics, even though the more flexible liberal leaderships may sometimes have taken them up. The urban artisanate and petty bourgeoisie, the independent peasantry, and eventually the industrial working class, were the main bearers of specifically democratic traditions in the nineteenth and early twentieth centuries, although the various situations in which democratic gains were actually secured – such as the inclusion of the universal (male) suffrage in the German constitutions of 1867–1871 – involved more complex negotiations and calculations than this straightforward statement of popular agency implies.

The three significant periods of nineteenth-century constitution-making – the failed ones surrounding the revolutions of 1830 and 1848, and the successful one of the 1860s – all show this to be the case, as do countless national instances of less dramatic change. It was not really until the next great moment of European constitution-making in 1917–1923 that liberals properly embraced democratic principles. The prevailing ideology that brought the First World War to a close, that of the self-determination of peoples, combined with the need to respond to the working-class insurgency that overtook most of Europe between 1917 and 1921 to engage liberals prominently in the democratic politics of those years, usually in the effort to contain any more radical breakthrough to socialism. This was how strong forms of cooperation among liberals and reformist social democrats were first shaped. Later, with the rise of fascism in the 1930s, and the politics of Popular Front and anti-fascist war – and a further period of constitution-making in 1945–1949 – the basis of liberal integration in the Left became even broader, as communist parties also discovered the value of bringing liberals in, before the onset of the Cold War engineered a new process of fracturing.

We are not likely to get very far in this discussion of democracy unless we combine a careful specification of formal criteria with a similarly careful historicization of democratic gains. I would like to close by suggesting some means of doing this, partly by abstracting from my specifically German discussion above, partly by further elaborating it.

(1) To conduct a sensible discussion of the conditions of possibilities of democratic politics before and after the First World War, we need to remind ourselves of the extremely limited progress made by democratic principles of political order in European terms before 1914; and to do that, we need a strict formal definition of the legal and constitutional conditions of democracy. Building on the work of Göran Therborn, I would propose the following: popular representation on the basis of free, universal, secret, adult, and equal suffrage, buttressed by legal freedoms of speech, assembly, association, and press. Therborn expounds this definition partly by distinguishing the four main bases of exclusion from the franchise – by class, race, sex, and opinion (as in the proscription of radical left or right-wing parties). On this basis, by 1914 "only three peripheral capitalist states could have been described as democracies: Australia, New Zealand ... and Norway. If we disregard sexism and include male democracies, then two more examples could be cited: France and Switzerland."[34]

(2) This definition seems to me superior, for instance, to the typically vague and idiosyncratic definition offered by Barrington Moore, as "a long and certainly incomplete struggle to do three closely related things: 1) to

check arbitrary rulers, 2) to replace arbitrary rulers with just and rational ones, and 3) to obtain a share for the underlying population in the making of rules."[35] On the other hand, Moore's definition *does* move us towards the dynamic societal context of social and political contestation. Moreover, in practice my own discussion of Germany above has likewise reached beyond Therborn's necessary context of constitutional law (citizenship rights in the formal sense) to the less firmly bounded context of contingency and contestation – of the specific struggles that define the political effectiveness of those constitutional rules and procedures at any one time.[36] In a sense, this is the distinction between the *formal* and the *dynamic* conditions of democracy – between on the one hand the strengthening of parliamentary representative institutions and citizenship rights under the law; and on the other hand the more extensive and radicalized conception of social rights that accompanies the rise of the welfare state, an expanded understanding of citizenship capacities that may or may not become institutionalized under the law, and the strengthening of an increasingly mass-mediated public sphere.

Once we begin historicizing the circumstances under which democratic forms were proposed and secured, it becomes harder to confine the discussion of democracy to formal juridical terms, least of all to liberal conceptions which identify democratic politics with the securing of parliamentary constitutions of the classic pre-1914 type, as opposed to other possibilities such as the strengthened republican constitutions that commonly emerged from the insurrectionary turbulence of 1917–1921. Struggles around parliamentary sovereignty in the formal constitutional sense have certainly been key to popular-democratic mobilization (whether before 1914, during 1917–1923, in the resistance against fascism, or most recently during 1989–1992), but there are other dimensions of democratization that go beyond this rather limited context.

The effects of social movements such as trade unions, women's movements, moral reform campaigns, and so on, which involve collective action and organization in a wider societal field, would be one major instance, requiring the constitutional definition of a democratic polity to be complemented by some developed conception of civil society.[37] The formation of the welfare state would be a second major instance. Yet a third dimension, concerning processes dismissed by German historians such as Wehler and Rosenberg as "pseudo-democratizations," is more difficult and ambiguous in character – namely, popular mobilizations which may have an *anti*-democratic orientation in terms of their conscious demands, but whose emergence and activities practically expand the bounds of participation within the public sphere, in ways that are extremely important for democracy and its dynamic possibilities; this is how I understand aspects of the non-socialist popular mobilizations in Germany in the 1890s. Finally, this broader conception of democracy should also include direct-democratic and community-based forms of participatory politics, which acquired explosive resonance during the revolutionary conjuncture of 1917–1923.

(3) There is a transnational European context to the historicized problematic of democracy, for the parameters of democratic politics have been set to a great extent beyond the borders of particular national histories in a series of horizon-expanding and limit-setting Europeanwide conjunctures between the eighteenth century and the present. I would suggest five such conjunctures, all of them transnational constitution-making moments of European history through which the limits and possibilities for democracy were established for the succeeding epochs: 1776–1815, 1859–1871, 1914–1923, 1943–1949, and 1989–1992. For our purposes, the 1860s provide the base-line of discussion, laying down the legal-constitutional and institutional terrain of popular-democratic politics until radicalized contestations began to dissolve this settlement in the years between 1905 and 1914. Likewise, the conjuncture of war and revolution in 1914–1923 produced a further generalized redrawing of the map, setting the scene for the polarized politics of revolution and counter-revolution that generated fascism.

In the 1860s, for instance, liberal constitutionalism registered an impressive international increment, through a series of state reorganizations and recognitions of popular rights, most importantly in relation to the franchise, but also including the limited legalization of trade unions on a local and national scale. This process embraced the creation of new constitutional nation-states in Germany and Italy, the Second Reform Act and associated social and political reforms in Britain, the constitutional compromise of 1867 between Austria and Hungary in the Habsburg Empire, the liberal revolution in Spain in 1868–1869, the collapse of the Second Empire and foundation of the Third Republic in France in 1871, together with the constitutional reforms in Greece (1864) and Serbia (1869), and even the reforms of 1861–1864 in Tsarist Russia. Moreover, the constitutional frameworks fashioned in the 1860s proved remarkably resilient. Of course, stability sometimes had to be secured through major feats of constitutional accommodation to popular pressure – for instance, the Third Reform Act in Britain (1884), the Belgian Constitution of 1893, the concession of universal manhood suffrage in Austria (1907) and Italy (1912), and the Scandinavian liberalizations in Norway (1898), Denmark (1901), Finland (1905), and Sweden (1907). But in each case the new settlements were negotiated by constitutional means. Even if extra-parliamentary in form, popular-democratic aspirations were articulated within and not against the liberal constitutional framework, and stability was secured *through* the available parliamentary forms.

If the experience of the 1860s established a lasting set of parliamentary constitutional norms for European political life, the next transnational conjuncture of constitution-making, which reshaped those norms, came in the aftermath of the First World War. Here I am concerned less with the insurrectionary revolutionary projects of the Bolshevik and other insurgent Lefts than the reformist initiatives such challenges precipitated. Thus even where the revolutionary Left was at its weakest and socialist parties recorded relatively modest gains in post-war elections, this effect could clearly be seen – as in France (with a law on collective agreements, the eight-hour day, and an electoral reform between March and July 1919); in Belgium (the eight-hour day, a progressive tax reform, social insurance legislation, and electoral reform during 1918–1921); and the Netherlands (the eight-hour day and 45-hour week, social insurance legislation, public housing, corporative involvement of the trade unions in the new Ministry of Social Affairs, and votes for women during 1918–1920). Similar effects could be seen in Britain and Scandinavia. In Germany and Austria, and in the new successor states of East-Central Europe, new republican sovereignties were constructed via processes of national-democratic revolution, accompanied with varying degrees of social reform. Finally, in most of the successor states and some others – Romania, Yugoslavia, Bulgaria, Greece, Czechoslovakia, Poland, the Baltic States, and Finland – there were also major land reforms.

This was a major increment of reform. In a large part of Europe – essentially the pre-war Central and North European "social democratic core" where socialist parties had achieved 20 percent or more in parliamentary elections (Austria, Germany, Czechoslovakia, Switzerland, and all the Scandinavian countries), together with France, the Low Countries, and Britain – the position of the Left had become much stronger than before. Yet this took a very specific form – that is, not a specifically socialist advance, so much as a further strengthening of parliamentary democracy in its democratic dimensions, the expansion of workers' rights under the law, further recognition of trade unions, growth of civil liberties, and significant social legislation, which in some cases amounted to the beginnings of a welfare state. In particular, the enhancement of the public sphere – in parliamentary, publicistic, and cultural terms – was a major strategic gain, especially in countries where public freedoms had been cramped and harassed before 1914. This toughening of civil society through the enhancement of the public sphere was a vital dimension of democratization, and in the newly created sovereignties of East-Central Europe – including the new republican sovereignty of Weimar Germany – the legal constitution of the public sphere was a vital process in the overall project of nation-forming.

(4) Lastly, I want to close with some observations on gender and the democratic access of women, not as an afterthought, but as a deliberate positioning, as a way of upsetting in the most radical way the more formal and customary ways of conceptualizing the conditions of emergence of democracy. One way of raising this set of questions is certainly through the feminist critique of political theory by deconstructing the gendered discourse of citizenship and political capacities descending from the Enlightenment and French Revolution. By now, feminist theory has shown just how fundamentally the terms of modern social and political identity – of class, citizenship, "race," nationhood, religion, the very category of personhood and the self – have been constituted from dichotomous assumptions about what it has meant to be a woman or man, producing the pervasive dualisms which organize dominant understandings of the social and political order in this respect. Inscribed in the language of identity have been definite notions of masculinity and femininity that have limited "women's access to knowledge, skill, and independent political subjectivity," as Sally Alexander has said.[38]

The basic category of civil society presumed the exclusion of women via the construction and naturalizing of claims about sexual difference, and as Carol Pateman has argued the demand for women's inclusion as fully qualified citizens consequently makes it "necessary to deconstruct and reassemble our understanding of the body politic."[39] Any adequate retelling of the German story before 1914 would require this gendered dimension of disablement and exclusion. For immediate purposes, however, my main effort has focused on showing how a formal perspective on democracy needs to be complemented by a more dynamic understanding of how democratic capacities become shaped, and from this point of view the question of women is vital to the early twentieth-century dialectic of containment and excess, or the limits and potential enlargements of democratic life. From this point of view, my question is: what is the appropriate ground from which a democratic politics of gender in the early twentieth century could be addressed?

The late nineteenth and early twentieth centuries provide a particularly informative context for considering this question – partly because it sees the first concerted challenge to existing conceptions of political and social authority on the part of both mass socialist and feminist movements before

1914 (thinking again in general European terms); partly because the years 1914–1923 see an unprecedented destabilizing and renormalizing of existing gender regimes; and partly because the politicizing of domestic life during the First World War was also accompanied in the early twentieth century by the emergence of an increasingly visible and extensive mass culture of entertainment and pleasure, which created a space of public recognition which in its sociology and discursive definition was distinctly female, in that women were and were thought to be disproportionately involved. What I want to suggest is that the years 1914–1923 see a very important transition in the terms within which women's political identities were understood.

If before 1914, advocates of women's emancipation mainly sought political enfranchisement and the enlargement of constitutional rights – the classic terrain of formal democracy – *after* 1914 women's citizenship was increasingly conceptualized via the validation of motherhood, so that the main ground of contestation around gender relations and women's emancipation shifted away from notions of productivism and political rights and toward ideas of *moral order*. Of course, there is always a counter-discourse to the discourse of emancipation and freedom, and that is the discourse of disorder and danger. During the First World War and the 1920s, maternalism supplied the main political language for both Right and Left, through which this opposition now became handled. Moreover, by the end of the 1920s the maternalist resolution of conflicts and debates around women's place was occurring in ways particularly inimical to possibilities of women's emancipation, and in some cases (notably Germany) provided the ground from which that feminist emancipatory project could be effectively destroyed. The question remains: were there other possibilities, given the circumstances of the early twentieth century, which may have allowed this political question to have been differently posed?

Where can we find a distinct space for feminist politics between the wars and after the (transnationally uneven) concession of women's right to vote, a space where the possibilities of women's politics escaped both the productivist demotion of women's interests and concerns behind the priorities of economics in industry and the maternalist normalization of women's difference within the emerging project of the social democratic welfare state? This question is all the harder to answer, because the explicit feminisms of the 1920s also found it difficult to escape from this frustrating and ultimately disabling dilemma themselves. But if the main story is the one which the women's history of the last two decades compellingly describes, if the female independence and visibility generated by the First World War was generally contained during the post-war turbu-lence and restabilizations, then where can we find some excess, where women's agency may have evaded control, escaping the maternalist and productivist normalizations I have just described?

We should look carefully at aspects of the 1920s that are certainly well known, and which have in fact been receiving growing attention from women's historians, but which until recently have not been conceptual-ized as being particularly relevant to the question of democratic political consolidation. On the one hand, there is the general area of "body poli-tics," organized around the moral and reproductive domains of social policy innovation in the early twentieth century, including maternal and child welfare, reproductive technology and regulation (contraception, abortion, sterilization), eugenicist social engineering, public health, poli-cies for the control of youth, and the general regulation of morality and sexuality. On the other hand, there is the emergent culture of mass con-sumption – the new culture of the movies, the dance halls, advertising, smoking, cosmetics, cutprice hedonism, and bodily display; a culture, as Judith Williamson puts it, in which "the conscious, chosen meaning in most people's lives comes much more from what they consume than what they produce."[40] These were the twin domains – the politics of the body, the politics of consumption – which the interwar Right, sometimes conser-vatively (as in Baldwin's Britain), but sometimes with activist aggression (as in fascist Italy and Nazi Germany), was able to bring ambitiously together.

Accordingly, if a democratic politics of gender is to be retrospectively constructed, it is to the areas of dreaming and pleasure, sexuality and recreation, that we will also need to look. These were the areas that began to emerge in the 1920s as a special domain, one that for women refused to be disciplined quite as easily into the familial sphere of maternalist responsibility and political dependency which virtually all parts of the political spectrum were so avidly constructing. In other words, alongside the social history of class relations at work, and the conditions and conse-quences of regulation and innovation through the welfare state, we also need to write the history of the politics of culture. If politics organizes at the intersection of public and personal life,[41] colonizing our imagination, shaping our needs, and inscribing our everyday transactions with its rules, then the same process also describes a key space of resistance; and a democratic politics of empowerment and opposition has to work creatively on this ground.

This is the note on which I prefer to end. The more familiar social and political histories dealt with earlier in this chapter are clearly important.

But if we are to take the social construction of democracy seriously, and therefore the complex production of political capacities, then it is to this other context – the domain of ordinary desire – that we must also attend.

NOTES

1. See especially Geoff Eley, "The British Model and the German Road: Rethinking the Course of German History before 1914," in David Blackbourn and Geoff Eley, *The Peculiarities of German History. Bourgeois Society and Politics in Nineteenth-Century Germany* (Oxford, 1984), 39–155; Eley, "What Produces Fascism: 'Pre-Industrial Traditions' or a Crisis of the Capitalist State?" *Politics and Society*, 12 (1983): 53–82; Eley, "Liberalism, Europe, and the Bourgeoisie, 1860–1914," in David Blackbourn and Richard J. Evans, eds., *The German Bourgeoisie. Essays on the Social History of the German Middle Class from the Late Eighteenth to the Early Twentieth Century* (London, 1990), 293–317; Eley, "Die deutsche Geschichte und die Widersprüche der Moderne. Das Beispiel des Kaiserreichs," in Frank Bajohr, Werner Johe, and Uwe Lohalm, eds., *Zivilisation und Barbarei. Die widersprüchlichen Potentiale der Moderne. Detlev Peukert zum Gedenken* (Hamburg, 1991), 17–65.
2. M. Rainer Lepsius, "Parteiensystem und Sozialstruktur: Zum Problem der Demokratisierung der deutschen Gesellschaft," in Gerhard A. Ritter, ed., *Die deutschen Parteien vor 1918* (Cologne, 1973), 56.
3. Barrington Moore, Jr., *Social Origins of Dictatorship and Democracy: Lord and Peasant in the Making of the Modern World* (Harmondsworth, 1967).
4. Alexander Gerschenkron, *Bread and Democracy in Germany*, 2nd. edn. (Ithaca, 1989, orig. pub. 1943); Hans Rosenberg, "Political and Social Consequences of the Great Depression of 1873–1896 in Central Europe," *Economic History Review*, 13 (19), 58–73; Rosenberg, *Bureaucracy, Aristocracy, Autocracy: The Prussian Experience, 1660–1815* (Cambridge, Mass., 1958); Rosenberg, *Probleme der deutschen Sozialgeschichte* (Frankfurt am Main, 1969); Thorsten Veblen, *Imperial Germany and the Industrial Revolution* (Ann Arbor, 1966; orig. pub. 1915).
5. Ralf Dahrendorf, *Society and Democracy in Germany* (London, 1968), 397.
6. Dahrendorf, *Society and Democracy in Germany*, 404.
7. Leonard Krieger, *The German Idea of Freedom* (Chicago, 1957); Mack Walker, *German Home Towns. Community, State, and General Estate, 1648–1871* (Ithaca, 1971); Fritz Stern, "The Political Consequences of the Unpolitical German," in Stern, *The Failure of Illiberalism* (London, 1972), 3–25.
8. Talcott Parsons, *Essays in Sociological Theory* (Glencoe, 1964).
9. Lepsius, "Parteiensystem und Sozialstruktur," 64ff., 73.
10. For an excellent summary of the debates around these perspectives, see Robert Moeller, "The Kaiserreich Recast? Continuity and Change in

Modern Germany Historiography," *Journal of Social History*, 17 (1984): 655–83.

11.   Hans-Ulrich Wehler, "Wie bürgerlich war das Deutsche Kaiserreich?" in Wehler *Aus der Geschichte lernen? Essays* (Munich, 1988), 214.

12.   Hans-Ulrich Wehler, "Industrial Growth and Early German Imperialism," in Roger Owen and Bob Sutcliffe, eds., *Studies in the Theory of Imperialism* (London, 1972), 84.

13.   Wehler, "Industrial Growth," 78.

14.   Wehler, *Aus der Geschichte lernen?* 269.

15.   See Blackbourn and Eley, *Peculiarities of German History*; Helga Grebing, *Der "Deutsche Sonderweg" in Europa: Eine Kritik* (Stuttgart, 1986); David Blackbourn, "The German Bourgeoisie: An Introduction," in Blackbourn and Evans, eds., *The German Bourgeoisie*, 1–45; Eley, "Die deutsche Geschichte und die Widerspruche der Moderne"; Jürgen Kocka, "German History before Hitler: The Debate about the German Sonderweg," *Journal of Contemporary History*, 23 (1988): 3–16.

16.   Jürgen Kocka, "Ursachen des Nationalsozialismus," *Aus Politik und Zeitgeschichte*, 21 June 1980, 11; Heinrich August Winkler, "Die 'neue Linke' und der deutsche Faschismus: Zur Kritik neomarxistischer Theorien über den Nationalsozialismus," in Winkler, *Revolution, Staat, Faschismus. Zur Revision des Historischen Materialismus* (Göttingen, 1978), 83.

17.   Heinrich August Winkler, "Wie konnte es zum 20. Januar 1933 kommen?" *Aus Politik und Zeitgeschichte*, 29 January 1983, abstract.

18.   Hans-Ulrich Wehler, "30. Januar 1933 – ein halbes Jahrhundert danach," *Aus Politik und Zeitgeschichte*, 29 January 1983, 53, 52.

19.   Stanley Suval, *Electoral Politics in Wilhelmine Germany* (Chapel Hill, 1985), 55–119.

20.   Suval, *Electoral Politics*, 36.

21.   Suval, *Electoral Politics*, 257.

22.   Suval, *Electoral Politics*, 149–60. This is also the theme of Geoff Eley, *Reshaping the German Right. Radical Nationalism and Political Change after Bismarck* (London and New Haven, 1980; new edn. Ann Arbor, 1991).

23.   For further discussion of this point, see Blackbourn and Eley, *Peculiarities of German History*, 29ff.

24.   Eley, *Reshaping*; David Blackbourn, *Class, Religion and Local Politics in Wilhelmine Germany: The Centre Party in Württemberg before 1914* (London and New Haven, 1980); Blackbourn, "The Politics of Demagogy in Imperial Germany," in Blackbourn, *Populists and Patricians. Essays in Modern German History* (London, 1987), 217–45; Wolfgang Mock, "'Manipulation von oben' oder Selbstorganisation an der Basis? Einige neuere Ansätze in der englischen Historiographie zur Geschichte des deutschen Kaiserreichs," *Historische Zeitschrift*, 232 (1981): 358–75.

25.   See Eley, *Reshaping*, 319f; and Dirk Stegmann, *Die Erben Bismarcks. Parteien und Verbände in der Spätphase des Wilhelminischen Deutschlands. Sammlungspolitik 1897–1918* (Cologne, 1970), 368–80.

26.   See Hans Rosenberg, "Die Pseudodemokratisierung der Rittergutsbesitzerklasse," in *Probleme der deutschen Sozialgeschichte*, 7–49.

27. Klaus Saul, *Staat, Industrie, Arbeiterbewegung im Kaiserreich. Zur Innen- und Sozialpolitik des Wilhelminischen Deutschland 1903–1914* (Düsseldorf, 1974), 188–282.

28. John C. G. Roehl, *Germany Without Bismarck* (London, 1967); and especially Stegmann, *Die Erben Bismarcks*. For the context of the Fischer Controversy see Fritz Fischer, *From Kaiserreich to Third Reich. Elements of Continuity in German History 1871–1945* (London, 1986).

29. David Blackbourn, "The Discreet Charm of the Bourgeoisie: Reappraising German History in the Nineteenth Century," in Blackbourn and Eley, *Peculiarities of German History*, 277.

30. See the much older work by Werner Frauendienst, "Demokratisierung des deutschen Konstitutionalismus in der Zeit Wilhelms II," *Zeitschrift zur die gesamte Staatswissenschaft*, 113 (1957), 721–46; and the two useful but problematic books by Manfred Rauh: *Föderalismus und Parlamentarismus im Wilhelminischen Reich* (Düsseldorf, 1972), and *Die Parlamentarisierung des Deutschen Reichs* (Düsseldorf, 1977). It is important to add that my argument about practical constitutionalism and the limited stabilization of parliamentary norms is not to be equated with a whiggish notion of democratization or the growth of "freedom."

31. See Michael Sturmer, "Staatsstreichgedanken im Bismarckreich," *Historische Zeitschrift*, 209 (1969), 566–617; Egmont Zechlin, *Staatsstreichpläne Bismarcks und Wilhelms II, 1890–1894* (Stuttgart, 1929); Roehl, *Germany Without Bismarck*.

32. Bülow to Stolberg-Wernigerode, 7 January 1904, Zentrales Staatsarchiv Potsdam, Rkz., 1391/5, cited Eley, *Reshaping*, 228.

33. Eley, "The British Model and the German Road," 148.

34. Göran Therborn, "The Rule of Capital and the Rise of Democracy," *New Left Review*, 103 (1977), 19. See also Therborn, "The Travail of Latin American Democracy," *New Left Review*, 113–14 (1979), 71–109; and Atilio Boron, "Latin America: Between Hobbes and Friedman," *New Left Review*, 130 (1981): 45–66.

35. Moore, *Social Origins*, 414.

36. For Therborn's own analysis of this kind, see Göran Therborn, "Why Some Classes Are More Successful Than Others," *New Left Review*, 138 (1983): 37–55.

37. See John Keane, *Democracy and Civil Society* (London, 1988), and Keane, ed., *Civil Society and the State. New European Perspectives* (London, 1988); also Jean L. Cohen and Andrew Arato, *Civil Society and Political Theory* (Cambridge, Mass., 1992).

38. Sally Alexander, "Women, Class and Sexual Differences in the 1830s and 1840s: Some Reflections on the Writing of a Feminist History," *History Workshop Journal*, 17 (1984), 137.

39. Carole Pateman, "The Fraternal Social Contract," in Keane, ed., *Civil Society and the State*, 123.

40. Judith Williamson, *Consuming Passions. The Dynamics of Popular Culture* (London, 1986), 230.

41. Williamson, *Consuming Passions*, 10.

5 The Two Souls of American Democracy
Richard Oestreicher

In the closing decades of the nineteenth century and the first quarter of the twentieth century, in most of the industrialized world, large-scale mass production provoked increasing class conflict and accelerated the political mobilization of the working class. Large-scale, capital-intensive industries concentrated workers in strategic urban areas where they came in contact with radical intellectuals and were socialized into the shopfloor cultures of earlier generations of working-class activists. Reorganization of work methods in mass production also broke down some of the craft and sectoral barriers which had previously divided workers. Combined with the effects of the First World War, this second industrial revolution led to fundamental political challenges to ruling elites and to the symbolic vestiges of *anciens régimes*.[1] The political situation varied from country to country, but in most industrialized countries the first quarter of the twentieth century was a historical moment when demands for long-sought expansion of democratic rights meshed with industrial class conflict to produce an atmosphere of political crisis, if not potential revolution. While democratic institutions and values by no means triumphed universally, in many countries workers, peasants, and other subordinate groups fought for increased power in the street, at the ballot box, and in the parliament.

In the United States, widespread popular politics with largely unrestricted speech and assembly and other norms of democracy had already been in place for several generations before the second industrial revolution. Egalitarian rhetoric had long dominated American political culture. Universal male suffrage had been achieved in the 1860s, at least in theory, as an outgrowth of the Civil War. Nonetheless, the consequences of the second industrial revolution also triggered a combination of increased industrial conflict and mass social movements similar to that found in other parts of the world. However, because of the racial and ethnic cleavages of American society, the relationship of these movements to an agenda of expanded social and political democracy was divided and ambiguous. While members of these movements campaigned for expanded rights for themselves, they sometimes did so by tactically aligning themselves with forces pushing restrictions of the rights of others. The resulting divisions of subordinate groups against each other facilitated the efforts of business and corporate leaders to shape demands for social reform to their own ends, defeat labor insurgency, and dominate federal economic and social policy. The political conflicts from the 1890s to the 1920s thus eventually resulted in a narrowing of the opportunities for popular political mobilization and activity. Although the Great Depression triggered a new round of mass protest, a basic realignment of the political party system, and new forms of government intervention in industrial conflict, the New Deal, in the end, did not fundamentally alter the trajectory of narrowing political possibilities initiated earlier in the twentieth century.

RACE, ETHNICITY, AND SOCIAL MOVEMENTS

The United States had already been the world's leading industrial producer before the age of steel, electricity, and the internal combustion engine, but as late as the 1880s, in only a few industries had large, capital-intensive factories superseded small-scale craft production.[2] However, between the 1890s and the 1920s, American industrialists embraced mass production technology more enthusiastically than anyone else in the world. Indeed, the rest of the world so associated the new system of capital-intensive, flow-through production with the United States that Fordism, after Henry Ford, became its popular label.

As elsewhere, mass production had enormous social and political consequences in the United States. The strings of industrial monoliths lining the river banks of western Pennsylvania, the southern shorelines of the Great Lakes, or the the outskirts of Detroit, needed millions of workers. At the same time, expanded application of new technologies to transportation and agriculture undermined small-scale agriculture and rural handicraft production both within rural America and in the less developed regions of the rest of the world.[3] Millions of working people left Kentucky and Mississippi, Sicily and Croatia, Canton and Manila, Mexico and Cuba for New York, Pittsburgh, Cleveland, Detroit, Chicago, and San Francisco. As they poured into rapidly expanding urban-industrial areas they challenged not only their employers' efforts to regiment their labor but also the very fabric of urban cultural and political life: urban geography, neighborhood patterns, demography, schooling, public health. Politicians, social reformers, academic experts, middle-class homeowners, as well as employers and supervisors, all felt compelled to respond to the the presence of a vastly expanded industrial proletariat, a proletariat comprised largely of outsiders: people with different skin colors, languages, customs, and religions.[4]

The contradictory legacy of the American political system and political culture ensured that political responses to the newcomers would also be contradictory. America had no *ancien régime*.[5] For more than a century before mass production, America had been a militantly democratic egalitarian republic which proudly proclaimed its commitment to universal human rights. Like nowhere else in the modern world, democratic rhetoric, symbols, and values have reigned supreme in American political culture. Democratic supremacy has been so unchallenged in American history that most Americans are not consciously aware of its overwhelming hegemony. There are practically no political alternatives. The United States has had no monarchists, virtually no fascists, no clerical parties, no putsches, no coups, no Hitler, no Mussolini, no Stalin, no Perón, no Bismarck. Most of those in American politics who have called themselves conservatives have been classical nineteenth-century liberals: had they found themselves in most European or Latin American countries, they would have been more at home in political parties that called themselves Liberal than those that called themselves Conservative. The only era in which communists gained even a minor mass following was the Popular Front period between 1935 and 1945, when the Communist Party of the USA emblazoned the words "Communism is the Americanism of the Twentieth Century" on the mastheads of its literature.[6] That slogan paid obeisance to the most commonly stated definition of what it was to be an American: loyalty not to language or to territory but to ideology; to be American was to be loyal to "liberty and justice for all."

But the United States has also been a colonial settler society. The ancestors of the dominant White Anglo-Saxon Protestant culture group seized the land in centuries of genocidal warfare. The epidemics and massacres which decimated native peoples from their first contact with Europeans continued right up to the age of mass production with the slaughter of the Sioux at Wounded Knee in 1890. The Africans who had been enslaved to work the land stolen from Native Americans were still largely excluded from the polity after emancipation. Hispanics who found themselves within the borders of the United States as a result of the conquests of the Mexican War, or who migrated in succeeding generations, fared little better. Asians, who played a critical role in the development of the West Coast, were also systematically harassed. One hundred years ago, Frederick Jackson Turner argued that the frontier had been the cradle of American democracy. Perhaps Turner had it backwards. American democracy had usually been white men's democracy, in large part because the experiences of frontier conquest, enslavement, and racial hierarchy had left behind a profoundly undemocratic legacy to contest the heritage of 1776.

In the decades just before the rise of mass production, some Americans had made an effort to make good on the promises of universal rights allegedly guaranteed in the Declaration of Independence and the Bill of Rights. Radical Reconstruction had been a serious effort to push democracy beyond white men's democracy. Reconstruction not only attempted to reshape Southern society, but it also unleashed a democratic idealism nationally which stimulated the efforts of virtually everyone in American society who felt that democratic promises had not been fulfilled for them.[7] It is, thus, no coincidence that in the same era that Radical Republicans tried to integrate the freedmen into American democracy, feminism first became a mass movement, or that the Knights of Labor, for the first time, seriously committed the labor movement to organizing women, African-Americans, and Hispanics.[8] Champions of genuine democratic universalism and advocates of restricted political participation contended with each other well before mass production had taken hold. That heritage of political conflict shaped the way all political actors responded after 1890 to the issues raised by large-scale corporate mass production, increased immigration from southern and eastern Europe, Asia, and Latin America, the black diaspora out of the rural South, and the social and ecological consequences of rapid urbanization.

A succession of social movements which exerted increasing influence in American political life after 1890 – populism, progressivism, socialism, women's suffrage, trade unionism, and civil rights – can all be viewed, at least in part, as responses to the problems raised by industrialization, migration, and urbanization. All of these movements mobilized followers by invoking America's democratic tradition. Whatever their immediate policy objectives, each claimed that they would defend the heritage of 1776 from threatening encroachments.

Populism, for example, began mainly as a farmers' movement. The Farmers' Alliance, an organization advocating farming cooperatives, railroad and banking regulation, and easier access to credit for small, agricultural borrowers, provided most of the movement's initial political base. The People's Party, a national third party organized by Alliance leaders and other reformers in 1892, was a serious electoral contender only where the Farmers' Alliance was already well established. Yet the leaders of the People's Party saw themselves as nothing less than the defenders of a democracy being usurped and corrupted by a newly emerging corporate capitalist power. Intent on symbolically establishing this image, they held their nominating convention on the Fourth of July. They included pro-labor planks in the Farmers' Alliance program, expressed sympathy for the urban poor, and denounced business influence over politicians.[9]

Similarly, the Knights of Labor, as well as many other labor organizations, focused their appeal on the defense of pre-existing democratic rights which they believed were threatened by the new corporate order. Progressives, socialists, civil libertarians, and feminists all appealed at various times to this democratic-republican tradition.

Yet, despite their rhetorical appeals to democratic-republican universalism, each of these movements also mobilized their followers around nativist, ethnocentric, or racist programs. Populist denunciations of urban and monopolistic corruption, phrased in the fundamentalist Protestant language of sin and redemption, consciously harkened back to earlier nativist harangues against Papists, Shylocks, and bloody Irishmen. Despite the pro-labor planks in their platform, to urban, immigrant, Catholic, and Jewish workers, Populist voices echoed the sound of pogroms as much as of liberation.

The Populist insurgency in the South also accelerated the process of black disenfranchisement and the erection of the rigid Jim Crow system of legally enforced racial separation. While some white Populists fought bravely for racial equality, when Populists from the largely white upland counties of the Deep South found themselves politically overwhelmed in the black majority counties of the Gulf coastal plain, enough of them joined their upper-class political antagonists in the campaign for Jim Crow to push segregationist laws through Southern state legislatures. Although many poor white farmers found themselves disenfranchised by poll taxes and the other legal devices that were part of the Jim Crow system, they demanded the full enforcement of apartheid nonetheless. To rural African Americans, as well as to urban immigrant workers, the Populists, at best, seemed to have a divided heart.[10]

Likewise, trade union slogans about workers of the world uniting often did not ring true. Both the Knights of Labor and the American Federation of Labor (AFL) emblazoned their mastheads with such symbols of universalism as clasped hands superimposed over globes. But from their very beginnings, a central tenet of the doctrines of both organizations was the protection of "American" standards of wages and working conditions from those nationalities they deemed unable to assimilate into American culture. In the late 1870s and 1880s, even in those parts of the country where Chinese immigrants were virtually unknown, the labor movement placed anti-Chinese agitation at the forefront of its agenda. The Knights were among the key lobbyists for the Chinese Exclusion Act of 1882. The

AFL made re-enactment of Chinese exclusion in 1902 (when it was due to expire) its chief legislative priority.

The Knights had differentiated between Asiatic coolies and African-Americans. The latter they viewed more as victims than as threats. But after the decline of the Knights in the early 1890s, the AFL and most of its constituent national unions abandoned any pretense of racial equality. With only occasional exceptions, by the turn of the century most AFL unions had "whites only" clauses in their national constitutions. As immigration patterns shifted after 1890 from northern and western Europe towards southern and eastern Europe, this concern with the culturally unassimilable widened to include the new immigrants. The AFL campaigned ever more incessantly for broader immigration restriction. It celebrated each successive restriction on immigration as a victory, including the application of racially inspired national quotas which after 1924 essentially limited immigration to people from northern and western Europe.[11]

Ethnic and racial divisions among American workers limited the appeal of the labor movement and decisively weakened it. At the beginning of the era of mass production, the American labor movement was among the strongest in the world. By the 1920s, unions had been driven out of many industries where they had seemed well established a decade or two earlier. In the late 1920s a smaller proportion of American workers belonged to unions than in the 1880s.[12]

Likewise, clean government advocates who railed against political corruption often used the term as a euphemism for the political influence of foreign, working-class Catholics. Business and corporate leaders were usually the instigators of proposals to change the rules of electoral politics.[13] From the 1890s through the First World War, in various states and cities, they proposed voter registration, stricter residency requirements, at-large election districts, new voting procedures, non-partisan local elections, and professional city managers. Such measures were aimed not only at reducing graft, corruption, and electoral fraud but also at insulating policymaking from neighborhood-based popular pressures and reducing the influence of politicians responsive to workers, unions, and ethnic communities. Generating the electoral support necessary to get these laws enacted demanded extensive agitation and the building of political coalitions sufficient to overcome the opposition of incumbent politicians whose power rested on the existing political system. The intensely moralistic tone of the leaders of political reform was designed to capture political allies among clergymen and other middle-class professionals and among rural Protestants who viewed the cities as hotbeds of sin. To homeowners, political reformers offered the lure of lower taxes and of more efficient public services. And the often thinly veiled anti-immigrant and anti-Catholic tone of political reformers sometimes made their ideas appealing to nativist workers and union leaders who were also seeking to exclude immigrants from American life.[14]

Even women's suffrage, the one movement which appears to be an unambiguous campaign for wider political participation, had ambiguous political consequences. While the success of the women's suffrage movement added millions of potential voters to the electorate, the movement had achieved victory by joining the racist and nativist chorus in early twentieth-century American politics. There were notable exceptions, but the most influential proponents of women's suffrage made their strongest case for male political support by emphasizing how uneducated, non-white, immigrant, and Catholic males had greater rights than pure, white, native, Protestant women. Votes for women would, they argued, be a barrier against the immigrant onslaught.[15]

The effects of the contradictory postures of the key social movements representing the interests of workers, small farmers, and women were most decisive during and after the First World War. In those years, the federal government systematically suppressed the key organizations of the political Left – the Socialist Party and the IWW – with the active collusion of moderate union leaders. But AFL support for anti-radicalism gave it no insulation from the furious business counter-attack against the gains unions had made during the favorable bargaining circumstances of the wartime economy. Racial and ethnic conflict peaked in these same years, as the Ku Klux Klan became a mass movement in the North as well as the South, and as black migrants to northern cities were brutally attacked in a widespread series of race riots. Nearly two dozen urban race riots, mostly in northern cities, accompanied black migration out of the rural South between 1915 and 1919.[16] Organizations like the National Association for the Advancement of Colored People (NAACP), which had sought to resist black disenfranchisment and the spread of Jim Crow apartheid, were politically paralyzed. By the end of the 1920s, political participation and the possibilities for popular political mobilization were far more restricted in the United States than they had been in 1890.

THE CONSEQUENCES OF A CONTRADICTORY LEGACY

These changes in American politics between the 1890s and the 1920s cannot be effectively understood only by emphasizing class conflict between a growing industrial proletariat and the corporate elite. Class conflict was central to the political dynamics of American society, but subordinate groups also acted in collusion with political and economic elites to restrict the rights of other subordinate groups.

Despite these ambiguities in the political alliances which supported changes in the way the political system operated, the long-term consequences were quite unambiguous. In at least three fundamental ways, democratic political participation declined by the 1920s, and corporate and business influence in American politics expanded correspondingly.[17] Voter turnout declined sharply. Both the legal system and the courts placed new restrictions on freedoms of speech, assembly, and association. And legally sanctioned and illegal, but officially tolerated, violence and terrorism against non-whites and political dissidents became endemic to American political life.

From the 1830s to the 1890s, American political parties had developed elaborate infrastructures to mobilize their constituents. They held rallies, parades, barbecues, marches. They printed vast quantities of campaign literature and distributed a bewildering array of campaign ephemera: ribbons, badges, buttons, hats, banners, photographs, posters. Armies of party workers visited their neighbors urging them to vote, did favors to curry a sense of obligation, escorted voters to the polls. Between 1840 and 1872, turnout in presidential elections averaged 69 percent; from 1876 to 1900, 77 percent. But after the turn of the century, presidential election turnout fell, averaging 65 percent from 1900 to 1916, and only 52 percent in the 1920s. Voting for congressional, state, and local offices fell by similar proportions. African-Americans, other racial minorities, the young, the poor, immigrants, and women were over-represented in the increasing ranks of non-voters.[18]

Scholars have fiercely debated the relative significance of various causes of this decline in voter turnout. Among the factors advanced to explain it are black and poor white disenfranchisement in the South; the effects of voter registration and other legal changes in the rest of the country; attacks on partisanship in the press; a greater emphasis on the politics of personality, and the resulting erosion of the ability of party organizations to mobilize voters; the rise of the regulatory state, which removed many issues from the electoral arena; and the continuing cultural belief among some women that voting was inappropriate for females. Undoubtedly all of these played a role. However, more important than sorting out the quantitative significance of each is their combined political and cultural effect. Lower turnout was only the tip of the iceberg of a fundamental change in political style from boisterous, direct, popular participation to a pattern of periodic plebiscites, from candidates who touted their log cabin and rail-splitter origins to those who emphasized their managerial abilities.[19]

New restrictions on other forms of political activity may have had even more far-reaching consequences than changes in electoral behavior. In the late 1800s and early 1900s courts, legislatures, and city councils created a new battery of legal and judicial weapons to control crowd activity, to limit mass demonstrations, and especially to restrict the actions of the labor movement. Cities enlarged, reorganized, and professionalized their police forces. They built armories, bigger jails, and fortress-like court houses. After local militias had proven unreliable in suppressing crowds during the 1877 national railroad strike, state governments reorganized the militias to make them less responsive to popular pressures. City councils passed ordinances requiring parade permits for public demonstrations and restricting the rights of street speakers. Opponents of ordinances restricting public speech and assembly frequently challenged them by holding illegal demonstrations, defying the police to arrest them. In some cases the objective was to provoke judicial tests of the constitutionality of ordinances, but more often the intent was to nullify the laws by such massive civil disobedience that local authorities would not attempt to maintain enforcement. These free speech fights resulted in mass arrests in dozens of cities.[20]

The courts also systematically beat back the efforts of workers to use direct action tactics in their conflicts with employers. Probably the most important form of judicial intervention in public political behavior was the application of the court injunction to labor disputes. American unions had always been subject to judicial harassment. Starting in 1805, a flurry of convictions of union leaders for conspiracy in restraint of trade had hindered development of the incipient journeymen's societies.[21] Modification of the conspiracy doctrine in the 1840s did not reduce the frequency of such convictions. Indeed, during the course of the nineteenth century, penalties for those convicted became more, not less, severe.[22] However, court injunctions were not used in labor disputes until the 1880s.[23] They proved to be an even more devastating legal weapon. In order to obtain conspiracy convictions employers had to convince the courts to undertake lengthy trials. In cities where unions had substantial followings, such trials inevitably provoked widespread publicity, public demonstrations, and political pressure on the judges. Juries sometimes refused to convict.[24] In contrast, a court injunction could be obtained from a compliant or sympathetic judge in a matter of hours. Since the injunction was a court order, workers or union leaders who violated it could be sent to jail without trial.

First used in the 1880s, court injunctions in labor disputes were unusual before the mid-1890s, averaging only about a dozen a year. Thereafter, their frequency expanded geometrically, reaching a peak of several hundred per year by the 1920s. According to William Forbath's estimate, by the 1920s the courts issued injunctions in 25 percent of all strikes in the United States. Injunctions were even more frequent in large strikes, sympathy strikes, and strikes over union recognition.

Not only did the number of injunctions increase steadily after 1890, but so too did the range of union activities subject to judicial action. Peaceful picketing was found to be unwarranted intimidation, as were shouts of "scab" or virtually any other verbal abuse. Even peaceful persuasion of potential replacement workers was ruled as an interference in the employer's freedom of contract. In Pennsylvania and West Virginia coalmining counties, where signing yellow-dog contracts (contracts which make non-membership in the union a condition of employment) was a universal prerequisite to employment in non-union mines, judges issued restraining orders against union organizers forbidding them from "holding meetings, publishing information about the UMW [United Mine Workers Union], distributing food to miners striking for union recognition, and paying court costs for appealing evictions from company-owned houses."[25] Judicial action likewise drew a tighter and tighter net around boycotts, eventually placing such restrictions on what was permissible as to virtually outlaw effective boycotts. In effect, although unions were theoretically legal organizations, so many of their activities became illegal that union organizers and activists were forced into a semi-outlaw status.[26]

Their marginal legal status placed union activists and organizers in the nether world of those Americans routinely denied due process of law and subject to terroristic violence both from state authorities and vigilantes. African-Americans and other racial minorities had always been subject to such violence and terrorism, although some scholars believe that the extent of racial violence increased substantially after the end of Reconstruction. As a result, much of the South bore little resemblance to a democratic society. The police and the courts were sources of additional violence rather than protection from the Ku Klux Klan or lynch mobs. According to one estimate, between 1882 and 1903, 1,985 Southern blacks were lynched.[27] Another estimate places the total number of Southern black lynching victims between 1865 and 1955 at over 5,000.[28] No one knows how many more African Americans were beaten, tarred and feathered, or otherwise abused.

But such practices were hardly confined to the South, nor were their victims limited to African Americans. American class relations have been characterized by more violence than almost anywhere else in the world.[29] Deaths of union activists and strikers were not concentrated in periods of wider national strife or civil disturbance. They were a routine part of working-class life. In the United States in the 1890s, approximately two workers were killed and 140 injured for every 100,000 strikers. In France in the same years, only three workers were injured per 100,000 strikers and none were reported killed. Between 1902 and 1904, the injury rate in US strikes soared to more than 1,000 per 100,000 strikers, and 198 deaths of strikers were recorded in slightly over two years.[30] A few of the dead and injured were strikebreakers attacked by striking workers, but the overwhelming majority were strikers attacked by police, troops, or company thugs.

In key industrial states, rates of arrest and injury during strikes were even higher than the national averages. In Illinois, in the second half of the 1890s, over 700 were arrested for every 100,000 strikers, ten times the arrest rate in France in the same years; in New York the figure was over 400 per 100,000. Federal or state troops intervened in more than 500 strikes between 1877 and 1903.

Statistics cannot give the full flavor of the intimidating impact of state and company violence. Consider the following anecdotes from Western Pennsylvania, a small sampling of those which could be cited. In 1916, striking Westinghouse workers marching peacefully to the Edgar Thompson Steel Works in Braddock were dispersed by a private army of company guards, coal and iron police, and railroad detectives numbering 1,700 in all. Armed with rifles, shotguns, and machine guns, the guards opened fire on the crowd, killing three and wounding fifty or sixty others. Thirty strike leaders (and none of the company guards who fired on the crowd) were indicted as accessories to murder. The strike collapsed shortly thereafter. Eleven workers were eventually convicted (some on lesser charges) and sent to prison.[31]

During the 1919 steel strike, local authorities in the steel towns, many of them company officials, forbade all public gatherings of three or more persons. Hall owners who rented to union groups were forced to return rental fees. One hall owner in Rankin who refused had his establishment condemned by the local Board of Health. A member of the Interchurch World Movement, a commission of clergymen who investigated the strike, had his Braddock office invaded by state troopers after speaking briefly with a small group of strikers. In Sharon, Pennsylvania, workers were only able to meet by walking several miles across the Ohio state line.[32] As late as 1934, little seemed to have changed in the steel towns. In that year a union organizer, George Issoski, vanished suddenly from the streets of Aliquippa. Days later his distraught wife learned that he had been committed to a state insane asylum under orders signed by Jones and Laughlin Steel Company physicians. She was only able to obtain his release after

Clint Golden (then a Pennsylvania Department of Labor investigator and two years later a key official of the Steel Workers Organizing Committee of the Congress of Industrial Organizations (CIO) persuaded Mrs. Gifford Pinchot, the wife of the governor of Pennsylvania, to intervene in the case. The governor sent his personal physician to examine Issoski, who was only then certified sane and released. In an unwitting prelude to later revelations of Soviet psychiatric practices, state newspapers which covered the story described Aliquippa as the Siberia of America.[33]

As this press reaction suggests, limits on popular political participation, judicial activism against social movements, and suppression of civil liberties never met with the unequivocal or unified support of American elites. There are two souls in the American democratic tradition, and those who sought to limit popular democratic participation could never entirely escape the subversive implications of a literal reading of the Declaration of Independence and the Bill of Rights. But for millions of Americans between 1890 and 1930, and afterward, the realities of their daily experiences fundamentally contradicted democratic promises.

This contradiction was particularly sharp in the era of the second industrial revolution. The reason lies in America's racial heritage as well as in the strains of rapid industrialization and urbanization. The years from the 1890s to the 1930s were the nadir of American race relations, an era when not only demogogues, but also nearly all respectable authorities condoned racism. In this cultural atmosphere, academic experts as well as popular commentators routinely conflated the concepts of race and ethnicity. To old-stock Americans, the new immigrants from southern and eastern Europe – Italians, Slavs, Jews, Greeks – despite their white skin, seemed to fit more on the other side of the color line. They merited the treatment historically reserved for slaves, Indians, and others the majority culture deemed "savages." To be labeled a "hunky" or a "wop" or a "kike" was to be placed beyond the safe boundary of white men's democracy. The irony, and perhaps the promise, of American democracy is that so many of them enthusiastically identified with American democratic political culture nonetheless.

NOTES

1. Leopold Haimson and Charles Tilly, eds., *Strikes, Wars and Revolutions in International Perspective: Strike Waves in the Late Nineteenth and Early Twentieth Centuries* (Cambridge and New York, 1989).

2. David M. Gordon, Richard Edwards, Michael Reich, *Segmented Work, Divided Workers: The Historical Transformation of Labor in the United States* (Cambridge and New York, 1982), 79–90, 117; Daniel Nelson, *Managers and Workers: Origins of the New Factory System in the United States, 1880–1920* (Madison, 1975), 3–10.

3. John Bodnar, *The Transplanted: A History of Immigrants in Urban America* (Bloomington, 1985), 1–56.

4. Herbert G. Gutman with Ira Berlin, "Class Composition and the Development of the American Working Class, 1840–1890," in Herbert G. Gutman, ed., *Power and Culture: Essays on the American Working Class* (New York, 1987): 380–94; David Brody, *Workers in Industrial America: Essays on the Twentieth Century Struggle* (New York, 1980), 14–21.

5. While Louis Hartz was not always sensitive to the dark side of American liberalism, his exposition of this theme is still important reading for those who want to understand American political culture. See *The Liberal Tradition in America: An Interpretation of American Political Thought since the Revolution* (New York, 1955), esp. 3–32.

6. Earl Browder, "Who Are the Americans?" (New York, 1936), 1; Irving Howe and Lewis Coser, *The American Communist Party: A Critical History* (New York, 1962), 319–86.

7. Eric Foner, *Reconstruction: America's Unfinished Revolution, 1863–1877* (New York, 1988).

8. Norman J. Ware, *The Labor Movement in the United States, 1860-1895: A Study in Democracy* (New York, 1929), 346–9; Bruce Laurie, *Artisans into Workers: Labor in Nineteenth-Century America* (New York, 1989), 158–63; David Montgomery, *The Fall of the House of Labor: The Workplace, the State, and American Labor Activism, 1865–1925* (Cambridge and New York, 1987), 146–7.

9. Lawrence Goodwyn, *The Populist Moment: A Short History of the Agrarian Revolt in America* (New York, 1978).

10. C. Vann Woodward, *The Strange Career of Jim Crow* (New York, 1957).

11. A.T. Lane, *Solidarity or Survival? American Labor and European Immigrants, 1830–1924* (New York, 1987); Gwendolyn Mink, *Old Labor and New Immigrants in American Political Development: Union, Party, and State, 1875–1920* (Ithaca, 1986); Montgomery, *Fall of the House of Labor*, 85–7.

12. Richard Jules Oestreicher, *Solidarity and Fragmentation: Working People and Class Consciousness in Detroit, 1875–1900* (Urbana, 1986), 250–2.

13. Robert H. Wiebe, *Businessmen and Reform: A Study of the Progressive Movement* (Cambridge, Mass., 1962); Samuel P. Hays, "The Politics of Reform in Municipal Government in the Progressive Era," in Samuel P. Hays, ed., *American Political History as Social Analysis: Essays* (Knoxville, 1979): 205–32.

14. Walter Dean Burnham, "The System of 1896: An Analysis," in Paul Kleppner, ed., *The Evolution of American Electoral Systems* (Westport, 1981); Walter Dean Burnham, "The Changing Shape of the American Political Universe," *American Political Science Review*, 59, no. 1 (March 1965): 7–28. For a contrary view, see Jerrold G. Rusk, "Comment: The American Electoral Universe: Speculation and Evidence," *American Political Science Review*, 68, no. 3 (September 1974): 1029–49.

15. Aileen S. Kraditor, *The Ideas of the Woman Suffrage Movement, 1890–1920* (New York, 1965).

16. Richard Maxwell Brown, "Historical Patterns of Violence in America," in Hugh Davis Graham and Ted Robert Gurr, eds., *Violence in America: Historical and Comparative Perspectives. A Report to the National Commission on the Causes and Prevention of Violence, June 1969* (New York, 1969), 51.

17. For one of the most explicit expositions of the thesis that the net result of Progressive Era reforms was increased corporate control over national policy, see Gabriel Kolko, *The Triumph of Conservatism: A Reinterpretation of American History, 1900–1916* (Chicago, 1967).

18. Michael E. McGerr, *The Decline of Popular Politics: The American North, 1865–1928* (New York, 1986), 5–6; Paul Kleppner, *Who Voted? The Dynamics of Electoral Turnout, 1870–1980* (New York, 1982), 28–82.

19. McGerr, *Decline*, esp. vii, 211–19.

20. The free speech fights of the IWW in the Far West have been extensively described by historians and have assumed an almost folkloric quality. Among the many accounts of the IWW's free speech fights, see Melvin Dubofsky, *We Shall Be All* (New York, 1969), 173–97. It is less well known that such free speech campaigns were more widespread, carried on by a variety of groups in many parts of the country. Montgomery, *Fall of the House of Labor*, 318, mentions such activities in the Homewood section of Pittsburgh in 1912. For description of similar events in Detroit during the 1880 Greenback-Labor campaign, see Oestreicher, *Solidarity and Fragmentation*, 94.

21. Wythe Holt, "Labor Conspiracy Cases in the United States, 1805–1842: Bias and Legitimation in Common Law Adjudication," *Osgoode Hall Law Journal*, 22 (1984): 592–663.

22. On the use of conspiracy convictions in Pennsylvania in the 1880s, see Paul Krause, *The Battle for Homestead, 1880–1892: Culture, Politics, and Steel* (Pittsburgh, 1992), 88, 156–9; on the increasing severity of penalties, see William B. Forbath, *Law and the Shaping of the American Labor Movement* (Cambridge, Mass., 1991), 59–61.

23. Charles O. Gregory, *Labor and the Law* (New York, 1946), 95–8.

24. Forbath, *Law and the Shaping*, 99–100.

25. Forbath, *Law and the Shaping*, 116 n.67.

26. Forbath, *Law and the Shaping*, 79–94.

27. Brown, "Historical Patterns of Violence," in Graham and Gurr, *Violence in America*, 47.

28. James P. Comer, "The Dynamics of Black and White Violence," in Graham and Gurr, *Violence in America*, 426.

29. Robert Taft and Philip Ross, "American Labor Violence: Its Causes, Character, and Outcome," in Graham and Gurr, *Violence in America*, 270.

30. Forbath, *Law and the Shaping*, 106 n.30.

31. Montgomery, *Fall of the House of Labor*, 324–6.

32. Commission of Inquiry, Interchurch World Movement, *Report on the Steel Strike of 1919* (New York, 1920), 173, 236–7.

33. NA, "Clinton S. Golden in Aliquippa," *Beaver Valley Labor History Journal*, 1 (June 1979): 8.

Part Two
Creating Single-Party Dominance, 1930–1960

6 From Bureaucratic Imperium to Guardian Democracy: The Shifting Social Bases of Japanese Political Power, 1930–1960

Gary D. Allinson

How to interpret the significance of the decade after 1941 in the context of pre-war and post-war history is the most difficult challenge that faces scholars of twentieth-century Japan. Four years of total war followed by six years of foreign occupation create an image of sharp discontinuity, and until recently most historians dealt with this challenge by deflecting it. Those interested in the early twentieth century consistently brought their studies to a close in 1937, when Japan's military adventures in China began in earnest, or in 1945, when the Pacific War ended. Others interested in post-war developments just as consistently began their studies with the advent of the Allied Occupation in 1945 and proceeded forward. Very few scholars have ventured to examine systematically developments across this awkward historical divide.[1]

The invitation to analyze Japan's democratization after 1945 carries with it both the obligation and the opportunity to confront this historiographical challenge. I intend to do so by adopting an avowedly unconventional approach that embodies three objectives. First, I want to re-examine the role of the Allied Occupation of Japan by treating it, not as the virtually exclusive cause of change, but rather as just one of many forces for change in the early post-war period. Second, I want to highlight the continuities that span the years between 1930 and 1960, and to balance them against the apparent discontinuities that arose from war and occupation. And third, I want to accentuate the dynamics of internal social and political change because their understanding is essential to an appreciation of developments after 1960.

There are compelling reasons for adopting these objectives. For too long the role of the Allied Occupation has been exaggerated in American accounts of post-war Japan. As we have gained distance from that period, and as more scholarly studies of the immediate pre-war period and the lengthening post-war period have appeared, two things have become clearer. Many Occupation reforms built on changes that had taken place under largely indigenous auspices before 1945. And developments in Japan since 1945 often owe more to distinctive processes of indigenous change than they do to reforms of the Occupation era. These observations endorse the importance of continuities that span the years between 1930 and 1960, and they call into question the implicit concession to discontinuity that denies how persistent some features of Japan's political sociology have been in the twentieth century. These include the enduring authority of key institutions and groups, the relations among those groups and institutions, and the patterns of thought and behavior that animate and shape those relations.

In pursuing these historiographical objectives, I have another larger goal in mind. I want to retrieve the mid-century decades for Japanese history and to place them in the continuum of a longer period of Japan's historical evolution. There has been a strong tendency to view this epoch as an aberration during which Japan was drawn into an international vortex. Aberrant years of war were followed by an equally aberrant occupation. Its enduring label – "Japan's American interlude" – makes the period between 1945 and 1952 seem more a part of American than Japanese history.[2] There is no denying that the war and the Occupation were both disruptive episodes, or that they drew the nation inextricably into the currents of world affairs. But beneath the surface of events during those tumultuous years, life went on as usual for large numbers of the Japanese populace and most people, elites and subjects alike, cleaved to familiar beliefs. This dogged continuity in the face of episodic change demands new efforts at interpretation.

If democracy is a form of government in which the effective political leaders are popularly elected individuals whose policies reflect the articulated will of a majority of the electorate, then Japan was not a democracy before 1947. The nominal head of government served as a hereditary monarch and the effective political leaders were selected from a diverse array of elites and legitimated by imperial appointment. In limited ways some elites and a minority of the populace were employing democratic forms of government before 1945, but their actions were peripheral to the main currents of national politics. After 1947, a new constitution established the forms of democratic government by making popular election of the prime minister a legal requirement. Nonetheless, pre-war elites commanding deference and position governed subjects acting with a strong sense of duty – in contrast with citizens consciously exercising their rights – until well into the 1960s. As a consequence, Japan experienced, at best, a rudimentary and attenuated democracy for most of the first two post-war decades.

THE SOCIAL BASES OF POLITICAL POWER

A comprehensive understanding of the social bases of political power in Japan between 1930 and 1960 requires an appreciation of the country's social diversity and structural characteristics during that era. Diversity, both within and among groups, was far more pronounced than conventional views allow. It militated against consensus, fostered keen competition among political elites, and hampered integration of societal groups. Japan's structural characteristics were a product of relatively late industrialization. They had a critical bearing on the constellations of social forces that contended for influence and on the political outlooks that animated the struggle for ascendance. This part of the chapter examines these features of Japanese society in two sections. The first sketches the characteristics of bureaucratic, parliamentary, and business elites and the political resources they could marshal. The second illustrates the diversity of four societal groups and how structural characteristics shaped their political roles.

Elites

By the early twentieth century Japan's national civil service had assumed the structure and adopted the patterns of recruitment and promotion that continue to the present day. The foundation of the civil service was a competitive examination system established in the 1890s.[3] Based on the assumption that civil servants should be specialists trained in the law, the examination system has subsequently recruited into the highest, policy-making ranks of the government a disproportionately high percentage of graduates from the law divisions of two public universities, Tokyo and Kyoto. Throughout the 1930s, 1940s and 1950s, as many as 90 percent of the men (and they were virtually all men) who rose to the rank of section chief and higher were graduates of these two institutions.[4]

This merit-based system of recruitment established a body of national bureaucrats consisting of talented high achievers who came from virtually every social stratum in the country.[5] They were not, therefore, the representatives of a "narrow class interest," but rather the representatives of the nation itself. They possessed a certain haughtiness that was integral to their sense of *esprit de corps*. Before 1945 their position as servants to the emperor conferred special prestige, and even after the war, when they were transformed under a new constitution into public servants, many continued to think of themselves as the guardians of a nascent democratic citizenry.

Haughtiness and *esprit* were undergirded with both intangible and tangible political resources. A long history of bureaucratic governance, especially pronounced during the Tokugawa period (1600–1868), bestowed a high measure of popular acquiescence to bureaucratic authority. So also did the accomplishments of men who excelled academically at the nation's top universities and who passed highly competitive service exams. On a more tangible note, ministries had a range of formal and informal legal prerogatives that made them among the most influential political bodies in Japan both before and after 1945. In fact, when Occupation authorities made the strategic decision to rule Japan indirectly through a bureaucracy that was only thinly purged and minimally restructured, bureaucrats enjoyed a brief tenure as the most powerful agents in the post-war polity.[6]

Owing to their prestige, status, talents, contacts, and experience, bureaucrats could command position and place even after they left national service. The term used to describe their departure, *amakudari* or the descent from heaven, is telling in itself. Bureaucrats who descended from heaven could readily count on a variety of new career options. Some found work as highly paid executives in banks and industrial firms. Others assumed positions as leaders of trade groups and business associations. And still others entered elective politics. Recognizing the significance of their post-retirement careers enables us to identify two kinds of bureaucratic power. One consists of incumbent power exercised by bureaucrats in office; the other is a form of ramifying power wielded by former bureaucrats in many institutional and political arenas following retirement. The ramifying powers of ex-bureaucrats were especially significant in the post-war era.[7]

Bureaucrats constituted one of three discernible groups from which the conservative political parties recruited their members during the period under discussion. From the perspective of the parties, bureaucrats were valuable members because they knew how the government operated, they had younger associates on whom they could impose for favors, they were men of talent and energy, and they had a special status that made them strong candidates, especially in the rural constituencies from which many of them hailed. Former bureaucrats had been appealing candidates for national office from the inception of parliamentary politics, and throughout the twentieth century they have constituted a steady one-fourth of all national legislators and an even higher percentage in the ranks of the conservative parties alone.[8]

Career politicians comprised the second category of recruits to conservative political parties. Such individuals often began their careers in local office, or in prefectural legislatures. After service at these levels of the polity, they had usually acquired enough financial backers, party support, and loyal voters that they could run for national office. Such figures were often the products of a local political elite comprised of families with a long history of leadership in their village, town, or region. They were usually well educated and reasonably well off financially, but it was family pedigree as much as overwhelming wealth that brought them to office and kept them there.[9]

The third group of politicians making up the conservative parties was more diverse.[10] Some were businessmen. Before the war, leaders of major enterprises held Diet positions concurrently. After the war, successful businessmen who owned and operated small firms tended to replace officials from large firms. There were also some white-collar professionals, such as journalists, physicians, and educators. Lawyers were rare among elected politicians on the political right, owing to the historical weakness of the legal profession in a society where litigation and judicial resolution of disputes were generally avoided.

The very diversity of party politicians on the right vitiated their ability to represent exclusively a narrow class interest. There was certainly a bias toward politicians who were themselves members of the most privileged groups in Japan: bureaucrats, rural elites, businessmen, and professionals. But they could not, even before 1945, afford to represent only their class's interests, because that would have complicated re-election in districts where their class constituted a small minority. Rather than class, therefore, popularly elected politicians represented the interests of a locale. All elected politicians needed to develop pull at the center in order to deliver pork at home. At root, politicians on the right lived or died on their ability to play pork-barrel politics, and to ensure that their locales won as much in the competition for national resources as they possibly could. Each in his own way, the bureaucrat, the career politician, and the businessman, had to cultivate the knowledge, the contacts, and the bargaining prowess that promised success in these ventures.[11]

Politicians representing the socialist and communist parties, both before and after 1945, were exceptions to these characterizations in two ways. They did strive to represent the interests of what they construed as classes, for the most part workers and farmers. Moreover, the politicians themselves were often products of those groups. Many socialist politicians before and after 1945 were industrial workers with little formal education. Others were better educated teachers, attorneys, or technical specialists, but few of them were the offspring of privileged families. Leadership of dissident parties thus fell to people who were themselves of marginal social status, and this is one of many explanations for the marginal political status of dissident parties between 1930 and 1960.

At the outset of this period, few of Japan's large-scale industrial firms were more than fifty years old, and most were even younger, products of the early twentieth century or of the boom that accompanied the First World War. There were a few exceptions to this rule in commerce and banking. Such comprehensive conglomerates as Mitsui, Sumitomo, and Yasuda – known since the 1910s as *zaibatsu* – traced their origins to the pre-Meiji (pre-1868) era. But on the brink of this century's fourth decade, big business was still a fledgling in many ways and so was the body of entrepreneurs and managers who led it.

The social backgrounds of business leaders in the 1930s, 1940s, and 1950s were highly varied. There was a hereditary business elite in some of the *zaibatsu* organizations that had been in existence for two generations or more, such as the Iwazaki family at Mitsubishi. Former bureaucrats were a second source of leadership at some firms. As in politics, their expertise, contacts, and status made them desirable recruits. A third stream of business leaders consisted of college-educated men forming a class of professional business managers. They would eventually dominate the business world, but only after the 1960s. The fourth group included individuals who had risen by dint of hard work and good luck to build major corporations. Matsushita Kōnosuke and the leaders of the Toyota enterprise were among this category of business leaders.[12]

Men in these four groups were born and reared in families that spanned the entire social spectrum. Families such as the Iwazaki were among the wealthiest and most privileged in the country. They lived in lavish estates and sent their children abroad to study. In contrast, Matsushita was born into humble circumstances, received little formal education, and rose by determination and hard work. Some of the former bureaucrats who were business leaders also came from humble or middling social backgrounds, while the new class of professional managers seems to have arisen from the middle and upper reaches of old rural and new urban society. It is thus not surprising that big business often spoke with a cacophony of voices during the three decades after 1930.

This cacophony was accentuated by the variety of organizational vehicles on which business relied to articulate its political demands. There were peak business associations, such as the Japan Industrial Club formed in

1917 and the Keidanren (Federation of Economic Organizations) founded in 1946, that strived to represent the general interests of many firms.[13] There were also trade associations that articulated the demands of industrial groups, such as textile makers or steel firms. Until the *zaibatsu* dissolution program in the late 1940s, each *zaibatsu* functioned as an individual business interest. And inevitably single firms and the sometimes aggressive individuals who led them also served as political demand-makers.[14]

Big business had two resources that were exceedingly valuable for political purposes. It was a necessary ally in the pursuit of economic development and it was a key provider of campaign financing. At one level, therefore, it was relatively easy for big businessmen to find ground for consensus with national bureaucrats, elected politicians, and other powerholders. All agreed that economic development was a worthy cause, and that the financial support of elected politicians who supported that cause was a necessary evil. Disagreement arose over how best to pursue the broad objective, and disunity multiplied when specific policies affected firms, industries, or conglomerates differently. In contrast with the years after 1960, the three decades before witnessed far more economic volatility and far less agreement about how best to achieve the objective of becoming a strong economic state.[15] The heterogeneous origins of business leaders and the organizational divisiveness of the business community were two social phenomena that contributed to such volatility and disagreement. These circumstances, combined with the localistic orientation of elected politicians, provided bureaucrats with a clear edge in the competition for political power among elites between 1930 and 1960.

Societal Groups

Shifting our attention from political elites to larger societal groups, we encounter three unusual structural phenomena. First, as late as 1960 the agrarian populace in Japan was proportionately larger than in other advanced industrial societies. Second, Japan also had a disproportionately large number of firms in the small and medium-sized enterprise sector, both in commerce and manufacturing. And third, workers in manufacturing comprised an uncharacteristically small percentage of the labor force.

Cross-national comparisons clarify the differences with respect to manufacturing. Industrial workers in Japan, along with workers in transportation and mining, comprised 19 percent of the labor force in 1930. In about the same year, the secondary sector employed 31 percent of all workers in the United States, 41 percent in France and Germany, and 47 percent in England.[16] Both the number and percentage of workers in industry, mining, and transport rose steadily in Japan until about 1944, when a precipitous drop ensued. Almost a decade passed before employment regained its highest pre-war levels, but in the late 1950s a long period of virtually uninterrupted expansion began that would continue into the 1970s. Nonetheless, in 1960 Japan's secondary sector still employed only 31 percent of the labor force, whereas the comparable figure was 34 percent in the United States, 37 percent in France, 45 percent in England, and 48 percent in Germany.[17] We must begin this discussion of workers in mid-century Japan by recognizing, therefore, that they were never as numerous as they had been in the early industrializing countries of Europe. As a consequence, the social, political, and cultural force of workers in Japan has always been less salient than in England and Germany.

Like Japan's large-scale business organizations, the country's industrial labor force was also youthful in 1930. The modern textile industry was only about fifty years old. Since the late 1800s it had employed most of the labor force working in large, power-driven factories. Eighty to ninety percent of such workers were young women in their teens and early twenties who were short-term sojourners in the labor market. They usually worked for only three to six years before returning home to marry and rear families.[18] A stable industrial workforce comprised of adult males did not emerge until the 1910s, when a wartime boom fostered expansion in the metals trades and shipbuilding. Early entrants into these trades were often young men recruited from rural areas with no prior industrial experience.[19] Before 1945, therefore, Japan's industrial labor force consisted mainly of first-generation workers with limited experience of factory life, urban residence, and political activism.

Activism and the organization that it entailed were complicated by other features of the pre-war workforce. Workers were geographically dispersed in many different locations. While some large textile mills located in factory zones in the largest cities, just as many found sites in remote rural towns that put them close to their labor markets and kept employees from the enticements of urban living. Workers were also divided among an almost infinite variety of firms, most of them quite small. Large-scale enterprises employing 500 or more workers were relatively rare before 1945, and they never employed more than a quarter of the industrial workforce. The vast majority of workers toiled in small firms, some as tiny as two or three workers, where personal relationships and patriarchal supervision were constant impediments to dissent and organization.[20]

These many historical, personal, social, and structural features of the pre-war labor force were powerful impediments to organization and activism. Nonetheless, government authorities and business leaders went to some lengths to impose still more impediments. National laws prohibited strikes and the right to bargain collectively; they also restricted the right to assembly.[21] A domestic police force that operated as an arm of the central government enforced these rules with compulsive attentiveness, usually acting in close collaboration with business leaders and factory managers.[22] In addition, during and after the 1920s management strived assiduously to create a psychology of attachment to individual firms by harping on the *bifū* or beautiful values of social harmony, that drew workers and managers into a common, cooperative enterprise.[23] As a consequence of these efforts and other impediments to organization, only a few hundred thousand workers, about 8 percent of the eligible labor force, ever joined labor unions before 1945.[24]

However, when the Allied Occupation legalized unions, strikes, and collective bargaining in late 1945, some conditions changed dramatically. In a short period of time nearly half of the eligible workers joined unions. In some firms workers were so enthusiastic for this new form of organization that they recruited everyone in the company to join and made the president chairman of the union! This kind of naive enthusiasm dissipated quickly, however, amidst the difficult economic circumstances of the late 1940s.[25] It diminished even more when the occupying authorities began around 1948 to restrict rights granted to workers in 1945, a legal reversion that management heartily applauded. By the 1950s, organization rates had dropped to the 33 percent level, where they remained for the next quarter-century. Worker devotion to adversarial relations proved to be a short-lived phenomenon of limited appeal.

Even though industrialization drew many workers from the countryside, the farm populace continued to dominate Japanese society during the mid-century decades. When this period began, farm households constituted more than half of the national total. Wartime industrialization lured many farm sons and daughters and some entire farm families to the cities, but they streamed back home between 1945 and 1946. As a consequence, the farm populace actually increased to over 50 percent of the national total in the early 1950s before the onset of the post-war economic boom initiated a rural exodus that still continues. Owing to this pattern of demographic change, Japan again presents a sharp contrast with other nations. As late as 1960, farmers still comprised 29 percent of the work force in Japan, whereas they were 20 percent in France, 12 percent in Germany, 7 percent in the US, and only 3 percent in England.[26] Their long-standing numerical importance has two critical implications. It fostered the retention of agrarian values well into the post-war era, and it made farmers a critical object of policy after 1930.

Four discernible groups made up the pre-war farm populace. At the top floated a thin stratum of exceedingly wealthy families. Numbering under 100,000 in a rural populace of more than 5.5 million households, such families owned scores or hundreds of acres of land, and they often possessed diversified portfolios that were already drawing them out of farming into commercial, financial, and industrial endeavors.[27] Three other groups of roughly equal proportion were distinguished by the varying size of their holdings. The best off among the three consisted of families that owned perhaps two to ten acres. Some worked their land themselves, but many hired tenants to do so. A second group consisted of families that owned some land and rented some. In this way they could assemble a holding of about two to three acres that made it economically feasible to sustain a livelihood. The third and worst off group consisted of tenants who owned little or no land. They lived on the brink of survival in a contest with creditors, tax agents, rent collectors, and Mother Nature.[28]

The socioeconomic diversity of the rural populace was reflected in differing organizational affiliations before 1945. At the turn of the century the government nurtured the creation of an Imperial Agricultural Society. Its membership came almost exclusively from families in the top two strata of rural society. As a quasi-official body, it always had close ties with the bureaucracy and with the established conservative parties. While it was formed with the purpose of improving farm management, it also functioned to thwart rural dissidence.[29]

A radically different kind of farm organization arose in rural Japan after the 1910s, the tenant union. Urban intellectuals and attorneys associated with the pre-war socialist and communist parties often lent tenant unions valuable support, but in many cases such bodies arose spontaneously under the leadership of farmers themselves.[30] Two spurts of rural unrest, one around 1920 and the other in the early 1930s, gave such farmers valuable lessons in political activism. They learned to organize, articulate demands, exploit their legal rights, and bargain with landlords, politicians, and bureaucrats.[31] However valuable such lessons were, only a small portion of the rural populace learned them. At the peak of membership in 1927, tenant unions attracted less than 7 percent of all farm households, and in the year of most active disputation (during the mid-1930s), only about 2 percent of all farm households participated.[32]

Under these circumstances, most of the adult males in rural Japan who voted before 1945 cast their ballots for conservative party candidates. Some did so for personal reasons, because the candidate was a friend, relative, or native son. Others bowed to the wishes of their social betters, out of a sincere sense of deference. Still others voted conservative because it was a pragmatic choice; conservatives were far more likely than Socialists to "bring home the bacon." And a few, who might have wished to cast a protest vote, were deterred from doing so because it was difficult in small, face-to-face communities to ensure the secrecy of one's ballot. Most rural voters were subject in some measure to all of these pressures, which drove farmers toward collective support of established, not opposition, political parties.[33]

The texture of social life in Japanese villages helps to explain this behavior. It varied widely depending on the history of a settlement, its ecology, and its landholding patterns. In some villages a few landlord families controlled the bulk of the land while many poor tenants did most of the work. One might imagine that such disparities in wealth and power would ensure conflict, and in some villages they did. But in others such disparities paradoxically fostered a sense of solidarity based on benevolence, reciprocity, and cooperative interaction. In other types of villages smallholders from the middling ranks might dominate. If the land they rented was controlled by outside owners, it was in this kind of apparently more homogeneous village where a strong tenant movement might develop. Despite the variety of social relations and economic structures, harmony, however tense, and cohesion, however precarious, seem to have been the prevailing conditions. The exigencies of poverty and labor exchange obliged people to cooperate out of necessity, and on this foundation arose the solidarity expressed so often in voting and other forms of political behavior. Village solidarity was both cause and effect of the widespread emphasis on pork-barrel politics. It was also a social form congenial to the dominant values of rural Japan.

The socioeconomic inequality of rural Japan was eased even before 1945 by government policies and it was virtually eliminated after the war by a thoroughgoing program of land reform. Between late 1945 and mid-1950, Allied authorities worked closely with Japanese bureaucrats in the Ministry of Agriculture (MOA) and a myriad of local committees to carry out one of the most ambitious programs of land redistribution in the twentieth century. During that period the portion of tenanted land fell from about one-half of the total to less than 10 percent, and landless tenants virtually disappeared from the countryside.[34] The land reform created almost overnight a rural populace of yeoman farmers – by Japanese standards. Most families came into ownership of two to three acres of land. More importantly, they were freed from the economic, political, and psychological inequities of tenantry and the deference that it entailed. Occupation authorities assumed that these farm proprietors would become the linchpin of a new kind of democracy in rural Japan, and they did. But like farmers everywhere, Japan's acted by their own lights, and they continued – as they had before the war – to support conservative political authority.

In the same way that Japan's agrarian populace survived far longer into the twentieth century than was the case in other advanced industrial societies, so also did small proprietors. In the late 1950s salaried employees still comprised only 65 percent of the non-agricultural labor force, at a time when most employees in England, Germany, and the United States earned wages or salaries by working for others. The 35 percent who were non-salaried employees fell into two categories. The majority were individual proprietors; the remainder were (often unpaid) family members who worked for them. Family-owned firms operated by family members were common throughout this period in commerce and manufacturing.[35]

Among commercial firms, small retail outlets selling a wide array of consumer necessities – food products, clothing, household wares – were the most numerous. Some of them were establishments that had been serving their neighborhoods since the Tokugawa era. Others had sprung up during the 1920s and the 1930s as old cities expanded and new cities emerged. Although such firms enjoyed great strength in numbers, their proprietors never organized systematically before 1945 on a national scale to make themselves a unified pressure group. They did organize, but they usually did so within the confines of a single business district (*shōtengai*) for purposes of luring customers and improving trade. One looks in vain during the years between 1930 and 1960 for the kind of shopkeepers' leagues that arose in France in the 1880s or the 1950s. The fierce self-reliance of the families that opted to run small commercial enterprises may be one explanation for this lack of organization. A lingering political diffidence characteristic of merchants in the Tokugawa period may be another explanation.[36]

Small proprietors in manufacturing present a somewhat different picture both socially and politically. Many small firms were subcontractors to larger industrial entities, and these firms and their managers were products of the industrial era. There were exceptions, especially in some traditional handicraft trades such as silk and cotton manufacture. But by the 1930s, most small and medium-sized manufacturing firms in Japan were producing components for large enterprises in chemical, electrical, metal, and vehicle manufacturing. Their owners were sometimes former managers from the large firm for which they produced, but more often they were former workers with technical skills, entrepreneurial energies, and good contacts who set themselves up in their own businesses.[37]

Manufacturing's small proprietors were far more likely than their counterparts in commerce to create organizations that advanced their collective, political interests. Such firms were especially vulnerable to arbitrary treatment by final producers, and they organized to protect themselves from such abuses. Moreover, during periods of high demand, small enterprises in booming industries found themselves with bargaining leverage that they were quick to exploit. Finally, dynamic personalities sometimes stepped in to provide valuable leadership to assist small proprietors; one such case was Ayukawa Gisuke, a prominent pre-war business leader who helped to organize a lobby for small and medium-sized enterprises in the 1950s.[38]

If we include unpaid family members along with the small proprietors, farmers, and workers discussed above, these groups accounted for about 75 to 85 percent of the Japanese labor force between 1930 and 1960. New urbanites formed an admittedly residual category that embraced the balance of the workforce. They were not seen as a definable social group during this period, and for good reason. New urbanites were the most heterogeneous among all groups discussed here, and they never assumed any measure of solidarity as a political force. In fact, they were barely an afterthought for bureaucrats, politicians, and political parties alike. It is their very lack of political importance that makes new urbanites significant to the argument of this chapter.

Lack of political solidarity is understandable in light of the social disparities among new urbanites. Some were among the wealthiest and most privileged people in the country. This was the case with university-educated professional groups, such as physicians, professors, and successful authors and critics. Other new urbanites formed the makings of a definably new middle class. They were modestly well-educated individuals pursuing salaried occupations as managers, supervisors, teachers, accountants, legal specialists, and so on.[39] Most new urbanites, however, possessed limited skills, earned low incomes, lacked job security, and moved frequently. They included clerical workers in small firms, sales personnel in commercial districts, young women employed for short stints as OLs or "office ladies," cooks and waiters in tiny restaurants, and many others even less advantaged than these.[40]

Partisan preferences among new urbanites were as disparate as the group itself. The better off among them appear to have supported the two established conservative parties before the war, and those parties' lineal successors after. Parties of the left, both before and after the war, drew some of their urban supporters from among the middle and lower ranks of the new urbanites. Many in this group, however, especially those in the lower orders who drifted from one job to another, never developed an attachment to a political party and never voted. They contributed to the low turnout rates in working class districts before the war and in urban areas after the war.[41] New urbanites, especially the less advantaged among them, were politically peripheral and recalcitrant to organization.

The social diversity and structural characteristics of Japan during this era shaped political competition in important ways. The pre-eminence of national bureaucrats conferred both incumbent and ramifying powers, lending them an advantage in the political competition with parliamentary and business elites. In contrast with European countries, Japan did not witness the emergence of a well organized, politically assertive working class owing to the relative smallness, youthfulness, transience, and fragmentation of its industrial labor force. The farm populace was also fragmented internally according to differences in status, wealth, and power, and it remained a rather somnolent mass that was a reliable base of support for conservative politics. Small proprietors formed a variegated segment of society, while they honored familial and patriarchal patterns of authority in their struggle to find a place in the volatile mid-century economy. Owing to these social and structural circumstances, each of these groups – in contrast with the new urbanites – proved receptive to political appeals couched in terms of communal symbols.

THE STRUGGLE FOR POLITICAL ASCENDANCE

Before, during, and after the years between 1930 and 1960, two broad visions of the polity contended for ascendance in Japan. In terms of indigenous political practice, one vision represented a mainstream or orthodox position. It advanced an organic view of society according to which, ideally, all cooperate for the good of the whole. This vision was premised on assumptions of hierarchy and inequality. It took for granted that differences in status, wealth, and power are natural features of society. These disparities may carry a potential for abuse of weaker individuals or groups, but such abuse will be ameliorated through the exercise of magnanimity, benevolence, and reciprocity. The haves will not ride roughshod over the have-nots. Instead, social superiors will assist their inferiors in times of distress, and they will never go so far in exploiting them as to drive them over the brink. In this regard, the polity and those who control it strive to subordinate social groups under forms of dependent tutelage. Many metaphors were invoked to express this vision of the polity, but reference to two primordial social groups was common. These were the family and the village. The patriarchal quality of relations within the family accorded nicely with the emphasis on dependent tutelage, and village solidarity offered a palpable referent for the aspiration to societal unity in pursuit of national goals.

The other vision was an anti-mainstream or heterodox view of the polity. It historically suffered two disabilities. It was associated with foreign or external, in contrast with indigenous, political ideals, and perhaps for this very reason, it attracted a minority of supporters. This vision of the polity eschews hierarchy and is premised on ideals of equality. Disparities in wealth, status, and power are viewed as obstacles to be challenged and removed in pursuit of a social order that minimizes such differences. It is not assumed that powerholders are by definition benevolent. Instead they are regarded as exploitative, controlling agents whose position must be contested. Solidarity is valued by adherents of this vision, but it is a solidarity that differs from that of the village. This solidarity is more likely to operate along class lines, and to lend coherence to disadvantaged groups engaged in adversarial relations while competing for their just deserts. Obviously, Marxian and socialist ideals underlie this conception of the polity, but it also draws inspiration from a wide range of liberal and democratic political theories, too.

At the outset of the 1930s neither of these visions enjoyed overwhelming domination, although the orthodox vision possessed a clear edge in power. Its adherents occupied many influential positions within the multivocal constitutional order of pre-war Japan. They included most members of the military bureaucracy, many members of the civil bureaucracy, the Imperial Household Ministry, most of the Privy Council, the upper house of the legislature, part of the lower house, and many leaders of big business. However, some politicians in the lower house, progressive bureaucrats in key ministries, a few military figures, leaders of some business firms, and some political leaders resisted the repressive and conformist polity that mainstream adherents sought. Within society itself, many workers, farmers, and small proprietors were either enthusiastic about the ideal of a family state presided over by the emperor as god/father, or they were willing to acquiesce to such a political system. Dissident members of tenant unions and organized workers in some cities were the principal contestants of this vision, joined in their opposition by a thin stratum of political activists and intellectuals.

By the mid to late 1930s, however, this condition of modest contestation gave way to a political order that granted visible dominance to adherents of the mainstream vision. Domestic economic crisis and external military adventurism enabled orthodox interests to advance their views more ardently. Right-wing terrorists, whose sporadic but successful attacks on outspoken politicians and prominent business leaders intimidated many anti-mainstream figures into silence, certainly helped their cause.[42] But the composition of the mainstream coalition was significant, too. Its foundation rested on the most pro-emperor, chauvinistic, and expansionist elements in the army and navy along with a segment of the civil bureaucracy. In the name of national unity, militarists and civilian bureaucrats used their strategic positions in the state administration to restrict dissent and to cultivate support for their cause.[43] These two groups dominated the bureaucratic imperium that sought empire in Asia under the aegis of the imperial will.[44]

Where disadvantaged social groups were concerned, the leaders of this bureaucratic coalition combined the stick of repression with the carrot of inducement in a manner that would have crucial long-term implications. An extended depression in agriculture obliged the bureaucracy to assist farmers in the early 1930s. This was done both to rectify economic distress in rural regions and to improve the quality of recruits for the military. With a wide range of complex policies, many aimed at enhancing the role of farm cooperatives, the bureaucracy shored up the position of middle-level farmers in rural villages, to some extent at the expense of landlords. These policies assumed additional momentum during the war with the creation of a price-support program for rice, and they established the rudiments of a more egalitarian rural society operating through a nationwide system of farm cooperatives, precisely the conditions that blossomed in the wake of the post-war land reform.[45]

Before and during the war the state also pursued a set of policies toward workers that had similarly unintended consequences. In the late 1930s the state created an imperial labor front that replaced labor unions and sought to bring industrial labor unanimously behind the war effort. This task was severely complicated by the keen demand for wartime labor and the high rates of job mobility that it stimulated. The labor front did, however, give workers practice at self-organization and plant-level bargaining. In the changed legal climate that emerged during the Allied Occupation, workers drew on their wartime experiences to develop a labor movement that, for a brief historical moment, operated with uncharacteristic intensity on an unprecedented scale.[46]

Although smaller in numbers and politically and historically less salient, small proprietors in commerce and industry also attracted the benevolent attention of the wartime ruling coalition. The most visible symbol of interest in small shopkeepers was the Large Store Law of 1937. Initiated by the Ministry of Commerce and Industry (MCI), pre-war predecessor to the Ministry of International Trade and Industry (MITI), the law restricted expansion of large department stores into commercial districts dominated by small shops, in order to protect small shopkeepers economically, and no doubt to purchase their political compliance as well.[47] MCI also recognized that small firms in manufacturing were indispensable contributors to the wartime economy, and it initiated policies aimed at increasing the stability of such firms and the quality of their output. One key official also saw them as a vehicle for upward social mobility that should be consciously enhanced, in the interests of promoting the well-being of Japanese society as a whole.[48] The war period thus brought the bureaucracy and the small enterprise sector together in a tighter embrace than before.

Repression of dissent, promotion of orthodox propaganda, benevolent state policies, and the exigencies of war all worked against expression of an anti-mainstream political vision after the mid-1930s. Many socialists and communists were hounded into silence, browbeaten into ideological conversion, or incarcerated.[49] A few continued to speak out publicly, but they so trimmed their sails that their message was virtually indistinguishable from that of the mainstream.[50] In 1940 both labor unions and political parties were officially disbanded in order to create a much ballyhooed New Order (inspired by Nazi models) that was more a rhetorical facade than anything else. Pressures to conform and to cooperate were overwhelming, and it appears that most opted to do so. There was no heroic resistance to the war, and even the most privileged and thoughtful intellectuals foreswore public criticism.[51]

Beneath the surface of events during the final years of war, however, critical changes set in motion earlier by the ruling coalition continued to gestate. Small landholders and some farm families that both owned and rented land continued to improve their positions relative to large landowners. Workers in large enterprises gained rudimentary experience at organization and bargaining. And small proprietors watched their status as politically constituted groups rise, and their claims on bureaucratic and financial resources expand. All of these changes entailed alterations to the structural features of the Japanese polity and they bestowed a political empowerment that Allied reforms soon enhanced.

Two significant effects of Occupation reforms were to discredit pre-war adherents of the orthodox view of the polity and to legitimate their anti-mainstream opponents. Implicated in the wartime defeat, the older leaders might have been discredited anyway. But the atmosphere of reform created by the Occupation and the purge of former officials that it carried out ensured the demise of wartime leaders for a short period, at least. Granting workers the rights to organize, strike, and bargain collectively authorized adversarial relations in a way that had not been tolerated before. Reforming landholding patterns eliminated inequities that had suppressed some and impoverished others. Creating an elected legislature and expanding the franchise endorsed expectations of equality and democracy. And eliminating the military and the Privy Council liberated the populace at the same time that it shored up representative institutions.

The initial reaction to these reforms was enthusiastic. Workers organized extensively and rapidly. They used their newfound collective strength to fight aggressively for material and other gains during the difficult early post-war years.[52] Farmers greeted land reform with gratitude and worked diligently to restore productivity.[53] Small manufacturers parlayed their wartime organizations and contacts with the state into an even closer relationship with both the bureaucracy and the political parties.[54] And small shopkeepers, while thrown awry by the heavy destruction to downtown business districts and by Occupation aversion to the Large Stores Law, nonetheless began to stage their own comeback in the late 1950s. Clearly, the Occupation reforms did legitimate a polity, premised on equality and devoted to democratic competition, that many groups in Japan found appealing and usable.

But just as many if not more Japanese still clung to an organic, hierarchical, and communal conception of politics. This was especially true of political elites in the bureaucracy, the conservative parties, and big business. Some of them could not act on their beliefs between 1947 and 1952 because they were purged from office. Others were too preoccupied with immediate duties to be able to take a leading position on national policies. And still others were temporarily overwhelmed by the democratic euphoria that Occupation reforms stimulated. Amidst such disarray, the heterodox vision of the polity enjoyed some ascendance, which culminated in a short-lived Socialist government in early 1948.[55]

However, almost as soon as they assumed ascendance, the socialist and labor movements began to wither in the face of a conservative resurgence. American anxieties about the Cold War and the rise of socialist and communist forces in Japan facilitated this resurgence, and the governments of Yoshida Shigeru between 1947 and 1952 abetted it.[56] But it was the return of pre-war leaders following the lifting of the political purge in the early 1950s that was most instrumental in restoring conservative elites to power. Two men who quickly reassumed influential positions were Kishi Nobusuke, a former MCI official who became prime minister under the new Liberal Democratic Party (LDP) in 1957, and Uemura Kōgorō, also a former MCI official who became a key leader at Keidanren in 1952. In the early 1950s many pre-war politicians also returned to their old seats in the Diet. Recognizing that the post-war constitution made the Diet a critical organ of state, former bureaucrats who had held strategic posts during the war joined them in significant numbers and began to use elective office, the Diet, and the cabinet as vehicles for the pursuit of a new vision for the nation.[57]

Men who had been leading figures during the war were able to return to high office in Japan by the 1950s for two reasons. First, having been victims of the searing experiences of Hiroshima and Nagasaki, many Japanese were cauterized against a strong sense of war guilt. Although some groups on the political left opposed the return of wartime leaders, many Japanese did not. Second, although Japan had mistreated Korean conscript laborers and domestic political detainees before and during the war, wartime indiscretions at home did not begin to compare with the magnitude and horrors of the Holocaust. Former wartime leaders did not therefore carry the stigma that afflicted former Nazi officials in post-war Germany.

The new vision that these elites created fixed firmly on economic growth as the highest national priority. They articulated their views most concretely at the very end of this period in the Income Doubling Plan. A Japanese version of the American aspiration to have two cars in every garage, the plan offered what many thought was an overly ambitious program for industrial expansion and consumer affluence. In the event, the goals of the program as it was articulated in 1960 were reached even more quickly than expected, and Japan found itself embarked on a heady period of exceptional growth.[58]

National commitment to growth and affluence elicited ready compliance from most members of the Japanese populace. Although the wartime boom had temporarily lifted some effects of the depression, many Japanese had suffered low or falling real incomes since the late 1920s.[59] The prospect of devoting national energies to higher living standards was extremely appealing. It carried with it none of the costs – such as personal insecurity and the loss of life – that had been an integral part of the wartime political bargain, and it offered prospects of material rewards that were both desirable and necessary. However, by accepting the national goals articulated by a political elite of bureaucrats, politicians, businessmen, and academics, many Japanese were also acquiescing to the reconstitution of a political order that was rooted in mainstream views.

Organized labor in the private sector gradually drifted into a position of still dependent tutelage under a new class of professional managers who began vigorously to assert their authority in the late 1940s. Emboldened by a second Occupation purge directed at 20,000 alleged Communists, and forced to address economic problems created by severe deflationary policies, business leaders at major corporations simply fired the aggressive, dissident leaders who had been the driving force behind unions in private firms. In their place they established leaders of "second" unions, men who were more moderate and accommodationist.[60] From the early 1950s onward, more and more workers in the private sector accepted the ethos of enterprise-based harmony and cooperation in return for better treatment and compensation.[61]

Japan's large farm populace also entered into the emerging conservative coalition. In the immediate post-war years, low productivity and high demand characterized the rural economy. Had landlords remained in place, conditions for an economically exploited and politically radicalized tenantry might have developed. However, the land reform completely forestalled such developments and instead made it possible for a homogeneous body of smallholders to reap the returns available.[62] Pragmatic to the end, these farmers used their local cooperatives as a vehicle for a unified national organization. By the late 1950s it was one of the most influential pressure groups in the country.[63] It functioned to elect conservative party politicians and to negotiate policies beneficial to the farm populace, which continued to harbor its longstanding alliance with conservative political authority.

The organization of small manufacturers that Ayukawa Gisuke spearheaded in the 1950s eventually became only one of many that articulated the interests of this sector. Post-war economic conditions reinstated precisely those circumstances that facilitated political activism among small manufacturers before the war: expansion and surging demand. In addition, bureaucrats at MITI and the Ministry of Finance took a growing interest in such firms, recognizing their centrality in the economy. And big enterprises eventually adopted a more beneficent attitude toward small manufacturers. In due course, the small enterprise sector became densely enmeshed in salutary exchange relationships with conservative political parties, key segments of the bureaucracy, and large business interests.[64]

By 1960 the fundamental outlines of a conservative hegemony – a guardian democracy – had emerged in Japan. Given the constitutional rules of the game, it operated through legislative and administrative organs of state as well as through key economic organizations. The elites who presided over this hegemony were pluralistic in composition. They included incumbent bureaucrats, former bureaucrats serving as elected politicians and business leaders, professional party politicians, and prominent members of the big business community. These were the guardians of Japan's embryonic post-war democracy. They incorporated the still large farm populace into the hegemony through ties among the MOA, the ruling LDP, and the national organization of farm cooperatives. They aligned private-sector labor with the hegemony through indirect means. Workers were supervised under the dependent tutelage of business leaders in large firms and of proprietors in the small enterprise sector. Most small proprietors were also drawn into the hegemony, either through an explicit exchange relationship negotiated through interest group politics or through incorporation at bureaucratic initiative.

There were groups outside this hegemony that maintained a dissident pattern of behavior. They tended to rally around the Japan Communist Party and the socialist movement. The latter, in an event symbolic of the fractious nature of the heterodox opposition, split into two parties in 1960 following a brief period of unity against the LDP. The outsiders included public sector workers affiliated with the political left, parts of the small enterprise sector, segments of the small retail sector, some farmers in areas with a history of tenant disputes, and, finally, some of those whom I have called new urbanites, especially the least advantaged among them. The latter had remained peripheral politically, because they posed difficult problems of integration. One policy might have drawn them into the conservative camp: adequate provision of low-cost housing. However, the emphasis on rapid growth, financial policies that favored large firms at the expense of others, and severe restrictions on consumer finance all militated against such a policy, and thus left outside the conservative hegemony many in the lower urban orders. Poorly mobilized by the parties on the left, too, they have remained the silent minority in Japanese politics, denizens of the city blithely resistant to the organizing metaphors of either village or class solidarity.

EPILOGUE

The guardians of this embryonic democracy remained in power, threatened but never dislodged, for the next dozen years while they presided over the most extraordinary economic expansion in Japan's history. Industrial output and exports both grew rapidly. Immensely profitable firms participating in a surging global economy won a new measure of autonomy; it enabled them to pursue their own course of action irrespective of government designs. Corporate wealth filtered into Japanese society in the form of higher wages, generous bonuses, and rising property values. Widespread affluence put more resources into the hands of individuals and interest groups, fostering their ability to press demands on the political system and to nurture advantageous contacts with elected politicians. And success at achieving high living standards enabled many to look beyond growth to other issues of political significance, such as education, welfare, and the environment. Finally, beginning in the 1960s farm mechanization gradually eliminated the need for cooperative labor exchange in rural Japan and with it a crucial underpinning for village solidarity.[65]

By the mid-1970s the structural and ideological components of guardian democracy had begun to disintegrate in many ways. Paradoxically, twenty years of leadership by former bureaucrats had by then fostered within the LDP increased influence for lifelong, career politicians. Former bureaucrats thus found themselves largely closed out of party leadership by the 1970s, at the same time that the business community was also rejecting them in favor of its own brash contingent of professional managers. Amicable negotiation gave way to more competitive negotiation among political elites who lacked the common backgrounds, experiences, and outlooks that their predecessors had shared during the 1950s and 1960s.

Competition also penetrated politics in other ways. The polity became a kind of marketplace in which citizens and interest groups exchanged votes and campaign largesse in return for favorable government treatment. The longstanding technocratic bias in policymaking gave way to more self-interested forms of demand-making, bargaining, and co-optation. Political pressures on the state expanded steadily after the mid-1970s, just as a national debt crisis restricted administrative and financial resources needed to resolve them. By the 1990s the polity groped for direction in a society where self-interest was corroding an earlier commitment to national interest.

More than constitutional revision and Occupation reforms, the dramatic economic expansion and social transformation of Japan after the late 1950s created the foundation for a new kind of political order. Bureaucratic dominance has declined. Business unity has frayed. The authority of the LDP hinges on a precarious "tacit covenant" with its ambivalent supporters.[66] And societal diversity has exploded in the wake of affluence and the self-indulgence it has stimulated. It is no coincidence that governments sought in the 1980s to revitalize a mainstream vision of Japanese society through programs of *furusato zukuri*. To *zukuru* is to build, mold, or create something. That something was a *furusato*, a term that invoked a nostalgic image of one's idyllic native village. Japan's political elites were trying to forestall the fractious, centrifugal, individualistic tendencies of an affluent urban and rural society to once again impose Japan's primordial social form on the nation's polity. But most Japanese families – worrying about college tuition, planning on trips abroad, and thinking about a leisured retirement – seemed far too distracted to heed the appeal. Their rejection of this rhetorical flourish may have signaled the end of village politics in the Japanese state.

NOTES

The author would like to thank the following scholars for their careful readings of, and helpful comments on, this chapter: Reid Andrews and Richard Smethurst of the University of Pittsburgh, Herrick Chapman of New York University, Donna Harsch of Carnegie Mellon University, and Hans Schmitt of the University of Virginia. He also expresses his appreciation to the Ellen Bayard Weedon Foundation for financial assistance that facilitated research and travel.

1.   One of the earliest efforts appeared in Gary D. Allinson, *Japanese Urbanism: Industry and Politics in Kariya, 1872–1972* (Berkeley and Los Angeles, 1975), and one of the most recent, in a set of essays in *Daedalus*, 119, no. 3 (Summer 1990), under the title "Showa: The Japan of Hirohito."

2.   *Japan's American Interlude* is the title of a seminal work on the Allied Occupation written by Kazuo Kawai (Chicago, 1960).

3.   Robert M. Spaulding, Jr., *Imperial Japan's Higher Civil Service Examinations* (Princeton, 1967).

4.   Akira Kubota, *Higher Civil Servants in Postwar Japan* (Princeton, 1969), and B.C. Koh, *Japan's Administrative Elite* (Berkeley and Los Angeles, 1989).

5.   Ibid.

6.   See, for example, Chalmers Johnson, *MITI and the Japanese Miracle* (Stanford, 1982) and T.J. Pempel, "The Tar Baby Target: 'Reform' of the Japanese Bureaucracy," in Robert Ward and Sakamoto Yoshikazu, eds., *Democratizing Japan* (Honolulu, 1987), 157–87.

7.   See Gary D. Allinson, "The Structure and Transformation of Conservative Rule," in Andrew Gordon, ed., *Postwar Japan as History* (Berkeley and Los Angeles, 1993), 123–44.

8.   Haruhiro Fukui, "The Liberal Democratic Party Revisited: Continuity and Change in the Party's Structure and Performance," *Journal of Japanese Studies*, 10, no. 2 (1984): 385–435.

9.   For a representative case, see Allinson, *Japanese Urbanism*, Chapters 4 and 5.

10.   Fukui, "The LDP Revisited."

11.   For an illuminating account of how the system worked, see Tetsuo Najita, *Hara Kei in the Politics of Compromise, 1905–1915* (Cambridge, Mass., 1967).

12.   Morikawa Hidemasa, "The Increasing Power of Salaried Managers in Japan's Large Corporations," in William Wray, ed., *Managing Industrial Enterprise* (Cambridge, Mass., 1989), 27–52.

13.   Gary D. Allinson, "Japan's Keidanren and Its New Leadership," *Pacific Affairs*, 60, no. 3 (Fall 1987): 385–407.

14.   For one such entrepreneur, see Barbara Molony, "Noguchi Jun and Nitchitsu: Colonial Investment Strategy in a High-Technology Enterprise," in Wray, *Managing Industrial Enterprise*, 229–68.

15.   William Miles Fletcher, III, *The Japanese Business Community and National Trade Policy, 1920–1942* (Chapel Hill, 1989).

16. Andō Yoshio, ed., *Kindai Nihon keizaishi yōran* (A Guide to Modern Japanese Economic History) (Tokyo, 1975), 25. (Hereafter cited as Andō, *Yōran*.)

17. Andō, *Yōran*.

18. E. Patricia Tsurumi, *Factory Girls: Women in the Thread Mills of Meiji Japan* (Princeton, 1990).

19. Allinson, *Japanese Urbanism*, Chapters 4 and 5, and Andrew Gordon, *The Evolution of Labor Relations in Japan* (Cambridge, Mass., 1985).

20. See Gary D. Allinson, "Japanese Cities in the Industrial Era," *Journal of Urban History*, 4, no. 4 (August 1978): 443–76, and William W. Lockwood, *The Economic Development of Japan* (Princeton, 1969).

21. Sheldon Garon, *The State and Labor in Modern Japan* (Berkeley and Los Angeles, 1987).

22. Andrew Gordon, *Labor and Imperial Democracy in Pre-war Japan* (Berkeley and Los Angeles, 1991) (hereafter cited as Gordon, *Labor*), and Elise Tipton, *Japanese Police State* (Honolulu, 1990).

23. W. Dean Kinzley, *Industrial Harmony in Modern Japan* (London, 1991).

24. Koji Taira, "Economic Development, Labor Markets, and Industrial Relations in Japan, 1905–1955," in Peter Duus, ed., *The Cambridge History of Japan* (hereafter, *CHOJ*),vol. 6 (New York, 1988), 606–53.

25. Joe Moore, *Japanese Workers and Their Struggle for Power, 1945–1947* (Madison, 1983).

26. Andō, *Yōran*, 25.

27. Ann Waswo, *Japanese Landlords: The Decline of a Rural Elite* (Stanford, 1977).

28. Nakamura Masanori, "The Japanese Landlord System and Tenancy Disputes," unpublished manuscript (Tokyo, 1989), and Ann Waswo, "The Transformation of Rural Society, 1900–1950," *CHOJ*, Vol. 6, 550–605.

29. Waswo, *Japanese Landlords*, Chapters 2 and 3.

30. Richard J. Smethurst, *Agricultural Development and Tenancy Disputes in Japan, 1870–1940* (Princeton, 1986) and Ann Waswo, "In Search of Equity: Japanese Tenant Unions in the 1920s," in Tetsuo Najita and J. Victor Koschmann, eds., *Conflict in Modern Japanese History* (Princeton, 1982), 366–411.

31. Waswo, "Equity."

32. Andō, *Yōran*, 129.

33. See Chapters 2 and 3 in Gary D. Allinson, *Suburban Tokyo: A Comparative Study in Politics and Social Change* (Berkeley and Los Angeles, 1979).

34. R.P. Dore, *Land Reform in Japan* (Oxford, 1959).

35. Andō, *Yōran*, 172–6.

36. Thomas C. Smith, "Pre-modern Economic Growth: Japan and the West," *Past and Present*, no. 60 (1973): 127–60.

37. Abe Takeshi, "Senkanki ni okeru chihō sangyō no hatten to kumiai, shikenjō (The Development of Local Industries and the Contribution of Trade Associations and Prefectural Technological Institutes in the Interwar Period)," in *Nenpō: Kindai Nihon kenkyū* (Annual: Research on modern Japan), Vol. 13 (1991): 225–48.

38. See Lockwood, *Economic Development*, and the chapter by Mike Mochizuki and Sheldon Garon in Gordon, ed., *Postwar Japan*.

39. Ezra Vogel, *Japan's New Middle Class* (Berkeley and Los Angeles, 1963).

40. Takeuchi Tsuneyoshi, "Shokaisō to sono dōkō (Social Strata and Their Tendencies)," in Shakai keizaishi gakkai, ed., *1930-nendai no Nihon keizai* (The Japanese Economy in the 1930s) (hereafter *1930-nendai*) (Tokyo, 1982) 187–278, and Chapters 7 and 8 in Andō Yoshio, ed., *Ryō taisenkan no Nihon shihonshugi* (Japanese Capitalism between the Wars) (Tokyo, 1979).

41. Gordon, *Labor*, esp. part 3.

42. Itō Takashi, "The Role of Right-Wing Organizations in Japan," in Dorothy Borg and Shumpei Okamoto, eds., *Pearl Harbor as History* (New York, 1973), 487–510.

43. Gregory J. Kasza, *The State and the Mass Media in Japan, 1918–1945* (Berkeley and Los Angeles, 1988).

44. Robert M. Spaulding, Jr., "The Bureaucracy as a Political Force, 1920–1945," in James Morley, ed., *Dilemmas of Growth in Pre-war Japan* (Princeton, 1971), 33–80, and Nagai Kazu, "Gunjin to kanryō: 15-nen sensōki ni okeru gen'yaku shōkō no kankai shinshutsu (Military Personnel and Bureaucrats: Inroads into the Bureaucracy by Active-duty Officers during the 15-year War Period)," in *Nenpō : Kindai Nihon kenkyū* (Annual: Research on Modern Japan), Vol.10 (1988), 284–309.

45. Waswo, "Transformation," and Mori Takero, "1930-nendai no Nihon nōgyō (Japanese Agriculture in the 1930s)," in *1930-nendai*, 325–33.

46. See Taira, "Economic Development," Allinson, *Japanese Urbanism*, Chapters 5 and 6, and Gordon, *Evolution*, Chapters 8–10.

47. Frank Upham, "Privatizing Regulation: The Implementation of the Large-Scale Retail Stores Law," in Gary D. Allinson and Yasunori Sone, eds., *Political Dynamics in Contemporary Japan* (Ithaca, 1993): 264–94. (Hereafter, *Political Dynamics*.)

48. Gordon, *Labor*, 325–6.

49. Tipton, *Japanese Police State*, Chapters 3 and 6.

50. Gordon, *Labor*, Part 3.

51. Andrew Barshay, *State and Intellectual in Imperial Japan: The Public Man in Crisis* (Berkeley and Los Angeles, 1988).

52. Moore, *Japanese Workers*.

53. Dore, *Land Reform*, and Waswo, "Transformation."

54. Mochizuki and Garon in Gordon, *Postwar Japan*, and Kent E. Calder, *Crisis and Compensation: Public Policy and Political Stability in Japan, 1945–1986* (Princeton, 1988), Chapter 7. For a dissenting view of the political economy of small enterprise, see David Friedman, *The Misunderstood Miracle* (Ithaca, 1988).

55. A good narrative analysis of these years appears in Richard B. Finn, *Winners in Peace: MacArthur, Yoshida, and Postwar Japan* (Berkeley and Los Angeles, 1992), Parts 2 and 3.

56. John Dower, *Empire and Aftermath: Yoshida Shigeru and the Japanese Experience, 1878–1954* (Cambridge, Mass., 1979).

57. See Ward and Sakamoto, *Democratizing Japan*, Chapters 11 and 12; Finn, *Winners in Peace*, Parts 4 and 5; Haruhiro Fukui, *Party in Power* (Berkeley and Los Angeles, 1970); and Muramatsu Michio, *Sengo Nihon no kanryōsei* (Postwar Japan's Bureaucratic System) (Tokyo, 1981).

58. See Gordon, *Postwar Japan*, especially the chapters by Gary D. Allinson, Laura Hein, Koji Taira, and Charles Horioka.

59.   Alan H. Gleason, "The Level of Living in Japan and the United States: A Long-term International Comparison," *Economic Development and Cultural Change*, 37 (January 1989): 261–84.

60.   How this process played itself out in the major firms in the auto industry is revealed in Allinson, *Japanese Urbanism*, Chapters 6 and 7, and Michael A. Cusumano, *The Japanese Automobile Industry* (Cambridge, Mass., 1985), Chapter 3.

61.   Ikuo Kume, Mike Mochizuki, and Yutaka Tsujinaka examine this process of moderation in their chapters in Part 3 of *Political Dynamics*.

62.   Dore, *Land Reform*, and Waswo, "Transformation."

63.   Aurelia George, "The Japanese Farm Lobby and Agricultural Policy-Making," *Pacific Affairs*, 54, no. 3 (Autumn 1981): 409–30.

64.   In addition to the chapters on this subject by Mochizuki and Garon, and by Calder, both cited above, see also, *inter alia*, Muramatsu Michio *et al.*, *Sengo Nihon no atsuryoku dantai* (Postwar Japan's Pressure Groups) (Tokyo, 1986).

65.   The ideas briefly adumbrated in this Epilogue are treated at greater length in *Political Dynamics*, especially in the chapters by Gary D. Allinson, Michio Muramatsu, and Margaret McKean.

66.   See Chapter 1 by Allinson in the preceding reference, especially pages 31–43.

7 Uncommon Democracy in Mexico: Middle Classes and the Military in the Consolidation of One-Party Rule, 1936–1946

Diane E. Davis

Mexico's political system defies easy categorization. In a region of the world known for violent coups, rapid regime change, and intermittent periods of military rule, Mexico stands apart. The same party has governed the nation since 1929, in one incarnation or another;[1] and for most of that time has done so under civilian rule with relatively little bloodshed. The last military general to hold the presidency was Manuel Avila Camacho, who took office in 1940. Since that time the armed forces have not played a visible role in national politics. Moreover, Mexico has held presidential elections regularly since 1929; and in these elections, the Partido Revolucionario Institucional (PRI) has consistently maintained its hold on power.

Given the nation's early transition from military to civilian rule, the ruling party's longstanding popularity and electoral successes, and the unprecedented political stability both have brought, Mexico breaks rank with its regional counterparts and appears closer to the "uncommon democracies" of Israel, Italy, Sweden, and Japan, recently analyzed by T.J. Pempel as notable for their civilian, one-party dominance.[2] Mexico differs from Pempel's uncommonly democratic countries, however, in one key way: its party system could hardly be called competitive. In Mexico, both right- and left-wing opposition parties do exist; yet until recently, they have not seriously challenged the ruling party. The most viable contender, the right-leaning Partido de Acción Nacional (PAN), had never received more than 20 percent of the vote in national elections, while left-wing parties fought among themselves to capture miniscule support. For years, in fact, most of these small left-leaning parties (and even the PAN) were referred to as the loyal opposition, in no small part because they refrained from publicly challenging the ruling party's claim to power during elections. Only in the past decade or so have opposition parties – both the PAN and the newly formed Partido de la Revolución Democrática – had any real impact on elections, and this appears to be primarily a local and regional, not national, phenomenon.

What accounts for Mexico's peculiar – if not uncommon – democracy, characterized by decades of civilian one-party rule? How has the PRI maintained its electoral hegemony without a military force in the wings to stem opposition, on the one hand, or without a viable or competitive party system to give it electoral legitimacy, on the other? How did Mexico chart a third political course somewhere between military rule and parliamentary democracy; and what trade-offs were made along the way? One way to answer these questions is to return to the historical period in which one-party rule and Mexico's political future were clearly up for grabs and military rule and competitive party politics were both still feasible options: the years between 1936 and 1946.

It was during this period that the PAN first organized itself as a forceful and potentially threatening political alternative to the official party. It made serious inroads into the ruling party's constituency by aiming its message primarily towards Mexico's middle classes, many of whom at the time felt disenfranchised by the labor and peasant orientation of President Lázaro Cárdenas. In this same period, the ruling revolutionary party, then called the Partido de la Revolución Mexicana (PRM), also faced an ongoing rebellion involving factions of the military in alliance with regional elites in several northern states. President Cárdenas weathered several armed uprisings against his government and managed to survive a failed military coup. Opposition to Cárdenas and the ruling party also surfaced in the presidential election of 1940, in which opposition candidate General Juan Andreu Almazán captured widespread electoral support from dissatisfied middle classes, the northern bourgeoisie, and much of the military rank and file.

If Cárdenas's military opposition had triumphed in their coup attempts, either before or after 1940, the ruling party would have been unable to maintain its hold on power and Mexico would have faced the threat of military rule. Or if the PAN and other opposition parties had continued to draw substantial middle-class or military support, Mexico might have developed a truly competitive political system. Yet we see neither of these outcomes. After 1940, Mexico's military practically disappeared as an autonomous institutional actor threatening the state, and the middle classes failed to actively support the PAN or other opposition parties to any significant degree. Instead, most middle classes and military personnel sided with the ruling party, primarily by collaborating in the programs and policies of the Confederación Nacional de Organizaciones Populares (CNOP), which was formally incorporated into the official party in 1943.

The CNOP gave institutional voice to those "popular middle classes" who had been ignored in the earlier party restructurings that accommodated peasants and the industrial working class. It also served as the principal sector of the party through which military personnel influenced policy and participated in party politics. It was with the establishment of the CNOP, in fact, that demilitarization occurred and the military became just another interest group in national politics. This stands in stark contrast to most other Latin American countries, where the military remained a highly autonomous and powerful force looming threateningly above or outside party and state structures, willing and able to stage a coup or impose military rule whenever conditions warranted.[3]

Accordingly, the foundation of the CNOP signalled a democratic opening in Mexican politics. The armed forces were practically eliminated as an external threat to governance, a state of affairs which reinforced the political system's democratic potential. Equally important, the ruling party recast its institutional contours to bring the forgotten middle into national politics and internal party decisionmaking. Almost immediately, the CNOP achieved parity with the party's other two sectors, holding 33.7 percent of total party membership by 1946. With all three sectors in place, the PRM governed Mexico with essentially all of the country's citizens formally at its side: labor, peasants, and popular middle classes alike. The CNOP's institutional relationship to the middle class, moreover, was democratically conceived in terms of its wide-ranging scope. This third sector of the party opened its institutional arms to a remarkably broad spectrum of the population, including artisans, small agriculturalists, professionals, youth workers, students, school teachers, bus drivers, street vendors, bureaucrats, small industrialists and shopkeepers, urban and agricultural cooperatives, neighborhood organizations, artists, and women's associations.[4]

MIDDLE-CLASS AND MILITARY INCLUSION: BEYOND POLITICS AS USUAL

In order to know more about how and why Mexico avoided military rule and institutionalized its uncommon democracy, we must examine the CNOP and its constituents more closely. Why was this organization so successful in attracting potentially challenging opposition forces into the official party? Why did military leaders slip so quietly into the political background to become just another social force within the CNOP? Why did Mexico's middle classes shun the competitive politics represented by the PAN and join the party-controlled CNOP instead? Indeed, what conditions would motivate middle classes to support a highly centralized party with a recent history of fraudulent and anti-democratic actions, especially if alternatives like the PAN existed?

These questions are absolutely critical to an understanding of democratization and its peculiar form in Mexico; so critical, in fact, that it is rather remarkable that we know so little about these class and social forces or about the CNOP during this watershed period. There are a few studies on the professionalization of Mexico's military,[5] and on middle classes and education policy,[6] but these works tend to focus either on the period up to 1940, as is the case with the military literature, or after 1946, as is the case with most studies of middle classes. No one has studied the critical period when the CNOP was founded and when demilitarization and middle-class inclusion were first achieved.

Given the absence of serious work on this topic, prevailing wisdom about the CNOP is that the organization was intended as a residual grab-bag, without internal coherence, whose principal function has been to send ideologically moderate candidates into electoral office and which was created merely to divide the labor movement and eliminate military resistance.[7] It is our intent to challenge this interpretation; and by doing so, to depart somewhat from prevailing theoretical views of Mexican politics. Most scholars of Mexico tend to see major political developments since 1929 as completely determined by a ruling party leadership able to co-opt, corrupt, or manipulate all major actors in national-level politics in order to maintain the official party's hold on power.[8] Occasionally, scholars have departed somewhat from this focus to examine labor's leading role in Mexican history and politics; but they too have tended to see labor's impact as mediated mainly by the party leadership. In this chapter, however, we extend our focus beyond the party leadership and labor to examine the actions and orientations of middle classes and the military in the construction of Mexico's political system.

Using secondary materials and primary documents, we argue that key elements of the middle class and military joined together to support the ruling party in the early 1940s, primarily because they shared a common political and social identity that linked them to each other and distinguished them from other class forces. Three factors in particular strengthened the elective affinity between sectors of the middle class and the military: (1) the strongly labor-oriented rhetoric, juridical reforms, and political practices of the ruling party from 1934 to 1940, which fortified middle-class and military attachment to more moderate political ideologies; (2) their agreement on basic economic development objectives, centering on national industrialization; and (3) the ideological and economic impacts of the Second World War.

We make our argument by focusing first on conditions in Mexico before 1940 and how they influenced the political orientations and actions of the military and the middle class. We then discuss the ways in which the foundation of the CNOP in 1943 responded to concerns shared by the two groups, and in turn produced a greater convergence of interests between them and the ruling party. Last, we explore the long-term economic and political consequences of the successful accommodation of middle classes and the military within the CNOP and the ruling party.

One brief definitional note before beginning. The term "middle class," used so loosely until now, is a problematic one, difficult to define even in advanced capitalist countries. In a developing country, and especially before the advent of comprehensive national industrialization, defining the middle class is particularly difficult. During the first decades of the twentieth century in Mexico, for example, the lines of demarcation among artisans, workers, and middle classes were elusive, subjective, and highly politicized. So too were the differences among military personnel, industrial workers, and white-collar employees, since many military pensioners were given jobs in government factories and state agencies. Given these complexities, we try not to impose on our primary or secondary materials any clear or rigid definition of the middle class, at least a priori. Instead, we take the "messiness" of middle-class categories, especially the problematic boundary between middle and working classes, as a principal point of departure in this chapter. Part of our task is to analyze the ways in which middle classes and the military identified themselves as distinct from working classes and similar to each other, how and why they did so, and with what implications for the CNOP and Mexico's overall political trajectory. By so doing, we will not only illuminate the middle classes' impact on politics in Mexico, but will also generate new insights into the process of middle-class formation, struggles over collective identities, and the role of both factors in the democratization process.

CLASS POLITICS SETS THE STAGE

The presidency of Lázaro Cárdenas (1934–1940) saw two related sets of changes in the ruling party that marked a break from prior practices and that alienated both the military and middle classes. The first was a move towards the left in the ruling party's ideology and rhetoric. The second was a programmatic emphasis on the policy demands of industrial labor and the peasantry. In 1936, the ruling Partido Nacional Revolucionario (PNR) founded the Confederación de Trabajadores Mexicano (CTM), an organization which united disparate federations of industrial laborers across the country. Cárdenas's goal in establishing the CTM was to make up for years of red-baiting and corruption in a labor movement that had established strong links to the conservative faction of the revolutionary leadership as early as 1918. In his efforts to restore class politics to the labor movement, Cárdenas placed under the CTM's jurisdiction those who "represented the most advanced fraction of the industrial proletariat" in terms of past struggles, commitment to union life, and location within the productive apparatus.[9] This generally meant industrial workers in larger firms, many of which were still foreign-owned.

Following the creation of the CTM, Cárdenas moved to incorporate the peasantry as well. In 1937 he founded the Confederación Campesina Mexicana, later renamed the Confederación Nacional Campesina (CNC). In that same year, Cárdenas and the CTM signed a pact with the Mexican Communist Party, an act which further underscored his administration's receptiveness to the radical, class-oriented demands of the proletarianized sectors of the industrial labor movement. With labor and the peasantry his main institutional allies in the party, Cárdenas introduced some of the most radical and far-reaching reforms Mexico had ever seen. In addition to recognizing the rights of all unions to exist, Cárdenas supported strikes by industrial workers for wage increases, fostered the elimination of company unions, mandated collective work contracts, and implemented a massive agrarian reform program.[10]

Almost immediately, Cárdenas's programs generated controversy, but not primarily from large capitalists, as might be assumed. At least in the first half of his administration, many employers saw possible benefits in the incorporation of labor into a state-managed federation. Where Cárdenas met some of his harshest opposition was among those who were institutionally excluded from the CTM and thus unable to participate in party politics to the same extent as industrial workers. Among these groups were artisans or craftsmen[11] and sectors of the so-called traditional middle class like shopkeepers, doctors, lawyers, and other professionals. These groups soon began to join together around their common sense of institutional exclusion and their shared rejection of Cárdenas's class-based rhetoric, using the banner of middle-class identity as a basis for organization.

In 1936, for example, the same year that Cárdenas established the CTM, a group of urban professionals founded the Confederación de la Clase Media (CCM). Claiming a membership of 162,000,[12] this organization sought to "protect the rights of the middle classes who felt threatened with extinction and who shunned religious or party identifications."[13] Unlike other opposition forces who joined the *sinarquistas*, a right-wing religious movement which opposed Cárdenas's anti-clericalism and the secularization of Mexican society, the CCM and its constituents did not necessarily oppose the basic principles of the Revolution. But they resented the clear preference given to labor and peasants in national politics and policymaking, and they saw themselves as losing the institutional capacity to push forward their own moral and political view of Mexico's future.

A 1936 pamphlet produced by the CCM claimed that under Cárdenas the ruling party "deliberately seeks the disappearance of the Middle Class, [which must] organize for the struggle and defend its interests." It was necessary to protect the middle classes, the CCM claimed, in order to protect all of "humanity," which would surely disappear "along with civilization, culture, and all the activities that dignify man," if working class preferences or antagonistic class rhetorics prevailed.[14] The perils of the time, the CCM argued with a "Fatherland and Rights" logo unfurled across its letterhead, were clear: communism, the moral disintegration of the family, irreverence toward family and country in public instruction, and the decline of the family firm. In order to guard against the elimination of these key institutions in Mexican society, polarizing class rhetorics should be abandoned and the common good emphasized instead.

Under a nationalist banner, the CCM called for credit to sustain family-owned industries; restrictions on foreign immigration; social and health policies to protect children and the family from such evils as prostitution and misery; and voting rights for women. Many in the CCM felt that female suffrage would bolster support for socially conservative, pro-family policies in national politics. The CCM also demanded civil and political rights for those employed in commercial and professional activities, including military service. These claims came in response to constitutional restrictions that legally prohibited military personnel from participating in political life or from striking; labor legislation that restricted hours and hiring practices in commerce; and the existing structure of the party, which ensured that commercial and professional employees were almost fully excluded from active involvement in party politics.

CLASS POLITICS IN THE PUBLIC SECTOR

Restrictions on the political and civil rights of state workers roused middle-class mobilization and anti-Cárdenas sentiment in the public sector as well. Since the CTM accommodated only industrial laborers and the more proletarianized sectors of the working class as its constituents, many occupational groups were left out. Public employees were among the most active of those groups, and in late 1935 a group of Mexico City-based state workers began to organize in protest. Their Alianza de Organizaciones de Trabajadores al Servicio del Estado included street-cleaners, teachers, and those employed in the water and sewage department, parks and gardens, graphic arts (i.e., newspapers), healthcare, communications and public works, and state-owned arms industries. Within a year, scores of other government agencies joined the organization, which was renamed the Federación Nacional de Trabajadores del Estado (FNTE).[15]

Because the FNTE defined itself as an organization of *trabajadores* or *obreros*,[16] one of the first political issues it tackled was the right to strike, something constitutionally denied to all state personnel. A second was the extension of state worker benefits – especially pensions – to military personnel employed in state-run factories and government agencies. In the process of struggling to extend industrial laborers' rights to state workers, the FNTE developed closer ties with the CTM, which supported the public workers' right to strike. But the CTM was an openly radical organization, and as the FNTE expanded its ranks to include white-collar administrators and technical staff (*empleados*) as well as blue-collar government workers, conflicts began to emerge. Some state workers, most notably teachers, remained avowedly leftist in orientation and in strong sympathy with the working-class causes advocated by the CTM. Others, however, had never been particularly radical. Many *empleados* had initially accepted the working-class language of the FNTE, and closer ties to the CTM, primarily as a means to defend themselves against political infighting within the bureaucracy or to improve working conditions within government agencies.[17] But as radicalized elements and the CTM leadership joined together to push a strongly laborist position, many state workers, especially higher-level administrators, began to express reservations about their alleged "proletarian" status and to tone down their demands for workplace rights. Instead, they called for a Ley de Servicio Civil that would merely regulate hours, wages, pensions, and promotions.[18]

In late 1937 President Cárdenas introduced into Congress an Estatuto Jurídico to protect state workers' rights. The statute distinguished between working- and middle-class state employees, granting the right to organize and strike to the former (*trabajadores de base*) and denying it to the latter (*trabajadores de confianza*), who held supervisory positions and considerable autonomy.[19] Still, this compromise did not end the ongoing conflict.

Many self-identified *empleados* were not high enough in the bureaucratic hierarchy to be considered *trabajadores de confianza*, and were thus lumped together with the *trabajadores de base*. Meanwhile, state workers who sought closer linkages with the CTM, especially teachers but also significant portions of the military rank and file, were not fully pleased either. For one thing, the statute mandated that state workers organize by agency rather than by job classification, a requirement which limited working-class solidarity. For another, these agency-based organizations could shun the CTM if so desired and affiliate with whichever federation they pleased.

With controversy continuing, the proposed statute remained stalled in Congress for almost a year, where debate over its implementation deepened the class faultlines among state workers and within Mexican society at large. Cárdenas's March 1938 oil nationalization further raised the stakes. Conservative voices both within and outside the FNTE denounced the government's steady march to the left and decried the chaos that would result if state employees could mobilize, like industrial workers, and paralyze the nation through strikes. Forces on the left feared that granting organization and strike prerogatives to state workers without also requiring them to affiliate with the CTM would strengthen conservative forces within both the union movement and the state itself.

Cárdenas's political problems reached a peak in May 1938 when right-wing military forces led by General Saturnino Cedillo attempted a *coup d'état*. Much of their opposition stemmed from the clear leftward turn of the administration, especially the oil nationalization. Yet many of the rebels were also disturbed by the growing solidarity between the military rank and file and the labor movement and by the involvement of military personnel in the party's labor and peasant sectors.[20] The proposed statute, which categorized military employees as state workers, heightened their concerns by juridically treating military personnel in class terms. Although most members of the army were to be classified as *trabajadores de confianza*, the statute categorized thousands of military men employed in the manufacture of armaments and other military goods as *trabajadores de base*, which meant that some members of the armed forces would have the right to organize and strike.[21]

Many high-ranking military officers interpreted the categorization of military personnel as state workers, both *base* and *confianza*, as well as the growing links between the armed forces and the union movement, as a threat to the military's independence from the state and to their own personal power. The move to treat military personnel as a category of state workers also exacerbated class tensions within the military in much the same way it had among government employees. Some in the armed forces were eager to ally institutionally and ideologically with the union movement or peasant federations, thereby asserting their own working-class or *campesino* identity.[22] Others saw themselves more in professional terms, and felt their classification as *trabajadores de confianza* linked them to higher-level bureaucrats and state employees with middle-class sentiments.

Growing opposition from senior military officers and high-level bureaucrats drove Cárdenas to a new compromise. Unwilling to drop the proposed statute and the rights it guaranteed, he instead reconstituted the party to provide distinct sectors for state employees and the military, thus distancing both groups from the CTM and from each other. In the new party, renamed the Partido de la Revolución Mexicana (PRM), the "military sector" did not have the federation structure of the original labor and peasant sectors; rather, it was created to allow soldiers, sailors, and airmen to participate in party politics as individuals rather than as corporativist groupings. They would enjoy constitutionally guaranteed "political rights and should exercise them," Cárdenas proclaimed.[23]

State workers were incorporated into the Federación de Sindicatos de Trabajadores al Servicio del Estado (FSTSE), which now included employees who had not been active or organized in the FNTE. Owing to its large and well-organized membership, the FSTSE formed the backbone of what was known as the party's "bureaucratic sector" and what Cárdenas occasionally called the "popular sector," foreshadowing its future role as the basis of the CNOP.

THE POLITICAL LIMITS TO CARDENAS'S REFORMS

Except for the fact that the military and bureaucratic sectors were institutionally distinct, these 1938 reforms were very similar to those that were formalized with the founding of the CNOP in 1943 during the administration of Avila Camacho. They signalled a broadening of party structures to include groups with an avowedly middle-class orientation. So why did Cárdenas continue to face rising middle-class and military opposition between 1938 and 1940? Why weren't the inclusion of the military and the creation of a "popular sector" enough to ensure political stability and widespread grassroots support?

In seeking explanations for continued middle-class and military opposition to Cárdenas, we must note the impact of his left-leaning rhetoric and class bias towards labor, which continued throughout his term. Yet neither totally disappeared after 1940, when languages of class struggle persisted and the labor sector remained at the forefront of party politics, despite the wave of political conservatism. Accordingly, a more fruitful line of inquiry focuses on the military and popular sectors constituted by the 1938 party reform: their functioning, composition, and utility for the military and non-bureaucratic sectors of the middle class, particularly professionals and small family firms in commerce, agriculture, and industry.

The party restructuring made Cárdenas popular with much of the military rank and file, who now received juridical status and political rights, as well as with many state workers. But it did little to stem opposition from powerful military leaders like Almazán. This was so not only because the basic ideological conflict still remained but also because the party's new structure limited the power of the conservative military *caciques* by bringing the rank and file directly into party politics as an autonomous organizational force. This move may have accomplished the objective of institutionally distancing military personnel from the labor movement and state workers, but it did not rid the military of radical elements. Many of the newly empowered enlisted men tended to be more progressive and supportive of Cárdenas's social policies than the conservative military leadership.[24] Equally important, the creation of a military "sector" that did not necessarily function as such in practice alienated even those higher-ranking military men who had no clearcut ideological reason to oppose Cárdenas. To the extent that the new military sector lacked the same political power and corporate rights as the other sectors, its leadership now had relatively little formal say in party politics, especially in relation to other class forces with well functioning sectoral structures, like peasants, labor, and bureaucrats.

Much of the upper ranks of the military was peopled by the sons of the provincial middle classes; the diminishing political power of these groups *vis-à-vis* laborers, peasants, and state workers, and growing ideological conflicts between officers and the radical rank and file, easily fed into pre-existing regional and class tensions, adding more fuel to Cárdenas's conservative opposition. The 1938 party restructuring also gave the PRM greater organizational control over the military rank and file, which worried many officers because it threatened to destroy the autonomous hierarchy of command within the armed forces.

Military unity was also limited by the dispersion of a small but notable proportion of the military rank and file across the party's sectors.[25] This occurred not only as a result of Cárdenas's decision to create agrarian militias that operated within the peasant sector,[26] but also because many veterans – who were still considered members of the military, covered by military benefits or pensions – worked in factories and government agencies and thus affiliated with the CTM or FSTSE. It also resulted from the classification of military personnel in arms-related manufacturing as *trabajadores de base*. Party leaders frequently insisted that soldiers "were no more than workers in arms," and in public pronouncements Cárdenas declared that Mexico's armed forces would "continue to identify with workers and peasants in their social activities and in the different phases of the class struggle."[27]

All these factors undermined ideological unity within the military, spurring some to identify with peasant comrades, others with industrial laborers, and still others with state employees, while at the same time eroding their allegiance to the upper echelon of officers. The military leadership thus felt just as threatened after the party restructuring as before.

But what about the middle classes? Why did they continue to form a strong core of opposition, lending support to conservative leaders like Cedillo and Almazán even when Cárdenas showed his willingness to include them in the party? The answer is relatively straightforward: Cárdenas failed to pre-empt middle-class opposition because his new "popular" sector did not adequately accommodate middle-class concerns and demands, either rhetorically or substantively.

Even though Cárdenas often referred to this new component of the party as the "popular" sector, it was clear that his principal concern in founding the sector was to politically accommodate state employees – especially those classified as *trabajadores de confianza*, who still lacked labor protections and other legal rights of organization and protest – rather than the middle class as a whole. The phrase "popular middle classes," used to identify this sector's constituency, did not come into common usage until after 1940. Before that time, Cárdenas called this fourth sector a popular sector primarily for rhetorical purposes, and infrequently at that, generally when he sought to demonstrate that the new party was open to other middle-class constituents besides members of the FSTSE.

Cárdenas's use of the term "popular" was thus intended, not to institutionally privilege the middle class, but to legitimate a politics of unity aimed at linking together constituents from different class and social backgrounds in support of the party leadership.[28] Most of the time he emphasized the importance of politically empowering workers and peasants in a popular front against fascism, imperialism, and unfettered capitalism. Thus the "popular" sector was intended to support the same working-class and peasant objectives of the party as before 1938, now presented in the language of populism rather than class.

Nor did the PRM leadership take Cárdenas's "popular" sector very seriously, at least as a format for a wide range of dissatisfied middle-class groups to participate in. Most party leaders saw the 1938 restructuring as intended primarily to unite disparate groups of state workers into one organization, in order to enhance their participation in politics *vis-à-vis* other "popular" groups. A June 1938 document of the PRM, for example, lists Trabajadores al Servicio del Estado and a category for Funcionarios Públicos y Empleados de Confianza as separate from each other and from the party's Sector Cultural y Popular. And in discussing this new "Cultural and Popular Sector," the document states that the party secretary "has not yet communicated ... the names of the organizations pertaining to this sector that are capable of contributing to the development of the politico-social program of the Partido de la Revolución Mexicana."[29] This does not necessarily mean that grassroots organizations were unwilling to join the popular sector, or that Cárdenas opposed their inclusion. He clearly relished support from popular and middle classes, if only to carry through with the developmental objectives of his administration. But the fact was that the PRM had no such groups readily at its side, and it lacked established relationships and/or a coherent position *vis-à-vis* their potential participation.[30]

PUBLIC SECTOR ACTIVITIES UNITE THE OPPOSITION

Perhaps most important in explaining why the reforms Cárdenas instituted in 1938 were not successful in stabilizing his administration is that they generated a new round of conflicts. Some of the most consequential stemmed from the earlier controversy over the class identities and the rights of state workers. With lower-rung state workers now allowed to strike, tensions between state workers *de confianza* and *de base* reached a new height. State administrators often found themselves directly challenged by the employees they supervised, especially when the latter went on strike. Further aggravating matters was the fact that strikes were often called for political purposes, that is, to express displeasure with the conservative actions or political orientations of higher-level bureaucrats.[31] And frequently, it was the public that suffered most from these strikes.

There were two specific issues which catalyzed class conflict among state workers and in society at large. One was education; the other, urban policy. Both issues generated public outrage; and their impact was magnified by the political alliances they produced. Controversies over education linked rural and urban middle classes in opposition against Cárdenas, while urban policy deficiencies brought the urban poor and middle classes together in questioning the Cárdenas regime.

The content of public education in Mexico had long been under dispute, owing to the post-revolutionary anti-clericalism and attendant prohibitions on private religious schooling imposed by the ruling party. When state workers were granted the right to organize as unions and strike, many in the public worried about the impact on education, since almost all school teachers were state workers classified as *trabajadores de base*. The teachers' union was known to be among the nation's most radical, and pedagogy was further radicalized by Cárdenas's support for teacher training using socialist models of education. A 1938 editorial in the leading Mexico City daily reflected the growing concern about public education when it argued that the government should promote nationalism over class consciousness. Most Mexicans "aren't reds," the author protested, and teachers should end their ongoing "fetishism over the right to strike," and stop filling children's minds with "Bolshevik propaganda."[32]

Public concern about communism among teachers was particularly strong in Mexico City, where the teachers' union was linked to left-oriented intellectuals and where most of the nation's middle classes resided. However, Cárdenas's use of *campesino* teachers to spread political education about class inequality and impoverishment in the countryside alienated rural populations too, especially those tied to Cedillo and other potentially rebellious regional elites. With both rural and urban middle-class opposition to the leftist orientation of Mexico's teachers, who used their juridical categorization as state workers to identify themselves as proletarian, both middle classes and the military leadership found themselves opposing Cárdenas and siding with the sentiments of right-wing clericalists linked to the *sinarquista* movement.

As concerns surfaced about communist control in the teachers' movement, Mexicans were also finding fault with government policymaking in the urban domain. Failures in this area stemmed from bureaucratic infighting and strikes in government agencies, which produced interruptions in critical public services, and from Cárdenas's longstanding bias towards peasants and labor, which led him to neglect critical urban services. Under his administration, public works received a declining proportion of the national budget, and new social programs mainly benefitted organized labor, including extensive investments in health, education, and new housing for CTM and FSTSE constituents only.[33] Fewer resources went to water, drainage, street paving, public lighting, and markets, which had been the principal demands of non-unionized and middle-class residents, especially shopkeepers and small industries which relied on these services for their livelihood.

The pattern of government social expenditures also confirms the privileging of rural over urban populations. For example, Cárdenas dictated that all "increases in the quantity [of resources] assigned to the Department of Health be destined completely for services in the interior of the Republic, since Mexico City has received constant attention in health matters and the sanitary needs in the States are much more urgent."[34] This not only alienated Mexico City residents, but also exacerbated tensions within the Department of Public Health between base workers and *confianza* workers, the latter of whom relied on a high volume of activities to sustain power or personal gain through bribes.

Cárdenas's neglect of urban services was an issue that united many against his administration. Insufficient access to water, drainage, electricity, and affordable housing angered the middle classes and urban poor alike, especially the self-employed urban poor who, unlike industrial laborers, lacked workplace benefits or government-provided housing. So too did growing transport problems, which accelerated as Cárdenas took little action against striking trolleyworkers. When floods paralyzed Mexico City in 1939, the government's neglect of the city's drainage system became a principal organizing issue around which a broad spectrum of the urban population rallied to express opposition. One such grassroots organization, the Unificación Popular del Distrito Federal, identified scarcities in public services as one of the four vital problems facing Mexico in the late 1930s, along with the economy, the administration of justice, and national defense.[35]

Urban middle classes and the poor were also affected by the inflation and rising costs caused by the oil nationalization of 1938. Self-employed street vendors, artisans, and shopkeepers were not covered by minimum wage legislation, unlike the industrial and state workers in the PRM, and suffered accordingly. And while Cárdenas proved willing to distribute urban and rural lands to workers and peasants, as well as construct housing for bureaucrats and industrial workers, he refused to respond to demands by well-organized and highly mobilized renters (*inquilinarios*) and small shopkeepers for legislation on rent control. Perhaps more than any other issue, the renters' movement brought together the urban poor and middle-class businessmen in an anti-Cárdenas alliance, and marches and rent strikes became common occurrences in Mexico City in 1938 and 1939.[36]

By 1939 it was clear that Cárdenas's institutional reforms had failed to stem citizen dissatisfaction. Indeed, many of his stances led groups and classes to unite in opposition to the PRM, either around substantive issues like urban policy, questions of political rights for the military and state workers, or ideological concerns like the threat of communism. These disenfranchised and dissatisfied forces became the political constituency for opposition candidate General Juan Andreu Almazán, who joined the presidential race in 1939.

CONSTRUCTING MIDDLE-CLASS IDENTITY: FROM ELECTORAL DEFEAT TO ORGANIZATIONAL TRIUMPH

With his military foothold in the northern city of Monterrey, Almazán rallied support from provincial opponents of the PRM, including conservative factions in the military elite, the northern bourgeoisie, and small farmers threatened by Cárdenas's land distribution and agrarian reform. But he also relied on support from groups who felt excluded by Cárdenas's classist, pro-union vision, especially professionals, small shopkeepers, alienated state workers, and the self-employed urban poor. In order to tap this constituency, Almazán inaugurated his national campaign in the nation's capital and largest city, Mexico City, where he generated a crowd estimated at between 200,000 and 250,000.[37] During the campaign, moreover, he appealed directly to white-collar state workers by arguing against the recently implemented Estatuto Jurídico. The PRM's candidate, Manuel Avila Camacho, responded by claiming that state workers had "class consciousness and won't swallow such clumsy bait or abandon their rights just for an attractive promise."[38]

In this verbal war over class and rights, Almazán's appeals struck a powerful chord. Employees in the Departments of Health, Pensions, Education, Economy, Agriculture, Lottery, Communications, and the Attorney General's office established pro-Almazán committees and publicly declared support for the general's candidacy.[39] So too did many of the rural middle classes, who responded to Almazán's call for an end to land reform and the restoration of protections on private property. Almazán's support for public housing delighted the lower-middle class and urban poor involved in the *inquilinario* movement; and his pro-Catholic stance and support for non-secular education appealed to those who worried about leftist pedagogy in Mexico's schools. He even won support from some sectors of organized labor, not because of his policy orientation but because they feared the anti-democratic consequences of the PRM's monopoly on political power.[40]

As it became clear that Almazán might triumph in the 1940 presidential election, armed conflict accelerated between PRM loyalists and Almazanista forces. In the election itself, the PRM frantically sought to manipulate voting results. It was most successful in doing so in rural areas;

and for that reason, it was able to claim a national electoral triumph. Yet Almazán captured massive support in the country's three principal population centers, Mexico City, Guadalajara, and Monterrey. In Mexico City, home to the largest concentration of state workers and middle classes, the PRM was forced to acknowledge that it had lost overwhelmingly.[41]

Faced with this obvious expression of urban discontent, the PRM now undertook a series of reforms aimed primarily at Mexico City. In April 1941 the party established the Confederación de Organizaciones Populares (COP) to serve as a coordinating body for a wide variety of groups in the capital, including renters, shopkeepers, artisans, and professionals who were excluded from the CTM and the FSTSE. Next, Congress modified the Estatuto Jurídico by expanding the category of workers defined as *trabajadores de confianza* (thus further limiting state workers' right to strike), implemented a new Ley de Servicio Civil that regulated wages, hours, and promotions of *confianza* workers, and reformed an existing Ley de Pensiones Civiles de Retiro in order to guarantee housing for state employees and members of the military. The party also introduced a strict rent control law for Mexico City, which addressed the housing concerns of those not covered by the new laws or previous labor legislation.

The PRM's next task was to reform the party's sectoral structure so as to incorporate the urban poor and middle classes alongside state workers. Because the Mexico City-based COP had served so well as a format for distinct occupational sectors of the urban middle class to participate in local politics, party leaders decided to use the same type of organization on a national scale. At its founding in 1943, this new national organization, the Confederación Nacional de Organizaciones Populares, became the third principal sector of the PRM. It replaced the military and bureaucratic sectors of the PRM and included within it many other predominantly middle- and lower-middle-class groups, such as shopkeepers, street vendors, small industrialists, family farmers, and women's organizations, to name but a few.

Among the CNOP's founding principles were several moderate – if not conservative – tenets that appealed to middle classes, both urban and rural, and that challenged the leftist orientation so evident in Cárdenas's initial class-oriented restructuring of the party in 1938. They included efforts to combat "prejudice and fanaticism" in education, to establish a full range of legal rights for professionals, to protect private property, to support small industry, to guarantee credit to small firms and farms, promote the formation of cooperatives, and to solve the urban housing problem and defend the rights of renters.[42] In stark contrast to the language used by Cárdenas a few years earlier, moreover, President Avila Camacho and party leaders were careful to claim that this new organization represented the "popular *middle* classes" (emphasis added), and by so doing cast their net broadly enough to tap the sentiments of the disenfranchised urban poor and middle classes.

In addition to incorporating middle classes and state workers, the CNOP also functioned as the party organization through which the military participated in national politics. It is commonly assumed by scholars that the military disappeared from party politics starting in 1941, once the military sector was eliminated as an autonomous institutional force in the PRM. But this was true in only a limited sense. Even without their own independent sector in the party, military personnel continued to participate, primarily through the newly formed CNOP; and they did so despite legislation that prevented those on active duty from running for office or participating in politics.[43] Thus after the formal dissolution of the military sector and its delegate bloc in Congress, "the majority [of military delegates] passed on to form part of the popular sector." With such a large number of military delegates adhering to the CNOP, moreover, they "soon acquired a numerical force that, in any given moment, could shift the balance of voting" in Congress.[44] The CNOP's first Secretary General was a military officer, Lieutenant Colonel Antonio Nava Castillo, who openly identified himself as such on party documents; military officers held two of the most criticial posts on the CNOP's National Executive Committee (Secretary of Finance and Secretary of Political Affairs); and a Secretariat of Pre-Military and Sports Activities was created to formalize the military's institutional presence and represent its programmatic concerns within the new "popular" sector.[45]

The CNOP's founding principles and the language with which it was presented to the public underscore the broadly defined common ground on which the self-employed urban poor, middle classes, and even the military could unite behind the party. They also highlight the shared sentiments, priorities, and class consciousness of these groups, much of which was forged in earlier battles over the juridical statute and urban policy. But to recognize this commonality of class identity and political ideology still does not completely explain the ruling party's political successes and the stability of Mexico's uncommon democracy after 1940. It does not explain, for example, why these groups – especially middle-class professionals and the military – would choose to join forces behind the PRM rather than within the right-wing PAN. The latter was not a far-fetched possibility: party documents suggest that the PRM leaders genuinely feared this and that they created the CNOP precisely to "counteract ... the demagogic activities that *sinarquista* leaders had carried out" in tandem with the PAN.[46] Why, moreover, did the political institutionalization of this alliance between middle classes and the military fail to alienate more progressive elements of the PRM, especially those affiliated with the labor sector, who remained loyal as well? After all, the military–middle class alliance produced far-right, if not fascist, rule in many other countries. If labor and peasant sectors had chosen to leave the party once the military and middle classes were institutionally linked to each other, one-party rule would have been unlikely, and disruptive political conflict probably would have continued. These questions suggest that what is still missing from this account is an understanding of why these more conservative social forces would join – and remain – with the PRM rather than the PAN and why the more radical sectors of the party would accept the CNOP as an equal partner within the PRM's formal structure.

BETWEEN COMMUNISM AND FASCISM: THE IMPACT OF THE SECOND WORLD WAR

Part of the answer lies in historical conjuncture and the advent of the Second World War. The war had a direct impact on the organizational successes of the CNOP and the longevity of one-party rule by uniting disparate class and ideological forces against an external enemy. It also limited the possibility of United States support for armed revolt, provided the ideological grounding for a centrist path between communism and fascism, and spurred the economy sufficiently to generate medium-term prosperity, thus sustaining the truce among labor, peasants, and middle classes long enough for Mexico's new party structure to become truly institutionalized.

The impact of the war was first felt in late 1940, after Avila Camacho's electoral triumph against Almazán. Refusing to accept the results of the election, Almazán and several of his military allies retreated north of the Mexican border and regrouped in San Antonio, Texas, where they declared a provisional government and began shipping arms to guerrilla forces in northern Mexico. Their struggle, however, was dependent on at least tacit support from the United States government, and that support was not forthcoming.[47] This was in part the result of Franklin Roosevelt's Good Neighbor Policy, which had foresworn US intervention in Latin America's internal affairs. Even when Cárdenas had expropriated US oil companies in 1938, Roosevelt had resisted domestic pressure to invade Mexico, asking only that the US firms involved be treated fairly. But the outbreak of the war in September 1939 provided further incentives for the

US to strengthen its relations with Mexico's ruling party and reject Almazán's pleas for support. The last thing the US wanted was a burgeoning civil war on its southern border, which would form both a source of instability in the region and an opportunity for "Nazis, Fascists, and Japanese to establish political, economic, and military beachheads in the New World."[48]

Almazán's appeal to Mexico's extreme right wing may also have been a concern to US policymakers. Despite Cárdenas's left-leaning rhetoric and his criticisms of bourgeois democracy, both he and Avila Camacho consistently took a strong public stance against totalitarianism and the imperial objectives of the Axis powers. Almazán, in contrast, was known to count on political support from the neo-fascist Gold Shirts, which hardly endeared him to a government intent on defeating world fascism. Thus the Roosevelt administration was eager to establish positive relations with both outgoing President Cárdenas – who now became Secretary of Defense – and incoming President Avila Camacho.

Although it helped, the US decision to side with the PRM was not enough to quell Almazán's revolt or to eliminate internal political opposition to one-party rule. Throughout 1941, even after Almazán had formally lain down arms, violent conflict continued between pro- and anti-Almazanistas, especially in the provinces.[49] Accordingly, explanations for the return to social calm, political stability, and one-party rule must also consider the Second World War's impact on internal conditions in Mexico.

The outbreak of the war distracted much of the officer corps from party politics, and the PRM leadership actively played this card to its advantage.[50] The government promoted a discourse of anti-imperialism and developed a massive campaign to "militarize" key sectors of civil society, mainly workers in factories, rural peasants, state employees, and local community organizations of *colonos* and *comerciantes*.[51] To militarize meant to teach skills of self-defense and to arm certain key populations; but it also served as a call to national unity, helping to reduce political differences and create solidarity among antagonistic class and social forces. Within the CNOP, this was accomplished through the creation of the 5000-man Civic Guard of the Mexican Revolution, a "semi-military" organization which served as a mechanism to link ideologically the sector's middle-class constituents to the nation's armed forces.[52]

Mexico stayed neutral for the first fifteen months of Avila Camacho's presidency, but when German submarines attacked Mexican ships in the Gulf in May 1942, the loss of Mexican life opened a floodgate of national support for the Allied cause. Thousands of citizens offered to join the

Mexican army, and the public began debating the evils of Nazi imperialism and the importance of national struggles for world democracy. This further united disparate social and class groups in Mexico at a time when continued internal conflict might have irreparably weakened the ruling party's hold on power. It also reduced both the motive and opportunity for military rebellion by fully engaging the armed forces in the privileged mission of national defense. This in turn allowed the PRM leadership to justify the military's organizational existence within the party to progressives and conservatives alike.[53]

One way the military's presence was legitimized was through the project of "militarization," noted above, which broadened the class and social basis of military activity and erased the boundaries between military and civilian groups. Yet party leaders also worked hard to present the armed forces as a democratic and equalizing force in society, introducing a program of military professionalization to help promote this new image. While in the past the army had been comprised of undisciplined renegades representing the "warrior soul of the race," it was now touted as an "institutional body with authentically legitimate and democratic roots ... formed of free and voluntary soldiers conscious of their responsibility" who deserved the "patriotic and enthusiastic" support of all the Mexican people.[54] In its new form, claimed General Felix Ireta, governor of Michoacan, the army "is the most alive, most pure, most perfect image of the Mexican Revolution. In it our workers, our peasants, our citizens of the middle class mix in a spirit of solidarity and fraternity."[55]

The discourse of national unity inspired a common language, somewhere between the rhetorics of communism and fascism, that at least temporarily served to reconcile different ideological tendencies and bring disparate class forces together behind the ruling party. However, the war effort brought much needed internal political peace and stability to Mexico not just because it was ideologically centrist, but also because it brought material results that benefited a wide variety of groups, beginning with the military.

Massive amounts of government resources were poured into special services for the armed forces, from housing to medical care to their own community schools. These benefits pleased almost all groups within the military, giving incentive to both its conservative leaders and the rank and file to remain loyal and work with the party leadership. They also helped establish an organizational logic to unite disparate social forces within the CNOP. For example, the military now joined state employees as the recipients of special housing services. This helped unite the two groups as a common constituency, and explains why provision of housing was a founding principle of the CNOP in 1943. In addition, much of wartime arms and machinery production was undertaken by military cooperatives, formed with government financial support under the guise of programs advanced by the CNOP. These policies brought the military's commitment to cooperatives as well, identified at the CNOP's 1943 founding as a policy issue particularly dear to artisans, small shopkeepers, and rural producers. Finally, much of the government money spent on *colonias militares* supported the establishment of small-scale service and commercial activities run by and for the military. These enterprises further linked the policy and political concerns of the military to those of other key middle-class constituents of the CNOP, like shopkeepers and self-employed artisans, while at the same time eliminating previous tensions between the military and industrial workers over the latter's special claims to social services under Cárdenas.

In addition to the effects of war-related social spending on the CNOP's internal cohesiveness, the war had a powerfully stimulating effect on the national economy as a whole. The United States renegotiated Mexico's foreign debt on highly favorable terms, requiring it to pay only 10 percent of the principal plus interest over a twenty-year period. The US also agreed to an annual purchase of Mexican silver, a $40 million credit to stabilize the peso, a $30 million line of credit at the Export-Import Bank, and a new commercial treaty that granted Mexico most-favored-nation status and that reduced trade barriers on manufactured and agricultural products.[56] New sources of public and private investment flowed from north to south to support infrastructural development (most notably new highway and port construction) and industrial production. Most of Mexico's exports during this period consisted of agricultural produce and textiles. But some of the most impressive growth took place in heavy industries directly involved in the war effort: iron and steel, motor vehicles, armaments, chemicals, and cement.[57]

The long-term effects of these investments would be felt in the import-substitution industrialization of the 1950s and the continuing expansion of the national economy, led in large part by industries that were first developed through the war effort during the early 1940s. It was in political terms, however, that the economic growth stimulated by the war had its greatest payoff, buying precious political time for the still fragile PRM. With new life breathed into the nation's manufacturing sector, for example, capitalists now found a reason to ally with the ruling party and its labor sector. The CTM was willing to go along because of the increased job prospects, and as a consequence the labor movement took a more conciliatory stance towards capitalists and their ideological allies in the middle class. Until the Cold War mentality penetrated Mexico after 1947, the capital–state–labor pact was a relatively successful one that gave the party leadership significant room to maneuver.

Wartime industrial growth, and the promise of more to come, kept the three-tiered party structure intact long enough to institutionalize solid political relations within and between each sector and the party leadership. In the 1946 presidential election, most of Mexico's citizens (77 percent) gave their approval to the party's new profile by supporting its candidate, Miguel Alemán, who promised to maintain good relations with the U.S. as he led Mexico down the path of rapid industrialization. The first civilian president of Mexico since 1911, Alemán came to office with particularly strong support from middle classes and the military. Labor, in contrast, split over his candidacy, with some of the most left-leaning sectors leaving the party to form the Partido Popular Socialista. Still, most of the labor movement stayed loyal, as did the peasant sector. This broad base of political support kept Alemán and subsequent party leaders loyal to the centrist politics and industrialization programs so successfully implemented during the war. The result: three and a half decades of unprecedented domestic peace, economic growth, and continued citizen support for the party responsible for both.

DEMOCRACY IN MEXICO? SOME CONCLUDING REMARKS

This examination of the period between 1936 and 1946 suggests that unprecedented political stability and the consolidation of civilian, one-party rule in Mexico were not an inevitable byproduct of the nation's revolutionary heritage. Rather, Mexico's unique political profile is owed in no small part to middle-class political allegiance and to the elimination of the Mexican military as a threatening and independent political force. Both of these outcomes were directly linked to the foundation of the CNOP; and this, in turn, can be traced to a common consciousness shared by the military and middle classes that pushed the party to extend its institutional arms beyond peasants and industrial laborers toward these middle sectors, and to the ideological and economic consequences of the Second World War, which linked the military and middle sectors to each other and to other class forces within the ruling party.

The establishment of the CNOP and its acceptance by other sectors of society signaled a critical turning point in the consolidation of Mexico's uncommon democracy. After 1943, Mexico's ruling party followed a much more centrist political path. It began to run the country with an eye to the concerns and demands of a wide variety of classes and social groups, not just labor, peasants, and bureaucrats, as had occurred before 1940 under President Cárdenas. This in turn meant that the party could not so easily be maligned for class bias or exclusivity, or even an anti-democratic character, since it now opened its arms to all.

The accommodation of middle classes and military personnel in the ruling party and the ideological centrism it produced paid off both politically and economically. With such a broad class-base of political support, not only did President Avila Camacho enjoy much greater legitimacy than Cárdenas; military opposition also was effectively squelched. Even more important, with the ruling party no longer seen as a conglomeration of revolutionary radicals beholden to labor and the peasantry, it also was capable of establishing a more collaborative, less volatile relationship with the country's capitalist class. Public and private capital flowing into Mexico during the war under the banner of continental solidarity set a solid industrial and infrastructural foundation for much needed economic growth. These strategic investments and the possibility of future prosperity gave domestic capitalists further incentive to support the PRI. And all this created a most uncommon democracy in Mexico: free of the threat of military rule, blessed with political stability and regular elections, political participation from a full range of social classes, yet all under the auspices of one-party rule.

At the outset of this chapter we argued that Mexico differs from other uncommon democracies because it lacks competitive party politics. The evidence presented here, however, suggests that something else is exceptional about Mexico: its institutional capacity to include middle classes, as organizationally distinct, within its corporatist structures of political participation. This may be what best explains Mexico's tremendous successes as an uncommon democracy and differentiates it from other corporatist regimes in Latin America, Europe, and Asia. Corporatism differs in Mexico because middle classes have their own institutional structure of participation within the larger system. Countries like Brazil and Argentina have used corporatist institutions mainly to structure their relationships with labor, leaving their middle classes to use parties or other mechanisms to press demands on the state. This has contributed to instability and frequent regime change, up to and including what scholars like José Nun have called middle-class military coups, in which the armed forces ally with dissatisfied or disenfranchised middle classes.

This is not to say that Mexico has avoided this path and achieved political stability because middle classes are more democratic social forces, or even more centrist by nature. Mexico has been successful in establishing political stability and a quasi-democratic character because middle-class inclusion occurred hand in hand with the inclusion of other classes and with the military. That is, it is the timing, nature, and broader class context of middle-class inclusion, and not their demands *per se*, that brings an uncommonly democratic process and content to politics in Mexico. This observation is lent credence by the crisis of one-party rule during the 1980s, a period when middle-class lifestyles, work prospects, and identities were seriously undermined. During the economic boom of the 1970s and the depression of the 1980s, the nation's middle classes were torn apart, some experiencing remarkable upward mobility, others pulled downward into proletarianization. This fragmentation gradually undid the carefully crafted relationship between middle-class identity and the organizational structure of the CNOP, with the result that the confederation was abolished in 1990.[58] This was the first institutional transformation in the structure of Mexican corporatism since 1943. Although it is too early to gauge the political consequences of this development, one can only wonder whether one-party rule, and thus Mexico's uncommon democracy itself, will be next.

NOTES

1. Mexico's Partido Nacional Revolucionario (PNR) was founded in 1929. With much of the same political leadership, the PNR was then transformed into the Partido de la Revolución Mexicana (PRM) in 1938 and eventually into the Partido Revolucionario Institucional (PRI) in 1946.

2. T.J. Pempel, *Uncommon Democracies: The One-Party Dominant Regimes* (Ithaca, 1990).

3. Alain Rouquié, *The Military and the State in Latin America* (Berkeley, 1987).

4. For a listing of the different occupations grouped within the CNOP, see Partido Revolucionario Institucional, *Historia documental de la CNOP*, vol. 1 (Mexico, 1984), 76.

5. Edwin Lieuwen, *Mexican Militarism: The Political Rise and Fall of the Revolutionary Army, 1910–1940* (Albuquerque, 1968); Jorge Alberto Lozoya, *El ejército mexicano* (Mexico, 1970); and Lyle N. McAlister *et al.*, *The Military in Latin American Sociopolitical Evolution: Four Case Studies* (Washington, DC, 1970).

6. Soledad Loaeza, *Clases medias y política en México* (Mexico, 1988).

7. Arnaldo Córdova, *La política de masas del cardenismo* (Mexico, 1974), 133; Pablo González Casanova, *El estado y los partidos políticos en Mexico* (Mexico, 1981), 124; Luis Javier Garrido, *El partido de la revolución*

institucionalizada: La formación del nuevo estado en México, 1928–1945 (Mexico, 1982), 305, 319, 323.

8. José Luis Reyna, "Control político, estabilidad y desarrollo en México," *Cuadernos del Centro de Estudios Sociológicos* (Mexico, 1974); José Luis Reyna and Richard Weinert, eds., *Authoritarianism in Mexico* (Philadelphia, 1977); Susan Kaufman Purcell, *The Mexican Profitsharing Decision: Politics in an Authoritarian Regime* (Berkeley, 1975).

9. Ignacio Marván, *La clase obrera en la historia de México: En el cardenismo (1934–1940)* (Mexico, 1985), 150.

10. For useful treatments of this period, see Nora Hamilton, *The Limits of State Autonomy: Post-Revolutionary Mexico* (Princeton, 1982) and Alan Knight, "The Rise and Fall of Cardenismo, 1930–1946," in Leslie Bethell, ed., *The Cambridge History of Latin America*, vol. 7 (Cambridge and New York, 1990).

11. During the 1930s, artisans and craftsmen frequently filled the ranks of the urban poor or so-called "popular" classes. They were employed in low-paying, unprotected jobs in small enterprises; and as factory industrialization advanced, they faced declining job security.

12. Archivo General de la Nación Mexicana (hereafter AGNM), Galería de Presidentes (Cárdenas), expediente 437.1/512.

13. Loaeza, *Clases medias*, 96.

14. AGNM, Galería de Presidentes (Cárdenas), exp. 437.1/512.

15. Among those who joined the Alianza in this second stage were those employed in the state-controlled telegraph industry, street maintenance workers, postal workers, employees in several government ministries (foreign relations, the treasury, public education, and *gobernación*), as well as office workers in the Mexico City municipal government.

16. When state personnel explicitly identified themselves as workers, or *obreros*, they used a strict labor–capital analogy and saw the state as similar to other employers. Sometimes state workers identified themselves as "*obreros profesionales*," who nonetheless had "proletarian aspirations and objectives." AGNM, Galería de Presidentes (Cárdenas), letter from the Unión General de Trabajadores de los Establecimientos Fabriles (20 Aug. 1935), exp. 437/104.

17. One 1936 document, arguing for state workers' right to strike, claimed that in many offices state workers were treated without respect – no better than "household help" – and asked to perform personal services at the whim of their supervisors. AGNM, Galería de Presidentes (Cárdenas), exp. 545.2/1.

18. For a detailed account of conflicts among state workers within one government agency, see Instituto Nacional de Estudios Históricos de la Revolución Mexicana, *Historia del Sindicato Nacional de Trabajadores de la Secretaría de Gobernación* (Mexico, 1986).

19. AGNM, Galería de Presidentes (Avila Camacho), Situación Jurídica de los Secretarios de Estudio y Cuenta de la Suprema Corte de Justicia de la Nación, exp. 542.2/10. The statute was eventually approved, with some modifications, as the Estatuto de los Trabajadores al Servicio de los Poderes de la Unión. See *Diario Oficial* (5 Dec. 1938).

20. Carmen Nava Nava, *Ideología del Partido de la Revolución Mexicana*, vol. 1 (Mexico, 1984), 286–7.

21. Lucio Mendieta y Núñez, *La administración pública en México* (Mexico, 1942), 181. Among workers categorized as *trabajadores de base* were those employed in the Dirección General de Materiales de Guerra, which reported directly to the Secretary of Defense.

22. A 31 Jan. 1938 document from the Frente Revolucionario de Intelectuales, signed by representatives from several organizations of state workers, health professionals, and artists, applauded Cárdenas for moves that appeared "to integrate a PARTY OF WORKERS AND SOLDIERS." AGNM, Galería de Presidentes (Cárdenas), exp. 544.61/103.

23. Pablo González Casanova, *El estado y los partidos políticos en México* (Mexico, 1981), 120; Nava Nava, *Ideología del Partido*, vol. 1, 67; Lozoya, *El ejército mexicano*, 66.

24. This was also the case with family farmers and agricultural producers in the provinces, who tended to ally with regional military elites in opposition to Cárdenas's agrarian reforms. These agriculturalists saw as threatening any reforms intended to educate and empower the military rank and file, since it was comprised mainly of poor peasants from rural areas who might challenge local elites' social and political power if not kept under tight rein.

25. Garrido, *El partido de la revolución institucionalizada*, 305.

26. McAlister, *The Military in Latin American Sociopolitical Evolution*, 203. Cárdenas found it necessary to create agrarian militias because regional military elites and provincial agriculturalists were carrying out an armed campaign of terror and violence against rural *campesinos* during the late 1930s.

27. September 1939 letter from General Heriberto Jara, President of the Central Committee of the PRM, AGNM, Galería de Presidentes (Cárdenas), exp. 708.1/19; Córdova, *La política de masas*, 140.

28. Córdova, *La política de masas*, 84. Cárdenas began to use the term "popular" in 1936, when he and party allies promoted a Frente Popular Mexicano within the PNR to bring peasants and laborers together with other social and class forces to strengthen the party against internal and external opposition. See Marván, *La clase obrera en la historia de México*, 238–301.

29. In this 14-page document, the popular sector is the only one which has no organizations listed under its heading. AGNM, Galería de Presidentes (Cárdenas), report from Elias Campos V. to Comité Nacional del PRM, exp. 544.61/103.

30. It is only in late 1939 that one finds any clear evidence of organized middle-class groups outside the bureaucracy proclaiming allegiance to the popular sector of the PRM. Many of these groups appear to have been organized by the party leaders themselves in response to growing social unrest and clear public support for Almazán's candidacy.

31. The inverse occasionally occurred as well, with conservative employees undertaking disruptive actions against leftist agency administrators. See AGNM, Galería de Presidentes (Cárdenas), letter to President Lázaro Cárdenas from the Congregación Ortíz, Municipio de Rosales (12 Jan. 1939), exp. 544.61/103.

32. *El Universal* (4 Jan. 1938), 3.

33. Manuel Perlo Cohen, *El cardenismo y la Ciudad de México: Historia de un conflicto* (Mexico, 1988), 7.

34. Perlo Cohen, *El cardenismo y la Ciudad de México*, 5.

35. AGNM, Galería de la Dirección General de Gobierno, Series 2, 331.9 (29) exp. 14.

36. Perlo Cohen, *El cardenismo y la Ciudad de México*, 38.

37. Ariel José Contreras, *México: Industrialización y crisis política* (Mexico, 1977), 143.

38. *El Universal* (5 Sept. 1939), 1.

39. AGNM, Galería de Presidentes (Cárdenas), letter from Ignacio García Telléz, Secretaría de Gobernación, to Dr. José Siurub, Jefe del Departamento de Salubridad Pública (14 Aug. 1939), exp. 531.2.

40. Contreras, *Mexico*, 140.

41. For detailed analysis of the election fraud, see Luis Medina Peña, *Historia de la revolución mexicana: Del cardenismo a avilacamachismo* (Mexico, 1976).

42. Confederación Nacional de Organizaciones Populares, *Primer Consejo Nacional* (Mexico, 1944), 2–4.

43. Frequently, military personnel simply took leave from active military service for the duration of their involvement in Congress or party politics, only to return once their term ended. For discussion of this and other ways in which military personnel bypassed constitutional regulations and actively participated in politics during the 1940s, see Rafael Coronado Barajas, *De las limitaciones impuestas al militar para actuar en política* (Mexico, 1949), 60–4.

44. Partido Revolucionario Institucional, *Historia documental de la CNOP*, vol. 1, 44, 45.

45. Confederación Nacional de Organizaciones Populares, *Primer consejo* (n.p.).

46. Partido Revolucionario Institucional, *Historia documental de la CNOP*, vol. 1, 62–3.

47. Lieuwen, *Mexican Militarism*, 138.

48. Charles D. Porter and Robert J. Alexander, *The Struggle for Democracy in Latin America* (New York, 1961), 184.

49. AGNM, Galería de Presidentes (Cárdenas), exp. 556.6/28; Galería de Presidentes (Avila Camacho), exp. 703.2/7.

50. Lieuwen, *Mexican Militarism*, 143.

51. AGNM, Galería de Presidentes (Avila Camacho), exps. 545.2/14-1 and 545.2/80.

52. Confederación Nacional de Organizaciones Populares, *Delegados de la Federación de Organizaciones Populares del D.F. en el Primer Consejo Nacional de la CNOP* (Mexico, 1944), 36.

53. By late 1941, even the right-wing Gold Shirts who had strongly supported Almazán now "frankly and loyally" pledged their cooperation with the governing PRM "for the patriotic good;" although this did not stop them in their search for "communist elements" inside the country's borders. AGNM, Galería de Presidentes (Avila Camacho), exp. 550/24.

54. AGNM, Galería de Presidentes (Avila Camacho), exp. 135.2/206.

55. AGNM, Galería de Presidentes (Avila Camacho), exp. 135.21/29.

56. Blanca Torres, *Historia de la revolucíon mexicana: México en la segunda guerra mundial* (Mexico, 1979), 37, 58, 160.

57. Alexander and Porter, *The Struggle for Democracy*, 184.
58. For an elaboration of these changes in the present period, see Diane E. Davis, "Urban Social Movements, Intrastate Conflicts Over Urban Policy, and Political Change in Mexico," *Comparative Urban and Community Research*, 3 (1990): 133–63.

Part Three
Democratic Movements, 1945–1990

8 Race, Equity, and Democracy: African Americans and the Struggle over Civil Rights

Earl Lewis

We have all heard the question asked before: "What does the Negro want?" In behavior, speech, folk traditions, and popular presentations, African Americans at different times and in different places have issued an answer to America's most vexing query. Writing on the eve of this country's entrance into the Second World War, Langston Hughes answered for himself and – we are led to believe – "thirteen million other American Negroes." Hughes's answer is simple: "[T]hey are the things any self-respecting citizen of the United States desires for himself regardless of color." He listed seven specific wants:

(1)   "a chance to earn a decent living";
(2)   "equal educational opportunities all over America";
(3)   "decent housing";
(4)   "full participation in Government";
(5)   "a fair deal before the law";
(6)   "public courtesy, the same courtesy normally accorded other citizens"; and
(7)   "we want social equality in so far as public services go."

"We want nothing not compatible with democracy and the Constitution," he concluded.[1]

The elimination of the visible signs of segregation between 1954 and 1968 followed an intense period of social activism and ostensibly rendered moot the question of what the Negro wanted. Henceforth, many hoped, African Americans would enjoy the rights and privileges bestowed on all Americans. Within a decade, prompted by claims equating affirmative action with affirmative discrimination, the country would find itself traumatized by a new and equally vexing set of questions about race, equity, and democracy.[2]

This chapter explores contemporary questions about race and democracy by exploring the meaning of equality for the generation of Americans who protested, went to jail, and contested conventions between the mid-1950s and late 1960s. After all, although African Americans had long challenged society's strictures, for a decade and a half the world witnessed one of the most sustained social, democratic movements in history. The successes of those efforts followed the maturation of the African American community's civil rights infrastructure, a significant demographic transition, and – for a moment at least – the clear articulation of a shared vision of democracy, a socially constructed vision.[3] This shared vision of democracy, expressed most powerfully and eloquently in the songs and speeches of the civil rights era, also exposed a deep rift in the polity, a rift that makes the question answered by Langston Hughes as powerful a concern today as it was half a century ago.

TOWARD AN UNDERSTANDING

The story of what blacks want, and how those desires became part of the social construction of democracy, dates from the signing of the Declaration of Independence and ratification of the Bill of Rights. These framing documents of the new republic expose in rare form the contradictory messages of life in an imperfect democracy. Freedom, according to Orlando Patterson, became slavery's companion, even as the notion of freedom became the core intellectual value of Western culture. Yet the men who wrote the Declaration of Independence, the Constitution, and the Bill of Rights consciously dodged the central question: how do we simultaneously reconcile slavery and freedom? They ducked the issue because owning slaves marked their own success, and few wanted to forego engaging in what Jefferson labeled the "execrable commerce." Fewer yet viewed Africans and African Americans as their social equals. Like many of his peers, "Jefferson," writes David Brion Davis, "had only a theoretical interest in promoting the cause of abolition."[4]

African Americans tapped an equally powerful impulse. From Perry Miller to Sacvan Berkovitch, intellectual historians have pondered Americans' belief in justice. Miller, and later Berkovitch, traced this tradition to the theological and philosophical perspectives of the Puritans. Political outsiders in Europe, these erstwhile social reformers associated the Old World with decadence, disease – profanity. The New World became a shining city on a hill, a beacon and harbinger of a more perfect union. Their journey to this unformed wilderness became a pilgrimage and the myth of America began. The political sermon or jeremiad surfaced as the chief vehicle for reminding others of their obligation to mold the shapeless, to transform the wilderness without contaminating its purity. And this myth of state-building, shaped by a broad set of cultural symbols, guides the national sense to this day.[5]

Moses, Blight, and Howard-Pitney have examined the African-American variant of this national myth.[6] Bear in mind, however, that for African Americans the consequences of an imperfect union could not be limited to philosophical exigencies. The imperfections were deadly. The Age of Revolution, after all, nakedly exposed the raw nerve of race. Rather than excise the cancer of human suffering, eighteenth-century republicans opted to prolong the agony. Blacks in America commented on the contradictions. But, as Howard-Pitney observes, the "black jeremiad tradition conceives of blacks as a chosen people *within* a chosen people."[7] African Americans remained forever hopeful that conditions would improve, that social justice would buy them peace and security in the land of plenty. In the process, they became partial architects of the construction that defined African-descended people as Negro, as black.

One of the central ironies of twentieth-century American history has been the use of race to erase considerable diversity. Race, the ultimate trope, created "the Negro" from the mosaic of people of African descent. Whites saw and blacks asserted a unanimity even when another reality better approximated the lived experiences of most. Beginning with the first attempts to codify a system of racial difference in the seventeenth century, through the *Dred Scott* decision of 1857, the 1896 *Plessy* decision, and a number of Jim Crow era ordinances and court decisions, the state played a central role in establishing "race" as an important category. In most instances, African people were defined as the "other." Therefore, even to ask what the Negro wanted was part of a larger strategy to define African Americans as marginal, the ultimate outsiders.[8]

The process of racial labeling had the added effect of creating a collectivity or group from the disparate communities representing African Americans. When called on to defend their place in America, to articulate their vision of America, they were no longer Masons or Elks, Baptists or Methodists, rich or poor. Certainly these differences remained, but they ceased to be the defining factors. A history of slavery and oppression, as well as cultural manifestations like folk tales, music, and language, created the contours of an "imagined community," as Benedict Anderson has noted in a different context. No person of African descent could admit to knowing all other members of his or her group; yet they imagined a connection, one born of their place in the social order.[9] This membership in an imagined community played a central role in the social construction of a racial identity. It also helped forge a sustained assault on racial segregation and on anti-democratic actions more generally.

Still, the attack on subordination seldom surrendered to an attack on the promise of democracy. Men and women of prominence and obscurity used the expanding institutional infrastructure in the black community to lay claim to a better America. Sometimes they were strident in their opposition and turned outside for direction and comfort, as in Langston Hughes's poignant yet controversial 1934 poem, "One More 'S' in the USA." More publicly than most, he turned to the Soviet Union for guidance and inspiration during the 1930s. Yet even Hughes held tenaciously to the promise of American democracy as he criticized the ugly harshness of the American present. In an earlier poem, that "depart[ed] from Walt Whitman's celebrated chant," he pleaded, "I, Too, Sing America." After recalling his treatment as a stranger in his own land, Hughes ended the poem with the reminder: "I, too, am America."[10]

This claim of a birthright focused the activities of thousands of black Americans between the 1930s and 1950s. A frontal attack on the edifice of Jim Crow began in earnest in the 1930s, after more than a generation of concerted institution-building. Between 1890 and 1930 dozens of societies, clubs, organizations, and associations sprang to life across Black America. Some appeared and disappeared with little notice; others started slowly and gained momentum and endurance. There were fraternal organizations like the Elks, Masons, and Daughters of the Forest; financial institutions like the Order of Saint Luke, North Carolina Mutual Life Insurance Company, and the Chicago-based Binga Bank; newspapers like the *Chicago Defender*, *Pittsburgh Courier*, *Baltimore Afro-American*, *Washington Bee*, and *Norfolk Journal and Guide*, among others; labor associations like the Transportation Workers Association, an all-black labor body in Virginia, the Brotherhood of Sleeping Car Porters, and black locals of national labor bodies; and civil rights organizations like the National Association for the Advancement of Colored People (NAACP), the National Urban League (NUL), and National Association of Colored Women (NACW).[11] With a few noticeable exceptions, most sought to improve conditions in the household and community (home sphere). Of course this does not imply that leaders or members of the organizations ignored work and labor conditions. On numerous occasions the well-being of black workers was advanced as a central element of any improvement in status. Rather, through the 1930s, improved living conditions and greater access to social and civic services received greater attention. More organizations, for example, concentrated on anti-lynching legislation than collective bargaining legislation.[12]

The NAACP, founded in 1910 to help ameliorate the nation's worsening race relations, played a leading role nationally. For several years, historians writing about black political and social activism have distinguished between the so-called direct-action phase of the 1950s and 1960s and the gradualist phase led by the NAACP from the 1910s through 1954. The NAACP was both lauded and castigated for adopting a dogged civil libertarian approach predicated on the gradual elimination of racial discrimination. Much has been written about the team of William Hastie, Thurgood Marshall, Jack Greenberg, Leon Ransom and others who systematically attacked the legality of segregation beginning in 1917 and continuing well beyond the landmark *Brown* decision, which ruled separate but equal unconstitutional.[13] For more than three decades the NAACP combatted segregation in housing and on public conveyances, desegregated graduate and professional schools, ended the practice of the white primary, and litigated on behalf of equal pay for equal work.

As they grew in status and in membership, the national office and its locals increasingly blurred the lines between direct action and gradualism. Starting with its first branch in Chicago, by 1921 the NAACP reported more than four hundred branches nationwide; as of 1940, the Association reported 481 branches, 77 youth councils, and 22 college chapters, with approximately 85,000 members.[14] Rather than following a national policy or a regional predisposition, these local branches displayed considerable autonomy. Some remained steadfastly conservative, while others moved well ahead of the national office. Branch members organized "don't buy where you can't work" campaigns, registered and organized voters, and spoke out against grievous acts of racism. Harry T. Moore of Florida, for example, championed a more aggressive approach and gave his life in the process. A high school principal, Moore spearheaded the Association's activities on behalf of equal pay for black school teachers, and was a forceful and vocal opponent of segregation and the broad range of racial and social inequities that it produced. In a period when the number of public lynchings decreased in the South, public assassinations became more common. Moore and his wife died in December 1952 when a bomb planted in their home exploded.[15]

Who belonged may not be as fine a barometer as who sought the NAACP's help and what they wanted. In many instances their pleas for help, given the social milieu, amounted to a form of direct action. The legal arm of the Association received hundreds of letters from average citizens who believed they had been wronged. A domestic in Baton Rouge,

Louisiana, complained of being physically assaulted by a white employer. A mother and son wanted to sue a Philadelphia hospital because an emergency room doctor attended the needs of a white female patient whose condition was less critical and who had arrived after them.[16]

Others wanted their property and persons protected. Typical was a 1945 letter from Virginia Tate, an eighth-grader in Nebo, North Carolina, and the fifth oldest of eleven children who ranged in age from seven to 25. Her three older brothers were in uniform, her mother languished in an insane asylum, and her uneducated but hardworking father had limited resources. Through a teacher she learned of the NAACP and wrote the national office, asking for help. On a recent night unknown assailants had torched the car of her older brother, who was stationed in France. The family lacked solid proof but believed envious white neighbors guilty of the deed. Her father, however, feared further retribution if they contacted the authorities. Virginia wrote New York:

> My father seems afraid to tackle and to be frank because he fears that they might come and burned [*sic*] us up alive[.] Will you please advise what we can do about this[?] We are wondering if there are any legal steps that we can do or take to have those punished or replace the car that my brother worked so hard in the coal mines of West Virginia to buy. To tell the truth we are desperate and do not know what to do. Will you please advise us?[17]

Knowing the dangers that lurked, the national office advised her to contact the local authorities, nonetheless. In an attempt to lessen the isolating effect of its recommendation, the Association promised to help if further violence occurred. National and local officials knew – like the scores of members and non-members who sought their help – that more was at stake than justice. They sought an equitable society, which required certain risks. Such risks were part of a process of social change, one informed by an abiding belief in the promise of democracy.

WAR, RACE, AND DEMOCRACY

A complex but interrelated array of factors gave form to the post-Second World War phase in the African American search for empowerment. Most noticeable was growing awareness of the international features of racism. Prior to the war black nationalist leader Marcus Garvey and his Universal Negro Improvement Association (UNIA) energized and galvanized approximately two million members throughout the African diaspora.

Through much of the 1920s, until his arrest, conviction, imprisonment, and deportation from the United States for mail fraud, Garvey and the UNIA called special attention to the interrelated plights of blacks world-wide.[18]

After the Second World War racism and colonialism became linked in a way that profoundly altered the world's map. First, the horrifying details of Nazi atrocities fueled the charge that European overlordship was bankrupt. Leading African-descended intellectuals linked Nazism to colonialism. For more than four decades Africans, Afro-West Indians, and African Americans had been meeting at Pan African Congresses to discuss their similar fates. During that period a number of Africans came to and were trained at historically black colleges and universities in the United States, including Howard and Lincoln, where they experienced the sting of American racism firsthand.[19] Therefore, Aimé Césaire's *Discourse on Colonialism* (1955) struck a responsive chord throughout the "colored" world. The Martinique-born poet and essayist, along with Léopold Senghor of Senegal (who became that country's first post-colonial leader) and Léon Damas of French Guiana, are considered the midwives of *Négritude*, the movement to reject European aesthetics and assert the value and beauty of African art forms and an African consciousness. The new emphasis had a great effect on a growing nationalist consciousness throughout sub-Saharan Africa. In indicting colonialism, Césaire insisted that "colonization works to decivilize the colonizer, to brutalize him in the true sense of the word ..." The West, he concluded, found Hitler's acts so atrocious because "he applied to Europe colonialist procedures which until then had been reserved exclusively for the Arabs of Algeria, the coolies of India, and the blacks of Africa."[20]

Second, the creation of the United Nations elevated the importance of human rights and showcased the contradictions between the American ideal and its less noble reality. Meeting in 1945 in San Francisco, delegates hammered out the preamble that affirmed the fundamental rights of all people of the world. With African American Ralph Bunche as a key member of the US delegation, and many black papers sending reporters to cover the event, the creation of this new organization received sustained coverage across Black America. Many were delighted when the preamble promised a commitment to "fundamental human rights, in the dignity and worth of the human person, in the equal rights of men and women and of nations large and small" as well as "[u]niversal respect for, and observance of, human rights and fundamental freedoms for all without distinction to race, language, or religion."[21]

Concurrently a demographic transition accelerated the pace of domestic change and gave birth to new organizations that rivalled and complemented the NAACP. Farley and Allen estimate that nearly three million blacks left the South during the period 1940–1960. Another 1.3 million left between 1960 and 1970, for a total of approximately 4.3 million. Many moved to urban-industrial centers in the North, Midwest, and West just as the economy began the awkward and uneven shift from the production of goods to the production of services.[22]

This urbanizing black population, radicalized by the experience of fighting for a war for democracy, openly expressed new expectations and created new institutions. With labor leader and longtime socialist A. Philip Randolph at its helm, the March on Washington Movement (MOWM) forced President Franklin Delano Roosevelt to sign Executive Order 8802, which prohibited discriminatory hiring practices at all national defense sites. The order led to the creation of the President's Committee on Fair Employment Practices (FEPC), which investigated charges of job discrimination at federal installations. Presaging a later event that would concretize the dreams of a generation, Randolph and others threatened a massive march on Washington in 1941 to dramatize the discordance between the promise and actuality of democracy in the United States, and "to secure full integration of Negro citizens into all phases of American life on par with other citizens."[23]

This and other acts heralded a new chapter in American race relations. A youth culture produced the image of the zoot suiter who was unwilling to compromise: a generation of youth like Malcolm X, who sought to avoid the constraints of wage labor. Meanwhile, coalitions of blacks and whites formed groups like the Congress for Racial Equality (CORE), which tried non-violent civil disobedience as a tool of social change.[24] As Paula Pfeffer has observed, the MOWM, CORE, and other groups signaled the coming of age of a cadre of black leaders determined to break the traditional client–patron relationship. Randolph's threatened march "introduced new rules into the old clientage politics game. Blacks were not supposed to make demands; they had always begged in the past."[25]

A simultaneous transformation occurred in the urban South. Between 1900 and 1920 more than 1.5 million African Americans left the rural South. More than half settled in the region's growing urban centers.[26] This growth accelerated after 1940, as blacks poured into defense centers like Norfolk and Mobile. They entered border cities like Washington, Louisville, and Baltimore. And thousands settled in the region's towns and cities, often the sites of major confrontations during the struggle over civil rights. Between 1940 and 1960, the black populations of Montgomery and Birmingham jumped 84 and 40 percent, respectively. During the same period Baton Rouge experienced more than a 300 percent increase in its black population.

In Washington the proportion of blacks in the city surged from 28 to 54 percent between 1940 and 1960, and in Baltimore from 20 to 35 percent.[27]

There were several immediate consequences of black migration to the region's cities. First, although disproportionately working class, blacks did realize an increase in earnings, narrowing the racial gap. In 1939 black men earned on average 41 percent of what white men earned, while black women earned 36 percent of what white women earned. By 1959 black men earned 47 percent as much as white men and black women received $0.62 for every dollar earned by white women. This national pattern was roughly repeated in the South. Black men earned a median income of $2,800, or 43 percent as much as white men in 1939; twenty years later they took home a median income of $5,900, or 47 percent as much as white men. Black women received a median income of $1,400 in 1939, or 31 percent as much as white women, and $2,600 in 1959, or 56 percent of the earnings of white women.[28] If we could separate urban from rural figures the gap would narrow further. Thus when economic boycotts were planned and executed in Baton Rouge, Montgomery and other cities in the region, they had a greater likelihood of being successful, reflecting the growth in the real and symbolic buying power of blacks.[29]

Second, black migration to Southern cities had a profound effect on the social construction of democracy and the issue of empowerment. For too long Rosa Parks's defiant act – the decision to ignore Montgomery bus segregation ordinances – that precipitated the 1954 Montgomery Bus Boycott appeared as an *immaculate conception*. Few scholars were aware of the daily resistance of black bus riders during the 1940s in the port city of Norfolk, Virginia or the industrial center of Birmingham, Alabama. The 1940s as a decade of planning in Baton Rouge, Birmingham, Winston-Salem and elsewhere went unnoticed as well.[30]

Yet during the Second World War African Americans in these and other cities across the South mounted daily assaults on the conventions of Jim Crow; they did so because they continually constructed an inclusive definition of democracy. As John H. Lewis, secretary of the Portsmouth, Virginia, Young Men's Civic Organization insisted:

> We as colored Americans know the law and we know right from wrong. We also know when we are treated wrong. We do not like to be treated wrong. We do not like to be made the victims of unfair court rulings … Several of the young men of our organization who are interested in this problem are now serving with the armed forces of America. They are fighting for democracy abroad. But what shall we tell them of Democracy at home?[31]

Such thought and action were very visible in Montgomery, often viewed as the birthplace of the "modern" civil rights movement. Capital of Alabama and the "Cradle of the Confederacy," Montgomery looked like a number of other medium-sized Southern cities. Racial protocol governed intergroup behavior; most whites believed that blacks knew their places, and at least publicly, few blacks did little to rob whites of this sense of comfort. But away from the spotlight residents like Rosa Parks attended workshops at the Highlander Folk School, headed by Myles Horton, in Monteagle, Tennessee. The school, which trained workers in Appalachia and later civil rights activists, showed citizens how to effect social change and empower themselves. There Parks learned the "strength to persevere in my work for freedom, not just for blacks but all oppressed people." On another front, community activist and local NAACP head E.D. Nixon belonged to the Brotherhood of Sleeping Car Porters, the country's most well known all-black union. His activities on the railroad plugged him into a regional and national network of blacks determined to change conditions.[32]

A number of reminiscences, essays, and articles have documented the essential roles played by African American women in the struggles of the 1950s and 1960s. According to Charles Payne, men may have led the movement, but women were the primary organizers in the Mississippi Delta, reflecting their key roles in central community institutions like churches.[33] Jo Ann Robinson and Mary Fair Burks have documented the response of women in Montgomery to the entreaties of social activists like Reverend Vernon Johns. Johns, who preceded Martin Luther King at Dexter Avenue Baptist Church, was a visionary who found segregation morally reprehensible and the quiescence of middle-class blacks unconscionable. Burks maintains that it was Johns's challenge, and her own experience of humiliation and degradation upon her return South, that led her to found the Women's Political Council, the organization that mobilized the black community to boycott the buses.[34]

Mary Burks founded the Women's Political Council in 1946 after a particularly harsh encounter with Montgomery's Police Department. A college graduate with advanced training from the University of Michigan, Burks returned to teach in the high school program at Alabama State, where she met and married her former professor and the school's principal. Comfortably sequestered in the black middle class, Burks knew that her social position protected but did not exclude her from the daily harshness of life in a Jim Crow city. One day she had an unplanned encounter with a white female pedestrian who entered the crosswalk as Burks, sitting in her car, began to accelerate. Black automobile owners were not uncommon in the urban South after the war; but the car did serve as an immediate marker of her status. This, however, did not prevent her arrest. "When the woman was located and pressured into making charges, I tried to explain that it was she, not I, using profanity, but I was stopped by a policeman's billy club," writes Burks.

The episode, including her white lawyer's ability to literally tear up the charges and have her released, reminded Burks that race narrowed the social divide between blacks of different socioeconomic levels. Despite her middle-class status, because race overshadowed other categories, Burks shared much with the black domestics who rode the buses and who suffered the near daily indignity of verbal and racial abuse. In response Burks formed an organization to improve conditions for *all* blacks.[35]

Yet Burks's efforts would have been for naught without the combination of changes which accompanied formal organization of the Council. Previous boycotts had been tried in Baton Rouge, details of which Montgomery residents knew. As important, the women in the Council had called for the hiring of black policemen and questioned the legality of the segregation ordinances for some time; they were just waiting for the right moment and the right individual to come forth. Finally, the rapid increase in the black population proved especially important. Blacks, particularly black women, relied on the bus for transportation to and from work, and as a group they accounted for a large percentage of bus riders.[36]

Thus when Council members heard of Parks's act they quickly mobilized the community, mimeographing more than 35,000 handbills calling for a mass meeting and a boycott of city buses. On the first day and many days thereafter up to 90 percent of those who normally rode the buses found other means of transportation. As later events demonstrated, so many blacks had suffered at the hands of arrogant and vicious bus drivers and bigoted white officers that the call struck a responsive chord throughout the community. Some were no doubt surprised that the boycott lasted more than a year. As Martin Luther King intoned during the initial meeting of the boycott movement, "There comes a time when people get tired. We are here this evening to say to those who have mistreated us so long that we are tired – tired of being segregated and humiliated, tired of being kicked about by the brutal feet of oppression."[37]

EQUITY, EQUALITY AND THEIR MEANING

During the 1950s and 1960s, in verse, song, and speech, blacks told the nation similarly. Their vision of life in a democratic society included justice, freedom, equality, and ultimately, equity. Equity meant more than equal opportunity; it meant some conscious attention to the legacy of discrimination and remedial actions to address those lasting disparities. Much later activists would invoke the image of a 400-meter race. Because the starting positions are staggered, at first glance the inside runner appears to have a disadvantage. However, the advantage is an illusion; without staggering the lanes, the outside runner would actually have to cover more territory to win the race. Here there was remediation to ensure equity. In fact, the power and consistency of that message is matched only by the power of those who have argued that blacks had somehow altered their commitment to "fair" play. "Illiberal," "politically correct," "reverse discrimination" – we have all heard the charges. It is easy to dismiss them as the ranting of conservative ideologues who fear their loss of power and privilege. Others might even say that this is a revolutionary period of disjunction characterized by immense disequilibrium; in other words, the acts and counteracts are part of the ebb and flow of historical change.

Instead, I believe the confusion stems from our inability to identify and interpret semi-hidden, coded social transcripts.[38] Examples of such semi-public transcripts abound. In one notable folktale passed about in the slave community, a group of slaves long for some meat. Just before a planned slaughter to fill the master's cupboards, not theirs, a fieldhand reports that seven hogs have succumbed to "malitis." The owner inspects the situation. He finds the dead animals and a group of slaves who profess some fear of touching them. The owner directs them to clean and dress the hogs anyway, and since he deems the meat of little value, gives it to the slaves. Later a mother explains to her child the origins of malitis. Apparently, before daybreak, one of the stronger members of the community "tapped Mister Hog 'tween the eyes with that mallet, [and] 'malitis' set in pretty quick."[39] Few could misinterpret this act: it was a clear sign of resistance. But what else do we see? The "taking" of the meat? The deft use of circumlocution to protect their gains? What about a comment on social inequities? Did the enslaved African Americans in the folktale seek equality or equity? Can we tell the difference? More often than not we see the public transcript, because it is obvious, and we seek to understand the hidden transcript because it seems elusive (my graduate students remind me often of the need to read the silence). But too little attention has been paid to the semi-public transcript, like the language developed to shield the "taking" of the hogs.

Both the hidden and the public or semi-public transcript educated a people about what existed, what could exist, and what was needed to transform the situation. Many have certainly heard a version of the humorous story of the African American, the Italian, and the Jew. In the version recorded by folklorist Daryl Dance, God instructs the trio to go out and bring back a stone. The African American is the first to return. He brings back a pebble. A little later the Italian returns with a wheelbarrow of stones. They wait and wait. Then they hear a thunderous rumble as the Jew finally pushes into place a mountain. God is impressed. He rewards the African American with a biscuit; the Italian with many loaves of bread; and the Jew with a bakery. God then grants the trio an opportunity to better their initial efforts. The Italian is the first to return, again with a wheelbarrow of stones. Much later the Jew comes back with another mountain. They wait and wait and wait and the African American finally arrives with a crash, rumble, and thunder. Improving on the record of the Jew, he has brought several mountains. God assesses their efforts. The Italian is given another wheelbarrow of bread, and the Jew another bakery. The African American anxiously awaits his reward. Whereupon God says, "Upon these rocks I'll build my church." The black man rails, "I'll be damned if you will. You gon' make bread today!"[40]

Buried in the humor we see the elaboration of a theme. Long criticized for being slow, late, and inattentive, the black man responded too quickly to God's entreaty. His contemporaries, unencumbered by this burden, responded differently and received a fuller reward. When given another opportunity, the black man was not to be outdone. Only this time the rules had changed, at least for him. Equality of opportunity did not bring equity. As the man reminded God, he sought equity.

Within the belly of the community blacks spoke in a language which connected the past and the present, the folktales of the slavery era and the oft-repeated joke on ethnic differences. Most illustrative of that talk and its ramifications were the songs generated by the civil rights workers – students, Southern blacks, organizers, etc.[41] In her introduction to *The Civil Rights Movement*, cultural historian Bernice Johnson Reagon complained:

> From the late 1950s through the mid-1960s, I celebrated and partici-
> pated in the wedding of our traditional culture with our contemporary
> struggle for freedom ... As I read the numerous studies on the Civil
> Rights Movement, I look for the people who made up the numbers; I
> look to see if they are a faceless mass or an eloquent and strongly
> focused community. The few successful studies acknowledge the songs
> as the language that focused the energy of the people who filled the
> streets and the roads of the South ... [42]

On warm days and hot nights, and on cool evenings darkened by the greyness of winter, women, men, and children crowded into churches, school gymnasiums, paddy wagons, and jail cells. Forced into these settings by the guardians of the citadels of segregation, the women, men, and children sang. The songs were old and new, traditional and modified, but in one way or another, they told what the Negro wanted.

Freedom was a recurrent theme. At mass meetings, in community-sanctioned space, songleaders and participants sang "Oh, Freedom" or chanted "Freedom Now." Students at Fisk University adapted the melody of Harry Belafonte's "Banana Boat Song" to accommodate the multiple meanings of freedom in "Calypso Freedom." Even songs like "Get On Board, Children, Children" reminded all inside the circle of community about the task at hand. The refrain acknowledges the fight for human rights.[43]

Like much in African-American literary history, the repeated reference to freedom was part of an evolving tradition of word play. Henry Louis Gates, Jr., insists that "the black tradition is double-voiced." Freedom in that sense became more than a metaphor; it functioned as a trope, a linguistic hint of a larger meaning. Chants of "Freedom Now" or "Get on Board, Children, Children" used the main text of freedom as a public transcript. Once again the double-voicing so central to the African-American vernacular tradition left unstated the larger purpose of freedom now or explained for those outside the circle why the children should get on board. But in the same fashion that blues artists, to borrow from literary critic Houston Baker, "offer interpretations of the experiencing of experience," the singers who sang the civil rights songs sought more than an abstract freedom. They expected jobs, peace, and dignity, they expected equality and equity. In singing about "freedom" they scripted a larger story, one often misread because it was centered in the tradition of African-American literary history and was retranslated by a larger society which understood only one definition, and quickly accepted it as the only possible explanation.[44]

In the summer of 1962, during the high point of the Student Nonviolent Coordinating Committee's (SNCC) fight to break down the fortress of segregation in Albany, Georgia, another song gained prominence. "Ain't Gonna Let Nobody Turn Me 'Round" had deep roots in the African American community. An old spiritual, now the words were changed but not the syntax. Like much that was modified, the new was as recognizable as the old, except that this version zeroed in on the challenge at hand:

> Ain't gonna let Chief Pritchard turn me 'round,
> Turn me round, turn me 'round,
> Ain't gonna let Chief Pritchard turn me 'round,
> I'm gonna keep on a-walkin', keep on a-talkin',
> Marching up to freedom land.

Subsequent stanzas inserted police dogs, nervous Nellie, Uncle Tom, segregation, and federal injunction.[45]

In the aforementioned example, we capture a glimpse of how African Americans socially constructed democracy. Freedom existed outside the boundary of the academic and abstract; freedom meant the dismembering of segregation. Moreover, citizens had the right and responsibility to change what was unjust. If this meant defying the local sheriff, mayor, federal government, and guardians of the status quo, so be it. As one resident said, "anybody who thinks this town is going to settle back and be the same as it was, has got to be deaf, blind, and dumb." This song and others like it exemplified a new language that "expressed a determination to seize the initiative in formulating goals and strategies away from local white, and in some cases, black elites."[46]

Moreover, such songs were part of a larger set of social signifiers. During the Freedom Summer of 1964, SNCC volunteers came to understand and appreciate why veteran activists held the federal government in such disdain. According to Doug McAdam, a sign in one Freedom House read:

> There's a street in Itta Bena called FREEDOM
> There's a town in Mississippi called LIBERTY
> There's a department in Washington called JUSTICE

This sign, laced with irony, drew a sharp contrast between expectations and reality. Unwilling to modify their expectations, the civil rights activists used music and other markers to focus their attention on changing conditions by forcing the hands of state representatives.[47]

The campaign for freedom and justice transformed the political as well. Public spaces became political spaces. Richard King observed, "in their willingness to spend time in jail, protestors undermined the traditional negative connotations of jail and turned it from a place of shame to one of political honor."[48] They did even more. Clusters of protest singers altered the measurements of public space. Whether congregating in churches, buses or prisons, singing protestors achieved spatial separation by sealing themselves off from an encroaching outside world. Congregation challenged the conventions of segregation, empowering African Americans for moments and hours at a time as they plotted to overthrow the entire system of racial superordination and subordination.[49]

In mass meetings or police vans, the songs demarcated the world created by the community from the world threatening the community. Paradoxically, what went on within the prescribed boundaries became both instantly recognizable and potentially incomprehensible. Those inside the boundary of community or home immediately comprehended the dual themes of justice and equity so much a part of the struggle's lexicon. When observed from the outside, justice and equity simply became equality. Thus the songs became a semi-public transcript.

Political rhetoric, although often well-intentioned and very useful, added to the misdiagnoses. In a report to Congress on the civil rights bill President Kennedy conflated justice, equality, and equity: "I emphasized that the events in Birmingham and elsewhere have so increased the cries for equality that no city or State or legislative body can simply choose to ignore them." He concluded his report, in which the word equity was used one time and justice a half dozen times, on this note: "I ask you to look into your hearts – not in search of charity, for the Negro neither wants nor needs condescension – but for the one plain, proud, and priceless quality that unites us all as Americans: a sense of justice."[50]

Away from the glare of public inspection Kennedy officials drafted details for an equal economic opportunity program. The document used the phrase "affirmative action," first used in federal legislation in 1935. The Wagner Act, which gave birth to the National Labor Relations Board, included the language. Few noticed or reacted to it at that time. But Kennedy's use of the phrase in the 1960s refigured the African American's plea for equity.[51]

The rhetoric of the federal government continued to shift in subtle but significant ways. In 1964 President Lyndon Johnson addressed Howard University graduates, delivering a speech influenced by Bill Moyers, then special White House assistant, and Patrick Moynihan, an Assistant Secretary in the Department of Labor. Saying what blacks had been saying for some time, that freedom was not enough, Johnson told the somewhat stunned audience, "We seek not just freedom but opportunity – not just legal equity but human ability – not just equality as a right and a theory but equality as a fact and as a result." In time, Johnson's rhetoric and federal policy became conflated. Whereas African Americans had long called for equity, federal policy became known simply as affirmative action. Thus affirmative action, which had been part of the nation's vocabulary for more than a generation, now acquired a more threatening, sinister meaning. In the process, what blacks wanted became more obscured and misinterpreted.[52]

By 1968 many believed the country was spiraling toward a racial cataclysm, a social abyss from which there was no return. Events on the evening news confirmed the worst fears. Little more than a year after Johnson's commencement address, and only weeks after the signing of the Voting Rights Act of 1965, a routine encounter between a black motorist and white policemen erupted into the worst urban disturbance seen in nearly twenty years. The nation watched as the section of Los Angeles known as Watts burned. When the smoke cleared, 34 people had died, and more than $35 million in property had been destroyed or damaged. Major disturbances soon rocked Detroit, Newark, and dozens of other cities. Many feared that African Americans had adopted social activist H. Rap Brown's line, "burn, baby, burn," as a personal credo.[53]

The year 1968 marked a clear transition in the national debate about race, equality, and democracy. On the one hand, the *Report of the National Advisory Commission on Civil Disorders*, or Kerner Commission Report, acknowledged the state's need to act to close the widening gulf between blacks and whites. The report recommended massive manpower programs, educational improvements, an overhauling of the welfare system, and a plan for integrating blacks into the mainstream of national life.

> The essential fact is that neither existing conditions nor the garrison state offer acceptable alternatives for the future of this country. Only a greatly enlarged commitment to national action–compassionate, massive and sustained, backed by the will and resources of the most powerful and the richest nation on this earth – can shape a future that is compatible with the historic ideals of American society.[54]

Any suggestion of a consensus was short-lived, however. In 1963 and again in 1965 more than half of Americans surveyed cited civil rights for blacks as the nation's number one challenge. By 1968 only a quarter of Americans believed civil rights to be the nation's number one concern, ranking it second on the list of national priorities. And by 1971 the status of blacks ranked fifth on the list, a lower priority than in 1962.[55]

Meanwhile, the federal government shifted from reluctant protector to hostile adversary. Johnson, prickly over any criticism, could not fathom blacks' opposition to the war in Vietnam. It seems few actually heard the freedom singers connect their struggles to colonial liberation efforts elsewhere. No one bothered to ask: was the song "Odinga Oginga" about more than colonial occupation of Kenya? Given *carte blanche* by Presidents Johnson and Nixon, J. Edgar Hoover instructed the FBI to take out the vanguard, or liberal and radical leaders, of the freedom struggle, believing that this would neutralize or eliminate opposition to state policies. He succeeded admirably until a decade later, when the cover on COINTELPRO was lifted.[56]

Others fretted that the Beloved Community had given way to something more sinister, un-American and undemocratic. As if to prove the point, King's words are often compared to those of Stokely Carmichael (a.k.a. Kwame Toure). Whereas King preached a tough-minded brotherly love,

Carmichael gained fame by invoking and advertising the phrase Black Power. King's "I Have a Dream" speech, shaped by an African-American idiom, a pervasive belief in the possibility of American democracy, and influences ranging from the Old Testament to modern philosophers, sounded authentically American in its pronouncements and hopes. As Carmichael somewhat sardonically hinted, Black Power conjured a different set of images and led the majority to a different set of conclusions. In a 1966 speech at the University of California at Berkeley, he told those gathered, "If we had said Negro power, nobody would get scared. Everybody would support it. And if we said power for colored people, everybody would be for that. But it is the word *black* that bothers people in this country, and that's their problem, not mine ... We are on the move for our liberation."[57]

Thus black Americans themselves gave the perception that the terrain had shifted. Many white Americans feared the implication of Black Power. The two words had never before been so publicly linked. Black domination, reminds William Van Deburg, is what many whites feared. James Brown's popular song, "Say It Loud: I'm Black and I'm Proud," meant little positive to them. As whites in Detroit railed after the 1967 riot, "Black takeover – Take over the world because that is what they want to do and they will. Why should they care? I am working and taking care of their kids." Harry Edwards's successful organization of a protest at the 1968 Olympics in Mexico City; the Black Panthers' armed promenade at the California legislature in Sacramento; the stylized donning of the Afro and the dashiki; additional racial disturbances and the takeover of college campuses by black activists – all of these events formed a kind of radicalized racial montage, certifying for some the end of Martin Luther King's earlier vision of a beloved community.[58] Few would accept this as social theater or the dramatizing of life in a post-industrial democratic society. It was easier to read the public transcript than to concern oneself with the meaning of the semi-public transcript, especially since it was clear that the former threatened their positions of power and privilege.

In the four years between Richard Nixon's election and re-election as president, tolerance levels plummeted even further. George Wallace's ascendancy as a viable third-party candidate signalled a clear backlash. He openly courted whites who felt disfranchised by governmental policy; in the process, writes Dan T. Carter, we witnessed the "southernization" of American politics. "What George Wallace did," Carter believes, "was to look out upon the disordered political landscape of the 1960s and give form to a nightmare." Wallace won five Southern states in 1968 and between 8 and 15 percent of the vote in more than a dozen states outside the South. In 1972, before an assassin's bullet nearly killed him, he had received almost as many popular votes in the primaries as George McGovern, the

Democratic party's eventual nominee, although he trailed McGovern in delegates. Most importantly, Wallace opened the doors to a highly successful Republican party strategy unabashedly built on the politics of race.[59]

During the Poor People's Campaign in 1968 a new song was written. It summarized the new feeling that everything had changed and everything remained the same. Entitled "Ev'rybody's Got a Right to Live," the song raised the possibility of a new emphasis in the black community: racial entitlement. The song recounted the tremendous contributions African Americans had made to creating the handsome reserves of wealth found in this country, and mentioned the toughening economic times and their consequences. The verses end with a plea for equity and justice:

> Now look a-here, Congress
> This is a brand new day
> No more full-time work
> And part-time pay.
>
> I want my share of silver
> I want my share of gold
> I want my share of justice
> To save my dying soul.[60]

During a period of economic constriction, if not outright slowdown, with evidence of a narrowing of the economic divide between middle-class blacks and whites, and a confused understanding of the relationship between individual discrimination and group rights, few whites favored programs that aided blacks or other racial minorities. Instead, hostility reigned. This was not because the list of black wants had changed that profoundly between 1941, when Hughes constructed it, and 1968, when the above song was penned. Rather, too few social analysts have read the semi-public as well as public transcripts created by African Americans. And those who have cannot reconcile the changing yet consistent themes of that message. With the scenes of a burning Los Angeles once again etched in our mind's eye, perhaps it is time to approach the age-old question with a new sensitivity. At the very least, it is important to remember that race and equity are key to understanding how African Americans constructed notions of democracy during much of the twentieth century.

CONCLUSION

Recent or forthcoming studies have forced us to rethink basic questions about the struggle over civil rights. Instead of a self-contained movement or an era with defined temporal boundaries, we have come to see that struggle as a long-term historical process, one deeply rooted in the African-American search for individual and collective empowerment.

Several points are worth repeating. First, the basic outline of what African Americans want has remained remarkably consistent, although the specific remedies have changed with shifts in the political economy. Second, to fully understand the contours of their outline of wants, we need to examine the social construction of democracy from the perspective of African Americans. Third, during the 1950s and 1960s, in communal settings and public spaces, blacks shared with the nation their perspective on democracy. The songs, shared in the defined space of community, became semi-public transcripts, audible but seldom completely comprehensible to those beyond the boundaries of "home." These songs functioned as texts that illustrate the relationship between the social construction of democracy and the social construction of race.

And fourth, several factors complicated receipt of that message in the 1960s. African Americans asserted the right to Black Power, which scared and confused many whites. Federal authorities became more aggressively hostile to black initiatives and movements. With complete impunity, they disrupted, killed, and distorted, making what blacks wanted less clear or recognizable to the white public. Images were critical, too. The earlier call for equity, always a semi-public transcript, became blurred or mistranslated as the potential subordination of whites. Busing, preferential hiring, reverse discrimination, crime – all of these concepts became part of a newly coded language that obscured earlier messages and meanings.

Regrettably, the issue of black wants is as salient a concern today as 25 years ago. Politicians from Richard Nixon in 1968 to David Duke in 1991 have inflamed public discourse by tendering their own answer to the question. Academics and intellectuals have been no less forthcoming, although as Omi and Winant remind us, in the process those uncomfortable with racial or group remedies recommend ethnic or individual solutions to social ills.[61] Oftentimes African Americans are said to favor quotas and seek guaranteed outcomes as well as assurances of equal opportunity. Affirmative action is portrayed as reverse discrimination, preferential treatment, unfair advantages for less qualified women and minorities.[62] How the concept of affirmative action originated as state policy in the 1930s and was updated and slightly modified in meaning in the 1960s is still little understood, as is the process by which its architects unwittingly (perhaps) redefined what African Americans meant by freedom, justice, and equality.

Clearly, the discourse has changed since James Brown intoned in 1969, "I Don't Want Nobody to Give Me Nothing. Just Open Up the Door and

I'll Get it Myself." Or has it? Are we the victims, or worse yet, prisoners, of our own rhetoric? Have we been too quick to assume that the distinctly public transcript is the one that guided black Americans these last forty years? Or do we conclude that the majority of African Americans have abandoned a nobler, purer vision? Moreover, where does this place people like Shelby Steele, who wrote that "after twenty years of implementation, I think that affirmative action has shown itself to be bad more than good and that blacks ... now stand to lose more from it than they gain."[63] Is he outside the traditional fold of African-American thought? More important, how did he get there?

As we pursue the artful quest for a fuller understanding of one of the world's most celebrated social movements, we are well advised to remember that African Americans, too, sang America. They did not always do so with one voice or one plan or strategy, but they did sing; in the process, they explained what they wanted. Our job as scholars is to do a better job of listening, translating, and interpreting their words and thoughts. Otherwise, we might never understand the relationship between race, equity, and democracy in the struggle over civil rights waged by African Americans.

NOTES

1.   Langston Hughes, "What The Negro Wants," *Common Ground*, 2 (Autumn 1941): 52–4.

2.   See, for example, Ronald Takaki, ed., *From Different Shores: Perspectives on Race and Ethnicity in America* (New York, 1987), especially 13–38, 215–50.

3.   By social construction of democracy I mean the ways in which individuals as members of a group create a shared view of rules, principles, and values and use that world view to negotiate with the state and its representatives to secure a fuller share of the state's resources and rewards.

4.   Orlando Patterson, *Freedom: Freedom in the Making of Western Culture* (New York, 1991), Introduction and Chapter 4. David Brion Davis, *The Problem of Slavery in the Age of Revolution, 1770–1823* (Ithaca, 1975), 178.

5.   Perry Miller, *Errand in the Wilderness* (New York, 1964); Sacvan Berkovitch, *The American Jeremiad* (Madison, 1978).

6.   Wilson Jeremiah Moses, *Black Messiahs and Uncle Toms* (University Park, Penn., 1982); David Blight, *Frederick Douglass' Civil War: Keeping Faith in Jubilee* (Baton Rouge, 1989); David Howard-Pitney, *The Afro-American Jeremiad: Appeals for Justice in America* (Philadelphia, 1990).

7. Howard-Pitney, *The Afro-American Jeremiad*, 15.

8. See, for example, Henry Louis Gates, ed., *"Race," Writing, and Difference* (Chicago, 1986), 1–37, 370–80; Abdul R. JanMohamed and David Lloyd, eds., *The Nature of and Context of Minority Discourse* (New York, 1990), 1–16, 37–49, 72–123.

9. Benedict Anderson, *Imagined Communities* (London, 1991), 5–7; see also Etienne Balibar and Immanuel Wallerstein, *Race, Nation, Class: Ambiguous Identities* (London, 1991).

10. As quoted in Arnold Rampersad, *The Life of Langston Hughes*, vol. 1, *1902–1941: I, Too, Sing America* (New York, 1986), 95, 285–6.

11. No one source fully delineates the development of the African-American institutional infrastructure during the Progressive period. The best general sources are August Meier, *Negro Thought in America, 1880–1915* (Ann Arbor, 1963) and John Hope Franklin and Alfred Moss, *From Slavery to Freedom*, 6th edn. (New York, 1988), especially Chapters 14–18. In addition see the following selected list: W.E.B. Du Bois, *The Philadelphia Negro* (Philadelphia, 1899), 221–30; Abram L. Harris, *The Negro as Capitalist* (New York, 1936); Edward N. Palmer, "Negro Secret Societies," *Social Forces*, 23 (December 1944): 207–12; Elsa Barkley Brown, "Womanist Consciousness: Maggie Lena Walker and the Independent Order of Saint Luke," *Signs*, 14 (Spring 1989): 610–33; William Muraskin, *Blacks in a White Society: Prince Hall Freemasonry in America* (Berkeley, 1975); Charles Kellogg, *NAACP* (Baltimore, 1967); Robert Zangrando, *The NAACP Campaign against Lynching, 1909–1950* (Philadelphia, 1980); and Jesse Thomas Moore, Jr., *A Search for Equality: The National Urban League, 1910–1961* (University Park, Penn., 1981). .

12. The distinction between home sphere and workplace is developed in Earl Lewis, *In Their Own Interests* (Berkeley, 1991), especially the Introduction and Chapter 1. Zangrando, *The NAACP Campaign Against Lynching*.

13. See among other studies, Gunnar Myrdal, *An American Dilemma* (1944; reissued New York, 1972), vol. 2, 819–36; Richard Kluger, *Simple Justice* (New York, 1977).

14. Myrdal, *An American Dilemma*, vol. 2, 820–6, 1402.

15. Moore's role in Florida is only now coming to light. See Stetson Kennedy, "Bid for Murder Tape Gets Cold Shoulder," *Crisis*, 90 (November 1983): 48–9. FBI documents surrounding the murder were recently found in local police files. Conversation with Professor Raymond Arsenault, 29 December 1992.

16. NAACP Papers, Box II, B-173, folder Legal T-1940-41.

17. Virginia Tate to NAACP, 6 April 1945; Edward R. Dudley, Special Assistant Counsel to Virginia Tate, 12 April 1945. NAACP Papers, Box II, B-173, Legal T-1940-41.

18. The literature on Garvey has grown considerably. For an introduction to Garvey and the movement he led see E. David Cronon, *Black Moses: The Story of Marcus Garvey and the Universal Negro Improvement Association* (Madison, 1955); Tony Martin, *Race First: The Ideological and Organizational Struggles of Marcus Garvey and the Universal Negro Improvement Association* (Westport, Conn., 1976); Lawrence Levine, "Marcus Garvey and the Politics of Revitalization," in John Hope Franklin

and August Meier, eds., *Black Leaders in the Twentieth Century* (Urbana, 1982), 104–38; Robert A. Hill, ed., *The Marcus Garvey and Universal Negro Improvement Association Papers*, 8 volumes to date (Berkeley, 1983–); and Judith Stein, *The World of Marcus Garvey* (Baton Rouge, 1986).

19. On pan-Africanism and international relationships among people of African origins, see A. Adu Boahen, ed., *Africa under Colonial Domination, 1880–1935* (Berkeley, 1985). On the making of transnational racial identities, see Evelyn Brooks Higginbotham, "African American Women's History and the Metalanguage of Race," *Signs*, 17 (Winter 1992): 251–74.

20. On *Négritude*, see Boahen, *Africa Under Colonial Domination*, 560, 564, 578–9, 768–81; and Aimé Césaire, *Discourse on Colonialism* (London, 1972), 13–14.

21. As noted in Franklin and Moss, *From Slavery to Freedom*, 406–8.

22. Reynolds Farley and Walter Allen, *The Color Line and the Quality of Life in America* (New York, 1989), 113.

23. Paula F. Pfeffer, *A. Philip Randolph, Pioneer of the Civil Rights Movement* (Baton Rouge, 1990), 45–88; Merl E. Reed, *Seedtime for the Modern Civil Rights Movement* (Baton Rouge, 1991).

24. CORE would garner headlines in the early 1960s for sending an integrated team of bus riders into the South to challenge the federal government's commitment to the non-segregation of interstate travel. Ironically, it had first done so, with less fanfare and violent consequence, in the 1940s. See August Meier and Elliott Rudwick, *CORE: A Study in the Civil Rights Movement, 1942–1968* (New York, 1973); Pfeffer, *A. Philip Randolph*, 61–88; Richard Dalfiume, "The 'Forgotten Years' of the Negro Revolution," in Bernard Sternsher, ed., *The Negro in Depression and War* (Chicago, 1969). On the radicalizing effect of the war on youth, see Robin D.G. Kelley, "The Riddle of the Zoot," in Joe Wood, ed., *Malcolm X: In Our Own Image* (New York, 1992), 155–89.

25. Pfeffer, *A. Philip Randolph*, 48.

26. Earl Lewis, "Expectations, Economic Opportunities, and Life in the Industrial Age," in Joe William Trotter, Jr., ed., *The Great Migration in Historical Perspective* (Bloomington, 1991), 22–3.

27. On the social consequences of the migration, see Constance McLaughlin Green, *The Secret City: A History of Race Relations in the Nation's Capital* (Princeton, 1967), 250–337; Lewis, *In Their Own Interests*, 168–98. Demographic patterns are discussed in Aldon Morris, *The Origins of The Civil Rights Movement* (New York, 1984), 6, 41; Gerald David Jaynes and Robin M. Williams, eds., *A Common Destiny: Blacks and American Society* (Washington, 1989), 62.

28. Farley and Allen, *The Color Line*, 298, 302.

29. Morris, *Origins of the Civil Rights Movement*, Chapters 2–3.

30. Richard H. King, "Citizenship and Self-Respect: The Experience of Politics in the Civil Rights Movement," *Journal of American Studies*, 22 (1988): 7; Robert Korstad and Nelson Lichtenstein, "Opportunities Found and Lost: Labor, Radicals, and the Early Civil Rights Movement," *Journal of American History*, 75 (December 1988): 786–811; Lewis, *In Their Own Interests*, 173–98; Robin D.G. Kelley, "'We Are Not What We Seem': Rethinking Black Working Class Opposition in the Jim Crow South,"

Journal of American History, 80 (June 1993): 75–112; Morris, *Origins of the Civil Rights Movement*, Chapter 2.

31. Quoted in *Norfolk Journal and Guide* (18 July 1942).
32. Juan Williams, *Eyes on the Prize* (New York, 1987), 64–9; Taylor Branch, *Parting the Waters: America in the King Years, 1954–63* (New York, 1988), 120-21.
33. Charles Payne, "Men Led, but Women Organized: Movement Participation of Women in the Mississippi Delta," in Vicki L. Crawford, Jacqueline Anne Rouse, and Barbara Woods, eds., *Women in the Civil Rights Movement* (Brooklyn, 1990): 1–11. See also Steven Lawson, "Freedom Then, Freedom Now: The Historiography of the Civil Rights Movement," *American Historical Review*, 96 (April 1991): 465–71.
34. Jo Ann Robinson joined the group in 1950 and headed it by 1955. Branch, *Parting the Waters*, 15–18; Jo Ann G. Robinson, *The Montgomery Bus Boycott and the Women Who Started It: The Memoir of Jo Ann Robinson*, David Garrow, ed. (Knoxville, 1987); and Mary Fair Burks, "Trailblazer: Women in the Montgomery Bus Boycott," in Crawford *et al.*, *Women in the Civil Rights Movement*, 71–83.
35. Burks, "Women in The Montgomery Bus Boycott Movement," especially 78.
36. For the best discussion see David Garrow, *Bearing the Cross* (New York, 1988), 11–82.
37. Garrow, *Bearing the Cross*, 11–82; Stephen B. Oates, *Let the Trumpet Sound* (New York, 1982), 70.
38. In large part I see this as a critique of James Scott, *Domination and the Arts of Resistance* (New Haven, 1991), 1–27.
39. Lawrence W. Levine, *Black Culture, Black Consciousness* (New York, 1977), 122–5; quoted on 127.
40. Daryl Cumber Dance, *Shuckin' and Jivin': Folklore From Contemporary Black Americans* (Bloomington, 1978), 9–10.
41. In preparing this chapter, I listened to or read the lyrics of more than four dozen songs sung or performed during the movement years. Most helpful was the three-album set arranged by Bernice Johnson Reagon and published by the Smithsonian Institution, *Voices of the Civil Rights Movement: Black American Freedom Songs, 1960–1966*, and Pete Seeger and Bob Reiser, *Everybody Says Freedom: A History of the Civil Rights Movement in Songs and Pictures* (New York, 1989).
42. Reagon, *Voices of The Civil Rights Movement*, 4.
43. Reagon, *Voices of the Civil Rights Movement*, side 2, side 1, and side 1, respectively. The three songs were recorded either in 1963 or 1964.
44. Henry Louis Gates, Jr., *The Signifying Monkey: A Theory of African American Literary Criticism* (New York, 1988), xxv; Houston A. Baker, Jr., *Blues, Ideology, and Afro-American Literature: A Vernacular Theory* (Chicago, 1984), 7.
45. For references to the text of the song see *Voices of the Civil Rights Movement*, side 4, and Seeger and Reiser, *Everybody Says Freedom*, 74–5.
46. King, "Citizenship and Self-Respect," 10.
47. Doug McAdam, *Freedom Summer* (New York, 1988), 128.
48. King, "Citizenship and Self-Respect," 12.

49. Congregation as an empowering practice is more fully delineated in Lewis, *In Their Own Interests*, 90–109.

50. Freidman, *The Civil Rights Reader*, 245, 260.

51. Hugh Davis Graham, *The Civil Rights Era: Origins and Development of National Policy* (New York, 1990), 33–6.

52. Quoted in Graham, *The Civil Rights Era*, 174–5.

53. The literature on racial violence in the United States is voluminous. For an overview, see Arthur Waskow, *From Race Riot to Sit-in* (New York, 1967); and Hugh Davis Graham and Ted Robert Gurr, eds., *Violence in America: Historical and Comparative Perspectives* (New York, 1969).

54. *Report of the National Advisory Commission on Civil Disorders* (Washington, 1967), 410. Hereafter called the Kerner Commission Report.

55. Jaynes and Williams, *A Common Destiny*, 224.

56. This literature is voluminous and growing. See especially Kenneth O'Reilly, *Racial Matters: The FBI's File on Black America, 1960–72* (New York, 1989), particularly Chapters 4, 5, 8–10.

57. For an examination of the language of King and its appeal to blacks and whites, see Keith D. Miller, *Voice of Deliverance: The Language of Martin Luther King, Jr. and Its Sources* (New York, 1992), Introduction, 142–58. Carmichael quoted in Philip S. Foner, ed., *The Voice of Black America*, vol. 2 (New York, 1975), 426–7.

58. On this period, see William Van DeBurg, *New Day in Babylon: The Black Power Movement and American Culture, 1965–1975* (Chicago, 1992); Detroit quote from 19.

59. Dan T. Carter, "From Foster Auditorium to Sanders Auditorium: The 'Southernization' of American Politics," in Harry J. Knopke, Robert J. Norrell, and Ronald W. Rogers, eds., *Opening Doors: Perspectives on Race Relations in Contemporary America* (Tuscaloosa, 1991): 64–76; quoted on 75.

60. Seeger and Reiser, *Everybody Says Freedom*, 226–7.

61. Michael Omi and Howard Winant, *Racial Formation in the United States: From the 1960s to the 1980s* (New York, 1986), 20–21.

62. See, for example, Dinesh D'Souza, *Illiberal Education: The Politics of Race and Sex on Campus* (New York, 1991) and the numerous responses to the book.

63. Shelby Steele, *The Content of Our Character* (New York, 1990), 113.

9 Black Political Mobilization in Brazil, 1975–1990

George Reid Andrews

This chapter examines the Afro-Brazilian political movement which emerged during the *abertura*, the eleven-year (1974–1985) process by which Brazil made a gradual, phased transition from military dictatorship to civilian democracy. The major scholarly treatments of *abertura* pay considerable attention to the organized opposition movements which emerged during those years; none of them, however, make any mention at all of the black movement.[1]

This neglect is doubtless owing to that movement's failure to exert much impact on electoral politics or policymaking either under the last years of the dictatorship (1964–1985) or the first years of the Third Republic (1985–present). Partly for reasons common to any popular movement in Brazil, and partly for reasons specific to the Afro-Brazilian population, the black movement proved unable to mobilize its intended constituency: the 45 percent of the Brazilian population which is of pure or mixed African descent.[2] Paradoxically, however, its lobbying and consciousness-raising efforts had considerable impact on white political, cultural, and intellectual elites. By the end of the 1980s, and despite their lack of a strong popular base, black activists had succeeded in provoking a vigorous national debate on Brazilian racial inequality and the role of Brazil's black population in national life. That debate centered on the concept of racial democracy, a semi-official ideology originally intended to describe and explain Brazilian society and culture but which, as its label suggests, has proven to be relevant to questions of political democracy as well.

RACIAL DEMOCRACY AND POLITICAL DEMOCRACY

The ideology of racial democracy asserts that Brazil is a land entirely free of legal and institutional impediments to racial equality, and largely (particularly in comparison to countries like the United States) free of informal racial prejudice and discrimination as well. The nation allegedly offers all its citizens, black, brown, or white, virtually complete equality of opportunity in all areas of public life: education, politics, jobs, housing. Thus, according to proponents of the ideology, Afro-Brazilians enjoy opportunities to better themselves, and the freedom to compete against their fellow citizens in the contest for public and private goods, to a degree unknown in any other multiracial society in the world.[3]

The roots of racial democracy stretch well back into the nineteenth century, in the form of observations by foreign travelers and by Brazilians concerning the relative mildness of Brazilian slavery and the broad range of opportunities for advancement and upward mobility open to free blacks and mulattoes. The ideology received its fullest and most coherent expression, however, during the 1930s as part of a broad-based national protest against the oligarchical authoritarianism and repressive social policies of Brazil's First Republic (1891–1930).

Despite its claims to being an electoral democracy, the Republic was an oligarchical regime thoroughly dominated by landowning elites. Suffrage was kept to a minimum (in only two presidential elections between 1890 and 1930 did voter turnout exceed 3 percent of the national population), party competition was virtually non-existent, and the nascent labor unions and other popular movements suffered severe repression.[4]

Reinforcing the trend toward political exclusion was a set of social policies based on the scientific racism and Social Darwinism dominant in Western thought at that time. In an effort both to "whiten" the national population and to reduce the planters' dependence for labor on their former slaves (final emancipation had been enacted in 1888), federal and state governments under the Republic actively promoted massive European immigration.[5]

Inevitably this campaign to "Europeanize" Brazil had severe impacts on the Afro-Brazilian population, especially in São Paulo and the southern states, where immigration was heaviest. European workers received both official and unofficial preference in plantation and factory hiring during this period, while black workers were relegated to the margins of the agricultural and urban labor markets.[6] However, the arrival of the Europeans proved problematic as well for white Brazilian workers, the middle class, and even the agrarian elites who had initially supported immigration. The immigrants, and later their children, posed direct competition to Brazilian-born workers, tradesmen and small merchants. And to the elites' horror, while immigrants undoubtedly contributed to the "whitening" of Brazil, they also contributed to the unionization of Brazil, helping organize and lead the numerous urban and rural strikes which reached a peak between 1917 and 1920.[7]

The Europeanization campaign combined with the corruption, oppression, and political stagnation of the Republic to produce growing disaffection and opposition to the planter state. Sporadic urban riots, rural rebellions, and strikes from the late 1890s through 1920 made clear the level of popular discontent. During the 1920s that discontent spread into the middle class and into the armed forces. Three unsuccessful military rebellions took place between 1922 and 1927, each led by disaffected junior officers, the *tenentes*. Following the presidential election of 1930, won as usual by the candidate of the Republican Party, the *tenentes* rose once again; supported this time by agrarian elites outside the coffee sector who felt excluded from national power by the southeastern planters, this fourth rebellion overturned the Republic and replaced it with a provisional government headed by the recently defeated presidential candidate, Getúlio Vargas.[8]

The "revolution of 1930" inaugurated a period of intense political and intellectual activity in Brazil. In the political sphere, the fall of the Republic opened the possibility of expanded electoral competition and participation. The Communist Party emerged from clandestinity to openly contest elections, as did the newly formed fascist party, the Integralists. The Constitution of 1934, while continuing to bar illiterates from voting, extended suffrage to women (only the second Latin American country to do so) and made voting compulsory. Completely reversing the Republic's antagonistic stance toward organized labor, the Ministry of Labor, created in 1930, proceeded to enact the labor code and system of state-regulated labor unions which would play such an important role in Brazilian politics during subsequent decades; social security, public health, and other programs of social provision also date from these years.[9]

Intellectually as well, the 1930s witnessed a remarkable burst of creativity as Brazilian thinkers pondered the failures of the Republic, and especially its ill-fated campaign to Europeanize Brazil. In trying to chart the course of Brazil's future development, its intellectuals now turned away from Europe and back to their own country, seeking in its past the historical foundations on which to build a new, genuinely Brazilian national identity. Inevitably, what they saw when they looked back was a history of plantation agriculture and African slavery – hardly a promising basis on which to build a modern, twentieth-century society.[10] Thinkers such as Francisco José Oliveira Vianna, Afonso Arinos de Mello Franco, and Azevedo Amaral rejected the possibility of governing such a society by democratic norms, and argued instead for an authoritarian regime, governed by educated elites who would guide Brazil down the road toward modernity.[11]

A more optimistic response, however, came from the young sociologist Gilberto Freyre. Beginning in the 1930s, and continuing until his death in 1987, Freyre developed the concept of Brazil as a "racial democracy," a "New World in the tropics" which had managed to escape the bane of European racism and create a society "beyond race" in which peoples of all colors lived together in relative peace and harmony. This had happened, Freyre argued, precisely because of Brazil's intense and extended experience with African slavery. Unlike many of the nineteenth-century commentators on whom he drew, Freyre readily acknowledged slavery's inherent violence and brutality. But he maintained that, despite slavery's negative features, it had also provided a setting in which Europeans and Africans lived together in close proximity and in which, over time, new social and cultural forms were created which were powerfully influenced by the slaves' African heritage.[12]

Slavery also provided the setting for widespread racial mixture between white masters and black slaves which in turn created a completely new racial group, the mulattos, who Freyre saw as the most tangible and conclusive expression of racial democracy. He noted that during the nineteenth century mulattoes had enjoyed broad opportunities for upward mobility in the skilled trades and the liberal professions, and that some even succeeded in becoming figures of national prominence in politics and the arts. The existence of this racially mixed group, and the ability of its members to rise to the highest levels of Brazilian society, constituted irrefutable proof, Freyre argued, of the absence of racial prejudice and hostility in Brazil, and of that nation's "racial democracy."[13]

Freyre went on to suggest that Brazil's slave past held within it, not just the seeds of racial harmony and equality, but of social and political democracy as well. The very label which he applied to his arguments – racial democracy – conveyed this point, as did his emphasis on "the democratic, democratizing, even anarchic elements always present in the amalgamation of races and cultures," and on how such amalgamation was breaking down the "recalcitrantly aristocratic" and "patriarchal" aspects of Brazilian life, replacing "subjects" with "citizens."[14] Even during slavery and under the oligarchical First Republic, he believed, Brazil had already achieved a form of "social democracy," by which he meant the inclusion of all Brazilians in a racially egalitarian society; and now that the Republic had fallen, that "social democracy" provided Brazil a basis on which to construct full-fledged political democracy as well.

The concept of racial democracy proved to be perhaps the most enduring and influential product of the intellectual ferment of the 1930s. In its rehabilitation of Brazil's past and optimistic forecast of its future, it proved enormously appealing to almost all Brazilians – black and white, elite and non-elite – and in the years since its initial formulation it has been elevated to the level of semi-official national mythology. It also attracted considerable international attention, particularly in the years immediately following the Second World War, when the Brazilian model of race relations was held up as a possible antidote to the evils of European Nazism and United States racism.[15]

This international attention led the recently founded UNESCO to sponsor a series of research projects during the late 1940s and early 1950s which sought to document how Brazilian racial democracy functioned in practice and whether it could be replicated in other countries. Instead of finding racial harmony and equality, however, several of the UNESCO research teams, especially those working in the more urbanized and industrialized South and Southeast, uncovered evidence of widespread racial inequality, prejudice, and discrimination.[16] Further research carried out by Brazilian and foreign researchers during the 1970s and 1980s has confirmed those initial findings and has led to an evolving critique both of racial democracy's questionable relationship to reality, and of its role as a bulwark and defense of racial hierarchy and inequality.[17]

Paradoxically, while racial democracy proclaims Brazil to be a land of racial harmony and equality, in fact the ideolopgy is based on an implicit assumption of black inferiority. It cites race mixture, and the ample opportunities offered to the products of that race mixture, the mulattoes, as prima facie evidence of racial equality in Brazil. But mulattoes are granted such opportunities precisely because European racial ancestry is viewed as superior to African; racial barriers to upward mobility are lowered only to the degree that Afro-Brazilians become less African and more European.[18]

One of the striking findings of the research of the 1970s and 1980s is that the ideology of racial democracy greatly exaggerates the opportunities actually available to mulattos. Taken as a whole, the mulatto racial group has achieved levels of education, income, life expectancy, etc., that are only marginally superior to those achieved by Brazilians of pure African ancestry, while both groups lag far behind the white population.[19] Nevertheless, there are enough upwardly mobile mulattoes to provide abundant anecdotal evidence in support of racial democracy's assertions of mulatto advancement. By offering the hope of such advancement to "browns," and categorizing them as a racial caste separate from the "blacks," racial democracy provides strong incentives for mulattos to distance themselves from their darker compatriots and try to assimilate into white society. Talented and ambitious Afro-Brazilians are thus encouraged to withdraw from the non-white racial group; and the non-whites they leave behind are in turn effectively divided into brown and black sub-groups which for the most part have not displayed much willingness to unite and combat the discrimination that in fact strongly affects both groups.[20]

This co-optation of potential Afro-Brazilian leadership, and the division of the Afro-Brazilian population into black and brown subgroups, have formed substantial obstacles to Afro-Brazilian political mobilization. Racial democracy further obstructs such mobilization through its promotion of a national consensus that, since Brazil is in fact a racially equal society, Afro-Brazilians have no legitimate grounds for protest or complaint. Indeed, such protests are seen as a direct threat to Brazil's highly valued racial harmony, and are denounced as *racismo às avessas*, or "reverse racism." Racism of any kind being a cardinal sin in a racial democracy, black organizations and activists go to considerable lengths to avoid such a charge – which in turn has significantly restricted their ability to mobilize and to place issues of racism and racial inequity on the public agenda.[21]

THE NEW BLACK MOVEMENT AND THE RETURN TO DEMOCRACY, 1975–1990

Given racial democracy's demonstrated ideological power, and the multiple ways in which that ideology works to undermine individual and collective efforts to combat racial inequality, it is little short of miraculous that black movements have existed at all in post-1930 Brazil. Nevertheless they have, in the form of the Frente Negra Brasileira of the 1930s, the cultural and political organizations of the 1940s and 1950s, and the black movement of the 1970s and 1980s. Each of these movements arose during periods of democratic "opening": Getúlio Vargas's provisional government (1930–1937); the populist democracy of the Second Republic (1946–1964); and the *abertura* years of 1974–1985. Black political mobilization has thus been closely tied to efforts to promote democratization more generally; and black activists have tended to justify such mobilization in terms of promoting the fuller participation in national political and economic life of a near-majority racial group which has historically been excluded.[22]

Those leaders and activists have been drawn mainly from an Afro-Brazilian middle class that prior to 1950 was miniscule in size, but which by the 1970s and 1980s had expanded dramatically. The 1940 census recorded fewer than 17,000 Afro-Brazilians, out of a total black and brown population of 14.8 million, as employed in professional, technical, or white-collar office work.[23] By 1980 that number had risen to 1.8 million, out of a total black and brown population of 53.3 million.[24] These increases in middle-class employment for Afro-Brazilians paralleled equally dramatic increases in Afro-Brazilian educational attainment. In 1940 only 20,000 non-whites had graduated from high school, and 4,000 from college. By 1980 1.1 million Afro-Brazilians had graduated from high school, and 172,000 from college.[25]

Much of this progress occurred during the "miracle" years of 1968–1974, when economic growth rates averaged more than 10 percent per year and the military government greatly expanded the nation's system of higher education. Both of these developments resulted in increased educational and job opportunities for Brazilians of all races striving to enter the middle class. But despite the undeniable progress which they made during those years, upwardly mobile Afro-Brazilians found themselves facing quiet and informal but extremely effective racial barriers which seemed to became more difficult to overcome as they climbed higher up the educational and vocational ladder. A series of studies on salary inequality employing government data from 1960, 1976, and 1980 demonstrated that, even after controlling for age, experience, education, occupation, and other factors, significant differentials in earnings persisted between Euro-Brazilians and Afro-Brazilians. Those differentials were relatively small at lower-skill levels of the economy but became increasingly pronounced at higher levels of the job market.[26] This research also found that the proportion of earnings differentials left unexplained by differences in education, experience, etc., almost doubled between 1960 and 1980, indicating a substantial increase in discrimination during those years.[27]

Even before the results of this research had become available and widely disseminated, a growing number of Afro-Brazilians were becoming increasingly exasperated by the racial barriers which were preventing them from receiving an equitable share of the benefits of economic growth. During the mid-1970s these Afro-Brazilians, many of them young and relatively well educated, began to debate and discuss among themselves the dilemmas of living in a society which was neither a political democracy nor, they had come to conclude, a racial democracy. These debates initially took place within newly founded organizations which, like their counterparts of the 1950s, tended to be primarily educational and cultural in orientation.[28] Many of the participants in these organizations soon concluded that an exclusively "cultural" approach was unlikely to have much immediate impact on patterns of discrimination and inequality. And in 1978 a number of these activists joined together to create a new, explicitly political organization, the Movimento Negro Unificado (MNU).

This decision to try to mobilize the Afro-Brazilian population for political purposes was motivated by events both in Brazil and abroad. Educated Afro-Brazilians were intrigued and inspired by what they saw as a surge in the "international black movement" world-wide: in particular, the struggles for independence in Portuguese Africa, and the civil rights and Black Power movements of the United States. In both instances black people faced opponents which Afro-Brazilians saw as quite similar to those which they themselves confronted in Brazil: in the case of Africa, the modern legacy of Portuguese colonialism enforced by a right-wing authoritarian dictatorship; and in the case of the United States, a social order which had abolished plantation slavery but had left racial hierarchy intact. As both movements seemed to reach peaks of power and influence in the 1970s, with the independence of the Portuguese colonies and the enactment and implementation of equal opportunity and affirmative action legislation in the United States, young Afro-Brazilians began to wonder whether it might be possible to imitate their achievements in Brazil.[29]

Within Brazil as well, the second half of the 1970s seemed to offer the conditions for successful political mobilization along racial lines. The military had seized power in 1964 in order to purge the Second Republic of its "populist excesses" and corruption and restore democracy to proper working order. By 1974 the military judged this cleansing process to be sufficiently advanced to permit the beginning of a second phase of military rule, a period of relaxation, "decompression" (*distensão*), and political "opening" (*abertura*), which would lead to a gradual transition back to civilian democracy. Relatively open Congressional elections were held in 1974, the "party reform" of 1979 permitted multiple opposition parties to organize, and open gubernatorial elections were held in 1982. Military rule formally ended in 1985 with the inauguration of President José Sarney, Brazil's first civilian president in 21 years.

The officers had intended *abertura* to be a process in which the military government would retain full control over the political system while overseeing a carefully planned, orderly transition back to a restructured, "sanitized" democracy. The reality proved to be quite different. Beginning with the resounding defeat of the government party in the Congressional elections of 1974, and culminating in the disintegration of that party in the presidential elections of 1985, the civilian opposition proved unexpectedly adept at recognizing and exploiting opportunities to contest power with the military government. The progressive wing of the Catholic church organized poor people and workers into "Christian base communities" which, working in conjunction with neighborhood and community organizations, brought pressure to bear on local and state government for improvements in services, infrastructure and schools. A militant "new union" movement appeared in the industrial belts of São Paulo state, launching a wave of wildcat strikes which spread throughout south-central Brazil in 1978. In 1979 that movement formed the basis for the creation of the Partido dos Trabalhadores, which ten years later came close to winning the Brazilian presidency. And at the level of the middle class, the Brazilian press and the Brazilian bar became much more aggressive in protesting human rights violations and other abuses of military rule and in pushing the process of democratization forward.[30]

Thus, by the second half of the 1970s, a number of factors were in place to encourage black political mobilization: a rising sense of frustration among middle-class blacks over the racial barriers which continued to bar their upward progress; concrete examples of successful black movements abroad; and the mobilization and organization taking place in Brazilian society at large as a result of *abertura*. Capitalizing on the energy gener- ated by the celebrations surrounding the ninetieth anniversary of emanci- pation – May 13, 1978 – the middle-class militants seized the moment and moved to create the Movimento Negro Unificado. Originating in São Paulo, the movement spread rapidly throughout Brazil, with chapters opening in Rio de Janeiro, Minas Gerais, Bahia, and the southern states.[31]

Its members envisioned the MNU, not as a formal political party, but rather as a popular movement which would lobby and put pressure on the government, the parties, and other important organized interests in Brazilian life – unions, academia, the bar, the Church – to combat racism within their own institutions and in the society at large, and to adopt poli- cies which would lead to the expansion of economic, educational, health, and other opportunities for the black population as a whole. The condi- tions and terms of *abertura* made the political parties in particular quite vulnerable to such lobbying. From 1965 to 1979 the military government had permitted only two parties to function in Brazil: the government party, ARENA, and the opposition party, the Movimento Democrático Brasileiro. In an effort to divide and weaken its opponents, in 1979 the government abandoned the two-party system and freed the opposition to dissolve into multiple competing organizations. While ARENA (now renamed the Partido Democrático Social) remained intact, the opposition divided into five new parties, each of which had to compete against the others for electoral support. Seeing a potential source of such support in the new black movement, all of the opposition parties hurried to display their commitment to combatting racial discrimination and inequality in Brazil. They inserted anti-racism planks into their platforms, and several created special commissions or working groups to examine the state of race relations in Brazil and formulate appropriate policy responses. The parties invited black activists to join their ranks and nominated an unprecedented number of Afro-Brazilian candidates for federal, state, and municipal office in the elections of 1982.[32]

Having won the attention of the parties, however, the black activists had to fulfill the second condition of a successful lobbying organization: delivering the goods agreed upon – in this case, votes for the opposition parties. The elections of 1982 saw resounding victories for the opposition parties in the states of the South and Southeast, where the black movement was strongest. But only in Rio de Janeiro, where longtime populist politician Leonel Brizola won the governorship on a platform of *socialismo moreno*, or "brown socialism," did the black vote prove decisive.[33] If anything, one of the notable outcomes of the elections was the poor showing of those candidates closely associated with the black movement. For example, of 54 Afro-Brazilian candidates who ran in São Paulo on major party tickets, only two – a state representative and a São Paulo city councilman – won election.[34]

As one of the black activists observed following the elections, "a lot of people were bluffing: they said they had X number of votes, and then when the election came, it turned out that they didn't have any."[35] Survey data collected in São Paulo showed that, even among Afro-Brazilian voters, fewer than a quarter had voted for black candidates. These proportions varied substantially by class background, however. Among upper-middle class blacks, 43 percent had voted for black candidates; among white-collar office workers, 27 percent had voted for black candidates; and among manual laborers (who formed the majority of voters polled, and the overwhelming majority of the black electorate), only 19 percent had voted for black candidates.[36]

Candidates associated with the black movement had appealed much more strongly to relatively well educated, upwardly mobile blacks than to poor and working-class voters. This was in part a reflection of the middle-class background and concerns of many of the black activists and candidates, which tended to distance them from the mass of Afro-Brazilian voters.[37] This distance in turn reflects the larger problem of the severe inequalities which characterize Brazilian society, and the obstacles which those inequalities pose to popular mobilization of any kind. Brazil has a longstanding history, dating back to slavery, of extreme concentration of wealth and power in the hands of a relatively small elite class.[38] The resulting exclusion of poor Brazilians from politics has had as a consequence that, "as a rule, popular sectors are somewhat skeptical about the possibility of effecting political change. Politics is seen as an elite struggle, and the State is perceived as a realm beyond the popular sectors." Given Brazil's historical experience, such attitudes are not at all unreasonable or unrealistic; they "nevertheless limit the possibility of collective action, for only at the point when people believe in the ... efficacy of collective action is it possible to organize a social movement."[39]

This skepticism clearly extends to the problems of racism and racial inequality. Surveys indicate that, regardless of their class background, most Afro-Brazilians have either experienced racial discrimination directly or are conscious of its existence. However, in discussing possible responses to such discrimination, only a handful of informants raise the possibility of organized political action. The most frequent responses are either that there is no solution to the problem, or that the informant has no idea what the solution might be.[40]

Such feelings of powerlessness and uncertainty reflect in part the pervasive and systemic quality of racial inequality, which is so deeply engrained in Brazilian life that it is by no means clear how it can most effectively be combatted and rooted out. But racial inequality also forms part of larger patterns of socioeconomic inequality which, as indicated above, have had the effect of excluding and marginalizing popular movements from participation in national politics and affairs of state. In such an environment, poor and non-elite Brazilians have tended to conclude that the most effective way to deal with the problems caused by poverty and powerlessness is not to organize collectively and press for political change. Rather, it is to establish direct personal ties with powerful patrons who can protect and do favors for their clients.[41]

Like other popular movements which appeared during the *abertura* period, the black movement proposed to repudiate this patronage-based model of social relations and politics and replace it with a "new social order" based on mass mobilization and collective action. Not surprisingly, most black voters, and especially most poor and working-class black voters, declined to throw in their lot with such a highly speculative enterprise.[42] The first casualty of their reluctance was the MNU itself, which never really recovered from the disastrous showing of 1982. While it continues to exist as a national organization with chapters throughout Brazil, one of its founders recalls that "it kept getting narrower and narrower ideologically, characterizing itself increasingly as a movement of the left ... losing militants and strength."[43]

As activists withdrew from the MNU, however, they by no means abandoned the struggle against racial inequality. Some continued the effort to organize poor and working-class blacks, though now under the aegis of more "mainstream" institutions such as the progressive wing of the

Catholic church or the left-wing political parties.[44] Others, however, moved their work to a different level and aimed their efforts at a different audience. During its initial years the MNU had devoted considerable energy to "consciousness-raising" among the black population, working to expose the internal contradictions of the doctrine of racial democracy and the disparities between that doctrine and the harsh realities of Brazilian racial hierarchy. Despite, or because of, the failure of those efforts to motivate Afro-Brazilians to join the movement in large numbers, a number of black activists now broadened their appeals to target a new and different constituency: the white population, and especially white cultural, intellectual, and political elites.

CONTESTING RACIAL DEMOCRACY

It was black intellectual and activist Joel Rufino dos Santos who first articulated how the concept of racial democracy, which formed such an obstacle to the mobilization of the black population, might prove to be an asset in lobbying white public opinion. Santos noted that, even if assertions of racial democracy found little support in empirical reality, they had nevertheless taught Brazilians to value highly the ideals of racial equality and harmony. He thus distinguished between the myth of racial democracy, "which is false," and the "burning desire for [real] racial democracy" that he believed most Brazilians share. If white Brazilians could be made to see the jarring disparity between the myth and the reality, perhaps they would be moved to take action against the discrimination and racism which sullied their national ideals.[45]

As with the "party reform" of 1979, again the specific conditions of the *abertura* years made white politicians and intellectuals particularly receptive to the black activists' appeals. Ever since the 1930s black activists had tried to draw public attention to the racial dimension of Brazilian inequality, arguing that neither political democracy nor racial democracy could be said to exist in Brazil until black people participated in national economic, political, and social life on equal terms with whites. These arguments began to be taken seriously by a handful of white intellectuals and academics during the 1950s and 1960s and then received wider currency in the work of a new generation of social scientists produced by the expansion of the university system during the 1970s. A number of these younger scholars took up the question of race as part of a broader critique of inequality in Brazilian society, and the ways in which that inequality posed fundamental obstacles to the construction of democratic norms and institutions. In so doing they made increasingly clear the connection between political democracy and racial democracy, arguing that, in a highly unequal, racially stratified society like Brazil, neither can exist, in any genuine sense, in the absence of the other.[46]

Meanwhile, politicans and intellectuals involved in opposition politics had also come to see the concept of racial democracy as a cornerstone of a larger ideological apparatus through which the nation's conservative elites sought to retain and justify their control over society. During the nineteenth century and the First Republic, landowning elites had repeatedly characterized the political system over which they presided as a participatory democracy when in fact it was a tightly controlled, oligarchical regime which, particularly after the electoral reform of 1881, sharply limited popular participation.[47] The result, argued Partido dos Trabalhadores theorist and general secretary Francisco Weffort, was "a legacy of equivocation" in which authoritarianism masqueraded as democracy.[48]

If one of the central tasks in constructing civilian democracy was to clear away that "legacy of equivocation," the aging and visibly false myth of racial democracy, which formed such an integral part of that legacy, seemed a good place to begin. Racial democracy was made even more vulnerable by the way in which the military governments had sought to cloak themselves in its folds. Despite the resolve with which they had seized power in 1964 and held on to it for the next two decades, the officers were never entirely at ease with their decision to close down democracy. They frequently reminded those who would listen that they had destroyed Brazilian democracy precisely in order to save it, and that their long-term goal was to clean up and restructure its institutions in such a way that democracy would eventually be able to function in Brazil free of the "excesses" and corruption which had marred it in the past.[49] In the meantime, during a period in which Brazil was clearly not a political democracy, it was helpful for the dictatorship to be able to claim that it continued to be democratic in at least one sense: that of race. Government officials made this point repeatedly, and classified any criticism of racial democracy as an act of subversion.[50] Thus by the time of *abertura*, the concept had been discredited as much by its political associations with right-wing authoritarianism as by its questionable relationship with reality. Not only was it easy to make a convincing empirical case against the concept; for many Brazilians it was also an act of political liberation, and an explicit rejection of the dictatorship, to do so.

The 1980s thus formed a propitious moment for the black activists to take on the national ideology of racial democracy, which they did in a variety of venues: public meetings and lectures, newspaper articles and editorials, debates and other features on radio and TV, academic conferences, and even popular songs and samba competitions. These activities reached a climax during the commemorations marking the centennial of the abolition of slavery, in May 1988.[51]

The content of those festivities, especially those sponsored not by the black movement but rather by such mainstream institutions as the Church, the universities, and federal, state, and municipal governments, makes clear the extent to which the national consensus on racial democracy had broken apart during the 1980s. Minister of Culture Celso Furtado, whose ministry coordinated the federally sponsored commemoration of the event, opened the festivities by proclaiming that "the idea that there is racial democracy in Brazil is false as long as the overwhelming majority of the black population lives marginalized and in poverty."[52] Partido dos Trabalhadores presidential candidate Luis Inácio da Silva, doubtless with an eye toward the elections of 1989, denounced racial democracy as "de facto apartheid."[53] The Catholic church, which had made race relations the central theme of its 1988 Brotherhood Campaign, issued an instructional text acknowledging past church complicity in slavery and racial discrimination and calling for systematic efforts to eliminate racial injustice in Brazil.[54]

In the press, the nation's two major news weeklies (comparable to *Time* and *Newsweek* in the United States) joined in consigning racial democracy to the dustbin of history. "The myth of racial democracy appears to be definitively in its grave," observed *Istoé*, while *Veja* implicitly dismissed the concept by opening its cover story with the observation that "one hundred years after Abolition, in Brazil there are two distinct citizenships – white and black."[55] The *Folha de São Paulo* ran a lead editorial on "the perception, ever more widespread, that 'racial democracy,' in its official and semi-official versions, does not reflect Brazilian reality . . ." In Rio, the *Jornal do Brasil* interviewed intellectuals and public figures who were virtually unanimous in their repudiation of the concept. Historian Francisco Iglésias curtly dismissed it as "foolishness," while his colleague Décio Freitas turned the concept on its head by insisting that "racial discrimination is the basis of Brazilian culture." Sociologist Octávio Ianni captured the mood of the day by observing that "more than anybody blacks know that racial democracy is a lie in a country in which there is no political democracy, much less racial democracy."[56]

Not all of the rhetoric surrounding the centennial was so revisionist in character. But the general tone of criticism and hostility toward the ideology of racial democracy marked a radical departure from traditional bland assurances of Brazil's racial harmony and equality. The policy proposals presented, and in some cases enacted, during the centennial year were no less dramatic. Inspired by US affirmative action policies, Minister of Culture Furtado called for "guaranteeing" a minimum number of slots in Brazilian schools and universities for Afro-Brazilian students. President Sarney established a new federal agency, the Palmares Foundation, encharged with promoting "a black presence in all the sectors of leadership in this country." And the newly enacted Constitution of 1988 included a provision declaring racial discrimination to be a criminal offense and denying the right of bail to defendants charged with that crime.[57]

CONCLUSION

Those policy initiatives, and the revisionist commemoration of the centennial, represent the highwater mark of the black political movement in Brazil. Since 1988 the movement has declined markedly in importance and influence, for reasons relevant both to the future of Brazilian democracy and to issues raised by other essays in this volume.

First, as in other cases documented in this book, members of the middle class, both black and white, played a prominent role in the events under discussion. Most of the leadership and motive force for the black movement came from upwardly mobile Afro-Brazilians denied admission to the middle class. And the movement found some of its most receptive audience, not among poor and working-class blacks, but rather among white intellectuals and activists who incorporated the issue of race into their general critique of inequality in modern Brazil.

Much of the movement's failure to mobilize the black population can be traced to the differences dividing middle-class activists from their poor and working-class constituencies. Even within the middle class, however, the black movement proved limited in its appeal, for a second reason which emerges repeatedly in this volume: the power of official and semi-official ideologies to set the terms on which political participation and competition take place. From the 1930s through the present, the ideology of racial democracy has played a central role in obstructing black political organization and in muffling public debate on racial inequality. It continued to play that role in the 1970s and 1980s, helping to alienate black support at both the middle- and working-class level.

Nevertheless, the power of such ideologies is not absolute, as evidenced by racial democracy's failure to survive the 1980s intact. That failure suggests that even the most potent and durable of national ideologies are inherently unstable; and those which base themselves on claims of justice and equality are perhaps the most vulnerable to being torn apart by their internal tensions and contradictions. In a skillful and creative act of political deconstruction, the black activists managed to turn the ideology which had been such a liability in their organizing work into a powerful tool for building alliances with white opponents of the military government. As part of their own campaign to tear down the ideological foundations of authoritarianism and overcome Brazil's longstanding heritage of social and economic inequality, opposition politicians and intellectuals made common cause with the black movement in denouncing the disparity between official claims of racial democracy and the objective reality of racial inequality and discrimination. The result was a marked transformation in the terms and content of public discourse on race in Brazil, and, as opposition parties came to power, the beginning of state action to combat racial inequities.

These changes in official rhetoric and policy had some immediate and measurable impacts on Brazilian race relations. In São Paulo state, following the centennial celebrations of 1988 and the adoption of strong anti-discrimination measures in the new constitution, nearly three times as many complaints of racial discrimination were lodged with the police in 1989 and 1990 as during the preceding 34 years (1954–1988) combined.[58] At the national level, the elections of 1990 brought three black state governors to power, an unprecedented event in Brazilian politics. Significantly, however, none of the three was closely associated with the black movement or had highlighted racial issues in his campaign; and indeed, by the end of the decade the political wing of the black movement was essentially defunct, playing hardly any role either in the presidential elections of 1989 or the Congressional and gubernatorial elections of the following year.[59] This in turn made it possible for defenders of the status quo to whittle away at the measures proposed or enacted during the centennial celebrations. Minister of Culture Furtado's proposals for an affirmative action policy in Brazilian education died aborning; the budget of the Palmares Foundation was eliminated in 1990 as part of President Fernando Collor's austerity program; and when Congress passed the enabling legislation for the anti-discrimination provisions of the new constitution, President Sarney vetoed the clause denying bail to persons accused of discrimination.[60]

These setbacks suggest a final conclusion: the severe limitations of a political strategy based largely on appeals to conscience and national values. They also suggest the perils of the black activists' embracing what in essence was simply a new variation of traditional patronage-based politics, in which articulate but powerless intellectuals sought support, protection, and favors from powerful white institutions and elites. The black activists were following the same time-honored approach employed by their poorer compatriots, relying on top-down patronage rather than collective mobilization and action. The rewards for such tactics can be substantial, as evidenced by the recasting of racial discourse which took place during the 1980s and the advances in the legal protection of black civil rights. But in giving up on efforts to mobilize a larger popular following, the black movement forfeited the possibility of acquiring the political weight required to turn those significant but isolated advances into a more comprehensive and effective campaign against racial inequality, and to push on beyond discourse to actual policymaking.

The durability of this patronage model of politics, even – or especially – within "progressive" political movements aimed at combatting the profound inequalities in Brazilian society and politics, suggests the continuing power of that model, and of the inequalities of which it is an expression, to shape the character of democratization in late twentieth-century Brazil. Patronage and clientelism remain bedrock features of political competition in Brazil; and even racial democracy, while largely repudiated among progressive elites, retains considerable vigor in the society at large. Democratization in Brazil is unlikely to overturn these structures, at least in the short run; if anything, one suspects that the institutions of the Third Republic will bear their visible imprint. Certainly racial inequality does not appear to be on the decline; on some indicators it actually increased slightly over the course of the 1980s.[61] The black movement's success in placing the issue of such inequality on the public agenda was a historic achievement; but its inability to provoke more systematic governmental action in this area leaves that issue unresolved for now and into the foreseeable future.

NOTES

1. See, for example, Maria Helena Moreira Alves, *State and Opposition in Military Brazil* (Austin, 1985); Thomas E. Skidmore, *The Politics of Military Rule in Brazil, 1964–1985* (New York, 1988); Alfred Stepan, ed., *Democratizing Brazil: Problems of Transition and Consolidation* (New York, 1989). On the black movement during those years, see Michael Mitchell, "Blacks and the *Abertura Democrática*," in Pierre-Michel Fontaine, ed., *Race, Class and Power in Brazil* (Los Angeles, 1985); George Reid Andrews, *Blacks and Whites in São Paulo, Brazil, 1888–1988* (Madison, 1991), 191–207, 216–33; Michael George Hanchard, "Orpheus

and Power: The Movimento Negro of Rio de Janeiro and São Paulo, 1945–1988" (Ph.D. diss., Princeton University, 1991).

2. Brazil's total population in 1980 was 119.0 million, of whom 64.5 million were white, 46.2 million brown (*pardo*), 7.1 million black (*preto*), 0.7 million yellow (Asian), and 0.5 million of undeclared race. Instituto Brasileiro de Geografia e Estatística (hereafter IBGE), *Recenseamento geral do Brasil – 1980. Censo demográfico* (Rio de Janeiro, 1983), Table 1.4, 10–11. In recent years IBGE researchers have combined *pardos* and *pretos* into a single "black" (*negro*) category; see, for example, Lúcia Elena Garcia de Oliveira *et al.*, *O lugar do negro na força de trabalho* (Rio de Janeiro, 1985). In the remainder of this chapter I will use "black" in this broader (and essentially North American) sense, to indicate people of both pure and mixed African ancestry.

3. On racial democracy, see Florestan Fernandes, *A integração do negro na sociedade de classes*, 3rd edition, (São Paulo, 1978), 1, 249–69; Emília Viotti da Costa, *The Brazilian Empire: Myths and Histories* (Chicago, 1985), 234–46; Thales de Azevedo, *Democracia racial* (Petrópolis, 1975); Carlos Hasenbalg, "Race Relations in Modern Brazil" (Albuquerque, 1985); Hanchard, "Orpheus and Power," 48–95 and *passim*.

4. On political conditions under the Republic, see Joseph L. Love, "Political Participation in Brazil, 1881–1969," *Luso-Brazilian Review*, 3, no. 2 (1970): 7–15; Joseph L. Love, *São Paulo in the Brazilian Federation, 1889–1937* (Stanford, 1980); José Murilo de Carvalho, *Os bestializados: Rio de Janeiro e a República que não foi* (São Paulo, 1987); June Hahner, *Poverty and Politics: The Urban Poor in Brazil, 1870–1920* (Albuquerque, 1986).

5. Between 1890 and 1930 Brazil received the largest volume of immigrants, 3.5 million, of any period in its history. The national population was 14.3 million in 1890, and 30.6 million in 1920. Thomas W. Merrick and Douglas H. Graham, *Population and Economic Development in Brazil* (Baltimore, 1979), 91. On Brazilian racial ideology during this period, and the "whitening thesis," see Thomas E. Skidmore, *Black into White: Race and Nationality in Brazilian Thought* (New York, 1974).

6. Andrews, *Blacks and Whites*, 54–89; Sam Adamo, "The Broken Promise: Race, Health, and Justice in Rio de Janeiro, 1890–1940" (Ph.D. diss., University of New Mexico, 1983).

7. Boris Fausto, *Trabalho urbano e conflito social, 1890–1920* (São Paulo, 1977); Sheldon Leslie Maram, *Anarquistas, imigrantes e o movimento operário brasileiro* (Rio de Janeiro, 1979).

8. Boris Fausto, *A revolução de 1930* (São Paulo, 1970); Silvio R. Duncan Baretta and John Markoff, "The Limits of the Brazilian Revolution of 1930," *Review*, 9, no. 3 (1986): 413–52.

9. On this period, see Robert M. Levine, The Vargas Regime: *The Critical Years, 1934–1938* (New York, 1970); and the essay by Barbara Weinstein in this volume.

10. Brazil received more African slaves than any other New World country, and approximately ten times as many as the United States; and it maintained slavery longer than any other Western nation, until 1888. On the importance of plantation agriculture in Brazilian history, see Gilberto Freyre, *The Masters and the Slaves: A Study in the Development of Brazilian*

Civilization (New York, 1946); James Lang, *Portuguese Brazil: The King's Plantation* (New York, 1979); and Stuart B. Schwartz, *Sugar Plantations in the Formation of Brazilian Society: Bahia, 1550–1835* (Cambridge and New York, 1985).

11. See, for example, Francisco José de Oliveira Vianna, *O idealismo da constituição* (Rio de Janeiro, 1927); Afonso Arinos de Mello Franco, *Introdução à realidade brasileira* (Rio de Janeiro, 1933); Azevedo Amaral, *O estado autoritário e a realidade nacional* (Rio de Janeiro, 1938).

12. See his *Masters and Slaves; The Mansions and the Shanties: The Making of Modern Brazil* (New York, 1963); *Order and Progress: Brazil from Monarchy to Republic* (New York, 1970); *New World in the Tropics* (New York, 1959).

13. Freyre, *Mansions and Shanties*, 354–99; see also Herbert Klein, "The Colored Freedman in Brazilian Slave Society," *Journal of Social History*, 3, no. 1 (1969): 30–52.

14. Freyre, *Mansions and Shanties*, 231–2; *Masters and Slaves*, xiv–xv.

15. See, for example, Frank Tannenbaum, *Slave and Citizen: The Negro in the Americas* (New York, 1946); David J. Hellwig, ed., *African-American Reflections on Brazil's Racial Paradise* (Philadelphia, 1992).

16. Luis Aguiar Costa Pinto, *O negro no Rio de Janeiro* (Rio de Janeiro, 1953); Roger Bastide and Florestan Fernandes, *Relações raciais entre negros e brancos em São Paulo* (São Paulo, 1955); Fernando Henrique Cardoso and Octávio Ianni, *Côr e mobilidade social em Florianópolis* (São Paulo, 1960). For more positive portrayals of Brazilian race relations, focusing on the Northeast, see Donald Pierson, *Negroes in Brazil: A Study of Race Contact in Bahia* (Chicago, 1942); Charles W. Wagley, ed., *Race and Class in Rural Brazil* (Paris, 1952); Thales de Azevedo, *As elites de cor: Um estudo de ascensão social* (São Paulo, 1955).

17. Nelson do Valle Silva, "Black–White Income Differentials: Brazil, 1960" (Ph.D. diss., University of Michigan, 1978); Carlos Hasenbalg, *Discriminação e desigualdades raciais no Brasil* (Rio de Janeiro, 1979); Fontaine, *Race, Class and Power*; Oliveira, *Lugar do negro*; Peggy Lovell, "Racial Inequality and the Brazilian Labor Market" (Ph.D. diss., University of Florida, 1989); Andrews, *Blacks and Whites;* Peggy Lovell, ed., *Desigualdade racial no Brasil contemporâneo* (Belo Horizonte, 1991).

18. Freyre himself confirms this point when, in discussing the frequency of upward mobility for racially mixed Brazilians, he notes that "naturally we refer to the light mulatto; barring favorable special circumstances, the situation of the darker ones was much the same as that of the Negro." Freyre, *Mansions and Shanties*, 410.

19. For example, in 1987 literacy rates in Brazil were 71 percent for *pardos* and *pretos* and 87 percent for whites. One percent of *pretos* and 2 percent of *pardos* had graduated from college, as compared to 9 percent of whites. Median years of schooling were 1.8 for *pretos*, 1.9 for *pardos*, and 3.6 for whites. *Preto* median earnings were 58 percent those of white median earnings, and *pardo* median earnings were 57 percent. IBGE, *Pesquisa nacional por amostra de domicílios – 1987. Cor da população* (Rio de Janeiro, 1987), vol. 1, Tables 2, 4–5, 9. See also sources cited in note 17.

20.   On these impacts of the "mulatto escape hatch," see Carl Degler, *Neither Black nor White: Slavery and Race Relations in Brazil and the United States* (New York, 1971), 272–81. Beginning in the 1930s and continuing to the present, Afro-Brazilian activists have sought to persuade *pardos* and *pretos* to see themselves as belonging to a common *negro* (black) racial category; but these efforts have been only partially successful.

21.   Bolivar Lamounier, "Raça e classe na política brasileira," *Cadernos Brasileiros*, no. 47 (1968): 39–50; Hasenbalg, *Discriminação*, 241–6; Andrews, *Blacks and Whites*, 182–6, 227–9.

22.   George Reid Andrews, "Black Political Protest in São Paulo, Brazil, 1888–1988," *Journal of Latin American Studies* 24, no. 1 (1992): 147–72.

23.   An additional 58,600 Afro-Brazilians were employed in state, federal, and municipal government, but this category does not distinguish between white-collar and manual workers. IBGE, *Recenseamento geral do Brasil – 1940. Censo demográfico* (Rio de Janeiro, 1950), Table 30, pp. 36–7.

24.   Data provided to the author by IBGE. Comparable figures for whites in 1980 were 6.0 million professional and white-collar workers out of a total white population of 64.5 million.

25.   IBGE, *Recenseamento, 1940*, Table 25, p. 30; IBGE, *Recenseamento, 1980*, Table 1.5, pp. 12–13. Among the white population in 1980, 4.4 million had graduated from high school, and 729,000 from college.

26.   Silva, "Black–White Income Differentials"; Nelson do Valle Silva, "Updating the Cost of Not Being White in Brazil," in Fontaine, *Race, Class and Power*; Oliveira, *Lugar do negro*, 47–53; Jeffrey W. Dwyer and Peggy A. Lovell, "The Cost of Being Nonwhite in Brazil," *Sociology and Social Research*, no. 72 (1988): 136–42; Lovell, "Racial Inequality," 136–9.

27.   Silva, "Updating the Cost;" Peggy A. Lovell, "Development and Racial Inequality: Wage Discrimination in Urban Labor Markets, 1960–1980" (unpublished paper presented at the Peopling of the Americas Conference, Veracruz, Mexico, 1992).

28.   Examples include, in São Paulo, the Centro de Cultura e Arte Negra (founded in 1974) and the Casa de Arte e Cultura Afro-Brasileira (1977), and in Rio de Janeiro, the Instituto de Pesquisa das Culturas Negras (1976). For a 1988 listing of 573 Afro-Brazilian organizations, most of them "cultural" in orientation, see Caetana Damasceno et al., *Catálogo de entidades de movimento negro no Brasil* (Rio de Janeiro, 1988).

29.   Joel Rufino dos Santos, "O movimento negro e a crise brasileira," *Política e Administração*, 2, no. 2 (1985): 287–307; see the periodic reports on black movements in the US and Africa in the monthly magazine *Versus*, to which a number of young black journalists contributed. On the disagreements between the "Africanists" and "Americanists" in the black movement, see Hanchard, "Orpheus and Power," 136–40.

30.   Skidmore, *Politics of Military Rule*; Alves, *State and Opposition*; Stepan, *Democratizing Brazil*.

31.   The founding of the MNU is discussed in Lélia Gonzalez, "The Unified Black Movement: A New Stage in Black Political Mobilization," in Fontaine, *Race, Class and Power*. See also Hanchard, "Orpheus and Power," 206–21.

32. The jockeying of the parties for the black vote is described in João Baptista Borges Pereira, "Aspectos do comportamento político do negro em São Paulo," *Ciência e Cultura*, 34, no. 10 (1982): 1286–94; Ana Lúcia E.F. Valente, *Política e relações raciais: Os negros e as eleições paulistas de 1982* (São Paulo, 1986).

33. Glaucio Ary Dillon Soares and Nelson do Valle Silva, "Urbanization, Race, and Class in Brazilian Politics," *Latin American Research Review*, 22, no. 2 (1987): 155–76.

34. Valente, *Política e relações raciais*, 73–8.

35. "Movimento negro avalia sua importância," *Folha de São Paulo* (15 April 1984).

36. Valente, *Política e relações raciais*, 139.

37. For complaints by working-class blacks concerning the "elitist" rhetoric of many of the black activists, see "Movimento negro já conta 400 entidades e cresce no Brasil," *Jornal do Brasil* (12 May 1985); Celma Rosa Vieira, "Negra: mulher e doméstica," *Estudos Afro-Asiáticos*, 14 (1987), 154–6; "Em pauta: O movimento negro," *Maioria Falante* (November–December 1988): 8–9.

38. Charles H. Wood and José Alberto Magno de Carvalho, *The Demography of Inequality in Brazil* (Cambridge and New York, 1988).

39. Scott Mainwaring, "Grassroots Popular Movements and the Struggle for Democracy," in Stepan, *Democratizing Brazil*, 183. See also Teresa Caldeira, *A política dos outros: O cotidiano dos moradores da periferia e o que pensam do poder e dos poderosos* (São Paulo, 1984); Nancy Scheper-Hughes, *Death Without Weeping: The Violence of Everyday Life in Brazil* (Berkeley, 1992), 505–16.

40. Valente, *Política e relações raciais*, 125–8; Jorge Aparecido Monteiro, "Cor e trabalho na empresa pública: Uma introdução," *Série Estudos IUPERJ*, no. 56 (1987): 45, 75.

41. See Roberto da Matta's characterization of Brazilian life as "a relational universe" in which "one can deny anything save the request of a friend"; or Roberto Schwarz's observation that, in Brazil, "the favor is our nearly universal mediation." Roberto da Matta, *A casa e a rua: Espaço, cidadania, mulher e morte no Brasil* (São Paulo, 1985), 55–80 *passim*; Roberto Schwarz, *Ao vencedor as batatas* (São Paulo, 1977), 16. On the historical roots of this pattern, see Richard Graham, *Patronage and Politics in Nineteenth-Century Brazil* (Stanford, 1990); Costa, *Brazilian Empire*, 188–96, 241–4.

42. Anthropologist Nancy Scheper-Hughes reports of her informants in a small NorthEastern city, all of whom are poor and most of whom are Afro-Brazilian, that "as *eleitor[e]s* they will vote for the local, regional, and national candidates who are most likely to win, and they will avoid association with likely losers, even if the 'weaker' candidate has expressed solidarity with their class. As Tonieta [one of the women in the community] qualified her support of local political leaders, 'If you're going up, I'll tag along with you. If you're going down, *adeus*, you can go without me.'" Scheper-Hughes, *Death Without Weeping*, 473.

43. "Movimento negro avalia sua importância."

44. See, for example, profiles of activist/priest Frei David Raimundo dos Santos, or Congresswoman Benedita da Silva, a *favelada* elected in 1986 on the Partido dos Trabalhadores ticket. Jane Kramer, "Letter from the Elysian Fields," *The New Yorker* (2 March 1987): 40–74; "One Woman's Mission: To Make Brasilia Sensitive," *New York Times* (9 February 1987): 4.

45. "Democracia racial, o mito e o desejo," *Folhetim, Folha de São Paulo* (8 June 1980): 7–11.

46. This argument is made most effectively in Fernandes, *Integração do negro,* and Octávio Ianni, "Diversidades raciais e questão nacional," in *Raças e classes sociais,* 2nd ed. (São Paulo, 1988). See also other works cited in note 17.

47. On the electoral reform, which reduced suffrage from approximately one million voters to fewer than 150,000, see Graham, *Patronage and Politics,* 182–206.

48. Francisco Weffort, *Por que democracia?* (São Paulo, 1985), 21–31. Weffort quotes historian Sérgio Buarque de Holanda, one of the seminal thinkers of the 1930s, who characterized Brazilian democracy as "always a lamentable misunderstanding, imported by a rural and semi-feudal aristocracy which tried to accommodate it … to their rights and privileges … "

49. Silvio Duncan Baretta and John Markoff, "Brazil's *Abertura:* A Transition from What to What?" in James M. Malloy and Mitchell A. Seligson, eds., *Authoritarians and Democrats: Regime Transition in Latin America* (Pittsburgh, 1987), 53–7.

50. Azevedo, *Democracia racial,* 53; see also Gilberto Freyre, "A propósito de preconceito de raça no Brasil," *O Estado de São Paulo* (25 June 1969).

51. For the events of the centennial, see Yvonne Maggie, ed., *Catálogo: Centenário da abolição* (Rio de Janeiro, 1989).

52. "Vem ai cem anos de ebulição," *A Gazeta* (13 May 1988): 13; "Prêmio Nobel cobra mais ação contra apartheid," *Folha de São Paulo* (13 May 1988): 11.

53. Luis Inácio "Lula" da Silva, "A mistificação da democracia racial," *Folha de São Paulo* (16 February 1988): 3.

54. *"Ouvi o clamor deste povo" … negro* (Petrópolis, 1987).

55. "Cem anos, sem quasi nada," *Istoé* (20 April 1988): 30–3; "Na segunda classe," *Veja* (11 May 1988): 22–30.

56. "Cem anos depois," *Folha de São Paulo* (13 May 1988): 2; "Cem anos de solidão," *Caderno B, Jornal do Brasil* (8 May 1988): 8. For other denunciations of racial inequality, see the supplements on "Abolição: 100 anos," *Diário Popular* (12 May 1988); "Vem ai cem anos de ebulição," *A Gazeta* (13 May 1988): 13–18; "Brasil: os negros, hoje," *Manchete* (21 May 1988): 4–9; "Another Myth Bites the Dust," *The Brasilians* (May–June 1988): 2.

57. "Abolição é exemplo de congraçamento e união," *O Globo* (13 May 1988): 6; "Racismo é crime," *O Estado de São Paulo* (3 February 1988).

58. "Racismo em São Paulo motiva 64 processos em 2 anos," *Folha de São Paulo* (27 January 1991).

59. "Negros no governo," *Veja* (5 December 1990): 40–1; "Em pauta: O movimento negro;" "A esquerda que o negro quer," *Maioria Falante* (December

1989–January 1990): 6–7; "Negros trocam militância por nova identidade," *O Estado de São Paulo* (12 November 1991).

60. "Sarney sanciona lei que pune os crimes raciais," *Folha de São Paulo* (6 January 1989).

61. George Reid Andrews, "Racial Inequality in Brazil and the United States: A Statistical Comparison," *Journal of Social History*, 26, no. 2 (1992): 229–63.

10 Modes of Opposition Leading to Revolution in Eastern Europe

Gale Stokes

With the exception of a handful of books on Poland, work by a few Western social scientists on factories in Hungary, and the studies of two notable anthropologists who worked in Romania, essentially no social history of the post-Second World War period comparable to the work that has been done for twenty years or more in the West exists concerning Eastern Europe before 1989. The most obvious reason for this is that the Communist regimes forbade such work, since the findings of any real social science were likely to undermine the claims of the vanguard party. The entire sociology department of Charles University in Prague was disbanded after 1968, and in Bulgaria the field of "anthropology" is a post-1989 product. The primacy of the Cold War paradigm also hindered the development of investigations in the West that were not overtly political or economic. Even Western interest in the democratic opposition in Eastern Europe tended to lead to theoretical constructs, such as the widespread use of the concept of civil society, rather than to concrete research projects that investigated the sociological ingredients of this opposition.

I begin with this disclaimer because I am about to make an argument that, with the exception of Poland, the revolutions of 1989 in Eastern Europe were not social revolutions in the way we have thought of them in the past. Whether this view is a construct of the data, or rather the lack of data, or whether it has a more substantial basis remains to be seen. We are only at the beginning of our investigations of these events, and it will be some time before we have the fine-grained analyses on which more substantial analysis can be based.

In Poland a self-activating workers' movement that created democratic forms of social interaction over a period of at least twenty years was the force behind the creation of Tadeusz Mazowiecki's government in August 1989, but none of the other countries of Eastern Europe experienced even a modest mobilization of either the working class or the peasantry prior to

1989. Neither did the new technocratic class provide a social basis for their revolutions, as some thought possible twenty years ago. In Hungary the growth of alternative forms of ownership and the reforms of the early 1980s that opened Hungary's internal market and its foreign trade furthered a process of embourgeoisement, but the beneficiaries of this policy played almost no direct role in Hungary's negotiated revolution. The social force of an aroused public did play a fundamental role in 1989, as demonstrators by the millions convinced Communist regimes that their time had come; but street demonstrations, whatever their short-term effects on public memory, are poor substitutes for the thick organization of pluralist societies, very little of which existed in any East European country by 1989.

The lack of obvious social determinants has caused some analysts to question whether the events of 1989 can be called democratic revolutions at all, especially because they lacked a level of violence normally associated with the concept of revolution. Even the Romanian events were small potatoes compared to the bloody traditions of the great revolutions. And in contrast to earlier social revolutions, the revolutions of 1989 were not progressive because they restored or sought to copy social and economic norms that had previously existed in Eastern Europe or that had proven successful elsewhere rather than opening new avenues for human development, as presumably the French Revolution did and as the Bolshevik Revolution claimed to be doing. Neither were they democratic in the sense that they created truly interactive forms of political discourse. The political mobilization of East European populations proceeds today not primarily by means of the self-activization of individuals forming primary groups but through appeals to the citizenry to join this or that political party formed and led by elites. For all these reasons I refer to the 1989 revolutions with a small "r" and with adjectival prefixes, such as "negotiated revolution."

But to deny that the events of 1989 were revolutionary because they were not sufficiently democratic or were not progressive is both to apply an ideal rather than a realistic standard to them and to miss their fundamental importance. None of the great revolutions actually produced an ideal democracy, a contested concept in any event; and the very notion of progressive was itself a product of the dialectical modes of thinking characteristic of the system that was overthrown in 1989. The term "progressive" is a product of nineteenth-century positivistic optimism and of its teleological relative, the dialectical process. Both ideas today have a distinctly anachronistic tone. The new notion in Eastern Europe is pluralism, which is not progressive, and not even a system, but rather a process whose outcome is unknown and whose structures vary, albeit within a particular type of world-wide economic system. Pluralism is not new, of course, since it emerged from the same eighteenth-century milieu from which Marxism emerged. But if the events of 1989 can be understood as the recognition that the centrally planned system failed, then it seems appropriate at the very least to term those events revolutionary in the negative sense that they interred any realistic hope that the teleological experiment in the use of human reason to transform society in its entirety might succeed. (The hope itself had died twenty years earlier.)

From a more positive point of view, the changes introduced in 1989 were startling. They hold significant hope for the development of the countries of Eastern Europe into functioning pluralistic societies. Not only were the former authorities overthrown, except perhaps in Romania, but the ideological justifications advanced by the vanguard party were rejected in their entirety; centralized planning was renounced, at least in principle; and private property was restored, once again at first mainly in principle. This latter change is now in the process of creating a basis for the emergence of another "new class" in Eastern Europe that eventually can be expected to fill the gap left by the decline and defeat of Djilas's "new class" of party and state agents that dominated the socialist societies of Eastern Europe since 1945. It is difficult to imagine a more sudden and more complete creation of the conditions for a social transformation than the events of 1989, especially if we understand that social change is the consequence of revolution just as much as it is the cause.

The revolutions of 1989 suggest in a newly powerful way that democratic forms are as much a product of the ethical and moral demands of the French Revolution, the calculus of freedom and the demand for equity, as they are of social determinants, although there clearly is a close relationship between pluralist economic systems and pluralist political forms. This is not to suggest that the question of how ideas turn into actions is not a fundamental locus of investigation or to deny that it is people who make history, not ideas. Neither should it be inferred that the revolutions took place entirely in the realm of ideas or that there were no underlying structural elements. In fact, it is highly unlikely that the revolutions would have occurred at all had not the centrally planned economies failed or had Mikhail Gorbachev not begun his reform process in the Soviet Union. The legitimacy of modern governments rests on their ability to deliver economic success, and East European governments were no exception. The extent of the economic failure of the centrally planned economies surpassed even the most pessimistic evaluations, and the responsible regimes paid the price of their failure. But if we concentrate on this factor alone or on the Gorbachev factor, we miss the most important part of the process – the utter moral rot that hollowed out the East European regimes and turned them into empty husks ready to be blown away with the first strong winds.

The initial Soviet incursion into Eastern Europe was no empty husk – it was the Red Army, which swept across the region in 1944 and 1945, and then, in varying degree, remained for the next 45 years. The entire history of Eastern Europe from 1945 to 1989, in fact, can be considered as one spasmodic imposition of Stalinism followed by forty years of adjusting, accommodating, opposing, reinterpreting, and rejecting. Naturally, this imposition did not occur on a blank slate. Each East European country had its particular historical background and characteristic political culture. Post-1989 events have suggested that despite the strenuous efforts of the Stalinists, these historical roots still exist and still play their role. But during the first few years of the Stalinist imposition, East European societies underwent a forceful transformation of enormous brutality that temporarily blotted out that past.

Naturally, the Communists who imposed Stalinism did not believe that they were creating a monster. Jacob Berman, interviewed in the early 1980s, believed that the Communists saved Poland from being crushed between a revanchist capitalism, by which he meant Germany supported by the United States, and an occupying army from the Soviet Union. Even at that late date Berman was still "convinced that the sum of our actions, skillfully and carefully carried out, will finally produce results and create a new Polish consciousness; because all the advantages flowing from our new path will be borne out, must be borne out."[1] Berman's lingering enthusiasm illustrates something that tends to be forgotten today. In the immediate post-war period many people, not only Communists catapulted to power by the Red Army, welcomed the chance to transform Eastern Europe. Charles Gati points out that approximately 50 percent of the Hungarian electorate in 1945 wanted radical change, and in Czechoslovakia all major parties favored nationalization of large industry, which actually took place before the final Communist takeover in 1948.[2] As G.M. Tamás puts it: "It is true that the Communist party dictatorship was brought to the small East European countries by the victorious troops of Stalin, but we should admit that we were ready for it."[3]

But since Stalinism was imposed by force, because it was perceived as being Russian, and because it did not work economically, it was only natural that opposition arose. In the 1960s the term *dissident* became the popular descriptive term for oppositionists in both the Soviet Union and Eastern Europe, but it was never a particularly good choice. For one thing, it hid the diversity of the opposition. Charter 77, for example, was made up of former Communist officials like Zdeněk Mlynář, revolutionary socialists like Petr Uhl, conservative Catholics like Václav Benda, and completely apolitical intellectuals like Václav Havel. The term *dissident* also implied that the opposition was static – a dissident in the Soviet Union in the 1960s being essentially equivalent to a dissident in Czechoslovakia in the 1980s. As the very term "Solidarity" suggests, the myth of a homogeneous opposition temporarily obscured the normal sociological facts of diversity and of process over time. In other words, opposition had a history.

That history is conceived here as the convergence of two originally antithetical tendencies that eventually came together in 1989. The first tendency began with the violent opposition put up by suicidal military and guerrilla movements that continued to resist Communist occupation in some places for several years following the Second World War. The second tendency began with the dissimulation practiced in the face of overwhelming force to which Czesław Miłosz has given the name "ketman."[4] The first might be termed the heroic strand of opposition, the second the survival strand.[5]

The violent military confrontations of opponents to the Communist regimes in the early post-war period have yet to find their historian, but their futility was heart-wrenching and complete. Facing a mobilized and energetic Red Army, or, in the case of the Chetniks, a mobilized and energetic Yugoslav army, traditional guerrilla movements were totally outgunned and crushed with complete finality. A significant number of people were involved in these actions, but most people in Eastern Europe who were unhappy with the new regimes and who were not killed or did not emigrate adopted a survival strategy of dissimulation, public accommodation justified with a whole variety of private reasonings. Czesław Miłosz describes many forms of this "ketman," as he calls it, such as the aesthetic person who conforms to all the canons of socialist realism in public life but maintains reproductions of "real" art on the walls of his or her flat, or the national dissimulator who hides his or her own nationalism under an exaggerated display of affection for the Soviet Union.

Almost all persons under Communist rule practiced dissimulation of this sort with varying levels of intensity throughout the entire socialist era, some quite cynically, and the majority of the population did not get much beyond this level even at the end. But dissimulation was the characteristic form of dissent only in periods of the most severe repression, which, not coincidentally, were the periods in which regimes were run by individuals who so strongly believed in their cause that they insisted on genuine conversion rather than mere observation of overt forms.

The Hungarian Revolution of 1956 was the polar opposite of accommodation, and it constitutes the next step in the heroic tradition of opposition.[6] It was a less violent confrontation than the post-war guerrilla wars if only because it took place in only one country and lasted only ten days. Following Stalin's death other countries had achieved some working space within the socialist commonwealth without violence. The Polish October (1956) was ecstatic but generally peaceful, although serious repressions took place in Poznań, and the right of Yugoslavia to tread its separate path to socialism had been recognized the previous year by Khrushchev. But in Hungary the unprepared events of October got out of hand. Whereas by 1956 the Yugoslavs had been thinking about how to construct a non-Stalinist socialism for five or six years, and in Poland vigorous discussions with the party, among the intellectuals, and at the workplace took place throughout 1956, Hungarians entered their revolution socially and intellectually relatively unprepared. Suddenly finding hundreds of thousands of people in the streets, Imre Nagy moved precipitately, declaring Hungarian neutrality and withdrawal from the Warsaw Pact. When the Red Army re-entered Budapest shooting, the Hungarians shot back. The Hungarian Revolution of 1956 was an unconsidered but heroic outburst of rage and defiance that ended, as romantic tragedy does, in death but not in ultimate defeat.

Stalin's death permitted the beginning of a new phase of the survival mode of opposition also – the Marxist critique. Agreeing that Stalinism was a distorted form of Marxism, both governments and oppositionists began a search for ways to create a better socialism. On the side of the governments, the main pressure came from economic reformers. Even the collegial leadership that came to power in the Soviet Union immediately following Stalin's death agreed that a "new course" was needed in the economy, and by the 1960s economic reformers were finding ways to introduce marketizing concepts while still using Marxist terminology. The publication of E.G. Liberman's famous article in *Pravda* in 1962 began a debate in the socialist countries of how best to reform their economies. In Yugoslavia Branko Horvat suggested that marginal prices were theoretically the best device for allocating resources, although, he claimed, they were not practical. In Poland, Oskar Lange proposed a "normal price" that sounded a good deal like Adam Smith's "natural price," while Włodzimierz Brus argued that indirect measures would be more effective than direct control for stimulating the economy. The Czechoslovak Ota Šik struggled to get a hearing for his "humane economic democracy," and in Hungary actual reform got underway after three years of detailed planning with the introduction of the New Economic Mechanism of 1968. Even East Germany and Bulgaria got into the act with superficial reform measures.

While none of these economic discussions were undertaken by oppositionists, they all posed the question of reform in ways that were antithetical to centralized planning and to direct party control of the economy. But all were couched in terms of Marxian economics. By the middle of the 1960s only a few persons had read any of the Austrian or neoconservative economists (Václav Klaus, later Czechoslovak Minister of Finance, came across Hayek while studying in North America in 1962, for example), and certainly no one was publicly advocating any sort of market economy.

Political oppositionists also presented their cases in Marxist terms. The most famous of these was Milovan Djilas, whose *The New Class*, published in 1956, remains in print today. Djilas had been a main player in Yugoslav communism since the late 1930s and had risen to be perhaps second in command of the new revolutionary state. But Djilas was and remained morally an adolescent, which is to say he never stopped asking sophomoric questions and therefore never lost his moral edge. After leading an underground Communist movement to power, he, unlike any other leader in Eastern Europe – or elsewhere, for that matter – refused to stop his critique of the abuse of power. His view that a new class of party officials had replaced the bourgeoisie as the dominant class in socialist societies, including Yugoslavia, remained a basic contribution, and his prediction of its end was positively prescient. "When this new class leaves the historical scene, and this must happen," he said in 1956, "there will be less sorrow over its passing than there was for any class before it."[7]

During the 1960s the most notorious critique of Polish socialism was, if anything, even more steeped in Marxism. It came from the pen of two young activists, Jacek Kuroń and Karol Modzelewski, today pillars of the post-1989 establishment. Although they are now embarrassed about their "Open Letter to the Party," which presented a Trotskyite interpretation of what had happened in Poland since the Second World War, the authors' style was wholly characteristic of opposition in the pre-Prague Spring era. The two authors agreed that Poland needed to develop economically and that a vigorous program of growth had gotten under way, but, like Djilas, they observed that the deadening hand of bureaucracy had stifled the country. Djilas did not offer any solutions to this problem, although he eventually went on to reject Marxism completely, but Kuroń and Modzelewski argued that only a direct workers' democracy would create the conditions for development in Poland. Their suggestions got them three years in prison.

The most sophisticated Marxist oppositionists in the 1960s were those surrounding *Praxis*, the Yugoslav journal that attracted socialist writers from around the world. The *Praxis* group consisted of a variety of intellectuals unified by their interest in the implications of the writings of the young Marx and their concern with problems of alienation. They not only did not believe, as even the relatively liberal League of Yugoslav Communists claimed, that socialism had put an end to alienation, they found that it was precisely the existing Communist parties that "cripple human beings, arrest their development, and impose on them patterns of simple, easily predictable, dull, stereotyped behavior."[8] They advocated free transformative activity and commitment that draws out genuine needs, not the false ones they observed around them. The *Praxis* group had begun to penetrate to the main theme of later oppositionists, the ethical vacuity of "real existing socialism," the difference between its claims and its actuality. Their project was not to abandon the claims but rather to adjust the actuality, since critical inquiry for them remained the only appropriate corrective.

The heroic tradition of opposition and the survival tradition, as represented by the economists and political theorists, came together momentarily in Prague in 1968. The Prague Spring was much better prepared than the Hungarian Revolution of 1956, in the sense that both the oppositionists and the party reformers had been advocating change in public forums for more than a year. But the main impetus for reform came not from civil society – indeed, no such entity existed in Czechoslovakia – nor from the working people, but from within the party, which meant that the Prague Spring remained a reform movement in the Marxist mold. The main vehicle the party proposed for improving political communication between the people and the regime, for example, was to be the National Front, in which differing views of public issues could be raised and forwarded to the party. But the abandonment of censorship that went with the airing of reform possibilities brought out not only oppositionists from the left but for the first time activists who suggested going beyond socialism. When Václav Havel suggested that perhaps it would be better having two political parties rather than merely permitting differing opinions to exist within the National Front, everyone was shocked, especially the Soviets. The economic reforms of the Prague Spring also remained in the tradition of tinkering with centralized planning, assuming that the dawn of the computer age would make a just and efficient plan possible through sophisticated technological innovations.

By the manner in which they suppressed the Prague Spring, the Soviets showed that they had learned something from 1956. Rather than marching in the Red Army shooting, they called upon their surrogates, the Warsaw Pact forces. When the Czechs and Slovaks did not shoot, the invaders did not shoot back. The Czechs and Slovaks resisted in ways calculated to annoy and to hinder the invading forces, and the Husák/B'ilak regime imposed a much longer-lasting regime of normalization than János Kádár had in Hungary, but in one sense August 1968 represented a significant de-escalation of violence in the heroic tradition of confrontation.

It almost goes without saying that 1968 destroyed any chance for socialism with a human face to be taken seriously in Eastern Europe, since the Soviet Union proved that it would not tolerate anything except its own rigid forms. The March Days in Warsaw and the student demonstrations in Belgrade, both of which occurred in 1968, reinforced that conclusion in Poland and Yugoslavia. With the exception perhaps of the Budapest School in Hungary and of East German oppositionists like Robert Havemann and Rudolf Bahro, both of whom continued to find Marxist discourse useful, and with the temporary exception of Romania, where Ceaușescu's non-participation in the invasion of Czechoslovakia produced a surge of party membership, the events of 1968 ended the viability of Marxist discourse in Eastern Europe.

Less recognized is the fact that Soviet decisions taken in 1968 constituted an economic watershed as well as a political and a psychological one. Politically the Prague Spring is remembered for the Brezhnev Doctrine, and psychologically it is the moment when belief became impossible. But economically, the decision not to permit socialism to evolve in a democratic direction also ended the possibility that the centrally planned economies would be reformed along the lines suggested in the 1960s by revisionist Marxist economists. Instead of rejecting the exhausted extensive strategy of development in favor of an intensive strategy, which presumed a competitive entry into the world market, Brezhnev scuttled the very modest Liberman reforms and forced his satellite states in Eastern Europe to hunker down once again within the sheltering arms of Comecon (Council of Mutual Economic Assistance, the Soviet-sponsored international trade organization for socialist economies). Every East European country, except Poland, which had not introduced significant reforms in the 1960s anyway, recentralized its planning and control mechanisms in the early 1970s, even Hungary and Yugoslavia. The East Europeans took these steps backward at a time when the environment of world trade was changing dramatically. During the 1970s the newly industrializing countries of the Pacific Rim began to come on line; the oil crises forced industrialized states to become more efficient; service industries began to replace manufacturing as the characteristic economic activity in the older industrialized states; and the information revolution began to transform the ways business was conducted. It may not have been possible to reform the centrally planned economies adequately in any event, but the almost complete failure to try sentenced the economies of Eastern Europe to permanent backwardness. The combined loss of ideological confidence and economic competence utterly destroyed the claims of the East European regimes to legitimacy.

Before 1968 many people had already recognized that their regimes were totally false, but it was still possible to hope that things could change, could be improved. After 1968 almost everyone in society understood that public life was a lie. Polish workers learned, both in 1956 and in 1970–1971, that regime reform promises would not be kept; economists learned that proposals that threatened major interests would be scuttled; ordinary citizens learned that suggestions of innovation or change would bring dismissal or disciplinary action. Millions of people sensed their own humiliation and even mentioned it to each other in private, but Soviet force made their situation seem hopeless. What to do in such a situation? Many decided to opt out, giving the state its minimal due and focusing instead on gardening, sex, or alcoholism. Some, like Milan Kundera, gave up and emigrated, arguing that it was a waste of time for intellectuals to send blurry carbon copies of each other's poetry to one another in the face of such overwhelming force. But these admissions of defeat were a dead end that left the entire field of public life in the hands of the false regimes. The new question after 1968 for those who did not give up was not how to adapt to the system or how to change it according to its own principles, but how to live an authentic life in spite of it. As Jacek Kuroń put it later, "What is to be done when nothing can be done?"[9]

Leszek Kołakowski provided one of the earliest and most compelling answers to this question in an article entitled "Hope and Hopelessness" published in the Paris journal *Kultura* in 1971.[10] The situation is hopeless, Kołakowski argued, because every effort at democratization in the Leninist state appropriates some aspect of the total control the regime enjoys and will not relinquish. But precisely because the leaders have no intention of relinquishing their power, they will be forced to cover the conflicts of interests that will inevitably occur among them with a false ideological screen. This will continually undermine their claim to meaning and therefore their claim to eternal power. But true hope does not lie in the working out of this historical process, which is in itself a false claim of the regimes, but rather with the power of individuals to believe that hope is possible. Hope lies in living an ethical life, not in forming an opposition party, which would only create the same desire to impose "correct" solutions on society that was the failing of the Communist regimes. As Adam Michnik put it later, "By using force to storm the existing Bastilles we shall unwittingly build new ones."[11]

Others in East Central Europe brought forward similar strategies in the hopeless situation. In 1967 Ludvík Vaculík had already enjoined his fellow Czechoslovaks to live "as if" they were free, and a decade later a group of Czechoslovak intellectuals formed Charter 77 to be a public, open grouping dedicated to the international norms of human rights. Charter 77 eschewed not only politics but any organizational structure at all. "Charter 77 is not an organization," the founding document stated. "It has no rules, permanent bodies, or formal membership. It embraces everyone who agrees with its ideas, participates in its work, and supports it."[12]

Václav Havel presented the most engaging and penetrating theory of the new style of antipolitics in his essay, "The Power of the Powerless." For Havel real life resided in the realm of the ethical, not in the realm of the political. "Under the orderly surface of the life of lies," he wrote, "there slumbers the hidden sphere of life in its real aims ... The singular, explosive, incalculable political power of living within the truth resides in the fact that living openly within the truth has an ally, invisible to be sure, but omnipresent: this hidden sphere."[13] This was the power of the powerless: to "live in truth." Only in this way could one experience the certainty that things make sense, and only in this way could one begin the hopeless project of creating a decent life.

The anti-political project constituted an entirely new phase of opposition, and a devastating one. No longer accommodating and no longer using Marxist discourse, the anti-politicians simply told people to ignore the regime and to live an honest life. Communist governments knew how to compromise dissemblers and how to silence oppositionists who spoke their own language, but now they found themselves contesting a space they could not even enter. One Polish author, Konstanty Gebert, put it this way: "A small, portable barricade between me and silence, submission, humiliation, shame. Impregnable for tanks, uncircumventable. As long as I man it, there is, around me, a small area of freedom."[14]

If anti-politics was a more thoroughly grounded and ethically engaging evolution of the survival strategy of opposition, the next stage in the history of East European opposition came from a genuine social movement that adopted an anti-political ethic. Solidarity transformed the ideal of living in truth, a strategy born of isolation and hopelessness, into a broad movement aiming to create an independent society in which all, or many, citizens could achieve a sense of freedom. By the 1970s every East European country, although some to greater degrees than others, possessed a population that was significantly alienated from its regime. But Solidarity was the only organization until 1989 that was able to tap that discontent in a politically forceful way. One reason was that the workers

of Poland were the only ones in the region to devise their own mechanisms for self-activization. It seems clear today from the work of Roman
Laba that the idea of an independent trade union, along with the tactics of
the occupation strike and the interfactory strike committee, were first
invented by the coastal dock workers of Szczecin in 1971, and that these
innovations, reinvented in 1980 by the workers of the Lenin Shipyard
under Lech Wałęsa's leadership, were the creative basis of Solidarity.[15]

Nevertheless, Solidarity was in intent an anti-political movement. Its
goal was not to create a political party that would try to seize power and
impose its views. That was the failure of the past. Solidarity simply sought
autonomy to pursue goals of interest to itself – the freeing of the workers
from the heavy hand of the party. Even in the strikes of 1970 and 1971 the
force behind the strikes was not, as one striker put it, "the compulsion, the
use of force so much, but the moral element, the element of honor."[16] The
second paragraph of the Solidarity Program of 1981 reads in part: "What
we had in mind were not only bread, butter, and sausage but also justice,
democracy, truth, legality, human dignity, freedom of convictions, and the
repair of the republic ... Thus the economic protest had also to be simultaneously a social protest, and the social protest had to be simultaneously a
moral protest."[17] Solidarity's position was also the position of the intelligentsia. Jan Józef Lipski, one of the organizers of the Worker's Defense
League (KOR), which was a group of intellectuals who came to the
defense of strikers in 1976 and formed the intellectual core of the
Solidarity movement, stated in his study of that organization that its
mission was "to appeal above all to ethical values and to general moral
standards rather than political attitudes," and after the Bydgoszcz crisis
within Solidarity in 1981 Andrzej Gwiazda said that in his view Solidarity
was primarily a "moral revolution."[18]

From the beginning the Solidarity movement was self-limiting, maintaining that it was simply a labor union and not a political opposition and
remaining as true as it could to its anti-political roots. Wałęsa and the
others feared the intervention of the Soviet Union, and they hesitated to
sacrifice labor union gains by forcing a political confrontation. But
Solidarity, despite its ethic, could not be an anti-political movement.
Politics is about power, and when a movement encompasses more than
half the active workforce of a society and has the ability to call these
workers out on strike, it has no choice but to enter the political arena.

The state recognized this better than Solidarity did. When it decided to
act, it did so brutally and with determination. Many were sent to prison
and others were badly beaten, lost their jobs, and experienced harrassment;
but in comparison with 1945, 1956, and 1968, the imposition of a State of

War, as martial law was called in Poland, represented another de-escalation of violence on the part of the Soviet Union, an amelioration of their response to heroic opposition. This time neither the Soviets nor their Warsaw Pact partners intervened, and there was no foreign occupation. Instead, a local surrogate who was far from being a Stalinist subdued Solidarity. At the time martial law in Poland seemed yet another example of how impossible change was in Eastern Europe and how certain repression was in the face of genuine aspirations. But the balance had tipped in a decisive way. After the Second World War the problem facing East European societies was how to adjust to the Stalinist state; after 1981 in Poland the question became how the state was going to adjust to society. Instead of dissimulating, reforming, or opting out, oppositionists had found a positive democratic agenda of their own that would reshape the state in a new form altogether.

This is not the way it looked at the time. The depression among polish oppositionists was as great in 1983 as it was among Czechoslovaks in 1970, but there was a difference. In Poland millions of people realized that opposition to the vanguard party and its state was possible for two reasons that were peculiar to the Polish experience. The first was the existence of a Polish Pope. In the late 1970s the activities of KOR, which included an impressive amount of underground publishing, mobilized many students and intellectuals and reached tens of thousands of workers, but it left most of society untouched. The elevation of Karol Wojtyła to Pope in 1978, however, and his visits to Poland in 1979 and 1983, galvanized millions of Poles and proved to them in a visceral way that another form of loyalty was possible. The second was underground Solidarity's success in keeping alive the flame of the movement that had attracted ten million members during its short existence. The breadth of underground publishing, radio broadcasts, videotape recording, and educational efforts during the years of martial law was amazing, so that by the late 1980s Solidarity was, in the minds of Poles, synonymous with democracy, unionism, pluralism – in short, of everything that the regime was not. The difficulties were great, the conflicts within the opposition epic, the discouragements profound, but the existence of a large public experienced in the memory of an independent church and a free union provided a unique resource for the ultimate transformation of Poland. General Jaruzelski eventually recognized this. In 1986 he began a series of moves that led to the round-table talks, the election of June 1989, and the installation of a Solidarity government.

The coming of Solidarity to power in September 1989 proved to be one of the most significant ingredients in the rush to revolution throughout the region that stunned the world the last three months of 1989. During that period the declining violence of Soviet reaction to heroic postures reached its ultimate conclusion – the Soviet Union did not intervene at all. This was not a simple matter of leaving the troops in the barracks. Given the dynamics of Mikhail Gorbachev's policies he no longer had the choice to intervene.

Gorbachev's new thinking had both a domestic and a foreign thrust. Coming to power at a moment when the Soviets realized they could not continue to compete technologically with the West in armaments, and understanding even more clearly that the Soviet Union could not sustain its great power status by simply being a Third World state with guns, Gorbachev undertook to restructure the Soviet economy. In order to push the painful changes called for by *perestroika*, he understood that he needed to mobilize both the intellectuals and the population at large. *Glasnost* was the device he proposed to engage the intellectuals; and *demokratsiya*, which meant free but still limited elections, was the device he hoped would engage the people. Gorbachev seems to have believed that appreciative intellectuals and grateful people would rally to his support, thereby outflanking the party stalwarts who stood in the way of change. In foreign affairs, Gorbachev decided to make a virtue out of the Soviet Union's inability to match the West technologically by signing the INF treaty (it abolished intermediate range nuclear missiles) and otherwise reducing arms, and to undermine the influence of the United States in Western Europe by pursuing the slogan "our common European home." Whereas Brezhnev believed in offering the West the vinegar of military strength, Gorbachev and Shevardnadze offered the honey of a secure Euro-Asian continent.

The dual thrust of Gorbachev's interrelated campaign constitutes the most daring and ambitious effort to transform the European geopolitical stage peacefully in the twentieth century. If the Soviet Union could become an economically viable country with moderately democratic forms, it might find itself accepted into Europe, thus enhancing its security by lessening American engagement. And if it could be accepted into Europe, it could find the credits and the technology that its economic transformation required.

Poland was best prepared to enter the space that Gorbachev opened up for Eastern Europe by 1988. Tested and well-known opposition leaders undergirded by a real social base produced a dramatic result. Only one other country in Eastern Europe was similarly prepared for change, and that was Hungary. There economic reforms begun in the 1960s and reinforced by important innovations in the early 1980s led to a process of embourgeoisement that invigorated the economy and encouraged reformers within the party. The emergence of a new stratum of private and semi-private economic actors constituted a potential social basis for the creation of a political movement. But the small anti-political opposition in Hungary did not base its claim to be heard on support from this new stratum. Whereas in Poland the organizational experience that made an independent society possible occurred in the workplace and in volved the initiative of working people, in Hungary the organizational experience that produced a new oppositional leadership grew out of public demonstrations.

Starting in 1985 with small demonstrations against the Gabčikovo-Nagymaros dam project and on the occasion of the May 15 anniversary of the Revolution of 1848, the Hungarian democratic opposition was able by 1988 to draw thirty thousand people onto the streets of Budapest to demonstrate against the dam, another thirty thousand to protest Ceauşescu's village reconstruction plan, and ten thousand for the May 15 celebration. The meetings' organizers, who were mainly Budapest intellectuals and student leaders, provided the nucleus of democratic leadership that emerged in that year.

The episodic generation of street demonstrations did not have the organizational thickness that interfactory strike committees gave to Solidarity, but they nevertheless proved to be a vital form of social mobilization against the totalitarian state. The demonstrations gave the organizers experience, a temporary constituency, and public visibility. They tapped the widespread alienation of those parts of the urban population who knew the regime was false but had never known what to do about it. But street demonstrations are not broadly based social movements. In Hungary they mobilized a very large proportion of the urban young and the more educated middle classes, but they were very thinly populated with workers and peasants. In fact "people power," as it has been called since Corazon Aquino's rise to power in the Philippines in 1986, is a fickle form of social mobilization whose democratic content depends greatly on the elites who call it forth. Whereas in Hungary, Czechoslovakia, and East Germany the leadership came from highly ethical anti-political backgrounds and were able to focus the crowds on democratic change, in Serbia a narrow and self-interested leader was able to draw hundreds of thousands of people onto the streets in support of a racist ideology and in support of a vicious civil war. The key element in the revolutions of 1989, therefore, was not so much the mechanisms of street demonstrations that provided the impetus for change but the fact that they were fomented by a leadership committed to a democratic outcome. Of course the Hungarian opposition used nationalist arguments – their rallies were skillful evocations of

Hungarian historical moments – but they did not evoke racial hatred or make irredentist claims, as Slobodan Milošević did in Serbia.

At the same time a Hungarian opposition leadership was discovering its voice on the streets of Budapest, a reform wing was achieving power in the Hungarian party. In Poland the most reform-minded group within the party were the three main generals who ran the country. It was they who forced the Polish party in January 1989 to accede to round-table discussions. A reform wing had always existed in the Hungarian party, and when Gorbachev came to power it began to elbow the aging János Kádár aside, which it accomplished in 1988. Gorbachevian in their plans for Hungary, leaders like the economist Rezső Nyers undertook measures to push Hungary back into the world economy, such as a banking reform and an income tax, while political reformers like Imre Pozsgay, hoping to mobilize broader social support, entertained democratizing reforms.

The dramatic moment in which the street met the reforming party was the rally held in June 1989 on the occasion of the reburial of the remains of Imre Nagy. The climax of a year of change in the party and increasing pressure from rallies, this emotional occasion symbolized the restoration of Hungarian dignity. Everyone believed that the Hungarian Revolution of 1956 had not been a retrograde counter-revolutionary outburst, as the party had maintained for thirty years, but that it had been a nationwide effort to take Hungary back from the Russians and the Communists. With that historical memory now restored, the two parties – the oppositional leadership now gathered together in a number of protopolitical parties on the one side and the reform Communists on the other – undertook their own round-table discussions that led eventually to the creation of the current Hungarian democracy.

In the other countries of Eastern Europe, nothing similar to the mobilizations that took place in Poland and Hungary occurred. As of 1985 Romania and Bulgaria had no opposition at all, while in East Germany opposition consisted of only small groups of church-supported peace advocates. The only major opposition grouping in these four countries was Charter 77 in Czechoslovakia, and even it was pitifully small. In the other three countries the first glimmerings of a substantial political opposition occurred only in the late 1980s. In Bulgaria Ecoglasnost, an environmental group growing from protests in Ruse in 1987, enlisted members of the Bulgarian intelligentsia, and in Sofia a democratic discussion group entitled the Club for the Discussion of Perestroika and Glasnost emerged in 1988. In Czechoslovakia oppositionists specifically decided to become more political in 1988, while in East Germany the democratic opposition coalesced into a political organization only in September 1989. Romania did not even have such a group, although individuals made brave gestures and in 1989 a group of six very senior party members dared to write Ceauşescu demanding changes.

All of these oppositional movements endorsed the anti-political view that the party had destroyed normal life. Under "real existing socialism" it was impossible to live as a person in the twentieth century had a right to live, that is, as an autonomous individual making his or her own choices about religion, politics, art, sexual preference, or ethics. But because of repression none of the oppositional movements in these four countries penetrated very far into society, they were all small, and – worse – they did not know how to translate their growing understanding that society at large despised their regimes into effective political action. No East European country outside of Poland had a self-activating workers' movement. Occasionally work stoppages occurred in each country, even quite severe ones such as the demonstrations in Braşov in 1987, but regimes had always been able to prevent the communication of whatever lessons these strikes offered to those who had not participated directly in them. Except in Poland and Hungary, therefore, very few persons in Eastern Europe had any experiential knowledge of autonomous participation in public life. Because of the lack of a workers' movement, the Polish experience offered inspiration more than a usable organizational example, although the round-table proved to be a useful device everywhere.

East German collapse was set off when Hungary opened its borders in May 1989. When the August vacation season hit, thousands of East Germans crossed the border into Austria en route to their final destination, West Germany. In the early 1980s some scholars detected a distinct East German national feeling, a sense the regime assiduously nourished. But the GDR had always labored under the burden of being "the first workers' and peasants' state on German soil" rather than being simply Germany, as the Federal Republic of Germany styled itself. In other parts of Eastern Europe democracy was considered a desirable goal, but the concept was more or less empty, since the broad ranks of society had very little direct contact with the West. In East Germany, however, constant contact between East and West made the notion real and specific: it meant life as lived in West Germany. The mass mobilization of the hundreds of thousands of emigrants in 1989 did not emerge from the self- activated mobilization of the citizenry into a civil society so much as it did from a yearning for a better life constructed from the images of West Germany. This is one of the reasons why the East German opposition, many of whom regretted the thirst for capitalism, were swept aside so easily by the organized parties of the West in the elections of 1990, even though it was they who had provided the impetus for the peace rallies in Leipzig and other cities that toppled the regime.

Elsewhere in the region the roots of alienation lay to the East, in Soviet domination and in the sense that one did not have control over one's own life. East Germans felt the same alienation, but their attention focused on the West rather than the East. Most East Germans did not want to follow their democratic opposition and to build their own pluralist society, thereby creating the conditions for re-entering Europe – they wanted to enter the West directly. When the GDR joined West Germany it was left with no indigenously developed democratic tradition. The utter dominance of the West German political parties, economic administrators, and even professoriate pre-empted the public space in eastern Germany, leaving little room for self-activated movements there. The East German revolution was a social revolution in the sense that broad masses of the population were involved, and it was democratic in the narrow sense that democratic forms now exist in a formerly totalitarian country. But mobilization did not occur on behalf of an indigenous democracy, and the new forms were imposed from the West, albeit on a willing population, without preparation, so that it will take time to fill them with real democratic content. Perhaps the form will create its content, but the resentments unification has created are immense and account in significant measure for the antisocial behavior that characterized public life in the five east German *Länder* in the two years following unification.

The democratic turn in Bulgaria was not a broad popular movement, since it was initiated by party reformers who pushed Todor Zhivkov out in November 1989. In Bulgaria, the mobilization took place after the change, which makes it interesting that the course of developments there give promise that an indigenous and stable democratic system will take root. Todor Zhivkov was forced out the day after the Berlin Wall fell, but the transfer of power to the democratic opposition was only completed with the election of Zhelyu Zhelev to a five-year term as president in January 1992. Historically, Bulgaria has never had the same sort of antagonistic relationship with Russia as have the other peoples of Eastern Europe. The Russian army liberated them in the nineteenth century, and even in 1945 the Red Army did not stay long enough in Bulgaria to create the antagonisms it did elsewhere. Many Bulgarians speak Russian, and all educated Bulgarians can read it. In addition, from the late 1970s one of the three Bulgarian television channels was a Russian channel. Bulgarians could follow Gorbachev's progress toward reform more directly than could any other non-Soviets. By 1987 Russian newspapers regularly sold out, an unprecedented event in Eastern Europe, and Bulgarians had become obsessed with Gorbachev, whose program cast a very poor light on the phony reforms attempted by their own leaders.

Still, no truly popular movement emerged in Bulgaria until reformers in the party itself began the process by ousting Zhivkov. Once again the main experiential learning came in the street, the organization of which after November 9, 1989, provided the United Democratic Forces, the coalition of the new democratic parties, with its first public education. The process of creating new parties in Bulgaria was not as artificial as it was in the former GDR, where foreign parties simply imposed themselves, but after the first few months the process of mobilizing a democratic opposition proceeded mostly through the mechanisms of party and union organization, that is, not through grassroots self-activization but rather through the propagation of formally inclusive structures by elites. Even this innovation was so novel in Bulgaria, however, that more than 80 percent of the eligible voters turned out for the fall 1991 elections to the national assembly, a significantly greater proportion than in other East European countries.

The difference in Czechoslovakia's velvet revolution lay in the quality and availability of its leadership, not in the emergence of a civil society there. The Jakeš regime proved able to contain street demonstrations late in 1988 and early in 1989 and was able to argue that Czechoslovakia was in better economic condition than Poland. But after the Berlin Wall came down the pressure in Czechoslovakia escalated. When the government brutally suppressed a student demonstration on November 19, allegedly killing a student, the crowds that gathered on the streets of Prague shouted "This is it" and "Now is the time." The opposition leadership available from Charter 77 emerged from the cellars and doorways to create Civic Forum, and the government collapsed. No civil society existed in Czechoslovakia, although the Catholic Church did provide a node of attraction for many, especially Slovaks, but the existence of a recognizable anti-political leadership permitted a rapid transition to democratic forms to take place.

The leaders of Civic Forum saw themselves as guiding a movement of national regeneration, not a political party. They had worked together for years despite fundamental political differences, and they believed that the spirit of change that suffused the velvet revolution should carry over to the transition period. The leaders of Solidarity had much the same feeling. The leaders of the Union of Democratic Forces (UDF) in Bulgaria, however, as well as those of the democratic opposition (DEMOS) in Slovenia, specifically created their organization as a coalition of protoparties that agreed to come together for the purpose of contesting elections with a united front. Therefore, whereas Civic Forum and Solidarity did secure a genuine popularity in the beginning, they both disintegrated and thereby undermined their self-actuating mythology. Nationalism and regionalism, which are not inherently democratic, emerged to threaten the ethical spirit of cooperation characteristic of the anti-political opposition. In Bulgaria the UDF also split, but this did not undermine the fundamental goal of the main coalition, which met with success in the election of 1991, when it achieved a plurality and took power. A similar contrast exists in Hungary between the Free Democrats, the leaders of which were the main oppositionists in the 1980s and which split and lost its momentum, and the Young Democrats, who consider themselves an electoral party and who are in the political ascendency.

Finally, Romania. The conditions surrounding the revolution there remain murky, with plot theories abounding, but the initial outburst in Timişoara, at least, seems to have been an authentically indigenous moment. When authorities attempted to remove a Hungarian reform minister from his parish, an ethnically mixed group of parishioners and townspeople surrounded his house and prevented it. This led to rioting in Timişoara, intervention of the army that led to a number of deaths, and the outbreak of spontaneous demonstrations in other parts of Romania. The most important of these was one convened by Nicolae Ceauşescu himself in Bucharest, during which the crowd turned against the dictator. In a series of violent and still confusing events a group of leaders emerged, formed a National Liberation Front, and took over the revolution.

The Romanian revolution remains, however, a revolution *manqué*. The brief outburst of violence that brought people into the streets for a few days was quickly over. New authorities presented themselves and established their position with very little or no preparation of their public. They had not been an anti-political opposition, they did not emerge from a workers' movement, and they had not even organized substantial street demonstrations. Indeed, most of them were lifelong party members in good standing at the time of the revolution. This meant that not only were they unprepared by experience with the mechanisms of democratic opposition, but citizens too were unprepared by any but the briefest experience in self-activization. Romania's leadership consists entirely of refurbished Ceauşescu Communists who sometimes find it useful to bring the equivalent of brown shirts to Bucharest to beat up opponents. The Democratic Convention is trying its best to encourage the growth of a pluralist politics, but the pre-revolutionary lack of any substantial opposition has made its task extremely difficult.

The history of opposition to Communist regimes in Eastern Europe had two tendencies: a declining violence of intervention by the hegemon, and progression of opposition from simple dissimulation to a Marxist critique, thence to anti-politics, and finally to a reassertion of politics. One of the strengths of Communism was that for approximately one hundred years it occupied the high moral ground of opposing oppression. The loss of this high ground in Eastern Europe, especially after 1968, when a large proportion of the citizens came to recognize that the regimes were totally false and supported only by force, created a reservoir of discontent waiting to be tapped. The most thoroughgoing process of reasserting politics took place in Poland, where the creation of a civil society over a period of fifteen years by Solidarity created a social basis for Solidarity's electoral victory in 1989. Czechoslovakia did not develop such an independent society, but the anti-political Charter 77 movement identified leaders with the moral stature to step in when a spark brought the people onto the streets. In Hungary, where a reformist party elaborated its own means of destruction, the creation of alternative forms of ownership prepared the way for Hungary's post-1989 economic success but did not create a civil society that formed a social basis for Hungary's negotiated revolution. East Germany's case was unique, since its mobilization was based on the promise of unification. Neither Bulgaria nor Romania experienced much pre-1989 social mobilization.

Behind the collapses of the East European regimes lay their moral hollowness. No regime in the world can make good on all its promises. There is a cant and a bluster about modern politics that every thinking person recognizes. But in pluralist societies the level of distrust and resistance to this falsity remains on the surface, a matter for debate and conversation but not a deep humiliation, because whatever the realities might be, there is always a feeling that change is possible. In Eastern Europe distrust and resistance penetrated deeper because domination by the Soviet Union suppressed the sense of possibility. The events of 1968 confirmed that economic and political change was impossible and that public life would remain monochromatic. The result was a malaise that went beyond politics into the personality itself. "Even if people never speak of it," Vaclav Havel said in his open letter to Gustav Husák in 1975, "they have a very acute appreciation of the price they have paid for outward peace and quiet: the permanent humiliation of their human dignity."[19] Restoration of dignity is what the social movement Solidarity sought, what the anti-politicians of Charter 77 sought, and eventually what the street demonstrators in Leipzig and Prague sought too.

In most of the revolutions of 1989 the main social element was people power, crowds on the street. There was a contagious quality to these demonstrations, first gathering momentum in Hungary, then in Leipzig and throughout East Germany, then in Sofia and Prague, and finally in Romania. But street demonstrations, whatever useful organizational lessons they teach their sponsors and whatever lingering memories of participation they may leave in the minds of their participants, are no substitute for the longer-lasting and more varied experiences of pluralism. They do not create habits of dialogue and compromise that are the lifeblood of democracy, however it is defined; they do not formulate programs or policies useful for transition; and they do not create structures of interaction. The real social basis of the revolutions of 1989, therefore, did not come before the events but are currently in the process of creation, as each society attempts, within the boundaries of its own historical experience, the qualities of its leadership, and the intensity of its ethnic problems, to create a democratic society.

NOTES

1. Teresa Torańska, *"Them:" Stalin's Polish Puppets* (New York, 1987), 354.
2. Charles Gati, *Hungary and the Soviet Bloc* (Durham, 1986), 69.
3. G.M. Tamás, "Farewell to the Left," *Eastern European Politics and Societies*, 5 (1991): 92.
4. Czesław Miłosz, *The Captive Mind* (New York, 1981). Miłosz says he found the term "Ketman" in a book by Gobineau dating from the middle of the nineteenth century. Gobineau used it in describing the Shi'ite tradition of *Taqiyya*, or religious dissimulation while maintaining mental reservation.
5. For an extremely interesting argument that heroism in the modern world is the act of surviving, not of storming the barricades, see Terence des Pres, *The Survivor: An Anatomy of Life in the Death Camps* (New York, 1976).
6. It is curious that many Hungarian intellectuals do not wish to give the name *revolution* to the events of 1989, despite the fact that they changed almost everything, and insist on using the term for the events of 1956, which consisted in part of the restoration of the parties of 1945 and ended by changing nothing.
7. Milovan Djilas, *The New Class* (New York, 1967; 22nd printing as corrected), 69.
8. Mihailo Marković, "Marxist Philosophy in Yugoslavia: The *Praxis* Group," in Gale Stokes, ed., From *Stalinism to Pluralism* (New York, 1991), 120.
9. Ted Kaminski, "Underground Publishing in Poland," *Orbis*, 31, no. 3 (Fall 1987): 328.
10. Leszek Kołakowski, "Hope and Hopelessness," *Survey*, 17, no. 3 (Summer 1971): 46.
11. Adam Michnik, *Letters from Prison*, translated by Maya Latynski (Berkeley, 1985), 86.

12. H. Gordon Skilling, *Charter 77 and Human Rights in Czechoslovakia* (London, 1981), 211.
13. Václav Havel, *Living in Truth*, edited by Jan Vladislav (London, 1968), 57.
14. Konstanty Gebert, "An Independent Society: Poland under Martial Law," *Alternatives*, 15 (1990), 359 (quoting his own work originally published in February, 1982).
15. Roman Laba, *The Roots of Solidarity: A Political Sociology of Poland's Working Class Democratization* (Princeton, 1991). For another excellent interpretive study of Solidarity see David Ost, *Solidarity and the Politics of Anti-Politics: Opposition and Reform in Poland since 1968* (Philadelphia, 1990).
16. Laba, *Roots of Solidarity*, 65.
17. Stokes, ed., *From Stalinism to Pluralism*, 209.
18. Jan Józef Lipski, *KOR: A History of the Workers' Defense Committee in Poland* (Berkeley, 1988), 44–5; and Timothy Garton Ash, *Solidarity* (New York, 1984), 280.
19. Havel, *Living in Truth*, 31.

Part Four
Democracy and the
Welfare State, 1930–1990

11 The Welfare State and Democratic Practice in the United States since the Second World War

Samuel P. Hays

INTRODUCTION: DEMOCRACY AND WELFARE

The theme of this volume, "The Social Construction of Democracy" and the theme of this section, "The Welfare State and Democratic Practice," are particularly applicable to the United States. For here major changes have taken place in the last half century in both participation in decision-making and the consequences of those decisions. These changes are particularly identifiable if one emphasizes the transforming years of the Second World War rather than the Great Depression. New Deal America belongs to a previous period of historical evolution and the war and the decade of the 1940s sets the nation's public affairs off in a new direction.

In probing the details of these changes I wish first of all to modify the terminology of "democratic practice" and the "welfare state." For the United States, at least, those terms obscure more than they clarify.

The term "democratic" usually refers to two subjects: how widely distributed is the ability to shape policy and how widely distributed are its benefits. The first focuses on participation and power and the second on the distribution of outcomes. Here I will avoid the use of the terms "democratic" and "welfare state" and use the more generic terms "participation" and "social service state," which provide a greater opportunity for clearer analysis.[1]

What is the problem that lies behind this matter of terminology? First, whereas the ideology of democracy is widely used as evidence that political demands arise from a broad popular base, investigations indicate that these demands are much more limited in active support. "Democratic" ideological statements often mislead historians. Once having found that what is known from ideological evidence as democratic in origin is in fact far more narrowly based, one is compelled to distinguish between ideology and practice and to be more realistic about the source of a political demand.[2]

The more fundamental question is quite simple: who participates and why? But the question is more complex than it appears. Participation involves not only the legal right to participate, but also the desire to participate and the availibility of resources required to participate. All of this has implications for describing the evolution of political "participation" in the last half of the twentieth century.

To provide some foreshadowing of my later discussion, I will argue that in the years since the Second World War, the main new ingredient in participation has been the increasingly elaborate political organization of the mass middle class, defined here as the portion of the inequality spectrum from roughly the 90th down to the 30th percentile. At the same time, the long-term decline in participation in voting has reflected the relative decline in participation by those in the lower third of the income spectrum. In so far as one wishes to use the term "democratic" to involve some check "out there" in the body politic to the dominance of political affairs by elites, then one would have to argue that the political mobilization of the "mass middle class" is the main element in the "social construction of democracy" in the United States since 1950.

There is also a problem with the term "welfare" that is far more subtle, because the term calls up paradoxical meanings. On the one hand we are tempted to acknowledge that it involves a range of state policies that are more social than economic and which encompass the whole range of twentieth-century "public" social objectives. Yet the historical origin of the term and its use in contemporary political debate in the United States convey a more limited meaning that emphasizes public policies for the benefit of those in the lower third of the income scale. While such historic policies as pensions for the retired, or minimum wage, or workmen's compensation, or health insurance have implications far beyond that strata of society, the use of the term at least in public debate and in much of the conversation among academic analysts seems to convey the meaning of public policies for the less advantaged.

Here I seek to avoid that implication by dropping the term "welfare state" and substituting the term "social service" state. Beginning in the 1930s and evolving especially during the 1940's and again in the 1960s and beyond, the direction of policy in the United States has been toward new social objectives ranging from health services, to education, programs for the elderly, civil rights, environmental progress, the disabled, women and children, and on to culture and the arts. Because of the meaning implicit in its origins and contemporary debate, the term "welfare" cannot convey effectively this range of evolving public policies. Some more comprehensive language is needed.

A more suitable language must expand the traditional meaning of "welfare" in two directions. First, it must incorporate a full range of "human services" beyond those for the lower end of the income scale to services for people of many income levels; this expansive meaning is applicable especially to health, education and senior citizen programs in which the mass middle class is vitally interested. Second, it must also incorporate newer programs not readily thought of as human services, but which are equally fostered by the mass middle class as desired public benefits: legal assistance in the form of civil rights for blacks, women, and the disabled, and the right to sue in the courts; environmental benefits in the form of expansion of natural lands, and reduction of pollution; and expansion of arts and cultural services. It is especially important to incorporate the second set of services because the significance of the modern social service state lies in the transition from a politics overwhelmingly emphasizing production to one in which consumption of social services plays a much larger role. In order to bring together all of these new governmental services for this analysis I use the generic term "social services," and the generic concept the "social service state."

To put the argument of this chapter precisely, in terms of who participates and who benefits, the central theme of American politics in the years since the Second World War has been the creation of a social service state for the benefit of the mass middle class. This is not to omit the politics of either the top 10 percent or the bottom 30 percent. Each plays its own role, and with far different degrees of participation and benefits. But whereas the top 10 percent has long played a major role in public affairs, as regards both participation and benefits, and the bottom third has steadily declined as a significant element in either participation or benefits, the major change in post-Second World War American public life has been the emergence of a firmly based and continuously influential social service state for the middle class.

PARTICIPATION

Two major social changes underly the changes in political participation in the twentieth-century United States, one in the way society is organized and the other in demography.

Organizational changes underway for a century, spreading slowly and steadily throughout the society, have greatly reordered the context of political choice from the smaller community to the wider society. This shift greatly reduced the more limited family and community social context that in earlier years fostered participation and enhanced the more personal setting of public affairs; that setting sustained the ability of the individual to feel a compelling link between individual choice and wider public policy.

This change has been reflected in rates of voting participation that began to decline in the 1890s and, with a short-term slight reversal in the 1930s, continued to do so to the present day. Paul Kleppner has produced the most convincing explanation of this decline by contrasting the close link in the primary group relationships of the small community in which ethno-cultural factors, religion, and ethnicity played such a compelling role with the loosening of those ties as one generation succeeded another to participate in a wider network of economic, social, and political activities. Earlier popular voting participation, in other words, was mediated by a community context of human relationships, issues, duties and obligations. With time these weakened and so did participation. That process continues to the present day.[3]

Demographic change, on the other hand, modified considerably the drive and capacity to participate on the part of the general public and especially among that segment that was growing in education and economic resources. Participation now required not just the right to vote, but the desire to participate in more demanding circumstances and the resources to understand issues and exert influence. A new set of participatory conditions involving issues on an organizational level far above the community required a new set of skills beyond just the act of occasional voting. Hence, as popular voting declined, a new kind of participation increased that was more focused on the organization of issues around the specialized concerns of individuals who sought to influence public affairs; the so-called "interest groups" of the twentieth century organized around issue lines.

The initial basis of the organization of such groups lay in economic concerns as labor, agriculture, and business each came together to advance their interests in public policy. This development constitutes a major element of the history of American public affairs up to the Second World War. Thereafter, however, a new set of "public interest" political movements arose that expanded this dimension of functional political organization to social services beyond economic benefits: housing, education, health and medicine, civil rights, environment, the conditions of women and children, the disabled, the elderly, arts and culture. They generated organized political activities that set "interest group" alongside "party" as a major mode of political participation. This new form of participation did not replace party activity, but it often established the issues to which political parties felt compelled to respond. Participants in interest-group political organization often then sought to shape electoral activity in terms of their own specialized objectives.[4] A new form of participation established new directions that brought the old and the new together.

Interest group participation did not reverse the inequality reflected in the decline in popular voting, but reinforced it or, perhaps more accurately, reorganized it. The new organizational context of issues and decisionmaking that prompted many voters to become divorced from wider political affairs in terms of voting guaranteed that they would be relatively uninvolved in interest group political action as well. This declining involvement was underscored by the fact that the very sense of ability to influence public affairs and the resources to do so were far greater among those who acquired higher levels of education and income. A division arose in both the desire to participate and the ability to participate, stemming from the new organizational society and its requirements for effective public action.

This transformation in political participation was an integral part of specialization in economic, social, and political life that also shaped the way in which public issues were dealt with. Specialization marked the way in which legislative, administrative, and judicial bodies were organized. It also shaped the information needed to take part effectively in public affairs. One could not participate now with general sentiment and opinion; information, often of a highly technical kind, was required.

This new setting generated a comprehensive condition of inequality in the capacity to influence decisions and to partipate in that process. It was well nigh impossible for the individual citizen to play a significant role in this context of decisionmaking; it could be done only through the organization of many individuals in a collective effort. Even if one wished to participate as an individual, the information requirements were far too costly. While one could obtain a rudimentary sense of issues through the general media, a relatively inexpensive source of information, to be sufficiently informed required more knowledge. Specialized newsletters arose to fill this need, but they were costly, ranging from several hundred to over a thousand dollars a year – beyond the reach of the average citizen but not of the lawyers, administrators, legislators, and public interest organizations to whom they were directed. The cost of acquiring information about public affairs guaranteed that individuals could not themselves participate as individuals but required organizations through which to do so.

The new participating public in the United States in the years after the Second World War was distinctively middle class, and its most significant strata ranged in the income and education hierarchy from the 90th percentile down to the 30th. One could call this a "mass middle class" not because it was homogeneous but because it tended to support a general program of social services in its behalf.[5] Surrounding this mass middle class were those in the upper 10 percent who at times supported the mass middle-class participants but who often also carved out their own benefits and methods of political involvement, and those in the lower 30 percent who for the most part remained far less involved and who relied for benefits almost solely on initiatives taken by those higher up the hierarchy of the income and educational scale.

These changes in participation gave rise to a marked change in the political consequences of education. In earlier years, much of the drive for increased high school education was justified by stressing its role in fostering civic education. There was a close link between advanced years of schooling and participation in governing as a voter. One hardly hears mentioned these days such a purpose of secondary education; the term "high school civics" is a thing of the past. But as participation in public affairs has become more complex, requiring higher levels of education and skills, a similar self-conscious effort to foster greater political participation might have developed where it might be most appropriate, namely in college education. But it did not.

On the contrary, education for the new citizenship takes place outside the formal institutions of higher education and is increasingly organized by citizens engaged directly in public affairs. Citizen organizations prepare manuals for their members about the workings of government and the details of the specific issues in which it is involved. They track legislative and administrative decisions and urge their members to participate more fully. There is a significant carry-over from communication and research skills acquired in higher education for academic subjects to information and communication skills applied to quite different purposes of political participation. But the context of substantive political education now is not the institution of higher education but the citizen "public interest" organization itself.

BENEFITS

If political affairs in the United States now emphasized mass middle-class participation, so it also emphasized mass middle-class benefits. The new phase of this policy development began with the 1930s, sharpened in the 1940s and grew steadily thereafter. One can trace the historical development partly through new legislation, but more distinctly through evolving administrative arrangements and budgets at the federal, state, and local levels. The benefit side of the social service state interwove programs at all governmental hierarchies, with accompanying tensions among them but with a similar policy direction.

The New Deal, long considered to be primarily a political drive on behalf of those at the lower rungs of the economic ladder, was more accurately the first stage of the new social service state for the middle class. Its initial action on this front was housing, not public housing but private housing bolstered by federal refinancing, initially to save mortgaged homes and then soon to construct new homes. The services were eminently successful, initiating a major expansion of home ownership.[6] This, it should be noted, was not a program for the poor; efforts at public housing for lower income groups were far more limited and received only peripheral support in contrast with financing for home buying. Federal mortgage financing obtained further significance when Congress approved low-interest housing loans for veterans during the Second World War.

Another New Deal Program with similar meaning was rural electrification. This initiative also was eminently successful; as a result rural America had by the 1950s made great strides in acquiring access to electricity.[7] The rural poor, of course, obtained electricity in the process. But these were "tag-along" benefits. Those in the farm economy who organized the rural cooperatives and were the major users of electricity were hardly from the bottom third; they were the more substantial elements in rural areas. The main long-term effect of rural electrification was to foster more intensive agriculture, as well as to bring benefits to farm homes, and then to shape a federal subsidy program for rural development as a more traditional "economic development service" rather than a "social service program."

Old age pensions were the third major "social service" program of the 1930s. Over the years, social security has played an important role in establishing a floor of minimums under the income of the elderly. But both the political drive behind the federally organized social security system and its benefits feature far more the mass middle class than the poor. The main point about social security as a social service is that it is an integral part of mixed private–public earnings on the part of the middle class elderly. Whereas for the poor social security is a sole reed for economic security, for the mass middle-class it constitutes only 23 percent of a retirement package that includes private investments and earnings, private pensions and public pensions.[8] This partial but crucial role of public pensions arouses the intense interest of the mass middle class, and even the upper 10 percent, in social security and sustains that program's political support.

While the general ideology of the New Deal would identify these programs as benefits to those at lower income levels, a closer examination would root them in an emerging political movement on the part of the mass middle class that had its first success in securing benefits in the 1930s and continued with more benefits in later years. These are not "welfare programs" but "social services" and in that form they constitute a beginning to the central tone of American politics from 1929 onward. The truly "welfare" elements of public policy in the 1930s, such as work relief and the programs of the Farm Security Administration, had little staying power; many were scuttled by Congress and disappeared early in the Second World War. A few programs such as aid to dependent children, remained and were bolstered by new programs in the 1960s, such as Medicaid. But on the whole these programs are politically far more fragile and seem to be rather minor amid the vast array of social services that have evolved over the years for other social strata.

To define the historical role of the New Deal and the 1930s, one must emphasize not just what the Roosevelt administration did provide in new social services but what it did not. Significant proposals arose in the mid-1930s for a number of new social services such as education and health. Their champion was Senator Robert Wagner of New York. In almost every case Roosevelt turned them down. Senator Wagner did obtain Roosevelt's support for a public housing program as a pilot venture, which by the end of the 1930s took shape as a tag-along program to the more powerful political campaign for urban redevelopment that city governments and real estate and construction interests were leading.[9]

The social service state took a major leap forward, however, during the 1940s with the support of Harry Truman. Especially prominent were education, health, and civil rights. the Second World War gave each of these a major boost, bringing from the back to the front burner those issues that had emerged in the 1930s but without much effect.

In matters of housing, health, and education it was the GI that focused attention. When health examinations for the draft revealed that a very high proportion of young men were not physically fit for the army, the public became more aware of the condition of the nation's health than was the case during the 1930s. When Congress sought to reward those in the armed services in ways other than the traditional forms of free land in the West or a money bonus, it chose education and established the GI bill. When blacks protested that they did not receive equal opportunities in employment and marched on Washington to reinforce demands for better treatment, they made the civil rights issue more prominent than it had been in the New Deal.[10] Truman responded more positively to all of these emerging demands when Roosevelt had not and in the 1940s the social service state moved to a new stage of evolution.

The 1960s provided still another stage. While older objectives were solidified, new issues emerged: environmental; culture and the arts; benefits to women and children; loans to college students generally; Medicare and Medicaid. The range of social services continues as reflected in the recently established programs for the disabled. The historical significance of civil rights programs of the 1960s was that they fostered upward mobility among blacks and created a new black middle class as part of a new structure of inequality in the black community. Meantime, the earliest beginnings of the social service state, loans for housing and pensions for the elderly, continued.

Each step in the evolution of these social service policies was subject to intense controversy and frustrated their advocates who emphasized the slow pace and magnitude of change. Yet if one takes the larger historical view, from 1930 on to 1992, the pattern of innovation is unmistakable: a major transformation took place in public policy that can be summed up as the creation of a social service state quite new in American history. Especially significant were those periods of consolidation where, after surviving intense opposition, the new policies reached a new stage of acceptance and became more firmly embedded in American public affairs. The Eisenhower administration witnessed a consolidation of the innovations of previous years, an interpretation that one might apply to the creation of the Department of Health, Education, and Welfare. The Reagan–Bush administrations witnessed a similar consolidation of the innovations of the 1960s and 1970s.

This remarkable resilience reflects the deep roots of these policies in the mass middle-class body politic. True, the ideology of reducing the role of the social service state abounds, and the budgetary implications are ever-present as public issues. Yet, as one looks at the course of policy, program, and budget one observes not only that the bulk of the programs persisted but in fact often increased during the Reagan years. If, during his presidential campaign of 1980, Ronald Reagan issued a massive challenge to the social service state, almost from the first day in office he had to backtrack. He retreated, for example, from the campaign promise to abolish the Department of Education. The significant historical fact is not what he was able to abandon, but what he was forced to keep. This staying power of the social service state becomes visible especially as one probes the inner recesses of the federal budget for a host of health, education, arts, and environmental expenditures, and the vast array of experimental programs that Congress worked into larger bills.

George Bush resisted less and gave in more. By employing a more limited rhetoric of reducing the size of the state he was freer to permit its growth. In 1991, at the same time that Bush was touting his new privatized education system, the Senate voted 92–6 to develop innovations in federal education programs. To cite another example, appropriations for the federal endangered species program more than tripled under the Bush administration. Beyond the rhetoric of anti-statism lies a record of legislation and budgetary expenditure extending rather than dismantling the social service state. George Bush was far more inclined to take the political heat from increasing taxes than from reducing social services.

Demands for such services remain intense, of course, and funds are not there to fill them. Indeed, those demands eat up potential finances long before they are available which accounts for the subtlety with which the government has handled the "peace dividend." The public debate has conveyed the notion that one first declares a peace dividend and then spends it on domestic policy. It actually happens the other way around. One carves out claims on available funds and then military spending is reduced little by little in order to provide funds for the expansion of the social service state.

The "welfare" dimension of the social service state is of course an important element of the story. There are food stamp programs, aid to dependent children, and special programs for the elderly poor, such as Medicaid. But the crucial element is that these features of the social service state depend far less on the political participation of the poor than on the desire of a distinctive segment of the mass middle class to include some such features in the social service package, albeit as only a relatively small part.

Historians have frequently conveyed the notion that public policies on behalf of people in the lower end of the income scale are implicit in the natural order of things, and as a result they devote much time to explaining why people oppose them. The limited expansion of "welfare" policy, however, has less to do with middle-class opposition than the weakness of the poor as a political force. Efforts to empower the poor have had few results save to further the advance of some of them into the mass middle class. It has remained for the mass middle class to give its selective attention to the "welfare" state.

That attention has varied in the nation's past, depending largely upon the occasions that the poor have become visible and hence more a subject of public debate and action. The depression of 1929, the urban riots of the 1960s, the widely known statistics of increasing inequality in income and wealth of the 1980s constitute such occasions. The middle class retains much of the national self-image that relative equality is inherent in the American "system" and inequality – or rather excessive inequality – should not be tolerated. This belief is often bolstered by the oft-expressed concern by those in the upper half of the income scale that the uneducated poor represented a wasted human resource and should be made more productive for the nation's benefit. At such times the "welfare" state becomes a more significant part of the larger "social service" state, but again the resulting mix has stemmed less from the power of the poor than from the determination of middle-class reformers to redress some inequality through larger policy initiatives designed above all to benefit the middle class.

THE URBAN CONTEXT

The social service state has evolved within a distinctive urban context in which the mass middle class emerged as the dominant force in the years after the Second World War. As American society became urbanized, new populations with new ideas about public affairs exercised an increasing influence in American public life. At each decade since the first population census of 1790 urban areas constituted a larger share of the population. In its earlier stages, the impact of this change on pre-existing rural society and politics was limited. But as time passed, urban populations grew steadily and persistently, and after the Second World War urbanization in the West and then the South made its mark. This pattern is easy to chart on the graphs of the decade-by-decade percentage of urban people in the total population. After an occasional census, such as in 1850 or 1920, the American people suddenly became more aware of what was happening to their society, and in later years the census had to change its classifications of urban places in order to chart the change more accurately. City growth constituted a relentless historical force that increasingly shaped public affairs.

The effect of urbanization on political life took place at several conjunctures in the course of the twentieth century. As for the 1910 census, Congress decided no longer to expand the size of the House of Representatives in line with population growth. However, when Congress came to apportion seats after the 1920 census it was stalemated for a decade. The issue was a simple one of relative power between rural and urban areas, between those formerly dominating the nation's political life and those who were now making claims on it.[11]

The first major claim of the cities on the nation's resources came in the 1930s. This change was the overarching historical significance of the New Deal. The cities came on with a rush as the Democratic Party gathered urban voters into its fold with the realignment of 1934 and piled up unpredecented majorities for Roosevelt in the election of 1936. Two issues in particular shaped the resulting political alignment between city and country: trade union organization and collective bargaining on the one hand, and work relief on the other. Both were urban policies; they came into prominence because unemployment was most dramatically an urban phenomenon and because the public associated organized labor and strikes with the cities. These perceptions shaped intense rural–urban divisions within the Congress and the nation at large and set off a dramatic, but in historical terms rather short-lived, phase of the rural resistance to the political rise of the cities.

Steps in the evolution of the new social service state in the 1930s and 1940s charted the direction of change which the cities would continue to pursue thereafter. Much of the electoral base for policy innovations in the 1930s came from blue-collar labor. But even at that time the urban political constituency was rapidly changing. Amid the successful labor bargaining of the 1940s, blue-collar workers acquired aspirations of upward mobility that prompted them to ally with the middle class in a common drive for health, education, and civil rights as well as publicly financed private housing and social security. It is important, therefore, to link these urban-rooted social service demands not with a static demography but one that was rapidly changing from an older blue-collar base into a more elaborate one, including blue- and white-collar workers combined in a mass middle class.

Changes in the cities themselves marked these stages of development. The mid-twentieth century phase of suburbanization that had long taken place in American cities brought about a decline in the old blue-collar factory city and the rise of the suburban city where older and newer population groups came together. By the time a full-fledged urban politics had emerged after mid-century to set the basis for the social service state, the city itself was undergoing massive change. Urban people came to think of their cities as not merely places of work but as residential communities with social services to improve their standard and quality of living. The "liveable city" came to be a major element in urban public affairs.[12]

By the 1960s a major thrust of the new urban drive in American public life focused sharply on the apportionment of legislative seats, more so than even in the 1920s. At that time Congress had capped the total number in the House of Representatives, but had left states to work out the boundaries of the congressional districts which they had been assigned. Moreover, the earlier action had not touched the state legislatures which, despite provisions in state constitutions, had been left unrevamped for decades and led to persistent over-representation by rural areas. Rural over-representation became more striking with each decennial census. Joined by organized business and industry, rural representatives staved off attempts by urban legislators to foster urban-based policies.

The cities overcame this opposition partially in Congress but not in the states. However, in 1962 in *Baker* v. *Carr* the Supreme Court decided that the existing malapportionment was unconstitutional, a violation of the principle of equal representation, and in a series of cases in 1964 the Court elaborated on the application of this principle. From that time on district lines would be redrawn each decade. The initial political impact of the change was felt in the election of 1970 and it grew persistently along with urban population growth.[13]

A second phase of this development came with the growth of suburbs and the gradual shift of political power within urban America from the central cities to the outlying areas. Even as the reapportionment battle was raging observers noted that the central cities, like the rural areas, were now over-represented and that it was the suburbs that were under-represented. Within a few years continued reapportionment would lead to the growth of suburban political power and by 1992 observors would note that the presidential election of that year would be the first in which the nation's suburban voters constituted a majority of the electorate. Much of the drama of politics in the evolving social service state arose from this shift in demography, political power, and issue interest within the cities.

Equally striking, however, was the steady decline in the political power of farm representation in the US Congress and in the states, and the recasting of farm bills to include significant elements of urban-inspired agricultural policy. In short, reapportionment set free urban political ambitions to work their way far more readily than in a political culture long dominated by rural America, and with time the national political agenda would be shaped ever more fully by the mass middle class of suburban America.

The social service state continues its evolution and not without considerable resistance. Voting patterns in state and federal legislatures display important rural–urban differences. But the full power of the combination of business and industry on the one hand and rural areas on the other, once described as the "deadlock of democracy," has diminished, and the wide majority of issues today are debated within the context of urban America rather than between urban and rural America. Moreover, as political debate proceeds, demands for a marked reduction in public services call up little support. While limitations on funds do discipline the choices of which programs to support, the social service state steadily advances.

THE IMPACT ON POLITICAL INSTITUTIONS

These urban-based patterns of political participation and political benefits had profound effects on the nation's political institutions. They helped to reshape party affiliations, the party composition of Congress, the internal structure of parties, federal–state relationships and the relationships between presidency and Congress.

Dealignment and Issues

Political observers have recently emphasized the decline in party identity and the change from historical patterns in which marked shifts in party voting support took place at particular times, called voter realignment, to a general decline in voting participation, known as voter dealignment. Parties, so the argument goes, do not attract the persistent loyalty that they did in the last half of the nineteenth century.[14] Voting turnout has steadily declined. While political observers after the Second World War charted the patterns of party realignment in the 1850s, the 1890s and the 1930s, the realignment that they predicted for the 1960s did not occur. Instead decline in party turnout, indifference to party affairs and the rise of issue-oriented political action through interest groups continued.[15]

   True enough. But this now-conventional analysis misses several features of the change. First, voter realignment *has* taken place. But, contrary to the historic pattern, during the 1960s it took place *within* political parties rather than between them. Realignment as observed by political historians concerned the fit between changes in the wider body politic and changes in parties. As the society and voter interests changed, the then dominant party did not respond sufficiently and hence voters shifted their party loyalties. A similar problem of fit occurred in the years after the Second World War with the rise of new voting interests associated with an expanding mass middle class. This created the possibility that the Republican Party might seize the opportunity to represent these new voter interests, and the Democratic Party might be removed from power. But precisely the opposite happened. The Republican Party did not take advantage of this opportunity while the Democratic Party did, bringing about a steady realignment within its ranks.

Secondly, some party voter dealignment did occur, as we have already noted in the shift from a party to an interest focus in political participation. But the reorganization of participation around interest and issues did not replace parties; rather it became integrated with parties. Party organization remained strong as an instrument for expressing the new issue interests, though there was considerable difference in the responses of the two parties to the new issue-objectives of the mass middle class. This was not party dealignment, but rather a reorganization of political participation and issues that brought together interest organizations and parties into a new working alignment.

Democratic Dominance in the House

These changes have given rise to one of the most important phenomena in American political history, the dominance of the U.S. House of Representatives by the Democratic Party since 1930 – for 62 years. On only two occasions, in 1947–1948 and 1953–1954, was that long-term dominance interrupted. No party has ever before approached such a long-term dominance of any one branch of the federal government. Several decades ago historians emphasized the unusual degree of Republican Party dominance in the Congress between 1894 and 1910 and the presidency between 1896 and 1912. But compared to the more recent 62-year Democratic dominance in the House, that 16-year stretch is far less significant.

A more dramatic way of describing this Democratic dominance is to observe its increase over the years, an evolution occurring in cycles around an upward secular trend. While Truman's Congress averaged 248 Democratic seats, that of Kennedy–Johnson reached 266 and that of Carter 284. During sequences of Republican administrations, a similar upward movement took place though at lower levels than during Democratic presidencies: from 225 Democrats under Eisenhower, 245 under Nixon, 255 under Reagan and 263 under Bush. To put it rather strikingly, by the Reagan–Bush years the Democratic congressional contingent in a Republican administration had reached a higher level than it had during the Democratic Truman administration.[16]

Why this Democratic dominance? Because the Democratic Party has been the major instrument of the new mass middle class in its drive for the benefits of the social service state. The Democratic Party has constituted the leading edge of these issues, whether it was social security in the 1930s or programs for the disabled in the 1990s. There has been a significant symbiotic relationship between the electorate's desire for an expanded social service state and the Democratic Party's role as the leader in such innovations. The Republican Party, on the other hand, has held back, at first in opposition, then accepting innovations, arguing that it could do a better job of it than the Democrats, but always giving the impression that it was the reluctant partner. The Democrats have spearheaded change in accordance with the wishes of the electorate; the Republicans have built those changes firmly into the nation's body politic by first resisting them and then accepting them in the institutional framework of government and confining their role largely to paring down their cost rather than their substance.[17]

Internal Party Divisions on the Issues

Realignments within the two parties led to a more workable consensus among the Democrats and a deeper division among the Republicans.

The Democratic Party had long been divided internally as a result of the Civil War on the one hand and the incorporation of many new urban voters, especially immigrants, into the party on the other. Two wings arose that had continuing difficulty in working together effectively. Urban voters became increasingly important for northern Democrats; the Confederate South continued to shape the southern party. The southern wing solidified its role within the party with the rule that a presidential nominee receive two-thirds of the convention votes, a policy that gave the South a veto over the decision. Even in the 1930s the two wings confronted each other forcefully; that confrontation reached its height in 1948 when the South left the party's convention on the civil rights issue to establish its own States Rights Party.

But this act of independence failed. Despite the southern revolt Truman won re-election, demonstrating that the South could no longer dictate to the national party. The key element was the expansion to the upper Midwest and then to the West Coast of the urban thrust in the Democratic Party, so that by the 1960 party convention the civil rights plank that had so divided the party in 1948 now received wide endorsement. Even more important, rapid urbanization in the South gave rise to a new urban-based politics which brought that region into a workable concensus with the Democratic Party in the rest of the nation. In terms of voting patterns in the Congress, where these relationships can be identified more precisely than through presidential elections, the South of 1992 was far more in agreement with the national party than it was in the 1930s.

For the Republican Party, however, the new social service state, its mass middle-class base, and the role of the city in American politics created a far more difficult situation. Rather than fostering greater internal agreement the new issues led to greater internal division. The problem became clear almost from the start of the urban claim on the federal government in the 1930s, when, in contrast with rising Democratic urban strength, the Republicans came to be dominanted by segments of the party based largely outside the cities. Two wings arose, the "old guard" and the "progressive," reflecting, respectively, the older rural and small-town America and the new urban America. The battle was joined most visibly on the level of the presidency; from 1940 on the progressive wing controlled the presidential nominations with Wilkie, Dewey, and Eisenhower. In 1964 the "old guard" rebelled, struck back with Goldwater, then accepted a "middle of the road" candidate with Nixon, and then achieved victory with Ronald Reagan.

A similar pattern was being worked out in Congress, where intra-party divisions sharpened between the North on the one hand and the South and the West on the other. The northern wing of the party tended to focus more on issues of practical substance to urban America while the southern and western wings focused more on ideology. On a number of occasions a crucial number of northern Republicans in the Congress provided significant support for social service policies and enabled Congress to override Reagan and Bush vetoes or to persuade the president not to risk a veto.

At the same time Republicans from the South and the West often were able to block action in Congress much to the consternation of the party's eastern contingent by supporting Reagan and Bush threats to veto legislation. The key element in this coalition was the group of Republican senators from the Mountain and Plains West, who now played a significant historical role in this drama of the rise of urban politics. Changes in the House reflected the political strength of an urbanizing America; but in the Senate where states with smaller populations retained disproportionate power, western Republicans constituted a key bloc of votes that served as a bulwark of resistance to the social service state.

The internal divisions within the Republican Party were hidden during the Reagan administration because of the unifying power of presidential personality and ideology. But close attention to patterns of congressional voting demonstrates the depth of internal divisions within the Republican Party. In environmental affairs, for example, while the nation's regions within the Democratic Party forged greater unity between 1970 and 1989, the regions within the Republican Party became more divided.[18]

Changing State–Federal Relationships

The political rise of the cities deeply affected state policy and reorganized the relationships between state and federal governments. In earlier years in the twentieth century, state legislatures had been deadlocked in the conflicts between growing urban and declining rural areas. Frustrated by unresponsive state legislatures, the nation's larger cities had turned their attention to the federal government, organizing in the late 1920s into the U.S. Conference of Mayors to spearhead the drive for federal urban assistance. In response to the ensuing federal initiatives, business interests and rural legislators teamed up at the state level to defend themselves against the closer ties between city and federal government.

Reapportionment and the continued growth of cities, however, reshaped these patterns. A more dominant urban contingent in the state legislature now served to create broader support for issues arising out of the majority urban populations of each state and by reducing longstanding rural–urban gridlock to provide a clearer sense of direction to state policies. This led directly to an increase in the governing capacity of the states. During the 1970s and 1980s that governing capacity grew sharply, a development reflected in the numerous organizations of state legislators, governors, and state attorneys general, to name only a few, and in new publications that reported on this larger role of state governments.[19]

As state governing capacity increased it led to new state initiatives in social service programs throughout the country. In the 1980s one began to hear of the states as "laboratories" in which new policies could be designed and carried out more effectively than at the federal level. Those opposed to such initiatives, in response, turned their attention to federal authority as a possible means to pre-empt state initiatives. They sought federal statutes and worked through executive agencies such as the Office of Management and Budget and the Council on Competitiveness to override state and local action.

Pre-emption now became a major issue in state–federal relationships, little noticed in the general public debate, but of vital importance to the institutional actors in the drama of political choice. The rise of the city to shape state government and policy tended to foster state initiative and autonomy, but it also gave rise to counter tendencies in which opponents to those policies in agriculture and business sought the executive power of the presidency and federal legislation to restrain the states. The relative balance between the two sets of forces was often tenuous, but it marked a major departure from the earlier dominant role of agriculture and business in state affairs which at that time had given rise to a vigorous opposition to federal action and the defense of "state's rights."

The Congress and the Presidency

The social service state played a major role in reshaping the relationships between the Congress and the presidency. Since the 1950s Congress has usually innovated in policy and the president has held back. At the center of this contest were the administrative agencies. Congress found that agencies were reluctant to implement the statutes. Hence it developed oversight hearings to review implementation and often brought the agencies to task. This led to legislative investigations and to increasingly prescriptive legislation.

The constitutional tussle between Congress and the agencies was sharpened by the growing tendency of the Executive Office of the President to enter the fray, often through the Office of Management and Budget.[20] Inaugurated as the Bureau of the Budget in 1921, then expanded by President Nixon into the Office of Management and Budget, and with increased authority granted by President Reagan, the office developed into an instrument of executive policy rather than mere budget management. Its power increased greatly because it was authorized to supervise attempts to reduce governmental paperwork and used that authority to veto or modify a host of substantive administrative actions. At the same time, it conducted its work in secret, justifying its exemption from the openness required under the Administrative Procedures Act on the grounds that the Executive Office of the President was free from such restrictions. When Congress required some public scrutiny of OMB decisions, the Executive Office created a new branch, the Council on Competitiveness, to review administrative rulemaking without public scrutiny.

It is not too much to say that a newer and sharper constitutional division has emerged between Congress and the Executive Office of the President. Arising from the contest over the evolution of the social service state, these tensions between Congress and the Executive Office of the President constitute an example of the way in which our constitutional system evolves not by an elaboration of the doctrines of 1787 but by incremental change arising from the give and take among political impulses in the body politic.

THE PERSISTENT CONTEXT OF POLITICAL INEQUALITY

These changes in American public life with respect to both participation and benefits have taken place within an even larger context of persistence in political inequality that has characterized the United States throughout its history. We usually think of the evolution of American society as a cycle of periods of inequality followed by periods of equality, within a general trend toward greater equality. Yet the evidence makes clear that in terms of property and income, the pattern of inequality has remained rather stable over the years and provides a continuous context for the analysis of both participation and benefits.[21]

The development of a social service state for the mass middle class represents not a greater political equality or homogeneity but a new stage in the continuing dynamics of inequality that has long characterized American public life.[22] We can observe this in several ways. One is to track changes in political participation not only in voting but also in the desire and ability to participate in an era when participation goes far beyond the suffrage. The organizational, communication, and information requirements of modern political participation are distributed quite unequally, and one might argue that those requirements build inequality more firmly and irrevocably into the political order than did earlier restrictions on the suffrage. These recent changes in the conditions for participation establish a more permanent condition for political inequality than the nation has known before.

Especially compelling is the role of personal commitment of time and energy to political participation. The vast range of human activities in which one can engage in this day and age have given rise to major shifts in personal choices as to how one spends limited time and energy. Time spent in religious affairs characteristic of much of the nineteenth century now has been replaced by leisure time activities. And so with political affairs. Earlier party affiliation meant not just voting but participating in political clubs that met regularly and provided an opportunity for male social life. But such activities have given way to other activities that are more private and less public in their focus. Consequently, a major feature of contemporary political participation lies in these alternative choices made by citizens in the mass middle class to fund or contribute time and energy to organizations that represent them. Much of what we know as political apathy reflects a choice to allocate resources more to private than to public affairs.

Yet even the inactive mass middle class that is drawn away from public affairs desires to receive the benefits of the social service state and so there is the tenuous and often paradoxical relationship between participation and benefits. On the one hand, the desire for benefits is continuous and strong, but expressed only sporadically when those benefits are not sufficiently forthcoming. But on the other, the sustained interest group political support required for sustained benefits is sporadic because of its demands on limited personal time and energy. This constant tension between the desire for benefits and the requirements of political action is one of the main sources of volatility in political participation by the mass middle class.

In exploring the role of persistent inequality in American public life we should also bear in mind the persistent tendency of the American people to elect leaders who are at the upper levels of the socioeconomic order. A host of historical studies make clear that in every electoral context – township, county, city, state, and nation – the elected leaders were drawn from the top quarter and most often from the top 10 to 15 percent of the social order from which they are elected.[23] One can conclude, certainly, that inequality in the personal circumstances of elected political leaders has been as longstanding and persistent as inequality in income and wealth.

Given these inequalities in personal resources and political leadership, what about benefits? Despite a variety of public policies ostensibly intended to reduce economic inequality, one is struck by their limited impact. The policies of the 1930s had little effect on the pattern of income distribution, and the limited tendencies toward equality that occurred prior to the 1950s came as a result of the Second World War rather than the New Deal. Measures in the 1960s did increase the real income of those at the lower end of the scale. And tax policies in the 1980s increased benefits to those at the upper end of the income scale and reduced those at the lower and middle. But how these short-run changes will affect long-term trends is not clear.

Inequality in the distribution of benefits from public policy tends to reinforce inequality arising from the private market. Some public policies tend to counteract such inequalities: public streets and highways, public health policies such as water, and air quality, public access to outdoor recreation on the public lands, and waters, and social security pensions.[24] But other policies reinforce inequalities, especially where public benefits require a significant degree of resources to take advantage of them, such as education, health care, housing, and even civil rights. Studies of the distribution of selected public benefits often provide some insight as to the distribution of benefits in the short run, but less with respect to the degree to which over the long run policy benefits reduce, reinforce, or increase the rather powerful tendencies toward inequalities in American private life.

CONCLUSION

The emergence of the social service state for the mass middle class provides a thematic framework for the analysis of American public policy over the past six decades. It reflects widespread demographic change in the form of the evolution of the mass middle class, the resulting innovations in demands for new types of public services, and the consequences of these new political developments for the evolution of state and federal government. In a far broader context, these developments in recent American politics reflect the gradual evolution and impact of urban society in America with its concomitant features of rising personal standards of living, higher levels of education, and specialization in economic, social, and political activities. At the same time, however, these innovations express in new form the longstanding inequality in American private and public life. A long-run perspective places these recent changes in a longer context of political inequality which the new social service state, despite its new content, continues to display.

NOTES

1. It is recognized that these problems of terminology may not apply universally, but I suggest that they might well be relevant to the analysis of Western-style industrial societies beyond the United States.

2. See my first statement of this problem, "The Politics of Reform in Municipal Government in the Progressive Era," *Pacific Northwest Quarterly*, 55, no. 4 (1964): 157–69.

3. Paul Kleppner, *Who Voted?: The Dynamics of Electoral Turnout, 1870–1980* (New York, 1982).

4. John Allswang has found that these "interest" lines in politics arose even early in the twentieth century out of the use of the "direct democracy" initiative in California. The initiative was described as an issue of the "people versus the interests," but as soon as it was put into practice many different proposals arose in which one group proposing an issue differed markedly from another group. See John M. Allswang, "The Origins of Direct Democracy in California: The Development of An Issue and Its Relationship to Progressivism," unpublished paper.

5. Two striking examples are the American Association of Retired People, with over thirty million members, and the environmental movement, a wide complex of local, state and national organizations that draws support in varying degrees from about three-quarters of the American people.

6. Owner-occupied housing dropped from 47.8 percent of all housing in 1930 to 43.6 in 1940 and then rose to 55 percent in 1950 and 72.9 in 1970.

7. In 1930 10.4 percent of farm homes in contrast with 84.8 percent of urban and rural non-farm homes had electricity; in 1956 the figures were 95.9 percent and 99.2 percent.

8. Among those aged 65 and over in 1990 and with incomes of $20,000 or more, 32 percent of income came from savings and investments, 24 percent from earnings, 23 percent from social security, and 20 percent from other pensions. *USA Today* (19 August 1992), 5A.

9. Joseph J. Huthmacher, *Senator Robert F. Wagner and the Rise of Urban Liberalism* (New York, 1968).

10. Herbert Garfinkel, *When Negroes March: The March on Washington Movement in the Organizational Politics of FEPC* (Glencoe, Ill., 1959).

11. Margo J. Anderson, *The American Census: A Social History* (New Haven, 1988).

12. Janet R. Daly, *The Changing Image of the City: Planning for Downtown Omaha, 1945–1973* (Lincoln, Nebr., 1992).

13. Gordon E. Baker, *The Reapportionment Revolution: Representation, Political Power and the Supreme Court* (New York, 1966). See also Robert B. McKay, *Reapportionment: The Law and Politics of Equal Representation* (New York, 1965) and Nelson W. Polsby, ed., *Reapportionment in the 1970s* (Berkeley, 1971).

14. Joel Silbey, *The American Political Nation, 1838–1893* (Stanford, Calif., 1991).

15. Byron E. Shafer, ed., *The End of Realignment? Interpreting American Electoral Eras* (Madison, Wis., 1991).

16. One way of describing this trend is to chart the average Democratic margin in the House of Representatives over time:

1942–1958	23	1975–1980	138
1959–1966	114	1981–1992	82
1967–1974	58		

17. One example concerns scores on environmental votes in the US House of Representatives, 1970–1989, which on a 0–100 scale averaged 65 for the Democratic Party and 33 for the Republican. For a more detailed analysis of regional and party environmental voting patterns over time see Samuel P. Hays, "Environmental Political Culture and Environmental Political Development: An Analysis of Legislative Voting, 1971-1989," *Environmental History Review*, 16, no. 2 (Summer 1992): 1–22.

18. Hays, "Environmental Political Culture," 7.

19. See, for example, *Governing* (Washington, DC, Congressional Quarterly, Inc., 1987–) and *State Legislatures* (Denver, Colo., National Conference of State Legislatures, 1975–).

20. See the publications of OMB Watch, Washington, DC, particularly its periodical, *Government Information Insider* (Washington, 1991–).

21. Lee Soltow, *Men and Wealth in the United States, 1850–1870* (New Haven, 1975); Jeffrey G. Williamson and Peter H. Lindert, *American Inequality: A Microeconomic History* (New York, 1980); Carole Shammas, "A New Look at Long Term Trends in Wealth Inequality in the United States," paper presented to the December 1991 meeting of the American Historical Association.

22. Thomas Byrne Edsall, *The New Politics of Inequality* (New York, 1984). Edsall presents charts that describe the variation in voter participation by

family income and occupation and the variation in Democratic and Republican Party support by income.

23. Eugene J. Watts, "Property and Politics in Atlanta: 1865–1902," *Journal of Urban History,* 3, no. 3 (May 1977): 295–322. This study, comparing the property holdings of successful and unsuccessful candidates for mayor, alderman, and council, found that voters consistently elected those with higher levels of wealth.

24. Inequality in private pension coverage, mitigated in some degree by social security, can be observed in the following percentages of income classes who have pension coverage other than social security (1983):

$5,000	–9,999	28.5%
$10,000	–14,999	51.0%
$15,000	–19,999	66.8%
$20,000	–over	75.9%

12 French Democracy and the Welfare State

Herrick Chapman

The expansion of the state's role in social welfare during the twentieth century has been both bane and boon to democracy.[1] Giant welfare bureaucracies have enhanced the authority of administrators at the expense of parliaments and citizens. The sheer scale of programs in health, education, and welfare have made many social programs remarkably resistant to partisan pressures, Margaret Thatcher and Ronald Reagan notwithstanding. Welfare policy has also served undemocratic rulers, especially during the fascist era in Europe and more recently in many non-European nations, as a means of weakening the appeal of democratic movements. Bismarck, after all, created the first national programs of social insurance for workers with just such motives in mind.

And yet there has also been a democratic side to the welfare state. In many countries since the late nineteenth century, working- and middle-class interest groups have fought to win government protection against the risks of injury, disability, sickness, unemployment, and old age. Social policies of this kind certainly helped stabilize democratic regimes at critical times, from New Deal America to war-torn Western Europe in the late 1940s. Welfare policy has also served as a focus for new political movements, be they American welfare rights activists in the 1960s or British feminists in the 1970s attacking the sexism of family policy. By shifting responsibility from private charity to government, the rise of the welfare state has politicized activities – caring for elders, healing the sick, attending to abused children – and hence enlarged the potential domain for democratic action.

Because the welfare state has become virtually synonymous with the state itself and claims a huge share of government budgets, the future of democracy in many countries may depend on how democratically social policy can be shaped and implemented. It may depend, too, on how effective and equitable welfare policies prove to be. State welfare provisioning, at least in theory, should have democratic consequences – by nurturing a sense of solidarity, by helping people secure the health, learning, and leisure they need to take part in the civic culture, by providing a focus for the kind of "rational-critical discourse" Jürgen Habermas has associated with the creation of a public sphere. But too often in recent years welfare policy has divided the public, broken budgets, and fed prejudice rather than empathy. Issues of representation in social policymaking, on the one hand, and the social effects of policy, on the other, trouble even the most stable democracies. A better historical understanding of the relationship between welfare provision and democratic practice, then, has value not only for scholars studying the social history of democracy in the twentieth century but also for citizens grappling with current policy.

One way to advance that understanding is to look at how the rise of the welfare state shaped and responded to the development of democracy in particular countries. France deserves attention for several reasons. First, the French built their own peculiar form of welfare state in the twentieth century over the course of several decades and in the context of several political regimes, namely the Third, Fourth and Fifth Republics. This protracted process involved three critical turning points: the creation of the social insurance law of 1930, an ambitious set of structural reforms in 1945–1946, and a more complex, piecemeal set of changes in the 1960s and 1970s. Other countries, such as Britain, built welfare states in a similar sequence of pivotal moments, but not with the same changes in political regime. The French case offers the unusual opportunity to see welfare state building in the context of three different democratic regimes and three different eras of political mobilization.

Second, since 1945 the French have experimented with an unusual form of popular participation in the administration of social security programs that made the French system of social security at least potentially more democratic than elsewhere. Representatives of various contributor and beneficiary groups sit on administrative boards at the local and national level, an arrangement that has changed in important ways over time. A look at this experience reveals both the possibilities and the obstacles to representative democracy in the welfare state.

Third, gender relations also played a crucial role in giving the French welfare state its unique qualities, especially its heavy reliance on family allowances. In a country where women won the vote only in 1945 and where leaders had, since the 1880s, been obsessed with the birth rate, women have had belated but important success winning a voice in post-war policymaking. In doing so they have called into question older assumptions about the aims of family policy as a keystone of the welfare state.

This chapter will explore the relationship between welfare state building and the evolution of democracy in France by examining each of these themes – the basic structuring of the system through three republics, the tensions between technocratic and democratic modes of authority within the system, and the gender politics at work in the making of family policy.

SOCIAL INSURANCE FROM THE THIRD TO THE FIFTH REPUBLICS

The architects of the 1930 law on social insurance had big obstacles to overcome in creating what proved to be the foundation of the French welfare state. By the 1920s France had clearly fallen behind Britain, Germany, Belgium, and Scandanavia in creating a coherent, national structure of social protection. To be sure, political leaders in the Third Republic had broken some important ground. A law on work injuries in 1898 required employers to compensate employees for accidents, unless employees themselves were at fault.[2] In 1905 parliament passed legislation that made municipal authorities responsible for poor relief (with some financial support from the central government), a major step in a century-long republican effort to shift charity from church to state.[3] But in comparison to Britain with its National Insurance Bill of 1911 and Germany with its Bismarckian programs for injury, unemployment and old age, France remained undistinguished in the field. Instead of a national program of social insurance the French had turned to voluntary, private solutions. By the 1920s a vast network of mutual aid societies and company funds had emerged. Working-class families fared poorly under this system. Although skilled workers had dominated the mutual aid movement a century earlier, by the twentieth century it was mainly a middle-class institution. Large employers, especially in mining, metalworking, and railroads, had created insurance programs of their own in an effort to shore up worker loyalty. Workers fortunate enough to have coverage under a company program bore the burdens of dependency on paternalistic employers. In a France still overwhelmingly dominated by small-sized enterprise, most workers lacked even a modicum of insurance protection.[4]

These limitations in welfare policy reflected the success, not the failure, in establishing democracy in the Third Republic. Ironically, it was precisely the absence of democracy in Bismarck's Germany that made the socialist movement so menacing to elites and government-mandated social insurance so appealing to Bismarck as a way to placate workers. In France universal manhood suffrage took the wind out of revolutionary sails, lowering the stakes of social reform.[5] More important, democracy empowered shopkeepers, small businessmen, and agriculturalists, the crucial constituency of moderate republicans and the Radical party which, as Philip Nord has emphasized elsewhere in this volume, dominated most of the governing coalitions of the Third Republic. In France, where urbanization and industrial concentration proceeded only gradually in comparison to Britain or Germany, small producers had inordinate power. And they hated the notion of a unitary, government-sponsored system of national insurance. They feared its costs and thought it would corrupt the working class.[6]

Suspicions about state power also inhibited social reform in the Third Republic. After the bloody defeat of the Paris Commune the far left distrusted the republican state as an instrument for social change and viewed social insurance as a palliative. Revolutionary syndicalists, extolling the virtues of worker self-help, hoped to revive mutual aid for workers without recourse to state intervention. Although more moderate trade unionists and socialists had fewer reservations about state-centered reform, they rejected contributory schemes of social insurance, at least before 1914, as an unjust tax on workers' wages.[7] If the left was divided over state intervention, the right was more united in its anti-statist stance. The far right fought to preserve a place for the church in social reform. Although center-right republicans opposed church intervention, they too preferred to address "the social question" through voluntary efforts in civil society rather than through the exercise of coercive state authority.

Yet these barriers to social insurance reform proved surmountable by the late 1920s when parliament passed two laws, one in 1928 and another in 1930, that created a national insurance system. The 1930 law was a turning point because it obligated employers and employees whose wages were below a certain threshold to contribute to any of a large number of social insurance funds covering health, disability, maternity, death benefits, and old age. Over 700 funds from the huge network of private insurance programs and mutual aid societies qualified for subscription, though employees could opt for a new state-sponsored fund established in each geographical department of the country, a *caisse départementale*. As a measure of how eager many people were to avoid the company funds that employers had long controlled, over 60 percent of the subscribers chose a *caisse départementale*. By the mid-1930s about 10 million wage-earners had come under the system, mostly manual workers whose wages were beneath the statutory ceiling and who were not covered by other programs, such as the railroad or civil service *caisses*, that had retained their independence.[8] The program fell far short of a full-fledged social security system, since it covered only a portion of the workforce and remained rooted in small, mostly private, funds that could spread the burden of risk only so far. Still, it marked a milestone in the struggle for social protection.

If the obstacles to social insurance reform loomed so large in the Third Republic, what made it possible to pass the 1930 law? For one thing, small producers had lost some of their power in parliament, as industrial growth and urbanization swelled the ranks of salaried employees and enhanced the political clout of large employers. Between 1926 and 1932 several center-right governments advocated ideas such as industrial rationalization, public investment in infrastructure, even planning, that were anathema to small-town republicans. André Tardieu's government of 1930 made a pitch for a big new program of "national retooling" along these lines. True, little legislation in the realm of economic policy actually ensued from these efforts. Parliamentary instability and then the depression put an end to the "neo-liberal" ambitions of the big business right. But in the realm of social insurance right-wing leadership with roots in big rather than small business proved essential in passing the 1930 law.[9] Large employers had come to see the advantages of a mandatory contributory system as a way to stabilize the workforce, standardize insurance costs, and avert the actuarial crisis that many company funds were beginning to face with an aging population of contributors.[10] A shift had taken place on the left as well. Socialists and moderate trade unionists had put social insurance at the top of their legislative agenda after the First World War. Even contributory insurance, they decided, would be better than nothing. Finally, the French recovery of Alsace-Lorraine in 1918 also made a difference. People there had no intention of giving up the social legislation they had come to enjoy as a part of Germany. The spoils of victory in the First World War forced the French hand, as did an awareness in government circles that France could not remain outside the drift of Europeanwide social policy reform forever.[11] All these factors combined to make coalition-building possible to pass the 1930 law.

The second pivotal moment in welfare state-building, in the first years after the liberation of France in 1944, transformed the basic structure of 1930 into a full-scale social security system. Impetus for change came from a number of directions. The three political parties that emerged from the Resistance to form a governing coalition for the Fourth Republic – the Communists, Socialists, and Social Catholics (the MRP) – all stood firmly behind the notion of expanding the system of social insurance. Communists and Socialists in particular hoped to create a more unitary and universal structure. The collapse of the Vichy regime and its association with the Nazi occupation momentarily silenced the traditional right. As a result, big business interests placed their hopes in de Gaulle, and the Gaullists viewed an expanded system of social security, especially family allowances, as part of a larger crusade to regenerate the nation.

What emerged from the Liberation was a blend of technocratic planning and tough interest-group politics. The initial plan for reform came from de Gaulle's entourage. Pierre Laroque, the chief architect of the postwar social security system, designed a scheme that would bring all the many funds of the 1930 arrangement, and many of the special occupational funds as well, into a single *caisse.* He hoped to simplify the structure, broaden its base of subscribers to make it virtually universal, and hence provide a means for spreading the costs of social risks as widely as possible. Laroque drew much of his inspiration from Britain's Beveridge Report,[12] but retained two crucial features from the existing French system: financing through payroll taxes rather than income taxes, since the latter were still poorly developed in France; and preserving a quasi-private status for the *caisse,* which would be administered by a board of representatives of the contributors rather than by a government agency. This notion of representation stemmed directly from the mutual aid tradition and had in principle, though not very faithfully in practice, been preserved in the 1930 social insurance program. Keeping the *caisse* outside the state bureaucracy also spoke to widespread antipathy in 1944, after four years of Nazi occupation and Vichy authoritarianism, to concentrating power in the hands of state officials.[13]

A bitter political struggle reshaped Laroque's original plan. The notion of a single *caisse* fell by the wayside in a close vote in the planning committee. Social Catholics fought to preserve the separate status of family allowance funds, and trade unions defended special retirement funds for miners and railroad workers. The insurance industry, fearing the single *caisse* as a financial threat, lobbied to maintain multiple funds.[14] What emerged was a compromise. The government created a *régime général* of nationalized funds largely along the lines Laroque had proposed but let most of the special occupational funds continue. Furthermore, by adopting a ceiling on assessed wages, the government left in place the incentive for better paid occupational groups to maintain or create complementary funds.[15] The old age pension system, then, remained a mosaic of public and private funds. White-collar personnel in middle and upper management, what the French call *cadres,* chose to maintain their own funds rather than join the *régime général.* So too did the self-employed – farmers, artisans, shopkeepers, and liberal professionals.[16]

Despite these compromises, the reformers of the late 1940s achieved a great deal. They expanded family allowances to the whole population and brought the liberal professions under the national health insurance fund. Only agriculture remained as a large economic sector outside the health *caisses.* By 1950 the French people had a social security system roughly comparable in scope to what the British had created, with the one striking exception of unemployment insurance, which the government introduced only in 1958. Overall levels of spending on social insurance, however, were still low by European standards.

It took another series of reforms during the Fifth Republic to bring France into the front rank of European welfare states. Throughout the 1960s President de Gaulle and then his successor, Georges Pompidou, initiated a series of reforms that enlarged the scale of the system. These reforms extended unemployment insurance coverage to the whole population, brought the agricultural population into the health insurance fund, and created a minimal floor for retirement that, unlike the British system, virtually insured against old age poverty.[17] During this era, too, the Labor Ministry expanded its mission of providing social services and social programs, that network of activities in public health and social work that has become synonymous with the welfare state. A new Inspectorate for Social Affairs for the first time began to attract well trained civil servants to the social policy sector.[18] Although the French right reigned over the Fifth Republic throughout the 1960s and 1970s, it was under its tutelage that French welfare policy came of age.

The social security system also expanded from initiatives outside the state. The very occupational groups that had fought to retain their own separate pension funds in the late 1940s, especially the self-employed, now lobbied to join the national pension system. Faced with the economic effects of industrial and commercial concentration in a prospering France now linked to the Common Market, many small producers could no longer afford to spurn the *régime général*. Ironically, workers who could have benefitted from the self-employed being part of the system in the 1940s now wanted to keep them out, since aging and struggling artisans and shopkeepers could burden the funds. But small producers remained a potent enough political force, even in the Fifth Republic, to secure support from parties on both left and right to bring them into the system.[19] The French pension system still remained a complex multilayered web of public and private funds, but most people contributed in some fashion to the *régime général*. By 1980 France stood only behind Denmark, the Netherlands, and Sweden in the size of its social security expenditures as a percentage of GDP. Indeed, France led all nations in Europe in the proportion of public expenditures allocated to social security programs.[20]

PATTERNS OF CONTINUITY AND CHANGE

This brief look at the three phases of welfare state building in the Third, Fourth and Fifth Republics reveals several patterns of continuity and change in the politics of social reform. For one thing, in all three phases right-wing leadership played a critical role in orchestrating the politics of reform. France may not have had a Bismarck, but it did have men on the right like André Tardieu in 1930, and Charles de Gaulle in both 1945 and the 1960s, to neutralize the traditional right-wing opponents of social legislation and to put a conservative stamp on the social insurance system. In each case the context for right-wing support had special qualities. The interest of large employers in rationalizing wage policy, along with other aspects of the business environment, gave Tardieu the political courage to oppose petty bourgeois preferences. In 1945 de Gaulle lent conservative legitimacy to what was essentially a left-wing project of reform. Gaullism as an ideology, moreover, provided conservatives with a way to combine their traditional nationalism with an enlightened view of social policy. France, in their view, needed more babies and healthy workers if the country hoped to return to international prominence. Gaullism gave social security a patriotic aura.[21] Likewise, in the Fifth Republic social policy served the Gaullists as a crucial political instrument. It helped build middle-class support for the regime at a time when Gaullist economic policy promoted big business interests at the expense of small producers. Social security provided the easiest way to buy back loyalty from the losers of economic modernization.[22] Gaullist technocrats also viewed a strong social security system as good economics – a way to boost consumption and improve the quality of the workforce – reflecting a Keynesian consensus that government spending on social programs could serve as a positive tool of macroeconomic management. Above all, social policy served the nationalistic end, central to de Gaulle's vision of the state, of projecting an ever stronger and more modern France into the international arena. Right-wing leaders, and especially de Gaulle, expanded social insurance as a means of enhancing the state itself.

If right-wing leadership proved essential in all three phases, so too did left-wing pressure. To be sure, France lacked the kind of social democratic movement and powerful trade unions that set the social policy agenda in Britain and Sweden. Still, the French Socialist party and moderate labor movement put national insurance policy on the table in the first place during the 1920s and remained essential to the parliamentary alliance which passed the bill of 1930. Without the left-wing electoral insurgency of 1945 a plan of the scope Pierre Laroque proposed would have been a dead letter from the start. Indeed, the leap in 1945 to a truly national system of social security and a participatory structure to administer it became possible only because of the peculiar historical circumstances that gave a parliamentary majority to Communists, Socialists and left-wing Catholics. Just as Gaullism brought the right into the welfare state game, so too the transformation of the Communist Party into an essentially nationalistic and reformist party of the left brought considerable momentum to the politics of social reform. And finally, in the 1960s and 1970s government initiatives in welfare policy were prompted in part by left-wing electoral pressure. Although the right ruled for 23 years after 1958, electoral competition remained keen for much of that time. Gaullists and Socialists both tried to woo support from the very groups that stood to gain most from expanding the social security system – white-collar employees and the self-employed. In the Fifth Republic as in 1930 and 1945, a basic pattern seemed to hold: major bursts in the welfare state expansion came with right-wing leadership and left-wing pressure – an implicit style of coalition politics that cut across left and right and across the class divide.[23]

Another pattern follows accordingly, namely the consistency with which governments accommodated middle-class interests over the whole half-century span of welfare state-building. Middle-class *mutualités* retained their independence, and middle-class occupational groups their right to abstain from the government-sponsored *caisses*, during the first two episodes of reform. When self-employed producers and liberal professionals joined the system after 1960, they did so voluntarily, not by force as some militants on the left had envisioned in 1945. The *haute bourgeoisie* fared well by reform as well. Paternalistic company funds in such big firms as Renault and Citroën in many ways served as the key point of reference for expanding social insurance through the 1930 law. Big employers retained a powerful voice on administrative boards of the funds, both private and public. True, employers lost ground to labor representatives after 1945 when the latter won the right to 75 percent of the seats on social security boards. But as we shall see below, employers recovered much of this ground in the Fifth Republic. Overall, as the French welfare state evolved it bore the heavy imprint of middle-class and big business influence. This pattern in the politics of social reform helps account for the tardiness of national health insurance and ironically its rapid growth after 1960. It accounts too for the complexity of a multilayered system combining a *régime général* with complementary quasi-private funds.

Business and middle-class influence also helps explain why the French welfare state, for all its size and range, ranks among the least redistributive in its impact. David Cameron has shown that in Sweden, Norway, and Britain over 60 percent of all transfer payments redound to the benefit of the poorest 40 percent of households. By contrast in France, benefits are distributed quite evenly across all quintiles of the population with no redistributive effect.[24] Some shifts in income clearly do take place – from the employed to retired and unemployed people, from young to old, from small families to large.[25] But relatively little distribution takes place from rich to poor, since the financing of the system is largely regressive. Payroll taxes with a ceiling on assessible wages are regressive from the start, and ultimately redound to consumers in the form of higher prices, as do the indirect taxes that finance the bulk of government subsidies to the insurance funds.[26] By avoiding much dependence on income tax, by preserving the traditional French reliance on contributory financing, and by keeping means testing for many social programs to a minimum, French governments throughout the post-war era have preserved a high level of middle-class support for the welfare state.

Perhaps a stronger, more unified left and trade union movement might have forced post-war governments to adopt more redistributive reforms. But even in 1945 the left lacked the power to recast social insurance in a truly egalitarian mold. By the 1960s the working-class left had become too ensconced in the post-war social security system to call its basic premises into question. When, for example, Gaullist technocrats tried to introduce means testing in a number of social programs, most notably in family allowances, as a way to trim costs and reduce poverty, they not only ran up against the expected opposition from middle-class groups; they encountered objections as well from trade unions and left-wing parties, including the Communists. Working-class families, especially those in the more organized sectors of the workforce, were riding the wave of post-war prosperity and watching their social security benefits grow accordingly. Many workers stood to lose ground if uniform allowances, for children, say, or for postnatal services, became adjusted for level of income. The welfare state, in short, had come to work well enough for the working and middle classes all to feel a stake in the benefit structure, even though benefit effects tended to rise with income.[27]

Left-wing ambivalence about means testing in the 1960s revealed something deeper about popular attitudes as well. As Stephen Cohen and Charles Goldfinger have suggested, people on both the left and the right had come to embrace an ideology of solidarity with regard to social security that gave little priority to redistribution. Solidarity meant sharing the nation's resources among its people for the general good, that is, for the good of the nation. Fairness mattered: everyone, the thinking went, had a right to social protection and to roughly equal service. But the main point of social security was not to transfer resources from the privileged to the poor. Even the Communists bought this view. They hoped to restructure the economic system, radically even, but not by manipulating social security.[28] The left, moreover, believed that by stressing uniform rather than redistributive rights, the French system averted the political dangers that came with invidious distinctions between different degrees of dependence on welfare provisions – distinctions that might divide better-paid workers from the poor.[29] When every family became entitled to child allowances and coverage under the national health insurance system, and when relatively high floors on old age pensions were established in the 1960s, few people spoke of the "undeserving poor" as in the United States.

So far this discussion has stressed continuities across the three Republics: the importance of right-wing leadership and left-wing pressure; the need to build coalitions, even momentary ones, across left and right to make breakthroughs in the structure of social security; the dominance of middle-class interests; and the survival of a solidaristic vision that helped sustain some consensus about social security, despite continuing conflicts over policy. But what of discontinuity? How did the structure of the three Republics, the way each governmental structure tended to institutionalize the power of officials, parties, and social groups, affect the politics of social reform?

The rise of executive authority and administrative expertise did make a difference. With each successive era of reform technocratic planners in the ministries played more prominent roles in shaping policy. In the 1920s plans for social insurance reform came as much out of the offices of leading employer lobbyists, such as Robert Pinot at the Union des Industries Métallurgiques et Minières, as from the bureaus of the Finance and Labor ministries. The doctors' organizations had a big say in shaping the policies that were proposed for insuring medical services. To be sure, high civil servants certainly played a role in helping to draft and modify legislation. But the power to promote reform remained fragmented by a parliamentary system which severely constrained executive authority. By 1945 the structure of power in the French state had changed. Charles de Gaulle's highly influential Labor Minister, Alexandre Parodi, had gathered around him a formidable team of high civil servants, including Pierre Laroque and Francis Netter, who were to remain central figures in social policy for a generation. They never had the power to dictate policy. Indeed, Laroque presided over a process which whittled away at his original plan. But by the early Fourth Republic the power of initiative had shifted decisively into the bureaus of the ministries. And doctors, for example, were given little role in policy planning.

This trend accelerated in the Fifth Republic. Strong presidential government gave technocratic planners in the ministries even more official sanction than before to serve as reigning experts over major domains of public policy. Ministers themselves, moreover, could also acquire a similar status since under the constitution of the Fifth Republic ministers no longer had to hold seats in parliament to win appointment. The blue-ribbon commission of experts became the vehicle of choice for putting social security reforms on the table. The very complexity of the system, and government ambitions to coordinate social security with wage policy, training programs and immigration policy, gave administrative experts added authority. So too did a penchant for Gaullist governments to make major reforms in the system by decree. By 1960 state officials even felt strong enough to issue a decree that would indirectly control medical fees through the reimbursement policies of the social security system.[30]

To be sure, social policy remained subject to interest-group pressures. Many a minister in the Fifth Republic felt compelled to back away from blue-ribbon commission recommendations.[31] Government proposals to shift social secruity financing away from payroll taxes in 1960 aroused rebellion from labor and business alike, and several attempts to introduce means testing in the family allowance system ran up against a hostile family lobby. The rise of an administrative technocracy, moreover, did nothing to depoliticize social security policymaking. On the contrary, administrative experts remained closely associated with a regime with a reputation for catering to big business in matters of social policy, just as it had in industrial policy and labor relations. This image was particularly credible in 1967 when the government decreed a sweeping set of changes – altering the composition of *caisses* boards and prohibiting the transfer of funds among the pension, health, and family allowance programs – that echoed what the big business lobby had long said it wanted. Still, the pattern of change from the Third to the Fifth Republic was unmistakable. Although partisanship found ample expression in the Fifth Republic, much of the power to initiate change had shifted from societal groups to state officials.

REPRESENTATION IN THE SOCIAL SECURITY SYSTEM

This tension between the growing strength of technocratic state authority and the continuing efforts of interest groups to exert influence became manifest in the administrative boards which supervised the many *caisses* in the post-war period. The reforms of 1945 stipulated that each of the *caisses* in the *régime général* have a governing board of contributors and beneficiaries. Boards were established in some 250 local and regional *caisses*, as well as at the national level. Local and regional boards had considerable authority over employees in the social security bureaucracy, as well as over discretionary funds for summer camps, vacation supplements, and other social activities.[32] This extraordinary feature of the French welfare state derived above all from the mutual aid tradition, which had made oversight by fund participants a sacred principle, a tradition that made employers, workers, and Catholic spokesmen all hostile to direct state control of the system. The 1930 law had preserved the principle of independent boards, much to the benefit of employers who dominated them. But when left-wing parties had the upper hand in 1945, the scale of representation tipped decisively toward the unions. In the new system employees had a right to 75 percent of the seats and employers the rest. The social security system suddenly became an unprecedented experiment in popular participation in the welfare state.[33]

Popular participation in the administration of social security took one other form as well. Trade unions succeeded in organizing the employees in the system, especially social workers, into a union, the Fédération nationale des organismes de la sécurité sociale, or FNOSS.[34] Local and national leaders of this body claimed an important say in the late 1940s and 1950s over how funds should be spent and social services organized. More important, they acquired influence over hiring and promotions within the social service bureaucracy. Like the *caisses* boards, leadership posts in FNOSS became the objects of intense competition between rival factions of the blue- and white-collar unions.

These participatory features of the French welfare state made the social security administration subject to the same kind of partisan struggles that were taking place in the trade union movement and in national politics. From the start the Communist wing of the labor movement secured a dominant position on the boards and within FNOSS. Riding a wave of post-Liberation popularity and real organizational strength in most industrial branches, Communist representatives held a majority of employee seats in the *caisses*. But Cold War politics and the slow decline of the left during the course of the Fourth Republic reduced the Communists to a strong but minoritarian position in the 1950s. *Caisses* board politics became a complex business of shifting coalitions, sometimes pitting employee representatives against employers, other times producing cleavages between Communists and the rest. Similarly, the competition for influence in FNOSS became more balanced among Communist, non-Communist leftists, and moderates.

Political combat at this level of intensity obviously came at a cost to bureaucratic efficiency. But it did engage the public in social policy debates to a remarkable degree. Every several years employees and employers throughout the country voted for their representatives, who campaigned as candidates put up by unions, mutual aid societies, and employer associations.[35] Every major trade union faction fought hard in these campaigns, since militants regarded the results as a measure of their strength in the workplace. These elections provided voters a multiplicity of views on social policy questions and a chance to register their preferences accordingly.[36] Levels of voter participation in the social security elections throughout the Fourth and Fifth Republic in fact remained respectable – abstention rates in the 1970s were about 30 percent – roughly comparable to rates for municipal elections.[37]

Over time, however, this participatory dimension of the French welfare state suffered with the rise of state administrative power. To some extent, of course, the growth of the social service bureaucracy was bound to strengthen the administrative hierarchy at the expense of board control. But the concentration of power in the hands of state officials had more direct causes as well. Officials in the Labor and Finance Ministries, with sanction from prime ministers in the Fourth and Fifth Republics, deliberately tightened the grip of state supervisory authority. How much these officials were motivated by narrow partisan aims, by sympathies for employer interests, by organizational ambitions, or by deep-seated notions of state, remains hard to say and begs for more historical research. What is clear is that state officials encroached on the autonomy of the boards in three different periods. First, in the late 1940s, as Cold War tensions reached their height in French domestic politics, state officials sought to limit the power of the left-dominated boards. They did so by requiring administrative approval of board decisions and by expanding the role of the Cour des Comptes, the powerful state auditing authority, over the caisses. Then in the reform decrees of 1960 de Gaulle's ministers diminished the power of the boards over personnel decisions, eliminated FNOSS as a hiring authority, and gave social service administrators at the local and regional level more autonomy from the boards. These steps produced an outcry, even from employer representatives, but to little avail.[38] Finally, in the reform decrees of 1967, the government restructured the boards to give employers 50 percent of the seats, and hence parity with employee representatives. Overnight this maneuver eliminated the effective control over boards that employee organizations had had since 1945. The effects obviously varied from board to board. But one analyst who studied these institutions in the 1970s found that employer representatives tended to give the boards a kind of managerial ethos, while employee representatives on the left settled into a role of militant opposition. Under these circumstances boards tended to replicate the larger ideological cleavages polarizing French society in the 1970s, at the price of inhibiting constructive dialogue among representatives.[39] The quality of boards as an arena of participatory democracy suffered accordingly.

Public reaction to the 1967 reform showed how seriously many employees took this attack on *caisse* representation. Every union, of course, issued its protest and made social security politics a centerpiece of labor agitation through the fall and winter of 1967. Opinion polls in the years immediately following the change revealed how unpopular the 1967 reforms really were, enough, it appears now in retrospect, to stoke the fires of rebellion in May 1968. When pollsters asked people on May 27, just before the settlement of the Grenelle labor agreements that helped put an end to the upheaval, "what good might come out of this crisis," 26 percent of the respondants pointed to a revision of the 1967 social security decree as their first or second preference.[40] But no such revision occurred. Parity between employers and employees remained in force.

The growth of state administrative authority at the expense of the boards and the unions in the supervision of social security funds paralleled a similar rise of centralized political control of the system in the course of the Fourth and Fifth Republics. The return of the left to power in 1981 did little to alter the trend. François Mitterrand's governments used a variety of technical initiatives to put the system on sounder financial footing, including loans from several private pension funds to help float the one major piece of social legislation the Socialists produced in the heady days of 1981–1982 – an early retirement option for people at age sixty. But the Socialists did not take it upon themselves to change the structure of representation on the boards or to restore lost authority to these representative institutions. True enough, in the late 1980s the government did invoke an old democratic tradition of calling an "estates general" of officials and representatives from throughout the social security system to consider new ways to improve the system. But little came of it.[41] As in other domains of policy, the Mitterrand regime did more to reaffirm than dismantle the technocratic character of the post-war French state. After 1982 Socialist government officials, struggling to implement an economic policy of austerity which included constraints on social security spending, had no desire to mobilize the public through a reinvigoration of the representative boards.

THE GENDER POLITICS OF FAMILY POLICY

State structure and the nature of democratic politics in France also played a role in shaping the gender politics of the social security system. All three major elements of French social security – old age pensions, health insurance, and family allowances – embodied assumptions about what roles men and women play in society, but nowhere were notions about gender more visible than in the family allowance program. Introduced in 1932 in legislation designed to supplement the 1930 social insurance law, family allowances soon became a centerpiece of the French welfare state. The 1932 law obligated employers to contribute to one of many approved funds that gave employees with at least two children a wage supplement to subsidize their households. Then in 1939 the Daladier government established the Family Code by decree. This ambitious pro-natalist program entitled every family to child allowances, which increased with each child, and was again financed mainly through a payroll tax. The Code also provided non-working mothers outside the agricultural sector with a housewife allowance. (Farmers' wives were thought to be able to handle childrearing and their domestic duties in the normal course of things.) Together these subsidies offered incentives to create what the Code's designers believed was the ideal household: a family with at least three children and a mother who stayed at home.[42]

This family policy brought to fruition a politics of pro-natalism that derived from three sources. First, for over a century Catholic familiarists had advocated support for the large patriarchal family as the single most important way to reverse the moral degeneration and social turmoil they associated with industrial change.[43] The second phalanx in the army of family reform came from the republican camp – secular pro-natalists who viewed population growth as essential to the future of France. Defeat in the Franco-Prussian War had made the country's demographic decline into an alarmist's cause of the first order. Staggering losses in the First World War and their long-term demographic effects further strengthened the movement. By the eve of the Second World War pro-natalism became synonymous with patriotism. Hitler as much as anyone helped pave the road to the Family Code.

Large employers became a third force behind the cause of family allowances, just as they were in the struggle for social insurance. Most employers, of course, waved their patriotic flags toward pro-natalism, like most good interwar bourgeois. But employers in some key sectors had by the early 1930s already experimented with family allowances for more immediate purposes. Textile employers in the north created *caisses* for family subsidies which they gave to men and women workers in exchange for rigorous attendance and refusals to strike. Employers in the Parisian metalworking industry used family allowances to hold down wage demands.[44] From the start family policy embodied the contradictory ambitions of employers who wanted to stabilize wage costs and keep women at work, on the one hand, and Catholic familiarists, on the other, who hoped to keep mothers at home. The Family Code of 1939 appeared to satisfy both sides. It created a national program modelled on what employers had already invented. It gave the Catholic family lobby the housewife allowance. But the latter remained a token, for non-working mothers received much too small an allowance to compensate for a working wage.[45] France continued to have one of the highest levels of female employment in Europe, despite the Family Code.

The breakthrough to the Family Code also reflected the relative power-lessness of women in the Third Republic. Not that most women opposed family allowances, especially at the relatively substantial rates of the Family Code. Nor was the Code as patriarchal as it might have been: allowances, in fact, were given directly to mothers in most cases, rather than to fathers who reformers feared might drink the proceeds. In contrast to Britain, where reformers introduced a more modest program of family allowances with the main aim of keeping married women out of the workforce and dependent on a husband's wage, in France the creators of the Code sought above all to promote childbearing, whether or not the mother worked.[46] Even so, the absence of a women's franchise in the Third Republic took its toll in the quality of debate about family policy. Left-wing radicals and the mainstream of the trade union movement at least in theory advocated the right of women to work at equal wages, and they viewed family allowances as an obstacle to the cause. But on the whole the left offered little in the way of an alternative, feminist vision of family policy.[47] Many politicians on the left dragged their feet on women's suffrage, for fear the Catholic right would benefit most from women's votes. Without a female constituency or the political will to create one, the left had little ammunition to counter the large employers, pro-natalist republicans, and the Catholic family lobby that coalesced behind the Family Code.

The Vichy regime further reinforced the conservative tone of the Family Code, which government officials enforced energetically during the German occupation. Marshall Pétain and other Vichy ideologues celebrated the family, in contrast to the individual, as the "cell of French life." They toughened restrictions against divorce. Fathers of large families were often given career advantages over other men. Although many women worked during the Occupation, as they traditionally had in large numbers in France, the government officially promoted the idea of motherhood as a full-time duty.[48] Vichy officials, in short, put the force of administration and propaganda behind a vision of gender relations they had inherited from the Family Code.

The Liberation, which ushered in important changes in many areas of social and economic life, did little to transform family policy. Although the Fourth Republic enfranchised women, and although the health insurance and pension provisions of the post-war welfare state treated men and women equally, it took some time to overcome much of the traditionalism in the family allowance system. To be sure, family policy lost some of the aura of Catholic conservatism that had surrounded the innovations of the 1930s. Another humiliating military defeat had made the left as pro-natalist as the right. Moreover, Antoine Prost may be right to suggest that an outbreak of family romanticism in the early post-war years – a desire to retreat into the couple and family as ideal sources of companionship, and a more open association of sexuality with marriage – created a pro-family ethos that took some of the conservative political undertones out of familiarist discourse.[49] The shift of many Catholics leftward in the 1940s also helped to neutralize the conservative side of the family lobby. Even so, the latter remained powerful, exerting its influence through the Union nationale des associations familiales and the new Social Catholic party, the MRP, which usually held sway over family policy in the parliaments of the Fourth Republic. Conservatives successfully fought off efforts by the unions, some feminists, and left-wing modernizers, such as Pierre Mendès France, to make the housewife allowance available to both working and non-working mothers.

By the 1960s and 1970s, however, a number of social and political changes converged to erode key features of French family policy and the gendered assumptions that had informed it since the 1930s. Broad shifts in social mores made the pro-family ideology of Catholic conservatives ring hollow in the ears of a younger generation. With the sexual revolution and the emergence of a stronger peer culture, young people loosened ties to their parents. The family lost its sanctity. Feminism, moreover, finally emerged as a powerful ideological and political force as women called for dismantling legal barriers to civic equality. A new marriage law in 1965 established legal equality for spouses. Parliament legalized contraception in 1967, abortion in 1975, and equal employment rights that same year. Women's rights, in short, emerged as something separate from the family as a focus for social policy.[50] Parties on the right as well as the left had to appeal to women voters first as citizens and only secondarily as mothers or wives. Finally, it mattered, too, that the MRP declined precipitously in the early years of the Fifth Republic, in part because a revived and powerful Gaullist party stole many of its voters. With the MRP's decay the family lobby lost its most potent parliamentary instrument.

This complex set of social and political changes altered the landscape for family policy in the Fifth Republic. Family allowances survived, largely because pro-natalist alarm revived when the birthrate fell in the early 1970s. By the 1980s allowances and tax deductions still offered substantial financial rewards for having a third child. But the older notion of using state power to promote a particular kind of family, especially one with a non-working wife, had become out of date. Gaullist technocrats, starting in the early 1960s, looked for ways to diminish the housewife allowance, which they viewed as an obstacle to part-time employment for women.[51] Government planners subordinated family policy to a labor market policy designed to boost industrial productivity. By the early 1970s officials in the Pompidou regime took the risk of attacking a central principle in conservative familiarist ideology – the notion that every family, regardless of income, should be entitled to the same allowances and hence the same incentives to produce more children. Means testing for certain benefits, despite the pro-family lobby, finally came to pass, especially for the housewife allowance, which was already on the decline.[52] If by the 1980s family allowances still remained in place as a hallmark of the French welfare state, they had diminished in importance. As a proportion of all social spending they declined to 14.7 percent in 1980, down from 21.2 percent a decade before.[53] Little remained in the structure of benefits to discriminate against women who worked. These changes in family policy during the Fifth Republic vindicated, ironically, both the large employers of the Third Republic who had always seen family allowances as perfectly consistent with female employment and left-wing radicals who had advocated gender equality in social insurance and the workplace. Shifts in family policy since 1960 also testified to the impact of integrating women into the polity.

CONCLUSION

The welfare state in France acquired its distinctive features in large part because of the way the French democratized their political regimes over the past century. The weight of conservative interest groups in the Third Republic left a deep imprint on the system of national insurance which remains to this day. The tardiness of the social insurance program, its decentralized and quasi-mutualistic structure, its regressive and non-redistributive financing, and its direct linkage to the place of employment – all these features reflect the resistance of small bourgeois interest groups and the formative role big business played in social policymaking in the inter-war years. The French welfare state began, and to a large extent remained, a product of *bourgeois* democracy. In this respect the Third Republic has cast a long shadow over the later history of French social policy.

The democratic politics of the early Fourth Republic made its mark as well when the Socialist and Communist left transformed the conservative achievements of the 1930 national insurance law and the Family Code of 1939 into a much more encompassing and solidaristic welfare state. The left also endowed the social security system with representative boards that made the welfare state a channel for democratic participation. In the end, however, the left conceded as much ground as it gained. The require-ments of coalition-building in the post-Liberation period forced Communists and Socialists to embrace a solidaristic notion of social insur-ance that limited the chances to use welfare policy to shift money from the rich to the poor. Middle-class occupational groups retained a veto on their own participation in the *régime général*. Nor could left-wing groups exploit their power on social security boards to great advantage. Cold War divisions disabled them, as did the growing power of state officials, policy experts, and eventually employer advocates in the social security system.

Finally, the recasting of French democracy through the creation of the Fifth Republic had complex consequences for the welfare state. Stronger executive authority made it possible for ministerial officials to enhance the power of social policy planners within government, who promoted the expansion of social security not merely for electoral advantage but also as part of a larger Gaullist ambition to strengthen the state, modernize the economy, and enhance the international prestige of France. Meanwhile, the decline of older parties and the rise of more mass-based and media-ori-ented parties on the left and right made it easier for new social groups – young professionals, young commercially oriented farmers, and above all women in various social strata – to become target groups for electoral appeals. The entry of women into the polity as voters, interest group advo-cates, and party activists no doubt helps account for a fundamental shift in the gender ideology of the welfare state. By the 1970s people who took part in political debate on social policy had to a large extent come to see women as citizens with individual interests, not as mothers represented principally through the institution of the family. In this respect welfare policy strengthened democracy in France, since it became a vehicle for incorporating women into the polity during the Fifth Republic, just as it had been for workers during the Fourth.

Still, developments during the Fifth Republic have largely preserved the bourgeois character of the French welfare state. Non-redistributive practices remain the norm, employer power within the system remains impressive, and efforts to contain costs have encouraged middle-class people to look to supplementary private insurance as a way to protect themselves against the rising costs of health care, infirmity, and old age.[54] The French working class, which fared comparatively well under solidaristic, non-redistributive programs during the first post-war decades of extraordinary economic growth, could stand to lose in the long run by the bargain. The underlying conservatism of the system also leaves the country vulnerable to bitter debate, just emerging in the past few years with the rise of the National Front, over the access foreigners should have to the social security system. If in the United States debate over social policy has focused on the distinction between the deserving and undeserving poor, in France it rests increasingly on an argument about who is French and who is not. As the French enter a new era of open borders, continued immigration, and policy coordination through the European Community, and as they struggle with the temptations to impede foreigners' access to citizenship, they are learning, as Americans did long ago, how corrosive prejudice can be to public debate about social policy. The French welfare state expanded during the past half century largely on account of a nationalist, pro-natalist consensus, an implicit cross-class alliance among workers, employers, and the middle class, and the state-building ambitions of the Gaullist right. Little in this history has prepared the country to handle the confluence of immigration issues and budgetary constraints that the current version of the "crisis of the welfare state" involves.

NOTES

1. I am grateful for helpful comments from Reid Andrews, Liz Cohen, Helmut Gruber, Kate Lynch, and Alberta Sbragia.
2. On the 1898 law on work accidents, see François Ewald, *L'Etat providence* (Paris, 1986).
3. On changes in policy and attitudes toward public assistance in the Third Republic, see John H. Weiss, "Origins of the French Welfare State: Poor Relief in the Third Republic, 1871–1914," *French Historical Studies*, 13, no. 1 (Spring 1983): 47–78.
4. On social insurance in the Third Republic, see Henri Hatzfeld, *Du pau perisme à la sécurité sociale, 1850–1940* (Paris, 1971); Ewald, *L'Etat providence*; Judith F. Stone, *The Search for Social Peace: Reform*

Legislation in France, 1890–1914 (Albany, 1985); Douglas E. Ashford, *The Emergence of the Welfare States* (Oxford, 1986); Abram de Swaan, *In the Care of the State: Health Care, Education and Welfare in Europe and the USA in the Modern Era* (New York, 1988); and Yves Saint-Jours, "France," in Peter A. Kohler and Hans F. Zacher in collaboration with Martin Partington, eds., *The Evolution of Social Insurance, 1881–1981: Studies of Germany, France, Great Britain, Austria and Switzerland* (London, 1982).

5. Peter Baldwin, *The Politics of Social Solidarity: Class Bases of the European Welfare State, 1875–1975* (New York, 1990), 103.
6. De Swaan, *In the Care of the State*, 197–204.
7. Baldwin, *The Politics of Social Solidarity*, 105.
8. De Swaan, *In the Care of the State*, 201–2.
9. Hatzfeld, *Du pauperisme à la sécurité sociale*, 153.
10. De Swaan, *In the Care of the State*, 202–3.
11. Hatzfeld, *Du pauperisme à la sécurité sociale*, 146.
12. The report of Sir William Beveridge, issued in 1942, which became the blueprint for major innovations in British social policy in 1945–1946.
13. Pierre Laroque, "*Social Security in France,*" in Shirley Jenkins, ed., *Social Security in International Perspective* (New York, 1969), 173.
14. On the opposition to a single *caisse*, see Henry C. Galant, *Histoire politique de la sécurité sociale française, 1945–1952*, préface de Pierre Laroque (Paris, 1955), 30–5; and Douglas E. Ashford, "Advantages of Complexity: Social Insurance in France," in John S. Ambler, ed., *The French Welfare State: Surviving Social and Ideological Change* (New York, 1991), 38.
15. Stephen S. Cohen and Charles Goldfinger, "From Permacrisis to Real Crisis in French Social Security: The Limits to Normal Politics," in Leon N. Lindberg, Robert Alford, Colin Crouch, and Clause Offe, eds., *Stress and Contradiction in Modern Capitalism: Public Policy and the Theory of the State* (Lexington, Mass., 1975), 58.
16. Baldwin, *The Politics of Social Solidarity*, 163–86.
17. Ashford, "Advantages," 45; Cohen and Goldfinger, "Permacrisis," 64.
18. Ashford, "Advantages," 43.
19. Baldwin, *The Politics of Social Solidarity*, 253–68.
20. David R. Cameron, "Continuity and Change in French Social Policy: The Welfare State under Gaullism, Liberalism, and Socialism," in Ambler, *The French Welfare State*, 62–3.
21. Cohen and Goldfinger, "Permacrisis," 59. On Gaullism and social policy see also Marc Sadoun, Jean-François Sirinelli and Robert Vandenbussche, with the collaboration of Martin Aubry, eds., *La Politique sociale du Général de Gaulle* (Lille, 1989).
22. Cohen and Goldfinger, "Permacrisis," 63–4.
23. On the importance of coalition politics in social policy, see Baldwin, *The Politics of Social Solidarity*, 288–99. See also Bruno Jobert, "Democracy and Social Policies: The Example of France," in Ambler, *The French Welfare State*, 238.
24. Cameron, "Continuity and Change," 87.
25. John S. Ambler, "Ideas, Interests, and the French Welfare State," in *The French Welfare State*, 12–13.

26. Ambler, "Ideas," 15. On the consequences of payroll taxes and indirect taxation for income transfers in the French social security system, see Wallace C. Peterson, *The Welfare State in France* (Lincoln, Nebr., 1960).
27. Cohen and Goldfinger, "Permacrisis," 84–5.
28. Cohen and Goldfinger, "Permacrisis," 59–61, 76–7.
29. Cohen and Goldfinger, "Permacrisis," 91.
30. On this innovation, and more generally on the role of doctors in the evolution of the social security system, see Henry C. Galant, "The French Doctor and the State" (Skidmore College, Faculty Research Lecture, 1966).
31. Cohen and Goldfinger, "Permacrisis," 81.
32. Ashford, "Advantages," 52.
33. On the political conflicts over how to constitute and modify the boards, see Galant, *Histoire politique*, 99–102, 116–22; Ashford, *The Emergence of the Welfare States*, 262–4, 284–8, 298–9.
34. On FNOSS, see Antoinette Catrice-Lorey, *Dynamique interne de la sécurité sociale*, deuxième édition, préface de Pierre Laroque (Paris, 1982), 220–30.
35. For leaflets, pamphlets, and other documentary material related to social security elections in the 1950s and 1960s, see Archives Nationales 39 AS 994 and 995.
36. Bruno Jobert warns against equating the organizational weakness of the French labor movement with low levels of social mobilization. See "Democracy and Social Policies," 55.
37. Dominique Schnapper, Jeanne Brody and Riva Kastoryano, "Les français et la sécurité sociale: sondages d'opinion, 1945–1982," *Vingtième siècle*, 10 (April 1986), 73.
38. Catrice-Lorey, *Dynamique*, 40–8.
39. Catrice-Lorey, *Dynamique*, 67–77.
40. Schnapper, Brody, and Kastoryano, "Les français," 71–2, 75–6.
41. George Ross, "The Mitterrand Experiment and the French Welfare State: An Interesting Uninteresting Story," in Michael K. Brown, ed., *Remaking the Welfare State: Retrenchment and Social Policy in America and Europe* (Philadelphia, 1988), 136.
42. Antoine Prost, "L'évolution de la politique familiale en France de 1938 à 1981," *Le Mouvement social*, 129 (October–December 1984), 8–10.
43. On bourgeois ideologies toward the family in nineteenth-century France, see Katherine A. Lynch, *Family, Class, and Ideology in Early Industrial France: Social Policy and the Working-Class Family, 1825–1848* (Madison, 1988), especially Chapter 2.
44. Susan Pedersen, *Family, Dependence, and the Origins of the Welfare State: Britain and France, 1914–1945* (New York, 1993), Chapter 5.
45. Pederson, *Family*, 401.
46. Jane Jenson, "Both Friend and Foe: Women and State Welfare," in Renate Bridenthal, Claudia Koonz, and Susan Stuard, eds., *Becoming Visible: Women in European History*, 2nd ed (Boston, 1987), 541–6.
47. On the weakness of left-wing feminism in the interwar period, see Miriam Cohen and Michael Hanagan, "The Politics of Gender and the Making of the Welfare State, 1900–1940: A Comparative Perspective," *Journal of Social History*, 24, no. 3 (Spring 1991): 469–84.

48. Remi Lenoir, "Family Policy in France since 1938," in Ambler, *The French Welfare State*, 150–1.
49. Prost, "L'évolution," 10–12.
50. Lenoir, "Family Policy," 168–9.
51. Lenoir, "Family Policy," 166.
52. Cohen and Goldfinger, "Permacrisis," 81–3.
53. Lenoir, "Family Policy," 174.
54. Ross, "The Mitterrand Experiment," 134; Laroque, "Social Security in France," 188–9.

13 Industrialists, the State, and the Limits of Democratization in Brazil, 1930–1964

Barbara Weinstein

The relationship between the expansion of the state's role in social welfare and subsequent "democratization" has been an almost obsessive concern for Brazilian scholars in recent decades. During the early to mid-1980s, when the transition to civilian rule initiated Brazil's latest attempt to create a more democratic political system and society, politicians, intellectuals, labor leaders, and Church officials all subjected to intense questioning the political and social traditions that had produced one of Latin America's longest-running military-authoritarian regimes (1964–1985).[1] Historians and social scientists in particular scrutinized the earlier dictatorship of Getúlio Vargas (1930–1945) since much of the legislation and institutional structure created under Vargas had survived into the 1980s. Many argued that the fatal fragility of Brazil's short-lived "populist republic" (1945–1964) could be traced back to the policies established under Vargas.[2] The failure of subsequent governments to purge the political and social systems of their authoritarian origins, according to this argument, had doomed the earlier experiment with democratization, and endangered contemporary efforts as well. Inevitably, current political concerns have vividly colored the debate over the legacy of the Vargas years.

It may be overstating the case to describe the state that emerged in Brazil during the period from 1930 to 1945 as a "welfare state." Given the central government's restricted resources, both financial and bureaucratic, and its limited ability – or determination – to enforce new regulations and benefits established during those years, it would be a somewhat distorting application of categories formulated elsewhere to talk of a Brazilian "welfare state". Having made this qualification, we should not underestimate the massive transformation of the role of the state in Brazilian social and economic life during the 15-year dictatorship of Getúlio Vargas.

315

Almost immediately upon seizing power, with support from a broad coalition of military reformers, middle-class technicians, and disgruntled elite politicians, Vargas and his advisors set about creating new agencies and legislation that affected nearly every sector of Brazilian society.[3] Among Vargas's first actions was the creation of a Ministry of Labor, Industry, and Commerce that began, in early 1931, to issue a steady stream of proposals for laws regulating paid vacations, the length of the workday, child labor, women's labor, and collective bargaining. During the more explicitly authoritarian period of Vargas's Estado Novo (1937–1945), the ministry also created a minimum wage law, labor courts for the adjudication of conflicts, and decrees regulating workplace safety and worker compensation. In 1943, this welter of new legislation was collected and further codified by the issuing of the Consolidated Labor Legislation (CLT), the bible of Brazilian labor law. Much of this legislation applied only to urban workers, a minority of the labor force at that time, and the actual enforcement of the new labor codes was uneven at best. But they represented a significant departure from the pre-1930 social legislation, which had been very limited in scope and met with near complete and overt resistance from employers.

Paralleling the creation of these labor codes was the construction of a corporatist union system based on the concept of the *sindicato único* – a single, government-accredited union for each trade or industry. According to the corporatist scheme, all registered workers in a particular industry automatically paid a "syndical tax" to the recognized organization, whether they officially belonged to the union or not. There was to be a single union for each industry in a designated municipality, which would then be affiliated with a state-wide federation for that industry, and then (eventually) with a legally recognized national confederation. Every union had to be registered with the Ministry of Labor, which would also disburse funds collected through the union tax at its own discretion. And any worker who wished to gain access to legal benefits and protections (such as paid vacations) had to register with the ministry and carry a *carteira de trabalho*, a workcard. In addition, all employers had to form *sindicatos* of the same sort to be registered with the Ministry. Thus, the Centro de Indústrias do Estado de São Paulo, set up in 1928, quickly registered itself as the Federação das Indústrias do Estado de São Paulo (FIESP) after Vargas's seizure of power, and became the officially recognized mouthpiece for the São Paulo industrialists and the state's employer *sindicatos*.[4]

Vargas and his advisors also oversaw the creation of agencies to perform some of the functions classically associated with a welfare state. The government set up social security institutes for registered workers in industry, banking, transport, and commerce, funded by contributions from the state, employers, and employees.[5] Their primary function was to establish a pension fund for workers in each particular sector, but the funds of the industrial workers' institute, for example, could be used for disability payments in the case of workplace accidents. The institutes also provided hospitalization and medical assistance of a very limited nature, though expenditures on medical coverage tended to increase over time. In practice, corruption, underfunding, and the eroding effects of inflation meant that workers' pensions and benefits from the institutes were often little more than symbolic, but they represented clear recognition of the legitimacy and need for the state to become involved in the provision of social services.

Before discussing the various tendencies in the historiography of twentieth-century Brazil, and how they have dealt with the legacies of the Vargas era, it is useful to consider how Vargas himself represented the various social laws, agencies, and institutions created under his dictatorship. In *getulista* discourse, the social policies of the Vargas regime were consistently represented as an *outorga* – a "grant" of benefits and favors to a weak and unprotected working class. Due to the benevolence and foresight of the central government, Brazilian workers had received, with a stroke of the pen, rights and benefits that European workers had won only at the expense of long and bloody struggles. The ideology of the *outorga* also emphasized the state's ability to rise above the immediate and short-sighted concerns of employers, thereby adopting laws that, by making industrial conflict unnecessary, served the collective welfare. In short, the Vargas regime was the smasher of the oligarchies, the savior (despite themselves) of the industrialists, and the champion of the workers – a benevolent state rising above petty class interests in a new Brazil.[6]

Scholarly treatments of the Vargas regime in the 1950s and 1960s did not necessarily accept this vision of the *outorga*. In this literature Vargas more often emerges as a canny opportunist than as a magnanimous "father of the people." But certain elements central to the ideology of the *outorga* did pervade the first wave of scholarship on the Vargas era, such as the notion that a weak, barely emergent working class had been prematurely granted extensive rights and benefits. Some lamented the allegedly demobilizing effects of the *outorga* on the labor movement, since workers (especially those of rural origin) learned from the outset that there was more to be gained by looking to a paternalistic state for benefits than from autonomous, grassroots organization and struggle. But virtually no one doubted the basic premise of the argument, and many social scientists explained Brazilian workers' "deviation" from the normative European pattern of unionization and political participation as resulting from Vargas's policies.[7]

Hand in glove with this view went the argument that the industrial bourgeoisie had also failed to play its proper historic role.[8] Weak, disorganized,
reactionary, this social group supposedly played no part in the reforms and
innovations of the Vargas period. Indeed, if anything, the embryonic
"national bourgeoisie" had opposed Vargas's labor laws and even allied
itself with segments of the traditional rural oligarchy. Taken to an extreme,
this argument presents Brazil as a nation without social classes. Neither the
proletariat nor the bourgeoisie could play their "historic roles," leaving it
to the state to oversee the transition to a modern society.[9]

The bleak implications of this interpretation for effective democratization are obvious. The labor movement, politically and psychologically
dependent upon the state, never develops sufficient militancy and autonomy to assert its own social agenda and to resist an onslaught from the
right. And the industrial bourgeoisie, also dependent upon the state, and
increasingly on foreign capital as well, never develops an independent,
progressive identity that would allow it to promote and defend democracy.
In other words, the pre-emptive role of the corporatist state had stunted the
growth of civil society.

If earlier scholars had regarded the *outorga* concept with a certain
amount of cynicism, post-1970 scholarship rejected it entirely. In light of
trends in social history and new theoretical approaches to domination and
resistance, conceiving of Brazil as a society without self-conscious classes
seemed increasingly untenable. Furthermore, the emergence on the
national political scene of the "new unionism" (*novo sindicalismo*) and
the dramatic metallurgical workers' strikes of the late 1970s moved many
scholars interested in labor history to re-examine their assumptions about
the weakness of the Brazilian working class and its alleged lack of
political consciousness.[10]

Reflecting the influence of the (then) new social history, as well as the
widespread view that *novo sindicalismo* had its roots in shopfloor militancy, Brazilian scholars eschewed their earlier emphasis on official union
politics and shifted their attention to traditions of workplace resistance and
combativity, especially prior to 1930.[11] The result was a rediscovery of
the working class, and a reformulation of the Vargas era. No longer did
scholars endorse the image of a weak, inept proletariat doomed to passiv-
ity by the benevolent and/or Machiavellian strategies of the state. In its
place emerged an even more tragic scenario: one of a militant,
autonomous working-class movement destroyed by repression and union
restructuring under Vargas, who was acting on behalf of the new industrial
bourgeoisie. Not only were the post-1935 unions tainted by their origins in
Vargas's corporatist union system, but even the organized left (i.e., the

Communist Party), due to its endorsement of the need for a strong central state, ultimately colluded with the process of "taming" an autonomous working-class movement.

The rediscovery of the workers as a self-conscious class also spurred a rediscovery of the bourgeoisie. No longer a weak, inarticulate, barely existing class dragged into the twentieth century by Vargas, the industrialists now emerged as a group with a well-defined project for the reorganization and rationalization of Brazilian society.[12] Edgar de Decca, in *O silêncio dos vencidos*, made the most forceful contribution to this new line of argument, claiming that by the late 1920s leading São Paulo industrialists, impelled by challenges from the workers, were already articulating the core elements of an ideology of national development. They were also assigning the state a significant economic and social role in the process of industrialization. It is this project for national development based on industrialization that Vargas supposedly adopted upon seizing power, ensuring the hegemonic position of the industrial bourgeoisie.[13] Thus in these recent historical studies Brazil has ceased to be a society without conscious classes or overt class conflict. Instead, Brazil is presented as a society with class-conscious workers and industrialists whose conflicts have been masked (or resolved in employers' favor) by a demobilizing state and a "mystifying" cross-class ideology of national development accepted by both the (orthodox) left and the right.

As should be apparent, these new scholarly studies view the ideological and political role of the state in a purely negative light, regarding it as strictly a detriment to genuine popular participation. The corporatist-populist era initiated by Vargas is seen as dooming autonomous labor movements, thereby defeating attempts at greater social or political democratization. Such revulsion against the concept of the "strong state" was probably both predictable and salutary in the context of the 1980s. But the wholesale condemnation of the post-1930 state has led both to caricatured portrayals of the Vargas regime and to a persistent romanticization of workers' struggles, neither of which have proved very illuminating for a careful discussion of the state and society in post-1930 Brazil. If the earlier view of Brazil as a society with a strong state and without classes now seems somewhat absurd, replacing it with images of an ever-hegemonic bourgeoisie and an always rebellious, but ineptly led, working class seems equally unsatisfactory.[14]

Fortunately, over the last few years new research has provided us with a more complex picture of the impact of the post-1930 state.[15] Whether explicitly or implicitly, this recent stream of studies offers us a more positive image of the Vargas legacy. State recognition of unions gave union members and activists some degree of protection and social legitimacy; populist discourse recognized the central role of the worker in the project of national development, and by extension, workers' rights within that project; and the CLT created a host of labor laws that, though unevenly enforced, added legitimacy to workers' struggles for such goals as a meaningful minimum wage, job tenure or a thirteenth-month bonus.

This new line of argument, by repositioning the state as a sometime ally of the labor movement, puts considerable emphasis on the political power of the industrialists, and their contribution to the ultimate failure of that movement. Recent research has revealed the extensive role of prominent businessmen and technocrats in creating an ideological environment conducive to the military seizure of power in 1964, and even in coordinating the actions of various groups within the military.[16] But the power and anti-democratic ideology of the industrialists, rather than simply constituting an explanation, have to be explained. And this is especially the case in light of attempts by Vargas and subsequent populist politicians to promote a cross-class alliance based on the ideology of national development. I will argue that the state, far from becoming the arena for social integration and reconciliation, became the site of intensifying conflicts that finally doomed the post-1945 experiment with democratic politics. And I will argue that there is a relationship between the reconfiguration of the state during the Vargas dictatorship and the breakdown of democracy in the early 1960s, but not precisely the one discerned by other historians.

My own research on the São Paulo industrialists and their strategies for labor control – including worker training and social services – has led me to compose a picture of the industrial bourgeoisie and the post-1930 state that does not fit comfortably into any of the categories that dominate the existing historiography.[17] Some of the same elements are emphasized: I agree with Edgar de Decca that the "vanguard" (my term) of the industrial bourgeoisie, and its technocratic allies, had by the late 1920s constructed an ideology of national development that required state intervention both to encourage industrialization and to foster "social peace." Despite some initial, and very serious, conflicts with the Vargas regime, leading industrialists and technocrats eventually occupied major positions within the government and exerted their influence in myriad ways, especially during the Estado Novo.[18] And many prominent industrialists enthusiastically endorsed the corporatist union system of the Vargas regime; at the behest of the Ministry of Labor, FIESP and the São Paulo textile manufacturers' *sindicato* twice during these years urged their members to collaborate actively in drives for unionization of their employees.[19] On May Day during the Estado Novo, the directors of FIESP regularly appeared with

Vargas or the Minister of Labor to celebrate, in a stadium full of workers (many transported by factory-owned vehicles), the collaboration of capital and labor in the campaign to industrialize Brazil.

The industrialist leadership, however, invested considerable effort in circumscribing the role and reach of the state in labor relations, defining a broad range of activities as more appropriate to the private sphere. The factory owners and industrial engineers (and many were both) who regularly served as the spokesmen for industry portrayed themselves as the vanguard of "rationalization" in Brazilian society. Indeed, during the 1930s the Paulista industrialists played a central role in the creation of the Instituto de Organização Racional do Trabalho (IDORT) and the Escola Livre de Sociologia e Política, both of which made pioneering contributions to the application of "rational" and "scientific" methods to the study and "management" of Brazilian society.[20] At the same time, the industrialists argued that only they and their technocratic allies had "hands-on" experience in industry and knew what types of regulations were "rational," whereas bureaucrats in the labor ministry who had little or no experience within the factory walls eagerly supported legislation that could have disastrous effects on industrial production.[21] In this same vein, factory-owners regarded with suspicion, and occasional alarm, Vargas's appeals to the working class – since the search for political support could translate into popular but less than rational regulations and reforms. The result was a markedly ambivalent relationship with the state, even at the height of the collaboration between Vargas and the industrialists, and a quiet but successful campaign to limit the state's control over the private sector.

The debate over vocational training – who should fund it, who should administer it, and who should have access to it – provides us with an excellent example of the "legislative process" under Vargas, and how the industrialists set limits on the state's control over services or activities they considered crucial to their interests. It also offers us a depressingly familiar picture of the way in which labor's perspective gets utterly marginalized, despite the supposedly pro-labor origins of the legislation, and of how social and political issues become the object of "technical" expertise and economic considerations.

SOCIAL PEACE THROUGH SOCIAL WELFARE: SENAI AND SESI

Vocational education, though never the most pressing issue for the state, employers, or workers, had long been an important agenda item in discussions of Brazilian industrial development. Since the early 1920s educators

in São Paulo – many of them closely tied to the emerging industrial bourgeoisie – had decried the inadequacy of existing methods of apprenticeship and training, particularly the informal means by which a young
worker – almost always male – gradually and "unsystematically" absorbed
techniques by observing an older worker. Such practices allegedly reinforced traditional methods, denounced as routinism or empiricism, and
made skilled workers resistant to innovation. To demonstrate the value of
systematic and "rational" training, Roberto Mange, one of São Paulo's
small coterie of industrial engineers, set up a school for training railroad
mechanics in the late 1920s, using techniques first developed for apprentices in the German railway system. Mange also trumpeted the value of his
training methods for producing workers with good "moral and civic formation," and condemned the traditional apprenticeship experience for
disseminating bad work habits and personal vices.[22]

In a 1931 speech, FIESP president Roberto Simonsen noted that industrialists and labor unions shared a concern for "the continuous development of technical and professional culture" in Brazil – a rare instance in
which an industrialist's claim to sharing the views of labor was probably
accurate.[23] Though from rather different motives, labor unions generally
echoed Engineer Mange's negative view of traditional apprenticeship
arrangements. The labor press tended to see the lack of organized and
formal training as undermining the status of the skilled crafts, and allowing the best-paid jobs to go to "foreigners" with access to the systematic
training available in more industrialized societies. Apparently Brazilian
workers were not immune to the appeal of educational credentials. And
during a period of increased mechanization and deskilling in some industries (printing, textiles), formal vocational instruction may have appeared
as an antidote to craft degradation.[24]

Worker training, then, seems the perfect issue for the evolving populist
politics of the Vargas regime: it could be presented as a benefit to both
workers and employers, as well as a "nationalist" initiative, and it would
provide for the more effective socialization of Brazilian worker-citizens.
Educational expansion and reform thus emerged as a major concern of the
Vargas administration, and Vargas repeatedly described vocational education (or to use the Brazilian term, "professional" education) as central to
the interests of both workers and industry.[25] Indeed, in 1939 Vargas
selected vocational training to be his by then traditional May Day "pledge"
to the Brazilian worker, announcing Decree-Law no. 1,238. According to
the text of the law, issued with uncustomary dispatch on the following day,
all factories employing over 500 workers had to set up training centers for
apprentices and adults. But the actual wording of the text is almost beside

the point since the law is most usefully regarded as a trial balloon, a proposal that Vargas used to goad the various interested parties into offering a feasible plan for the expansion of vocational training.[26]

The industrialists were initially very critical. The announcement seemed a perfect example of Vargas pandering to the masses, decreeing a law without consulting those best situated to define a national worker-training program. For the Paulista industrialists and their organizational representatives, the key preoccupation was to ensure a sufficient number of appropriately skilled workers – sufficient not only to fill the increasing demand for certain skills, but also to limit the wage levels and bargaining power of trained workers. And appropriate training meant the development of skills that could be applied immediately on the factory floor. Some of their spokesmen also emphasized the role of education and training in promoting efficiency, rational organization, and moral character among workers, but these were secondary themes.[27]

In contrast, the many educational reformers who filled the ranks of Vargas's bureaucracy viewed the purpose and promise of vocational education in the broadest possible context. While these educators and technicians shared with the industrialist leadership an enthusiasm for rational organization of work, scientific management, and industrial psychology (known as *psicotécnica* in Brazil), they were more likely to view vocational training from a socialization, rather than a labor supply, perspective. And they were more likely to see it as a vehicle to strengthen the worker's identification with the state.[28]

Immediately after issuing the decree-law, Vargas convened a six-member inter-ministerial commission to oversee its implementation, and this commission soon became the site of a battle over the meaning and objectives of vocational training. Among the members, Rodolpho Fuchs, a close collaborator of education minister Gustavo Capanema, emerged as the major advocate of a state-directed vocational training program based on instruction in the workplace. Fuchs's position on vocational training had been deeply influenced by his participation in the 1938 International Congress on Vocational Education, held in Germany. The report he presented on his return was an unabashed endorsement of the German training process, instituted under Nazi rule. The German system, with its mandatory factory-floor training for all males not going on to secondary school and its six-to-eight hours of weekly classroom instruction, obviously inspired Fuchs. He openly admired the way the Germans used training to instill discipline, comparing it favorably to the German Army and the Hitler Youth as a vehicle for socialization. He regarded the scheme for funding the program, which combined a tax on industry with government subsidies, as an excellent model for Brazil. And he especially lauded the strict separation of the sexes, which produced "feminine women and real men."[29]

FIESP spokesmen, meanwhile, rejected the idea of universal apprenticeship or training. And they objected even more vehemently to the singling out of firms with over 500 workers, as well as to assigning factory-owners the main burden of worker education. FIESP invited the commission to São Paulo precisely to allow its six members to gather information that would bolster the industrialists' version of rational worker training. As part of the carefully orchestrated visit, the commission toured several factories with over 500 workers, virtually all of them textile mills where most of the workers were semi-skilled "machine tenders" (an impression fortified by the large proportion of girls and women in the plants). In contrast, the one enterprise – a metallurgical plant – that employed a large proportion of skilled workers had a workforce of only 250. Thus, a "scientific" examination of industry had revealed that the designation of factories with over 500 workers (most of which, throughout Brazil, were textile mills) was arbitrary and inappropriate.[30]

During the commission's meeting with FIESP, Simonsen's close colleague, Roberto Mange, took the implications of this even further. Basing his argument on his "scientific" studies of Brazilian industry, Mange claimed that only 10 to 15 percent of the Brazilian industrial workforce needed extensive training and could be classified as skilled (in Mange's language, *braço pensante*). The majority of the workforce he classified as semi-skilled (*braço atento*), needing only rapid, on-the-job training, while the remaining 25 percent or so (*braço anatômico*) performed heavy, unskilled labor needing no training at all. According to Mange, whose views clearly had the blessing of FIESP, any joint effort by government and industry to train workers should concentrate almost exclusively on the upper tier of skilled workers, and should not operate in such a way as to challenge or disturb this basic, and rational, hierarchy.[31]

A few months after the visit, the commission issued a majority report that incorporated most of the opinions expressed by Mange and Simonsen. It concurred with the view that large factories should not be exclusively burdened with the cost and responsibility of vocational training, proposing instead community training centers operated jointly by several different factories. It proposed a tripartite funding system, with contributions from employers, workers, and the state. And each of these entities would be equally represented on the administrative bodies of the vocational training system. As for whom should be trained, the report enthusiastically endorsed Mange's argument that only 10 to 15 percent of the workforce actually needed extensive vocational instruction.[32]

The proposals contained in the commission's report seem almost completely compatible with the suggestions made by the FIESP leadership; yet in mid-1940, soon after the report appeared, Simonsen sent his own plan for a national apprenticeship system to the Ministry of Education. This new proposal maintained the central concept of apprentices alternating between classroom instruction and on-the-job experience, and predictably endorsed the 10–15 percent rule. But Simonsen now reversed his previous position on funding, arguing that industrial employers should accept the full burden of financing this vocational training system. In exchange, they would be granted full administrative control, with the state exercising only a limited administrative oversight, and unions being completely excluded from participation.[33]

Simonsen's exact motives for this change of heart are probably unrecoverable. But his proposal was generally consistent with the industrialists' claims that they were the best positioned to direct and define a vocational training system for Brazilian industry. The industrialist leadership may also have wished to head off initiatives being considered by the Ministry of Education, including calls for direct government supervision, for obligatory apprenticeship of male workers, and even for government interference in the labor market through compulsory hiring of trained workers. Moreover, the industrialists could now take full political credit for an economically and socially desirable program. As one political scientist later put it, "Simonsen had ingeniously turned the impending obligation into a political asset ..."[34]

Vargas eagerly jumped at Simonsen's generous offer, and promptly formed yet another commission to construct a vocational education system.[35] This new commission, however, had a very different composition. Its three members included Simonsen, Lodi and prominent businessman-economist Valentim Bouças, and all of its formal consultants were well-known technocratic allies of the industrialists. From the outset this *comissão de empresários* (employers' commission) framed its objectives in terms of the need for "a rapid improvement of the national economy ... through the greater industrialization" of Brazil. It also displayed symbolic allegiance to Vargas's corporatist ideology by arguing that the officially recognized employer federations in each region were the appropriate bodies for administering vocational training. With these two premises in mind the commision set about fleshing out Simonsen's initial proposal, and by December 1941 it had issued the text of a new decree-law that established a national industrial apprenticeship service eventually known as the Serviço Nacional de Aprendizagem Industrial, or SENAI.[36] Within weeks, Vargas had signed the proposed decree into law.

Not everyone in the Vargas administration shared the chief executive's enthusiasm for the plan. The powerful Minister of Education, Capanema, disliked everything about it, from the proposed name, which made no reference to education, to the near exclusion of the state from its administration. Capanema openly registered his disapproval of a vocational education program in which his ministry would play only a peripheral role, and which would treat worker education as a function of industrial demand. Instead, he suggested that the program be overseen by a National Commission of Professional Education staffed by educators rather than industrialists.[37] But his criticisms of the SENAI proposal, which was feasible and inexpensive for the state, were to no avail. Indeed, at a celebration of SENAI's first year of activity, Capanema capitulated and declared the agency "an extraordinary badge of glory for the employers and industries of Brazil." At the same time, he tried to reserve some credit for his ministry by citing Fuchs's 1938 report as the "seed document" for the subsequent formation of SENAI.[38] Fuchs, meanwhile, took little consolation from such attributions. Writing to Capanema just prior to the official inauguration of SENAI, he lamented that the new program treated apprenticeship as a function of "the necessities of the national economy" rather than the needs of Brazilian youth. Indeed, the new program, which targeted only a small percentage of young workers for formal training, was a far cry from the German model, with its obligatory apprenticeship for all incoming male workers. Defined in this fashion, Fuchs wrote, "industrial apprenticeship has not become the great protective armor of the Brazilian adolescent who works, but only the institute for technical upgrading of the labor force required by industry."[39] For Fuchs, who envisioned industrial training as a vehicle for discipline, social control, and worker integration into a state-directed project for national development, SENAI was a profound disappointment.

It is sobering to consider that Fuchs, the Nazi sympathizer, was the closest to being a champion of labor of anyone intimately involved in this "legislative" process. The almost complete absence of union spokespeople from the discussions indicates, in part, the weakness of the labor movement at the height of the Estado Novo's authoritarian policies. But it also reveals how completely the industrialists and technocrats had succeeded in defining this issue as a technical problem rather than a social question. In the documentation produced by the various commissions, only Fuchs emphasized the aspirations of the workers themselves. And even then he did so in a negative sense: his 1938 report ended by warning that "we should not have the slightest illusion in this respect ... either Brazil resolves to give [workers] a direct and secure path to professional education, or shortly we will see such demands become an arm of combat for the tireless communist agitators ..."[40] Indeed, his disappointment with the final version of the law reflected his sense that it would contribute little to "social peace."

Of course, Vargas had made his initial May Day pledge with labor in mind; to that extent, workers were represented in the government's discourse on vocational education. And in short order the highly compliant labor unions responded in kind; according to a 1943 issue of the São Paulo metallurgical workers' newspaper, "today, principally due to the protection of the Head of our Nation, there are competent mechanics everywhere, who learned the craft in Brazil and who are in no way inferior to the best mechanics of other countries." A few years after this declaration, the president of the metalworkers' union went even further: speaking at a SENAI graduation ceremony, he claimed that Vargas initiated the vocational training program directly in response to the appeals of union leaders.[41]

To be sure, SENAI enjoyed a generally favorable reception among Brazilian unions, few of whom questioned the way in which decisions had been made about vocational training. Yet it is important to emphasize that throughout the debate over what type of education different workers needed, and what positions were to be designated as skilled, workers themselves were excluded and the main participants operated on the assumption that such questions could and should be resolved in a "scientific" manner. Experts could determine precisely the attributes and knowledge necessary for a particular task, and approximately how many people industry needed to perform such a task, and could design an instructional system accordingly. Within this construct, the opinions and identities of the workers themselves became irrelevant. Of course, workers had rarely played a direct role in the formulation of Brazilian educational policy, but traditionally members of particular crafts had wielded some influence in the definition of skill in the workplace through informal and organized means of negotiation and resistance. Though certain occupations could be more easily represented as skilled crafts than others, workers and employers formed their notions of "skill" from a variety of elements that included the state of the labor market, craft-based protest, gender roles, and a sense (not necessarily "objective") of how difficult it was to learn a particular craft.[42] In contrast, the vocational program being developed by the inter-ministerial commission relegated the power to designate occupations as skilled or unskilled to educational experts whose decision would be based on narrow definitions of apprenticeship and industrial demand.

The subservient character of most labor unions in the late 1930s meant that these organizations were unlikely to contest the definitions of skill, or appropriate instruction, now being formulated by Vargas's industrial education experts. Many unions already found themselves incapable of resisting employers' attempts to reduce the standing of their craft; under such circumstances, the expansion of training opportunities and official recognition of certain occupations as skilled represented a partial victory for the labor movement. Yet there are also a few examples from this period of practitioners of certain crafts struggling to construct or retain their identity as skilled workers. According to an article in the official organ of the São Paulo textile workers, many textile factories were suffering from a shortage of weavers due to the low salaries being paid. Although the article was entitled "Salary, a social question," its author argued not in terms of social justice but rather in terms of the value and significance of the weaver's craft. Claiming that machines in many factories were idle because there were very few weavers "who deserved the name," the author insisted that weaving was indeed a skilled occupation.

> Look, a weaver, that is to say, a worker who acquires a certain technical knowledge through a period of apprenticeship, and another of practice that varies according to the branch of textiles and the article being produced ... A weaver is not a worker that can be made from one day to the next. [The weaver] is a worker who, little by little, goes on absorbing the secrets of the profession, and gathers an accumulation of small daily observations perhaps at great sacrifice.[43]

Such sentiments, however, found little resonance among Vargas's educational experts. Quite the opposite: it was precisely this type of "improvised" and "empirical" approach to skill acquisition that the rationalizers scorned.

The increasing tendency to mold "education" for sons and daughters of the working class according to the demands of the industrial labor market also evoked occasional criticism from labor organizations. During the 1930s the São Paulo printers founded the first union-sponsored Escola Proletária. According to one of its graduates, the school was of great importance for young workers due to the limited nature of public education.

> With the advent of industry and the rapid evolution of new production processes, that is, the rationalization of work, governments do recognize the necessity of administering elementary education to the proletariat. However, such education is strictly limited to [the knowledge] indispensable for the exercise of the respective trades.[44]

Again, these critical and alternative voices found expression only at the margins of the political process, drowned out by a discourse of rationalization and scientific management. And the ultimate configuration of SENAI eliminated any possibility that these discordant viewpoints would be given a serious hearing any time in the near future.

Moreover, SENAI was not an anomaly; a few years after its founding, the industrialist leadership, in collaboration with the state, extended its vision beyond vocational training to address the pressing need for new social services in post-war Brazil. In this case the role of labor militancy in spurring action by the bourgeoisie is quite apparent. The removal of wartime restraints on labor protest, combined with the devastating impact of inflation, had produced a wave of successful strikes throughout urban Brazil, with São Paulo being the most acutely affected. The central government responded by expanding some of the social welfare programs initiated during the war, including discount worker cafeterias and food depots, and by encouraging labor unions to found or expand cooperatives. Meanwhile the industrialist organizations began crafting their own response to the emerging crisis, including a FIESP proposal to set up a Fundo de Assistência ao Trabalhador based on voluntary contributions from employers.[45]

Despite a flurry of enthusiasm for the workers' fund, the industrialist leadership discovered that few contributions would be forthcoming on a strictly voluntary basis. Thus once again Simonsen presented a proposal to the central government (with Vargas's elected successor, General Dutra, now presiding) to create a national agency through an official decree-law. Like SENAI, the new agency – the Serviço Social da Indústria (SESI) – would be administered exclusively by the industrialist associations. And as in the case of SENAI, funding would come from a compulsory monthly payroll tax (set at 1 percent for SENAI and 2 percent for SESI), freeing the organization from dependence on the goodwill of employers. In short, SESI and SENAI were organized to combine the best elements of both worlds: the state's capacity for coercion and the private sector's preference for autonomy.[46]

Given the broader and more varied objectives of SESI, it is even more impressive that the industrialists managed to exclude all but the most minimal state intervention, and all formal labor participation in the new agency. During its first year of activity (1946) SESI focused on the most pressing needs, setting up 77 discount food posts in São Paulo alone.[47] But the directors of the new agency soon set about expanding its activities (all aimed exclusively at urban workers and their families) to include adult literacy and sewing courses, medical and dental clinics, home and factory visits by social workers and "social educators," legal services, courses on "human relations in the workplace," district kitchens, and recreational centers. SESI also quickly became a fixture of May Day celebrations with its elaborate parades and "Workers' Olympics." Some of these services and activities were being duplicated by government agencies, church organizations, individual firms, and the larger labor unions. But none could match SESI in scope or ambition.[48]

SESI also shared with SENAI a discourse that emphasized rationalization of all facets of Brazilian, and especially urban, society. Courses on human relations in the workplace treated industrial conflict as the result of poor supervision or inadequate understanding of human psychology. Home economics courses – one of SESI's most successful areas of activity in terms of enrollment – taught working-class women (identified as "housewives" rather than workers) to practice proper hygiene and stretch the family budget. Even the district kitchens and discount food posts were meant not just to relieve the pressures of inflation, but also to teach workers the rudiments of good nutrition. Indeed, according to the dominant SESI discourse, much of urban poverty in Brazil could be traced to workers' irrational spending and consumption habits. Hence wage increases alone would be of little use in improving living standards, and had to be accompanied by proper socialization.[49]

Perhaps the best example of a SESI operation that attempted to defuse an explosive industrial issue by removing it from the arena of class conflict and placing it within the realm of technical expertise was its Service for Industrial Hygiene and Safety, founded in 1948.[50] The purpose of this service was to assist employers in the formation of Internal Committees for the Prevention of Accidents (CIPAs), mandated by the CLT for all factories with over 50 employees, and to disseminate information on the prevention of workplace accidents and hazards. Given the notoriously high accident rate in Brazilian industry, this was a matter of considerable concern within the industrial sector, and an obvious source of tension between employers and workers.[51]

Having only an advisory and not a coercive function, SESI could not intervene in any dramatic way to improve workplace conditions, but it could play a central role in the way accidents were "represented." Predictably, some of the early SESI and SENAI literature placed the blame for industrial accidents on careless and ignorant workers or on incompetent supervisors. But not all of the articles authored by industrial technocrats adopted a crude "blame the victim" position that could easily be disputed by labor leaders. In a more sophisticated vein, a long article in the national bulletin of SENAI argued against distinguishing between "subjective" and "objective" causes of workplace accidents (that is, worker carelessness as opposed to dangerous work conditions). Such distinctions, the author claimed, were not only fruitless, but exacerbated conflict between workers and owners, with each party seeking to blame the other. Instead, the author proposed approaching workplace hazards in "organizational" terms; that is, even when it seemed that the worker was at fault, the real problem was probably poor (i.e., unscientific) personnel training and selection. Thus, both "subjective" and "objective" hazards could be reduced through rational organization.[52]

This approach still indirectly placed the burden of accident prevention on the worker, but transformed the issue from a moral or political matter to a technical question by making workplace hazards a problem to be resolved through scientific management. The widespread acceptance of this approach is indicated by the composition of São Paulo's Council on Labor Health and Safety, founded by Governor Lucas Nogueira Garcez in 1951. The governor appointed to the council representatives of SENAI, SESI, SESC (the commercial sector's version of SESI), the State Departments of Labor and Industrial Production, and IDORT, but did not include a single representative of organized labor, even though he himself was allied with Vargas's Brazilian Labor Party.[53]

The staffing of SESI's Service for Industrial Hygiene and Safety also reveals the ability of the industrialist-controlled agency to attract technicians and "reformers" who, in other national settings, would have been more likely to work within the state. The head of the service from 1953 on was Bernardo Bedrikow, Brazil's most prominent expert on accident prevention and industrial hazards. Given his prestige and reputation, Bedrikow was able to adopt positions on industrial accidents that were somewhat at odds with the general drift of SESI discourse. For example, soon after he assumed the directorship of the service, its monthly publication began to emphasize the need for industrialists to spend more money on machine guards and other protective equipment. But as an employee of an agency funded by industrialists, he was always careful to emphasize education, not compulsion, in his approach to eliminating workplace hazards.[54] And his situation was hardly exceptional. SESI and SENAI quickly became the largest Brazilian employers of social workers, social hygienists, experts in social law, industrial psychologists, home economics teachers, and basic literacy instructors. Even the renowned radical educator Paulo Freire began his adult-education career with SESI.[55]

While SESI tirelessly promoted the concepts of rational organization and scientific management, it never presented itself in a purely technical light, unlike SENAI, which always insisted that it had no political tendencies or objectives. Given SESI's founding in the midst of an unprecedented wave of strike activity, and a sudden, if brief, surge of popularity for the Communist Party, the agency from the outset acknowledged its anti-communist objectives, choosing as its motto, "For Social Peace in Brazil." In his speech at the inauguration of SESI-São Paulo, the ubiquitous Simonsen declared that the new organization would "enable the Brazilian working masses to cross the Red Sea of oppressive and inhumane totalitarianism without wetting their feet in it, and, after the undoubtedly arduous journey, [the workers] will breathe the clean Brazilian air, purified by our civic spirit and our vocation for democracy."[56] Yet even here the language of rational organization and industrial psychology applied: by raising the moral and cultural level of the typical Brazilian worker, by resolving maladjustments, and by contributing indirectly to a higher standard of living, SESI would maintain the social peace necessary for Brazil to become a productive and efficient society.

INDUSTRIALISTS AND THE FAILURE OF DEMOCRACY

Returning to the original concern of this chapter, we need to consider the implications of SENAI and SESI, and the industrialists' discourse, for the fate of democracy in post-war Brazil. One obvious aspect of the foregoing analysis is the impressive extent to which the industrialist leadership managed to keep under its direct control activities that in most other societies have been relegated to the state. The industrial elite's considerable independence from state supervision undermines both the old image of Vargas's strong central state and the newer image of a seamless collaboration of state and bourgeoisie. Yet we are not talking about a strictly private, "welfare-capitalist," factory-based substitute for the welfare state. Perhaps for analytical purposes it makes sense to think of the industrialists as creating a collateral "welfare state" in which they could develop social and educational programs free of influences from the competitive political arena or from organized labor. These programs also allowed the leading industrialists to develop educational and welfare services that reinforced their conception of their social class as the group most capable of overseeing the transformation of urban life, in alliance with an army of trained technicians and educators imbued with a rationalizing, "scientific" discourse. By the same token, they reinforced a conception of Brazilian workers as poorly prepared to participate in the resolution of these problems.

Industrialist control over vocational training and a wide array of social welfare programs also aided the industrialist leadership in one of its most pressing concerns: preserving management's near-complete authority within the factory walls. While leaders like Simonsen and Lodi might regard the "rank and file" industrialists as requiring a certain amount of re-education with regard to rational methods of organization and improvement of labor relations, they certainly preferred such education to come from industrialist-controlled agencies rather than directly from the state or, worse, the labor unions. Early on, FIESP and other employer associations had strenuously impressed upon Vargas their opposition to any policy that allowed union representatives to enforce regulations on the factory floor, describing such intervention as breeding "the greatest and most harmful evil, the weakening of the employer's authority."[57] And any attempt by government inspectors to assert a countervailing authority usually met with intense denunciations.

The very limited power of union representatives on the factory floor helps explain the near absence of a shop steward or factory commission network in Brazilian industry during the period from 1945 to 1964. Scholars have tended to explain the weakness of shopfloor organization by citing (in the earlier literature) the low level of class consciousness among Brazilian workers, or (in more recent studies) the bureaucratization and non-democratic character of the government-controlled union structure. Few have considered the near-absolute power of management within the workplace, based both on the logic of rationalization and on specific social and educational arrangements that reinforced the industrialists' position. Moreover, the massive influx of multinational capital in the late 1950s further solidified the position of management within the workplace.[58]

In his famous discussion of Fordism, Gramsci claimed that it was primarily in the factory that the "American" worker absorbed the values and practices associated with capitalism.[59] Perhaps this could be more accurately said of the employers and managers who directed the factories. And if so, in the case of Brazil, the concentration of technical and social authority within the factory ran counter to any reordering of industrialist ideology in favor of democratic values. Industrialists and technocrats saw the factory as the privileged space for rational organization and scientific logic; the political sphere, by contrast, with its highly conflictual, "irrational" and "unscientific" methods of decisionmaking, was the very antithesis of the factory, a potential threat to industrial development and "social peace."[60] And this was particularly worrisome since the industrialists, despite a considerable degree of autonomy, generally regarded the state as an inevitable partner in the process of industrial transformation. The contrast that leading industrialists perceived between the spheres of production and politics, combined with their ongoing dependence on the state, magnified the significance of gains made by worker representatives under the populist governments of the 1950s and early 1960s.

Weak and ineffective at the factory level, organized labor adopted a very different posture toward the public sphere, looking to the state for redress of its grievances, and seeking leverage from the political parties' competition for popular support. Throughout the 1950s and early 1960s the Brazilian union leadership repeatedly attempted, through the state, to obtain new benefits or higher wages (which could be achieved through a hike in the minimum wage or such laws as the thirteenth-month bonus). And as urban labor emerged as an important base for electoral success, even politicians like President Juscelino Kubitschek (1956–1960), who were only mildly populist, made some substantial concessions to the labor unions. Indeed, it was the pro-industry Kubitschek who, in 1957, issued a decree-law that reversed the strike prohibitions established during the Estado Novo, a move that elicited immediate condemnation from FIESP and other employer associations.[61] It was also under Kubitschek that labor unions finally gained representation in the bureaucracies of the state social security institutes.[62]

If the industrialists, through SENAI and SESI, had aspired only to controlling the world within the factory walls, the intensified labor mobilization of the late 1950s and early 1960s might not have seemed so threatening. Both agencies, however, had even more ambitious goals: they sought to construct a new Brazilian worker, committed to industrial progress and social peace. SESI in particular had long cultivated ties with moderate union leaders through the provision of funding, services, and personal favors. But in the late 1950s, an era of increasingly autonomous industrial unions, prominent labor leaders shunned or minimized relations with SESI, and avoided overt alliances with industrialist representatives. One union militant of this era claimed that by the early 1960s, SESI had "almost disappeared" from organized labor. And the phrase "social peace" became a favorite of the union press – used to underscore the hypocrisy or mock the rhetoric of the industrial bourgeoisie.[63]

During these years the union leadership viewed the state as an ally, and as the most opportune site for struggle over social issues. In contrast, the industrialists by the late 1950s regularly described the political system as being "in crisis," denounced the growing influence of Communists within organized labor, and feared that gains made by the labor movement would eventually threaten the internal order of factory life.[64] The state constructed by Vargas and his advisors during the 1930s was supposed to serve as an integrative mechanism, as a means to reconcile conflict and create cross-class alliances; instead, the state had become a locus of ever more acute conflict. Although SESI had, from the outset, represented industry as a bastion of democracy in Brazilian society, the industrialists and their allies had always framed their devotion to democracy in contingent terms – it was the preferred basis for politics only if the Brazilian people, and especially the Brazilian worker, learned to exercise their democratic rights in a "rational" manner.[65] Disappointed in their hopes, by the early 1960s a substantial portion of the industrialist leadership had begun to explore alternative political arrangements.

NOTES

1. See, for example, the writings of philosopher and political activist Marilena Chauí, including "Apontamentos para uma crítica da Ação Integralista Brasileira," in Chauí and M.S. Carvalho Franco, *Ideologia e mobilização popular* (Rio de Janeiro, 1978), 17–149, and *Cultura e democracia: O discurso competente e outras falas* (São Paulo, 1980).

2. Aside from the work of Marilena Chauí cited above, see Luiz Werneck Vianna, *Liberalismo e sindicato no Brasil* (Rio de Janeiro, 1976); Ricardo Antunes, *Classe operária, sindicatos e partido no Brasil* (São Paulo, 1982); Kazumi Munakata, *A legislação trabalhista no Brasil* (São Paulo, 1981); Amélia Cohn, *Previdência social e processo político no Brasil* (São Paulo, 1981); Edgar Salvadori de Decca, *O silêncio dos vencidos* (São Paulo, 1981).

3. On labor legislation before and after 1930, see Angela M. de Castro Gomes, *Burguesia e trabalho* (Rio de Janeiro, 1979). As Castro Gomes shows, Brazilian labor law did not originate with Vargas, but the new legal code was broader in scope, more "rationally" constructed, and somewhat better enforced.

4. Evaristo de Moraes Filho, *O problema do sindicato único no Brasil* (rpt., São Paulo, 1978; 1st edn., 1952); see also Kenneth Paul Erickson, *The Brazilian Corporative State and Working-Class Politics* (Berkeley, 1977).

5. Here again, Vargas based his "innovations" on existing institutions, specifically the Caixa de Aposentadoria e Pensões created by the federal government in 1923 as a pension fund for railroad workers. Cohn, *Previdência social*, 5–33.

6. Werneck Vianna, *Liberalismo e sindicato*, 87–153; on the ideology of the *outorga*, see John D. French, "The Origins of Corporatist State Intervention in Brazilian Industrial Relations, 1930–1934," *Luso-Brazilian Review*, 28, no. 2 (1991): 13–26.

7. See, for example, J.R. Brandão Lopes, *Crise do Brasil arcáico* (São Paulo, 1967) and *Sociedade industrial no Brasil* (São Paulo, 1971); Leôncio Martins Rodrigues, *Conflito social e sindicalismo no Brasil* (São Paulo, 1968); Asiz Simão, *Sindicato e estado* (São Paulo, 1966).

8. Fernando Henrique Cardoso, *Empresário industrial e desenvolvimento econômico no Brasil* (São Paulo, 1964) and Warren Dean, *The Industrialization of São Paulo, 1880–1945* (Austin, 1969).

9. In his early essays, Francisco Weffort described the arrangement that emerged from this apparent social vacuum as an "estado de compromisso." *O populismo na política brasileira* (Rio de Janeiro, 1978). For a blistering critique of this concept, see Kazumi Munakata, "Compromisso do estado," *Revista Brasileira de História*, 4, no. 7 (March 1984): 58–71.

10. Margaret E. Keck, "The New Unionism in the Brazilian Transition," in Alfred Stepan, ed., *Democratizing Brazil* (New York, 1989): 252–96.

11. Antunes, *Classe operária*; Margareth Rago, *Do cabaré ao lar* (Rio de Janeiro, 1985); Sidney Chalhoub, *Trabalho, lar, e botequim: O cotidiano dos trabalhadores no Rio de Janeiro da Belle Epoque* (São Paulo, 1986); Maria Alice Ribeiro, *Condições do trabalho na indústria textil paulista* (São Paulo, 1988); Maria Auxiliadora Guzzo Decca, *A vida fora das fábricas: Cotidiano operário em São Paulo, 1920–1934* (Rio de Janeiro, 1987).

12. For a discussion of how the rethinking of the working class prompted a similar re-examination of the industrial bourgeoisie, see Paulo Sérgio Pinheiro and Michael M. Hall, eds., *A classe operária no Brasil*, vol. 2 (São Paulo, 1981), 9–14.

13. De Decca, *O silêncio dos vencidos*, Chapter 4.

14. For examples of these romanticizing tendencies in an otherwise interesting and innovative study, see Joel Wolfe, *Working Women, Working Men: São Paulo and the Rise of Brazil's Industrial Working Class, 1900–1955* (Durham, 1993).

15. The two most ambitious "revisionist" studies are Angela M. de Castro Gomes, *A invenção do trabalhismo* (São Paulo, 1988), and John D. French, *The Brazilian Workers' ABC: Class Conflict and Alliances in Modern São Paulo* (Chapel Hill, NC, 1992).

16. René Armand Dreifuss, *1964: A conquista do estado* (Rio de Janeiro, 1981). Transcript of interview with Raphael Noschese (25 June 1990), Projeto Memória, SENAI-São Paulo. See also Philip Siekman, "When Executives Turned Revolutionaries," *Fortune* (September. 1964), 147.

17. I outline some of my arguments in "The Industrialists, the State, and the Issues of Worker Training and Social Services in Brazil, 1930–1950," *Hispanic American Historical Review*, 70, no. 3 (August 1990): 379–404.

18. M. Antonieta P. Leopoldi, "Industrial Associations and Politics in Contemporary Brazil" (D.Phil. thesis, St. Antony's College, Oxford, 1984), 133.

19. Arquivo da FIESP, Biblioteca Roberto Simonsen, Circular no. 59/43 (7 April 1943); no. 68/43 (28 April 1943); no. 120/43 (29 July 1943); no. 51/44 (22 April 1944).

20. Weinstein, "The Industrialists," 382–8.

21. See, for example, "Discurso de Aldo Mário de Azevedo na ocasião da 1a reunião do IDORT" (1931), Arquivo do IDORT; and "Confederação Nacional da Indústria" and "O ensino profissional no Brasil," in Roberto Simonsen, *Ensaios sociais, politícos e econômicos* (São Paulo, 1943).

22. Weinstein, "The Industrialists," 388–90.

23. "As finanças e a indústria," in Roberto Simonsen, *À margem da profissão* (São Paulo, 1931), 217.

24. *O Trabalhador Gráphico* (January 1906), 1–3; (26 September. 1906), 4. The resentment of "foreign" skilled workers may seem incongruous with

the immigrant origins of many Paulista workers; this referred specifically to highly skilled craftsmen from Britain, France, etc., often "imported" by firms to fill supervisory positions within the factories. See Stanley J. Stein, *The Brazilian Cotton Manufacture* (Cambridge, Mass., 1957).

25. In a 1933 speech, Vargas declared that "the education which we need to develop to the extreme limits of our possibilities is the vocational and technical kind. Without it, systematic labor is impossible, especially in an age characterized by the predominance of the machine." Getúlio Vargas, *A nova política do Brasil*, vol. 2 (Rio de Janeiro, 1938), 119.

26. Weinstein, "The Industrialists," 392; Castro Gomes, *A invenção do trabalhismo*, 235.

27. My sketch of industrialist attitudes and priorities is derived from the records of the inter-ministerial commission established to deal with this issue. These are available in the Center for Documentation (CPDOC) of the Fundação Getúlio Vargas (FGV) in Rio de Janeiro.

28. Simon Schwartzman *et al.*, *Tempos de Capanema* (Rio de Janeiro/São Paulo, 1984), 231–45.

29. FGV, CPDOC, Arquivo Gustavo Capanema, 35.12.00, doc. 1–10, "O ensino profissional na Alemanha" (1938). On the apprenticeship program in Nazi Germany, see John Gillingham, "The 'Deproletarianization' of German Society: Vocational Training in the Third Reich," *Journal of Social History* 19, no. 3 (Spring 1986): 423–32.

30. FGV, CPDOC, Arquivo G. Capanema, 38.04.30, doc. 2A–1, part 4, "Observações feitas em visita oficial da Comissão ao Estado de S. Paulo."

31. Mange published his views on this matter in the pamphlet *A formação dos técnicos para a indústria* (São Paulo, 1940).

32. FGV, CPDOC, Arquivo G. Capanema, 38.04.30, doc. 2A–1, part 6, "A aprendizagem nos estabelecimentos industriais." The author of this report was Joaquim Faria Góes Filho, who had emerged as the main spokesman for the industrialists.

33. FGV, CPDOC, Arquivo G. Capanema, 38.04.30, doc. 2A–1, letter to G. Capanema (7 July 1940).

34. Philippe Schmitter, *Interest Conflict and Political Change in Brazil* (Stanford, 1971), 184.

35. For a contrast between Vargas's positive response to the industrialists' initiative and Juan Perón's effort to have the Peronist state monopolize all such programs, see Robert J. Alexander, *Labor Relations in Argentina, Brazil and Chile* (New York, 1962), 18.

36. FGV/CPDOC, Arquivo G. Capanema, 41.09.13, doc. 1–1.

37. FGV, CPDOC, Arquivo G. Capanema, 38.04.30, doc. 2B–1, letter from Capanema to Vargas. See also Schwartzman *et al.*, *Tempos de Capanema*, 236–37.

38. FGV, CPDOC, Arquivo G. Capanema, 41.09.13, doc. 1–15.

39. FGV, CPDOC, Arquivo G. Capanema, 41.09.13, doc. 1–6, letter to Capanema from Fuchs (21 July 1942).

40. FGV, CPDOC, Arquivo G. Capanema, 35.12.00, doc.1–10, "O ensino profissional na Alemanha." In a dissenting opinion, Fuchs argued for making apprenticeship obligatory, claiming the government could not "abandon the hardworking adolescent, who … in the future will either serve

as the consolidator of social peace or the instigator of class revolt."
38.04.30, doc. 4–3.

41. *O Metalúrgico* (March 1943), 4; (August–September 1948), 4. In the latter
issue another article (p. 2) praised SENAI extravagantly, claiming that it
gave Brazilian workers "the sweet hope of better days ..."

42. Some recent works have stopped treating "skilledness" as a given, and have
paid more attention to the consistent underestimation of the skill levels of
tasks traditionally performed by women. See, for example, Wolfe, *Working
Women, Working Men*.

43. *O Trabalhador Textil* (November–December 1939), 4.

44. *O Trabalhador Gráfico* (7 February 1936), 3. This article is especially note-
worthy since it appeared after the union's subordination to government
control.

45. Arquivo da FIESP, Biblioteca Roberto Simonsen, Circular no. 75/46 (23
April 1946), "Fundação de Assistência ao Trabalhador."

46. Weinstein, "The Industrialists," 402.

47. SESI purposely located several of these *postos de abastecimento* in districts
where the Communist Party had established food co-ops; unable to compete
with SESI's better funded posts, the co-ops went out of business. SESI-São
Paulo, Atas do Conselho Regional (10 July 1947).

48. There were close ties between SESI and Catholic groups such as Social
Action (whose school for social work provided much of SESI's staff) and
the Workers' Circles. Labor unions sought SESI assistance in setting up
food co-ops, medical care services, and adult literacy and sewing courses.
Union newspapers regularly advertised social services sponsored by SESI.
See *A Voz da Construção Civil* (February 1951), 4; *O Metalúrgico* (March
1947), 9; *A Média* (June 1958), 1.

49. "Rumos da educação social," *SESI Jornal* (31 July 1949): 1–2; "Centros de
aprendizado doméstico," *SESI Jornal* (31 December 1955): 1–2.

50. On the Serviço, and later Subdivisão, de Higiene e Segurança Industrial, see
SESI-18 anos: Assistência social (São Paulo, 1966), 202–440.

51. See Amélia Cohn *et al.*, *Acidentes do trabalho: Uma forma de violência*
(São Paulo, 1985).

52. Pedro da Costa Rêgo, "Da natureza do acidente," Boletim do SENAI
(July–September 1945), 1–2.

53. *Boletim Informativo do Trabalho* (December 1951), 32–4.

54. See for example "Deficiência de segurança e higiene," *CIPA-Journal*
(January–February 1964), 7; "Campanha educativa," *CIPA-Journal*
(January–February 1966), 4–5; *SESI-18 anos*, 223.

55. On SESI's corps of social workers, see transcript of interview with Hugo
Guimarães Malheiros, Chief of the Social Service Subdivision, SESI-São
Paulo (13 April 1956), Robert J. Alexander Archive, Rutgers University.

56. Roberto Simonsen, *Discurso pronunciado em São Paulo, na instalação do
1o Conselho Consultivo do SESI* (São Paulo, 1946), 14.

57. Arquivo da FIESP, Circular no. 430 (19 July 1933); no. 451 (10 October
1933). Provoking this response was a proposal by union leaders that their
representatives on the shopfloor be allowed to enforce the "Two-Thirds
Law." While the enforcement of this law did not imply material costs for the
employers, it did challenge their control over hiring and firing.

58. See Claude McMillan, Jr., "The American Businessman in Brazil," *Business Topics,* 2 (Spring 1963): 68–80. McMillan observed that "organized labor is not a serious factor limiting managerial prerogatives," and that "unions are relatively weak, except as a political force."

59. Antonio Gramsci, "Americanism and Fordism," in *Selections from the Prison Notebooks* (New York, 1971), 298–310.

60. On the growing sense of political crisis among Paulista industrialists, see Maria José Trevisan, *50 anos em 5: A FIESP e o desenvolvimentismo* (Petrópolis, 1986), 43–7.

61. *Boletim Informativo da FIESP,* no. 247 (28 June 1954), 11–12; no. 319 (14 November 1955), 13–17; no. 431 (8 January 1958), 5; no. 522 (7 October 1959), 100–101. This last called the right to strike an "incentive to anarchy."

62. Cohn, *Previdência social,* 35–93; see also James M. Malloy, *The Politics of Social Security in Brazil* (Pittsburgh, 1979).

63. Interview with Affonso Deleles, former president and secretary of São Paulo Metallurgical Workers Union (18 July 1986). Transcript of interview with Olavo Previatti, president of the Federation of Workers in the São Paulo Paper Industry (27 April 1956), Alexander Archive, Rutgers University.

64. On the politics and policies of this period, see Miriam Limoeiro Cardoso, *Ideologia do desenvolvimento – Brasil: JK-JQ* (Rio de Janeiro, 1978), and Maria Victória de Mesquita Benevides, *O governo Kubitschek* (Rio de Janeiro, 1976).

65. Divisão de Orientação Social, SESI-São Paulo, *Boletim Interno,* no. 12, 17; DOS, SESI-SP, *O Voto,* Série Popular no. 6 (1955); *Boletim Informativo da FIESP,* no. 431 (8 January 1958), 5; Trevisan, *50 anos em 5,* 162. In his introduction to the handbook, *Seminário da formação cívica* (1957), Eduardo Gabriel Saad, director of the Divisão de Orientação Social, SESI-São Paulo, wrote: "We affirm ... that, as long as education has not reached the majority of our people, making them conscious of their rights and duties, one cannot think about true democracy."

14 Constituting Political Bodies in the Adenauer Era
Robert G. Moeller

In the first decade of their post-war history, West Germans were engaged in a process of political self-definition. The urgency of this task was self-evident; the pressure to establish models of democratic citizenship was enormous in a country burdened by the legacy of a failed experiment in parliamentary government, National Socialism, and defeat in war, and shaped by the post-1945 division of the world between East and West. In the late 1940s, the victorious British, American, and French Allies moved de facto toward establishing the economic and political boundaries of what would become the Federal Republic; but within this imposed framework, it was left to West Germans to create themselves. In the process, they defined themselves as male and female; the social construction of democracy and the language of political citizenship in a new post-war democratic West Germany were gendered. In describing the body politic, West Germans were also constituting political bodies.[1]

The forces of occupation were directly involved in economic and political restructuring in the West, but the same cannot be said of Allied concern about the status of women and the family. Administrative structures to analyze these problems remained poorly staffed and underfunded; they appeared as relative latecomers in the occupation bureaucracy. By contributing to the division of Germany, the Allies had ensured that discussions of women's status and the family's future would take place against the background of the Cold War and the establishment of the political boundary between East and West. But this was an indirect influence. Perhaps more than with any other part of social and political recovery, West Germans were left on their own when it came to renegotiating the boundaries between women and men in the context of defining a democratic political order.[2]

This chapter focuses on how legal reform and social policy described and delimited the status of women and outlined the dimensions of their citizenship in a democratic West Germany. It argues that in the Federal Republic, defining social and political citizenship for women was inseparable from defining a normative vision of the family. It examines two major arenas: (1) the prescription of women's equal rights with men in the Basic Law (*Grundgesetz*), the constitutional basis for a new West Germany drafted by the Parliamentary Council in 1949, and the implications of guaranteeing women's equality for a reform of German family law in the 1950s; and (2) debates over family allowances and the place of women in a reformulated West German welfare state. Borrowing from the categories laid out by T.H. Marshall, it was in the Basic Law that women were described as "civil" and "political" citizens, endowed with the same rights as men and equality before the law. In debates over family allowances, their role as "social citizens," their rights to economic and social security, were at stake.[3]

This chapter is devoted largely to an analysis of men's descriptions of "woman's place." Men – vastly over-represented in parliament, in the government, in political parties, in trade unions, and in the medical, legal and academic professions – dominated debates over national policies affecting women. By specifying their conceptions of women's rights and needs, however, men were also defining themselves and their vision of a just society. Thus, this chapter attempts to describe not only the reconstruction of "woman's place" in reconstruction West Germany; it also examines what the politics of gender can tell us about the larger process of framing political identities and a democratic order – for women and men – in the first decade of the Federal Republic's history.[4]

CONTEXTUALIZING THE "WOMAN QUESTION" IN THE LATE 1940s

Until recently, most accounts of West Germany's early history have paid scant attention to the place of women and the family in the politics of the post-war period. In the few general treatments of the late 1940s and 1950s that exist, the problems of reconstruction are the problems of Germans without gender.[5] The dearth of historical analyses of gender relations in Germany after the war contrasts sharply with the general acknowledgement by post-war West Germans that a reassessment of relations between women and men would be a crucial part of rebuilding. The salience of gender as a political category was hardly surprising. On the most basic level, relations between the sexes commanded attention because post-war Germany was a society where women far outnumbered men. As the journalist and political activist Gabriele Strecker put it, in purely visual terms, because of the high rate of male casualties in the war and the large number of soldiers detained in prisoner-of-war camps, post-war Germany was a "country of women."[6] As late as 1950 when many men held as prisoners of war had returned home, there were still more than 130 women for every 100 men in the age group 25–40.[7] This lasting demographic consequence of the Second World War combined in the late 1940s with the social dislocation and economic instability of the immediate post-war period to prompt widespread fears of the "crisis of the family." In a society where adult men were in short supply, this was a crisis of the status of women and gender relations.

Unlike the situation in Britain, France, and the United States, the problem for West German women was not how to adjust to their post-war demobilization from non-traditional occupations; they faced challenges of a very different sort. Until the late 1940s under Allied controls, shortages of all necessities became worse than they had been before the war's end, and the gradual release of men from prisoner-of-war camps, which continued into the 1950s, delayed family reunions. War deaths meant that many families remained "incomplete" (*unvollständig*) – without adult males – and many marriages collapsed under the pressure of long separations.

Women's hardships and the perceived disequilibrium of gender relations caused by women's altered status in the war and post-war years became central concerns of politicians and public policymakers. For women and men, from the Social Democratic Party (SPD) to the conservative Christian-Democratic/Christian-Social (CDU/CSU) coalition, there was a broad political consensus that the war had placed particularly great burdens on the family, and that "more than any other societal institution, the family had fallen into the whirlpool created by the collapse." This made the "family the central problem of the post-war era."[8] Everyone could agree that after the hard times of the war and its aftermath, the needs of women and the family deserved special attention.

In providing answers to the "woman question," West Germans also felt compelled to respond to the ideological legacy and practical policies of National Socialism. The Nazis had set out to revolutionize the family, transforming private spheres into public spaces, and identifying women as "mothers of the race."[9] From the perspective of West German policymakers, the Nazis had attempted to reduce women to breeding machines for the *Volk*, erasing the boundary between private families and public policy. Restoring women to an inviolable family, safe from state intervention, was a shared objective. West Germans renounced a past in which they had sought political stability in *Lebensraum* (living space) in Eastern Europe; they replaced it with a search for security in a different sort of living space,[10] the family, where a democratic West Germany would flourish. At the center of this construction was the German woman.

For the political definition of women and the family, communism was just as powerful a negative point of reference as fascism. In her perceptive study, *Homeward Bound: American Families in the Cold War Era*, Elaine Tyler May illustrates how metaphors of "containment" influenced not only United States foreign policy in the 1950s but also conceptions of gender relations and the family. "In the domestic version ...," she writes, "the 'sphere of influence' was the home."[11] In the case of the Federal Republic, the context of the Cold War was even less subtle and more significant than in the United States, because the West German discussion of "woman's place" repeatedly invoked the example of their German-speaking neighbors to the East; structuring much of the debate around policies that detailed "woman's nature" and "woman's place" were comparisons with conceptions of women's equality in the "Soviet zone of occupation."

Political responses to the "woman question" in the late 1940s and 1950s drew on a well-established repertoire. Advocates of women's equality returned to an agenda established in the late nineteenth century by the Social Democratic and bourgeois women's movements. Pressure for policies to "protect" families in the 1950s echoed longstanding demands for the "family wage," conservative pro-natalist enthusiasm for state support for families "rich in children," and anxieties, long predating the demographic impact of the Second World War, that family size limitation would cause Germans to "die out." Still, when familiar themes surfaced in post-war West Germany, they carried additional layers of meaning. In discussing "woman's place," post-war West Germans were constantly assessing the immediate past of National Socialism and the ideological alternative presented by those other Germans across the border to the East.

LEGISLATING WOMAN'S PLACE: THE *GRUNDGESETZ* AND FAMILY LAW REFORM

Concerns about the relations between women and men in post-war West Germany emerged clearly in the debates over the Basic Law, the new constitution adopted in 1949. Largely because of the forceful argumentation of Elisabeth Selbert, one of only four women delegated to the Parliamentary Council, and the insistence of other Social Democratic delegates, backed by a broad mobilization of middle-class and working-class women's organizations, the final form of the Basic Law prescribed that "men and women have the same rights" (*Männer und Frauen sind gleichberechtigt*). In part, this represented an acknowledgement of women's contributions to sustaining German society under the extraordinarily difficult circumstances of war and post-war privation. In part, it was the fulfillment of Social Democratic and liberal feminist demands for women's complete equality before the law which dated back to the late nineteenth century.[12]

The Basic Law also clearly articulated concerns about the family's future, echoing public opinion that after nearly a decade of hardship, women and the family were at risk, desperately in need of the state's protection. Explicitly addressing these concerns, expressed most fully by the CDU/CSU coalition, Article 6 of the Basic Law placed marriage and the family under the "particular protection" of the state.[13]

In a new democratic Germany, women and men were to have equal rights, but the Basic Law also located women squarely within families. This represented no contradiction, because all political parties agreed that equality must be compatible with a full recognition of the difference between women and men. For the CDU/CSU, this difference was sometimes rooted in a preordained, Christian order, sometimes in biology and nature. For Social Democrats, it was most often explained in terms of social function. But varying justifications led to the same end: a woman's principle identity was as wife and mother.

The SPD's insistence, articulated most fully by Selbert, on an "equality of rights ... founded on an equality of worth, which acknowledges difference,"[14] was an explicit response to the fears of *Gleichmacherei*, the bogey of an arbitrary levelling of difference legislated in East Germany. With the exception of the marginalized voices of a small Communist delegation, all representatives to the Parliamentary Council accepted that preserving and maintaining difference was essential for distinguishing the social order in the Federal Republic from the negative example of the East. Across the political spectrum, there was a broad consensus that behind Communist ideological formulations was nothing more than the cynical attempt to force women into jobs for which they were ill-suited, to make mothers carry a weighty double burden, and to destroy the family, leaving children to be charges of the state. In such formulations, the totalitarianism of the right was implicitly equated with the totalitarianism of the left; Communists shared with National Socialists a desire to subordinate families to the state. By situating women within the family, an ostensibly private sphere free from state intervention, the Basic Law sought to fortify boundaries between women and men; it also fortified boundaries between East and West in the present and distanced West Germans from their own most recent past.

The drafters of the Basic Law were fully aware that by calling for women to have equal rights with men, they were also mandating an overhaul of the Civil Code (*Bürgerliches Gesetzbuch*) that had been in force since the turn of the century.[15] The Civil Code's provisions governing relations within marriage were outspokenly patriarchal, and Social Democrats, organized middle-class women's groups, feminist lawyers, often experts in family law, and some liberals had criticized it on these grounds in the Wilhelmine period and in Weimar. When the newly elected Bundestag took up the reform agenda in the early 1950s, there was general agreement that laws granting a husband complete control over his wife's property and limiting a wife's right to work outside the home were inconsistent with the promise of women's equality in a free, democratic order. In properly constituted families, the workplace of wives and mothers was the home, but there was also a solid consensus that it was vital to emphasize that their unpaid household labor was the functional equivalent of the wages earned by male "providers" who went out to work.

Agreement collapsed, however, over provisions that left husbands the sole arbiters in all cases of irreconcilable marital dispute. For the Chancellor, Konrad Adenauer, and the ruling conservative CDU/CSU coalition, the stability of the family depended on the existence of a means for adjudicating differences of opinion; the husband should be judge and jury. The Basic Law legislated equality, but, argued Adenauer and the conservative coalition, where "objective biological and functional differences" distinguished women from men, men and women could be subject to differential treatment.

For the ruling CDU/CSU coalition and the Social Democratic opposition alike, biology and function led women directly to motherhood and housewifery. However, where unanimity did not exist was over what responsibilities and rights should come with these jobs. For the CDU/CSU, a mother's obligation to ensure her children's welfare and the stability of her marriage might entail subordinating her own opinion to that of her husband. Social Democrats and many Free Democrats opposed such clear survivals of patriarchal authority, and the absence of agreement meant that the Bundestag did not meet the Basic Law's April 1953 deadline for reforming the Civil Code.[16]

When the Bundestag finally agreed on the outlines of a revised family law after four more years of debate, it legislated a normative vision of the family where mothers and fathers were equal but separate. Women remained wives and mothers, men were "providers." Christian and Free Democrats insisted that failing to designate the home as a wife's principle workplace would potentially drive women to work for wages, "preparing the way to the collective," the path clearly outlined in the East. Social Democrats reminded their colleagues that during the period of post-war recovery some mothers might also be forced to work outside the home, but with equal fervor, the party's male leadership and its women's organizations advocated the goal of "an economic order in which no mother of pre-school or school-aged children should be forced out to work because of economic need."[17] In the long term, Social Democrats agreed that stable families and children's welfare were best secured by adequate male wages, not more work for mothers.

A narrow majority in the Bundestag continued to insist that when mothers and fathers disagreed over what best promoted a child's welfare, parental authority should become paternal authority; it was the right and responsibility of fathers to resolve any differences of opinion. To be sure, conceded one CDU spokesman, fathers might on occasion abuse their authority, but this did not justify "castrating" the family. There could scarcely be a more graphic expression of where authority should lie.[18]

Two years later, deciding a case supported by many middle-class women's organizations and brought by a number of "wives and mothers of minor children" who charged that to grant paternal authority in this form was a violation of the constitutional guarantee of their equal rights, the Federal Constitutional Court (*Bundesverfassungsgericht*), the highest instance of judicial review in West Germany, "castrated" the family; it declared unconstitutional the legal sanction of a father's ultimate determination of his children's welfare. Denying mothers equal rights with fathers, the court determined, "weakens the status of the mother precisely in that area – motherhood – where her essence is most deeply rooted and where she realizes herself." With this judgment, the court maintained its reputation for standing to the left of Adenauer's conservative government. Probably just as important for determining the outcome in this particular case was the presence on the bench of Erna Scheffler, the lone female justice on the court, who had a solid reputation as a feminist legal expert and whose voice resounded in the judgment upholding the principle of equality of authority within the family.[19]

The court decision of 1959 ended a decade-long debate over how to bring the laws governing family relations into accord with the equal rights for women and men guaranteed by the West German constitution. It also represented the culmination of the battle for the reform of the Civil Code that had engaged politically active middle-class women and Social Democrats since the 1890s. Still, both in parliament and the courts, even by those who advocated an expanded notion of women's equality, strengthening women's status was seen primarily as a means to strengthen families. The fiercest political battles over the meaning of women's equality during the "Adenauer era" were thus over the ideal conception of the family, where women were defined not as individuals but in terms of their relationships to others – to men and children, as wives and mothers.

MOTHER'S WORK IN THE WELFARE STATE

As the debates over the *Grundgesetz* made clear, any discussion of women's rights immediately raised questions about the family. The definition of women's political citizenship was inseparable from the linkage wife–mother. When it came to the definition of *social* citizenship in the reformulation of the West German welfare state in the 1950s, women's political identity was no different. While the Bundestag explored how best to define "woman's place" in a reformed Civil Code, it approached the same question from another perspective in discussions of how the state might most effectively support families. Citizenship was prescribed not only in terms of women's civil equality before the law in the categories of the *Rechtsstaat* (state based on law), articulated in the *Grundgesetz* and Civil Code; it was also specified in debates over the *Wohlfahrtsstaat* (welfare state). This was explicitly outlined in the parliamentary debates over family allowances, which revealed how the politics of the family constructed post-war West German conceptions of motherhood and how motherhood was the basis for women's "social citizenship" in a democratic welfare state.

"Money-for-children" (*Kindergeld*), the West German program of family allowances, was initially conceived as a response to rising prices and organized working-class protest over inadequate wage levels in the wake of currency reform in 1948. There was general agreement that assisting the family was vitally important, that the state was the most appropriate agent for making payments, and that for specifics, lawmakers could look to Nazi precedents, suspended by the Allies because of their racialist and pro-natalist content. There was much to be reclaimed from the National Socialist past. The representative from the Labor Ministry of North Rhine-Westphalia to a national commission mandated with formulating a program to implement *Kindergeld*, Jacob Schiefer, summarized the widely held view that "the principle of granting a state subsidy for children, established by the National Socialists, was correct, wrong was administering it according to considerations of race and population policies."[20] It was up to West Germans to define alternatives not similarly flawed.

Lawmakers also viewed stable families as the essential foundation for the post-war social order. Here, they echoed the arguments of many post-war West German sociologists, whose studies concluded that the family was a "vestige of stability in our social crisis."[21] It was a locus of constituted authority that had escaped Nazi invasion and Allied bomb attacks, a repository of uniquely German values that could be reclaimed as a basis for post-war reconstruction.

Policymakers also emphasized that in the post-war world, the family, not class, was the appropriate object of state assistance. Social policy had been tied to a "strata or class-bound" perspective for too long. Outdated measures had aimed at increasing chances for social mobility by encouraging the collective advancement of the working class. In the analysis of one leading post-war West German sociologist, Helmut Schelsky, the upward movement of some accomplished by these policies before the Second World War combined with the downward mobility of others, caused by the devastation of the war and post-war years, had created a "levelled-out petit-bourgeois *mittelständisch* society" (*nivellierte Kleinbürgerlich-mittel-ständische Gesellschaft*). German society was now "characterized by the loss of class tensions and social hierarchy, neither proletarian nor bourgeois."[22] Social differentiation continued to exist, but social conflict was now defined by organized interests, not synonymous with classes. At most, class was a residual analytic category that no longer described social reality.

The "end of ideology," measured in the 1950s by French and American intellectuals in terms of the decline of the political extremes of the interwar period,[23] registered in West Germany in discussions of a classless society in which families had become the fundamental unit of social analysis. Social Democrats did not challenge this consensus view any more than they disputed the assumption of the reformed family law that a woman's most important work was in the home. In neither context did they invoke that part of their ideological heritage that might have pointed in a different direction; in a world divided between East and West, Marxist theory, which etched a road to political consciousness through "socially productive labor" and described the true equality of proletarianized families, was abandoned to those other Germans across the border.

Social Democrats and the CDU/CSU coalition, the major proponents of competing family allowance schemes, differed not over the objective of supporting families, but over how best to achieve that end. According to CDU/CSU proposals, family allowances should not lead to the introduction of a "family wage." The determination of the "production wage" (*Leistungslohn*) was the business of the "social partners" – capital and labor – not the state. Allowing the state any direct role in regulating the system of family allowances represented a return to the institutional forms of National Socialism and mirrored the centralized planned economy in the Soviet-occupied zone; it was an intolerable and dangerous expansion of the state's authority over private relations. Rather, self-regulation by the private sector was the only acceptable administrative solution. Proposed was a system of employer contributions that would be redistributed to families with more than two children through the existing framework of occupational insurance providers. These principles embodied the CDU/CSU's commitment to the "social-market economy" (*soziale Marktwirtschaft*). Though it should not lose its social conscience, the German economy must be reconstructed according to the competitive laws of the market with as little state intervention as possible.

Doubtful that capitalism and less government would necessarily guarantee just solutions, critics from within the ranks of the opposition SPD, trade unionists, social workers, and some middle-class feminists were skeptical of CDU/CSU proposals. In particular, they argued that although wages *should* support a family of four, they might well not. In addition, excluding those with only one or two children from benefits would disadvantage widows and divorced women whose needs were just as great as those of low income family fathers; family allowances must also be extended to these families, who often still bore the scars of the war and post-war crises.[24]

Social Democrats subscribed enthusiastically to the theory that large families were the key to economic prosperity and future social security. Where they differed from the CDU/CSU coalition was in their demand that families of four needed help and that families without fathers were families as well. A policy of equal payments to all children and the elimination of the highly regressive system of tax allowances for dependents – a Nazi legacy that most helped the families who needed it least by granting a higher allowance to those with higher incomes – would permit all mothers to stay at home and would not limit benefits to certain groups.

The SPD countered fears that the costs of this alternative would be prohibitive with claims that family allowances would redistribute wealth to those lower income families, more likely to spend most of their earnings on consumer goods, thus stimulating demand, spurring economic growth, and generating more taxes. The party proposed a system of state administration, financed through a tax on the gross income of all wage-earners, and argued for the elimination of all other allowances for minor dependents.

Compared with their active engagement in debates over reforming the Civil Code, organized middle-class women's groups were relatively silent in discussions of "money-for-children" and the larger agenda of reforming the post-war welfare state. There were at least some women among the lawyers who could claim expertise in the intricacies of the Civil Code and family law; there were none among the professors of social policy who strongly influenced discussions of family allowances nor had women ever gained significant access to employment in state-run social welfare agencies.[25] When middle-class feminists did intervene, however, they too were committed to a politics of difference in which motherhood assumed a central place as the apotheosis of womanhood and in which the problem for working mothers was not inadequate training or career opportunities but inadequate wages for men.

The discussions of family allowances among academic sociologists, economists, demographers, policymakers, and politicians indicated clearly that the work of reproduction was on a par with the work of production; human capital accumulation was equated with other forms of created value. The "body of the population" was seen as part of the capital stock, and economic planning necessitated paying attention to the costs of production and circulation of this crucial resource. The emphasis in debates over "money-for-children" on the family, not class, as the vehicle for upward social mobility suggested that women's work in the home had intensified since the war. According to sociological investigations of women's unpaid labor, what time women gained from advances in the rationalization of housework and the transfer of some services from the home to the economy was now spent checking over children's school assignments and caring for their psychological as well as their physical needs.[26] The home was no "haven in a heartless world;" it was the site of important work. Family allowances could not compensate women fully for their labors, nor should they; love was work, but at the same time, women's care for their families was motivated by instincts that could not be measured in monetary terms.[27] Still, supplementary benefits could at least enhance a mother's ability to work at one job, not two. Totalitarian states forced women to carry a heavy double burden. In the West, social policy should aim at making women offers they would not refuse by allowing them to opt for the work of housewifery and motherhood.

"Money-for-children" represented society's recognition of the importance of women's work in the home and the need to elevate the value of this non-wage labor, but this recognition was to take the form of a supplement to a male wage. Fattening a family father's paycheck was a way to allow him to accept assistance without stigma. Male egos would be preserved, women's work could be accomplished, companionate marriages where women and men were separate but equal would flourish, and the next generation of Germans would thrive.

Bundestag elections in 1953 returned a dramatically increased CDU/CSU delegation with as many votes as all other political parties combined, leaving the conservative coalition in a position to define West Germany's family policy agenda. In his opening remarks to the newly elected parliament, Adenauer directly addressed the importance of the family's responsibilities for reproduction as a crucial part of post-war recovery. West Germany, he explained, was a rapidly aging nation. This threatened the future of economic growth and the stability of the social security system; at present, there was not a one-to-one relationship between those entering the labor force and those leaving it. Adenauer expressed his dismay over the "entire development of our era that is inimical to the foundation of a healthy family." Technological advance might slow down the corrosive effects of a declining birthrate, but it could not completely reverse a process that threatened to "destroy our entire population in the course of a few generations." A constant birthrate, not machines, was the best guarantee of prosperity and social security. "Only one thing can help: strengthening the family and thereby strengthening the will for children (*Stärkung des Willens zum Kind*)."[28]

The tonic intended to strengthen the "will for children" adopted in 1954 was that prescribed by the ruling CDU/CSU. The coalition railroaded through a law that provided monthly payments of 25 marks per child to wage earners with three or more children. The measure ultimately helped few Germans. Payments were inadequate to cover the costs of feeding and clothing a child, and most West German families included only one or two children living at home. Family size limitation remained the rule, and after a slight increase in the birthrate in the early 1950s, by the middle of the decade the trend reverted to the long-term tendency toward declining family size. On balance, "money-for-children" was far less significant for the material benefits it instituted than for the elaborate description of women's status as "social citizens" which it embodied.[29]

The same conception of "woman's place" in post-war West German democracy was written into the general overhaul of the welfare system, adopted in 1957. The Pension Reform Act of 1957 was one of the most important social welfare reform measures of the Adenauer era, the capstone of a much larger policy agenda set in place in the 1950s. Heralded as a path-breaking innovation, this measure indexed pensions, tying them to general changes in wage rates. In addition, it reduced the differentials in payments to wage-earners and salaried employees and increased the level of payments by as much as 65–70 percent. At these higher levels, pensioners might actually live from their retirement income, and the 1957 Act attenuated the almost axiomatic connection between old age and poverty that had characterized the lives of the overwhelming majority of Germans. Before this reform, payments out had been directly tied to payments in; retired workers had no hedge against general price increases and drew only on the resources they had accumulated over the course of their working lives. Now the younger generation's contributions financed the older generation's retirement.

As it had been since the founding of the German social insurance system under Bismarck in the 1870s, the basis for claims on the post-war welfare state remained employment status. Those who paid into pension funds when they were employed were entitled to receive payments from them when they were eligible to retire. The labor contract constituted the essential point of entry into the greatly expanded post-war social contract. The consequences of this system for women – both those who worked for wages and were insured and those whose unpaid and uninsured workplace was the home – were easily fathomed. Women who interrupted their lives as wage earners to devote themselves exclusively to mother's work paid less into social insurance funds and were entitled to take less out. In addition, the continued differentials in men's and women's wage levels translated into different levels of benefits, even for women who remained in full-time work. Women in part-time jobs received payments that reflected their reduced working hours and wages.[30]

Married women who did not work outside the home had claims to social security only through supplements for dependents paid to their husbands; for many adult women, access to the social contract came not through the labor contract but rather through the marriage contract. Despite all the political paeans to the value of women's work in discussions of "money-for-children," when it came to listing occupational categories or establishing the bases for accident and disability insurance, unemployment benefits, and retirement pensions, housewives and mothers had no jobs.

The debates over "money-for-children" made explicit where married women fit into the welfare state. To be sure, women were workers – indeed, their work was essential to the welfare state's survival. Without the next generation, the economy would falter, without new workers to pay into insurance and retirement funds, there would be nothing left to take out. Indexing pensions on the basis of wage-rates was cast explicitly as a "contract between generations," between one generation of workers paying into social insurance funds and another enjoying retirement.[31] As producers of the next generation, women could be part of this contract as well. However, they signed not with their wage work, but with their marriage vows and a lifetime of unpaid labor, through their status as wives and mothers, not as individuals. Social citizenship and social security in the Federal Republic were grounded in a productive order and the world of paid employment; they were also grounded in a reproductive order and the world of women's work in the home.

SOCIAL CITIZENSHIP AND THE SEXUAL CONTRACT [32]

The emphasis of West German social policy on women's dependent status within nuclear families reiterated themes already familiar from the public deliberations over the reform of the Civil Code. The constitutional guarantee of the family's protection was frequently invoked by those advocating family allowances. The Basic Law's promise of women's equal rights received no explicit mention, though discussions of "woman's place" in the West German welfare state underscored that difference was compatible with equality.

Alternatives to defining women's "social citizenship" in terms of their status as wives and mothers were not entirely lacking in other Western European countries. For example, in the categories of French social policy, high rates of women's labor force participation had long been viewed as crucial to dynamic economic development. State social policy acknowledged employers' reliance on a female labor force, and the French left accepted the ideal of women's wage work, because of its continued belief that women's entry into political consciousness would be facilitated by their entry into paid employment. This political combination led to emphasizing the right to work for all citizens in the post-war French constitution. On this basis, trade unions and the left supported demands for equal wages and equal treatment in the social security system for women and men. The other pillar of post-war French social policy, a system of family allowances, incorporated many of the nationalist and pro-natalist sentiments that were ubiquitous in the post-war West German discussion, but the French program included no assumption that only non-wage-earning mothers would raise children nor that only married couples were families; families in which parents were not married and single mothers were entitled to the same financial support.[33]

In post-war Britain, family allowances incorporated the same vision of a "normal family" enshrined in West German measures. Throughout debates over how best to aid families, however, there also resounded a feminist critique of women's dependency within marriage and wives' subordination to potentially abusive husbands, who might be as likely to spend their wages on drink as on their children. Although family allowances were ultimately much smaller than those proposed by feminists, the parliamentary decision in 1945 to issue payments directly to mothers, not as a supplement to a male wage, represented a clear concession to feminist pressures.[34]

In the Swedish discussion of family allowances that intensified in the 1930s, the needs of children without fathers and of unmarried single mothers had been at the center of policy formulation from the beginning, not treated as anomalous. Not the "family" but the "citizen" was the focus of social policy. From this starting point, it was possible to develop programs of income maintenance based on the assumption that all adults would work outside the home and that single women with children needed particular assistance so that their children's standard of living would not fall below that of families with two incomes.[35]

As in Sweden, France, and Britain, fears of population decline had also intensified the move toward a comprehensive family policy in Germany in the 1930s and 1940s. Nazi policies, however, were based on very different conceptions of "family" and "citizenship" and left no space for a feminist critique of married women's dependence. After 1945, the massive loss of adult male life led to exaggerated fears of the "surplus of women" (*Frauenüberschuβ*) and population decline and a resurgence of pronatalist rhetoric, despite the fact that gains from post-war immigration into West Germany more than cancelled out war losses. Indeed, between 1939 and 1950 the population of those areas constituting the Federal Republic grew by 7,600,000, an increase of 18.2 percent. Throughout the 1950s, a steady stream from one Germany to the other continued, dammed effectively only in August 1961 with the closing of the East German border.[36] Nonetheless, West German policymakers remained obsessed with declining birthrates, and these fears translated unambiguously into pro-natalist sentiments. To be sure, it was no longer the *Führer* that demanded population growth, but the needs of the economy, and the social security system delivered new justifications for familiar rhetoric.

Connecting economic prosperity to population growth raised difficult questions about where to set the boundaries between state social policy and the "private" sphere. The past of National Socialism made it even more important to provide clear definitions; memories of the Nazis' attempt to invade the family made it essential for the West German state to make explicit how its intentions differed from those of the state that had ruled from 1933 until 1945. Denise Riley, writing of post-war British attempts to define a language of pro-natalism distinct from that of fascist regimes in the interwar period, emphasizes how British policymakers were at pains to prove that "*we* were not Germans."[37] In the 1950s, West Germans had to prove that they were not *those* Germans either.

In the confused categories of totalitarian theory, it was possible to establish an identity as a new sort of Germany by associating National Socialist and Communist family policy, and, by rejecting both, to make claims to be something completely different. West Germans argued that the boundary between private and public was best maintained by harnessing the state in the service of families and protecting women as private, not public, mothers, not by making families into slaves of the state.

The emphasis on the value of women's unpaid labor as wife and mother in post-war West Germany was appropriate to a nation that found itself in the throes of economic reconstruction according to a capitalist blueprint. West Germans proclaimed that what they most needed in the collective project of building anew was hard work. Not politics but productivity would allow them to redeem themselves and to gain distance from the legacy of National Socialism. When the family, not class, was identified as the locus of individual social mobility, when human capital was just as vital to economic prosperity and growth as the capital invested in factories, women too had their work cut out for them. In the late 1940s, the "woman of the rubble" (*Trümmerfrau*) took on enormous significance as the symbol of a Germany clearing away its troubled past; in the 1950s, the work of the German woman became no less significant once she moved from bombed out buildings to protected homes. Her *deutsche Qualitätsarbeit* (German quality work) was now measured in healthy children and the strength of family ties; it was on this basis that she had claims to "social citizenship" in the West German welfare state.

GENDER AND THE SOCIAL CONTRUCTION OF WEST GERMAN DEMOCRACY

The difficulties of "representing difference as a relation of equality,"[38] of defining a language of political citizenship in which women and men can be different and equal, are enormous and by no means uniquely German. Indeed, they have defined discussions of the rights of women in Western Europe and North America since the late eighteenth century. What this chapter argues is that demands for women's equality and rights as citizens and demands for recognition of women's capacities, especially as real or potential wives and mothers, depend on the political rhetorics available in a particular historical context. This chapter has outlined a peculiarly German response to a not peculiarly German problem. In particular, it has emphasized that in the post-war period Cold War anti-Communism and the abandonment of Marxist theory to East Germany eliminated one socialist set of answers to the "woman question," which some within the SPD and KPD had still espoused in Weimar. It has stressed that within the governing CDU/CSU coalition, the Catholic church claimed a privileged voice in all discussions of social and legal policies affecting women and the family. It has illuminated a broad post-war consensus spanning the entire political spectrum that shaped a vision of the welfare state in which class divisions were waning, resilient families were the basis of West German reconstruction, and the reproductive work of wives and mothers was essential to economic prosperity and growth. These contingent elements limited the ways in which post-war West German social policymakers sought to reconcile the tensions between demands for women's equality and demands for an acknowledgement of the fundamental significance of sexual difference.

On this restricted terrain, advocates of women's rights were still able to win some victories. The final form of the revised family law and the Federal Constitutional Court decision of 1959 realized crucial parts of a feminist agenda that had been in place since the Kaiserreich. A political language of families' claims on the state, laid out explicitly in debates over "money-for-children," established categories of entitlement and rights that could be used in the 1960s and 1970s to make additional demands for improvement in this program and for expansion of benefits in other areas, such as subsidies for education and housing.

However, in the political context of the 1950s, the equal rights of husbands and wives were seen to be completely consistent with the explicit relegation of women to an unpaid workplace in the home. Even those most committed to women's equality with men did not dispute that German women were still defined by at least two of the three K's of Weimar and the Third Reich: for Social Democrats and liberal feminists, *Kirche* was rejected, but *Küche* and *Kinder* were still firmly in place. They maintained that accepting these roles should not deny a woman status as a *Kamerad*, as fully equal with men, but they also accepted that for women in a democratic Federal Republic, biology would structure and circumscribe the meaning of political, civil, and social citizenship for women.

Running throughout debates over family law and "money-for-children" was a language of "protection." The constitution guaranteed the "particular protection" of marriages and at least in theory, family allowances "protected" families by diminishing the likelihood that mothers go out to work. The West German experience confirms Carole Pateman's conclusion that "protection is the polite way to refer to subordination."[39] The acknowledgement of difference, defined by narrow conceptions of women's roles as mothers, was ultimately incompatible with equality and full rights of democratic political participation.

The process of redefining "woman's place" in post-war West Germany occurred not only in social policies that expressed how families *should* be, but in the lived experiences of families as they *were*; not only in arid social policy debates, but in movies, magazines, and other forms of popular culture; not only in debates about nuclear families, but in women's organized protests against the threat of nuclear annihilation. This chapter describes only one part of a much larger process. However, it was in debates over the reformulation of the welfare state and the revision of family law that the state pronounced most explicitly its conception of the dimensions of women's citizenship in a democratic order. These debates constituted a crucial arena where women's rights, responsibilities, needs, capacities, and possibilities were discussed, identified, and reinforced.

A growing body of feminist scholarship convincingly illuminates how established conceptions of gender difference influence public policy, and how social policy in turn shapes the objective conditions of women's social and economic status.[40] Yet it is startling to see how many historians, sociologists, and political scientists continue to ignore the ways in which state policy differently defines and delimits the rights and responsibilities of female and male citizens. In these accounts, the welfare state is viewed as a set of institutional arrangements aimed at meeting demands for greater socioeconomic equality in advanced capitalist countries. How these demands are met depends on the relative strength of the working-class movement and national histories of state–society relations. In one account, the welfare state appears as "one of capital's children out of wedlock – unexpected by protagonists and antagonists alike." The analysis of the welfare state is part of the project of "lay[ing] bare the complex processes of the conception and birth of capitalist democracies."[41] It is remarkable that in this and many other treatments, procreation acts only as metaphor; how the welfare state incorporates normative visions of relations between actual women and men receives no attention. For the most part, "social citizenship" remains a generic category, behind which stands a universalized male experience.

An analysis of the post-war West German experience underscores how important it is to recognize the gendered definition of citizenship and the prescriptive models of male–female relationships that are central parts of the social construction of democracy. A look at the West German case suggests that the welfare state – both in its origins and in its post-war form – represented a response not only to the crisis of liberal democracy and the challenge of the organized industrial working class, but also to the perceived crisis of *demography*, and concerns that women's increased involvement in production would interfere with their commitment to reproduction. The links between economic potential and reproduction, women's bodies and national strength, population size and population quality were not the exclusive preserve of the National Socialist warfare state; rather they were central to the formulation of the democratic West German welfare state. Recognizing that the post-war welfare state was constituted as a productive and a reproductive order contributes to understanding the different meanings of "social citizenship" for women and men. It illustrates how democratic state policy can shape and reinforce not just social hierarchies and definitions of political citizenship based on class; the state can also shape and reinforce social hierarchies and definitions of political citizenship based on gender.

One of the goals of this volume is to explore how to expand the possibilities for democratic political participation. This makes it impossible to avoid the relevance of this chapter's analysis of Germany's past for assessing the problems that confront Germany in the present. Historians are wise to leave predictions about the future to others, particularly when the most recent chapters of German history took everyone by surprise and left me hurriedly revising undergraduate lectures on the post-war years that were liberally peppered with ponderous phrases like "the irreversible division of the two Germanies." However, celebratory assessments that the post-war period is finally at an end obscure the extent to which Germans are once again embarking on a process of reconstruction in the wake of a war, though this time no armistice was signed and the conflict was one in which ideology was the dominant weapon. The analysis of the politics of *Frau* and family offered here should remind us that questions of women's status, family structure, the relationship between equality and difference, the limits to women's rights, the extent of women's responsibilities, the possibilities for women's participation in a democratic polity – concerns that loomed large in the post-Second World War II 1950s and circumscribed women's "civil," "political," and "social citizenship" – will be crucial to German self-definition in the post-Cold War 1990s.[42]

NOTES

1.   This article draws on research presented in much greater detail in Robert G. Moeller, *Protecting Motherhood: Women and the Family in the Politics of Postwar West Germany* (Berkeley, 1993). My thanks to Herrick Chapman, Donna Harsch, and Lynn Mally for their critical suggestions that greatly helped me to focus my argument. In what follows, I have attempted to keep references to a minimum.

2. For examples of those who argue that the United States imposed a new order in other areas, see Tilman Fichter and Ute Schmidt, *Der erzwungene Kapitalismus: Klassenkämpfe in den Westzonen 1945–1948* (Berlin, 1971); and Theo Pirker, *Die verordnete Demokratie: Grundlagen und Erscheinungen der Restauration* (Berlin, 1977).
3. T.H. Marshall, "Citizenship and Social Class," in *Sociology at the Crossroads and Other Essays* (London, 1963), 73–4; and the useful critique of Marshall from a feminist perspective in Jane Jenson, "Both Friend and Foe: Women and State Welfare," in Renate Bridenthal, Claudia Koonz, and Susan Stuard, eds., *Becoming Visible: Women in European History*, 2nd edn. (Boston, 1987), 535–56.
4. Joan Scott, "Rewriting History," in Margaret R. Higonnet *et al.*, eds., *Behind the Lines: Gender and the Two World Wars* (New Haven, 1987), 30.
5. See, for example, Theodor Eschenburg, *Jahre der Besatzung, 1945–1949* (Stuttgart, 1983), and Hans-Peter Schwarz, *Die Ära Adenauer: Gründerjahre der Republik, 1949–1957* (Stuttgart, 1981), parts of a massive multi-volume history of the Federal Republic.
6. Gabriele Strecker, *Überleben ist nicht genug: Frauen 1945–1950* (Freiburg im Breisgau, 1981), 53.
7. Ausschuß der Deutschen Statistiker für die Volks- und Berufszählung 1946, *Volks- und Berufszählung vom 29. Oktober 1946 in den vier Besatzungszonen und Gross-Berlin: Volkszählung, Textteil* (Berlin, n.d.), 36–7, 44–5, 58–9; and Adelheid zu Castell, "Die demographischen Konsequenzen des Ersten und Zweiten Weltkrieges für das Deutsche Reich, die Deutsche Demokratische Republik und die Bundesrepublik Deutschland," in Waclaw Długoborski, ed., *Zweiter Weltkrieg und sozialer Wandel: Achsenmächte und besetzte Länder* (Göttingen, 1981), 129, 135.
8. The quotations are from Bernhard Winkelheide, *Verhandlungen des deutschen Bundestags* (hereafter *VDBT*), Deutscher Bundestag, 162. Sitzung, 13 September 1951, 6959; and Winkelheide, "Warum Familienausgleichskassen?" *Soziale Arbeit*, 1, no. 3 (1951): 100.
9. On Nazi policies toward women, see in particular Claudia Koonz, *Mothers in the Fatherland: Women, the Family, and Nazi Politics* (New York, 1987); and Renate Bridenthal, Atina Grossmann, and Marion Kaplan, eds., *When Biology Became Destiny: Women in Weimar and Nazi Germany* (New York, 1984).
10. Indeed, Franz-Josef Wuermeling, Adenauer's Minister for Family Affairs, referred explicitly to social policy as the means to ensure the "freedom of the living space [*Lebensraum*] of the family." See, for example, Wuermeling, "Der Sinn der Familienpolitik," *Bulletin des Presse- und Informationsamtes der Bundesregierung*, no. 211 (9 September 1954): 1911–12; and Moeller, *Protecting Motherhood*, 137–41.
11. Elaine Tyler May, *Homeward Bound: American Families in the Cold War Era* (New York, 1988), 14.
12. Anna Späth, "Vielfältige Forderungen nach Gleichberechtigung und 'nur' ein Ergebnis: Artikel 3 Absatz 2 GG," in Anna-Elisabeth Freier and Annette Kuhn, eds., *"Das Schicksal Deutschlands liegt in der Hand seiner Frauen"* (Düsseldorf, 1984), 122–67.

13. For a summary of the discussion of these issues, see Gerhard Leibhold and Hermann von Mangoldt, eds., *Entstehungsgeschichte der Artikel des Grundgesetzes* (Tübingen, 1951).

14. Elisabeth Selbert, Parlamentarischer Rat, Hauptausschuß, Bonn 1948/49, 42. Sitzung, 18 January 1949, 539–41.

15. In general, see Thilo Ramm, *Familienrecht*, vol.1 (Munich, 1985), 76–94.

16. The arguments over reform of the Civil Code were presented in *VDBT*, Deutscher Bundestag, 239. Sitzung, 27 November 1952, 11052–73; and *VDBT*, Deutscher Bundestag, 258. Sitzung, 26 March 1953, 12514–27.

17. "Frau und Familie," *Gleichheit* 15, no. 11 (1952): 329. This was a repeated theme in the official pronouncements of the party and of its women's organizations.

18. Comments of the CDU's Eduard Wahl, "Protokoll der 68. Sitzung des Unterausschußes 'Familienrechtsgesetz' des Ausschußes für Rechtswesen und Verfassungsrecht am 26. November 1956," 30. And for the debates of these issues, *VDBT*, 2. Deutscher Bundestag, 206. Sitzung, 3 May 1957, 11761–801.

19. *Entscheidungen des Bundesverfassungsgerichts*, vol.10 (Tübingen, 1960), 59–89. And on the history of the Federal Constitutional Court, Donald P. Kommers, *Judicial Politics in West Germany: A Study of the Federal Constitutional Court* (Beverley Hills, 1976).

20. "Niederschrift über die vom Unterausschuß Kinderbeihilfen des Ausschußes für Arbeit und Sozialpolitik des Bundesrates einberufene Konferenz am 21.12.49," Nordrheinwestfälisches Hauptstaatsarchiv, NW42/547.

21. Helmut Schelsky, *Wandlungen der deutschen Familie in der Gegenwart: Darstellung und Deutung einer empirisch-soziologischen Tatbestandsaufnahme*, 4th edn. (Stuttgart, 1960), 13.

22. Helmut Schelsky, "Die Wandlungen der deutschen Familie in der Gegenwart und ihr Einfluß auf die Grundanschauungen der Sozialpolitik," *Sozialer Fortschritt*, 1, no. 12 (1952): 284, 287.

23. Daniel Bell, *The End of Ideology: On the Exhaustion of Political Ideas in the Fifties* (Glencoe, 1960); and Raymond Aron, "The End of Ideology and the Renaissance of Ideas," in *The Industrial Society: Three Essays on Ideology and Development* (New York, 1967), 92–183.

24. *VDBT*, Deutscher Bundestag, 60. Sitzung, 28 April 1950, 2196–206; and *VDBT*, Deutscher Bundestag, 162. Sitzung, 13 September 1951, 6569–78.

25. On this topic, see Young Sun Hong, "The Politics of Welfare Reform and the Dynamics of the Public Sphere: Church, Society, and the State in the Making of the Social-Welfare System in Germany, 1830–1930" (Ph.D. diss., University of Michigan, 1989); and "Femininity as a Vocation: Gender and Class Conflict in the Professionalization of German Social Work," in Geoffrey Cocks and Konrad H. Jarausch, eds., *German Professions, 1800–1950*, (New York, 1990), 232–51.

26. In general, see the insightful, critical analysis of Josef Mooser, *Arbeiterleben in Deutschland 1900–1970: Klassenlagen, Kultur und Politik* (Frankfurt am Main, 1984), 157, 159.

27. Marta Gieselmann, "Gedanken über die Hausarbeit," *Gleichheit*, 15, no. 8 (1952): 244–5.

28. *VDBT*, 2. Deutscher Bundestag, 3. Sitzung, 20 October 1953, 18.

29. In general, see Jutta Akrami-Göhren, "Die Familienpolitik im Rahmen der Sozialpolitik mit besonderer Berücksichtigung der Vorstellungen und der praktischen Tätigkeit der CDU" (Diss., Bonn University, 1974).

30. For a good summary, see Volker Hentschel, *Geschichte der deutschen Sozialpolitik (1880–1980)* (Frankfurt am Main, 1983), 168–72.

31. See the comments of the Labor Minister, Anton Storch, quoted in Werner Abelshauser, *Die langen Fünfziger Jahre* (Düsseldorf, 1987), 141.

32. I borrow the formulation from Carole Pateman, *The Sexual Contract* (Stanford, 1988). See also Monique Wittig, "On the Social Contract," in *The Straight Mind and Other Essays* (New York, 1992), 33–45.

33. Jane Jenson, "Both Friend and Foe," 541–5; the excellent study by Susan Pedersen, Family, Dependence, and the Origins of the Welfare State: Britain and France, 1914–1945 (NewYork, 1993), 357–411, and Karen Offen, "Body Politics: Women, Work and the Politics of Motherhood in France, 1920–1950," in Gisela Bock and Pat Thane, eds., *Maternity and Gender Policies: Women and the Rise of the European Welfare States, 1880s–1950s* (London, 1991), 138–59.

34. See Pedersen, *Family*, 138–223; John Macnicol, *The Movement for Family Allowances, 1919–45: A Study in Social Policy Development* (London, 1980); and Jenson, "Both Friend and Foe."

35. Rita Liljeström, "Sweden," in Sheila B. Kamerman and Alfred J. Kahn, eds., *Family Policy: Government and Families in Fourteen Countries* (New York, 1978), 19–48.

36. Castell, "Die demographischen Konsequenzen," 130; Ulrich Herbert, *Geschichte der Ausländerbeschäftigung in Deutschland 1880 bis 1980: Saisonarbeiter, Zwangsarbeiter, Gastarbeiter* (Berlin, 1986), 180–92; and Wolfgang Köllmann, "Die Bevölkerungsentwicklung der Bundesrepublik," in Werner Conze and M. Rainer Lepsius, eds., *Sozialgeschichte der Bundesrepublik Deutschland* (Stuttgart, 1983), 77–8.

37. Denise Riley, *War in the Nursery: Theories of the Child and Mother* (London, 1983), 159.

38. Sally Alexander, "Women, Class and Sexual Differences in the 1830s and 1840s," *History Workshop*, no. 17 (1984): 146.

39. Carole Pateman, "The Patriarchal Welfare State," in Amy Gutman, ed., *Democracy and the Welfare State* (Princeton, 1988), 238, 254; also Robert G. Moeller, "Protecting Mother's Work: From Production to Reproduction in Postwar West Germany," *Journal of Social History*, 22, no. 3 (1989): 413–37.

40. For good examples of historical studies that build on this theoretical insight, see Linda Gordon, ed., *Women, the State, and Welfare* (Madison, 1990); and Bock and Thane, eds., *Maternity and Gender Policies* (London, 1991).

41. Göran Therborn, "Classes and States: Welfare State Developments 1881–1981," *Studies in Political Economy*, 13 (1984): 7–41, quotation, 7.

42. See, for example, Hanna Behrend, "Women Catapulted into a Different Social Order: Women in East Germany," *Women's History Review*, 1, no.1 (1992): 141–53; and Irene Dölling, "Between Hope and Helplessness: Women in the GDR after the 'Turning Point,'" *Feminist Review*, no. 39 (1991): 3–15.

Part Five
Comparative Perspectives

15 Democracy is a Lake[1]
Charles Tilly

TIME FOR DEMOCRACY

Once theorists thought vibrant, viable democracy emerged from centuries of struggle or maturation. In such formulations as Barrington Moore's, class and politics interacted over hundreds of years to create democracy or its alternatives.[2] Disillusioned by the failure of various revolutionary programs during the previous two decades, bemused by the Cold War's ending, and enticed by the opportunity to prescribe programs of political change for Eastern Europe, Latin America, or Africa, recent theorists of democracy have moved away from the populism and revolutionism of the 1960s toward a remarkable elitism: suppositions that the masses have little to do with the making of democracy, that (however regrettably) presidents, priests, political patrons, planters, police chiefs, paratroop commanders, and plutocrats perform the essential operations producing durable democratic institutions.

Not all the change resulted from disillusion. Impressed by the rapid displacement of authoritarian regimes set in place by Franco, Salazar, or Brazilian generals, and pressed to formulate futures for Eastern Europe, Latin America, and Africa, recent theorists have accelerated the tempo so that at times the transition to democracy looks almost instantaneous: put the pact in gear, and go. After decades of bottom-up, deterministic, long-term theories, we now see top-down models, instrumental and constructivist approaches to democratization, and short-run analyses beginning to prevail. Top-down models specify what rulers and leaders must do to promote democracy, instrumental ideas make democratization seem a matter of social engineering (whoever serves as engineer), constructivist approaches assert that democracy depends on certain kinds of social beliefs, and short-run analyses say how polities move toward democracy today, this month, or this year rather than at a scale of centuries.

Timescale matters both theoretically and practically. Theoretically, democracy's time could resemble that of an oilfield, a cultivated garden, or something in between. An oilfield, the specific product of millennial history, conforms to regularities strong enough that petrogeologists can spot likely untapped deposits or explain how an oil well works. Yet experts cannot produce a new oilfield at will wherever they want. The presence of oilfields depends on long, long conjunctions of circumstances that appear rarely in history, and are little amenable to human manipulation.

Gardens are different. They will not flourish everywhere, but given adequate soil, sun, and precipitation, many different sorts of gardens grow in a variety of environments. As in the cases of oilfields, specialists in gardens are perfectly capable of explaining how they work, indeed of making contingent predictions about what will happen if X or Y happens first.

In both cases, experts know enough to intervene, within clear limits, to produce desired results with considerable probability. They know what aspects they cannot influence. They even know enough to identify a wide range of interventions which, however well meaning, are likely to fail. Differences between the cases do not concern the phenomenon's regularity or intelligibility, but the nature and timescale of the regularities involved, which in turn determine the phenomenon's susceptibility to deliberate promotion. We have no a priori warrant to think of democracy as resembling gardens more than oilfields. If oilfields offer the proper analogy, valid explanations of the presence or absence, waxing and waning, of democracy will combine very long histories with dense accounts of short-term dynamics. In that case, we might well conclude that Barrington Moore tells us how to analyze the foundations of democratization better than recent short-term planners.

Practically, the promotion of oilfield democracy will require the transformation of environments, indeed the creation of whole histories, over centuries or even millennia. Both planned ruling-class intervention and popular collective action will be irrelevant to the success or failure of democratic projects. The cultivation of garden-style democracy, on the other hand, can occur in a wide variety of environments with relative rapidity through many combinations of elite and popular action. If the garden analogy holds, the secret will be to find or create those environments that can support some sort of democracy, then adapt the design and cultivation to the capacities of each environment. Two essential points follow: (1) the validity of various theories and metatheories of democracy depends on the general character and timescale of the phenomenon, which remain highly contested; (2) the validity of theories and metatheories of democracy has profound practical implications. Both points are at issue in the effort to create a sound social history of democracy, constructed or otherwise.

A short timescale typically couples with an instrumental, top-down view of democratization. Distinguishing between "elite ascendant" and "mass ascendant" paths to democracy in Latin America, for example, Terry Karl declares that:

> To date, however, *no* stable political democracy has resulted from regime transitions in which mass actors have gained control, even momentarily, over traditional ruling classes ... Thus far, the most frequently encountered types of transition, and the ones which have most often resulted in the implantation of a political democracy, are "transitions from above."[3]

In a similar vein, Eva Etzioni-Halevy argues that:

> A central historical condition for the emergence of stable Western democracy was the development of the relative autonomy of elites from and within the state. Without it the chances for the stabilization of such democracy – whatever its achievements and drawbacks – would have been greatly diminished, and the chances for democratic breakdown would have been much increased.[4]

From Adam Przeworski we hear that "It seems as if an almost complete docility and patience on the part of organized workers are needed for a democratic transformation to succeed."[5] In place of yesterday's bottom-up histories of democratization, today only top-down views vie for acceptance. In today's context, the massive historical-comparative analysis of Dietrich Rueschemeyer, Evelyne Huber Stephens, and John D. Stephens, with its long timescale and its strong emphasis on working-class contributions to democracy, reads as a startling exception, an obvious holdover from the era of Barrington Moore.[6]

Recent views have an instrumentalist edge, assuming that leaders can engineer democracy, or at least foster conditions for its appearance. Giuseppe Di Palma's characteristically titled *To Craft Democracies*, for a case in point, sometimes refers to "the popular sector" as a party to democratization, but in general presents the crafty creators of democracy as "actors" or "players" in a game more closely resembling chess than rugby. Although it often fails, the creation of democracy becomes work for self-conscious fashioners of collective bargains, not for social classes or armies engaged in battles to the death.[7]

Instrumentalism couples oddly but firmly to the increasingly popular argument that democracy is, or results from, a social construction. The argument has many variants, but in essence claims that the basic operations constituting or creating democracy consist of changes in shared beliefs; from shared beliefs follow the necessary institutions and constitutions. The shift toward social construction then encourages a comforting conclusion: the way to build democracy is to change people's minds about what is politically proper and possible. Everything depends, of course, on how plastic and subject to deliberate alteration such ideas turn out to be. At the extreme, all hope of concerted action disappears in the grip of over-powering, autonomous, slow-moving ideas. Nevertheless in principle the emphasis on social construction complements the top-down, instrumental view of democratization.

People actually *construct* democracy, however, in two different senses of the word. First, they create a set of political arrangements whose effects are democratic, however we define democracy. This sense of "construct" has the misleading connotation of blueprints and carpenters, when over the last few hundred years the actual formation and deforma-tion of democratic regimes has more often resembled the erratic evolu-tion of a whole city than the purposeful building of a single mansion. Still, the first sense draws our attention to the ways that human agency, however consciously, produces and destroys the objective conditions for democracy.

The second sense of "construction" refers to the shared understandings, the culture, that people create for themselves. Extreme versions of linguistic skepticism reduce all social reality to construction in this sense, on an argu-ment that conflates epistemology and ontology: if social existence can only be known through language, it does not exist independently of language. Short of that extreme, however, even hardnosed realists recognize that people do construct shared understandings concerning their political arrangements. Indeed, shared understandings affect how those arrangements work. In the case of democracy, as Robert Dahl points out repeatedly, much depends on the readiness of political actors who lose in the current round of struggle to believe that they will get another reasonably fair chance to win later on. Adam Przeworski makes just such an institutionalization of uncer-tainty the hallmark of democracy.[8] That shared belief is a social product.

More generally, ideas of justice, of due process, of official propriety, of efficiency, of collective interest, of property, of rights, and of history pervade every set of political arrangements, including those of democracy. No system of parliamentary democracy, for example, can survive the gen-eralization of a belief (however false) that its elections are fraudulent and its officials powerless. The real questions are: (1) how such beliefs and their democracy-sustaining antitheses form, wax, or wane: (2) exactly what relation they bear to the political system's operation, routine or otherwise.

In principle, either form of construction – the deliberate creation or the imaginative formulation – could proceed at the timescale of an oilfield, of a garden, or in between. One can imagine with Max Weber that age-old and slowly-changing beliefs shape political institutions as they channel economic enterprise, with the consequence that only some select meta-physical traditions offer – and will ever offer – hospitable ground for democratic institutions. Thus some advocates argue that Islam has a unique affinity for democracy, while others consider Islam to be inher-ently authoritarian. Either view rests on oilfield reasoning. But garden-variety construction also offers a plausible model, as sweeping changes rush across the world transforming beliefs and social relations simultane-ously. In short, an emphasis on the social construction of democracy does not resolve, theoretically or empirically, the choice among timescales for its analysis.

Meanwhile, a historical puzzle arises. Broad-based democracy on a large scale first took shape in Western Europe. In the past, durable democ-ratic institutions emerged out of repeated, long-term struggles in which workers, peasants, and other ordinary people were much involved, even where the crucial maneuvers involved an elite's conspiring in small con-cessions to avoid large ones. Revolutions, rebellions, and mass mobiliza-tions made a significant difference to the extent of democracy in one country or another. Yet current theories of democratization give little place to popular collective action, emphasize instrumental maneuvers and bargains among elites, stress promulgated beliefs, and stage the critical political changes in the short run. Is the history revealed to us by Barrington Moore, Reinhard Bendix, or Stein Rokkan an illusion? Or have the conditions promoting democracy changed fundamentally?

TO CONCEPTUALIZE DEMOCRACIES

Before examining that question, let us do some conceptual construction. In order to get to democracy, we must work our way down a chain including state, polity, rights, and citizenship. Here is the chain:

State: an organization controlling the principal concentrated means of coercion within a delimited territory and exercising priority in some respects over all other organizations within the same territory.

Polity: the set of relations among agents of the state and all major polit-ical actors within the delimited territory.

Rights: enforceable claims, the reciprocal of *obligations*.

Citizenship: rights and mutual obligations binding state agents and a category of persons defined exclusively by their legal attachment to the same state.

With that conceptual chain in place, we can begin hauling up an idea of democracy as a particular form of citizenship. Democracy combines *broad and relatively equal citizenship with (a) binding consultation of citizens in regard to state personnel and policies as well as (b) protection of citizens from arbitrary state action.*

This definition stands between those emphasizing ideal outcomes and those stipulating institutional arrangements. Robert Dahl speaks of "a political system in which the members regard one another as political equals, are collectively sovereign, and possess all the capacities, resources, and institutions they need in order to govern themselves."[9] As Dahl himself stresses, such a definition is not only problematic in detail (do children, convicts, and students from other countries, for instance, all qualify as "members"?) but also empirically empty (no large state has ever met its requirements). Yet it states a standard against which we can array real political arrangements.

Rueschemeyer, Stephens, and Stephens, on the other hand, offer an eminently institutional definition of democracy:

> It entails, first, regular, free and fair elections of representatives with universal and equal suffrage, second, responsibility of the state apparatus to the elected parliament (possibly complemented by direct election of the head of the executive), and third, the freedoms of expression and association as well as the protection of individual rights against arbitrary state action.[10]

For some questions (for example, what political arrangements are worth sacrificing for?) the ideal definition serves best, while for others (for example, what sort of government should we now organize in our new country?) the institutional definition makes much more sense. My definition lies between the two.

An intermediate definition, on the one hand, makes problematic the relationship between institutions and their consequences or correlates, whereas it facilitates, on the other hand, the linking of theories of democratization with theories of nationalism, citizenship, revolution, political conflict, and change in state structure. I claim that different institutional arrangements – town meetings in some settings, secret ballots for party-nominated candidates in others, and so on – promote democracy within different sorts of social structure, hence that strictly institutional criteria of democracy yield misleading conclusions on a large scale. To repeat, democracy consists of *broad and relatively equal citizenship with (a) binding consultation of citizens in regard to state personnel and policies as well as (b) protection of citizens from arbitrary state action.*

Notice what this conception does *not* do. It does not make general equality of means or opportunity a criterion of democracy; equality only refers to claims on and from the state in a person's capacity as citizen. As much as it invites a search for institutions guaranteeing democratic outcomes, it does not stipulate any particular political institutions as defining features of democracy. It ignores the unequal treatment of non-citizens, disregarding any disabilities they suffer with respect to binding consultation and protection from arbitrary state action. It certainly does not require intelligent communication, patriotism, legitimacy, happiness, or prosperity. It leaves theoretically and empirically open the relationship of democracy to general economic equality, care for non-citizens, social justice, communication, and innumerable other features that people sometimes consider inseparable from democracy. It excludes many connotations of the word "democracy" on the ground that including them all would bar any effective theoretical or empirical investigation of the subject.

The proposed conception of democracy *does*, on the other hand, declare that a polity is undemocratic to the degree that citizens' political rights and obligations vary by gender, race, religion, national origin, wealth, or any other general set of categories, that it is likewise undemocratic to the extent that large numbers of people subject to the state's jurisdiction lack access to citizenship. It makes binding consultation and protection from arbitrary state action, furthermore, matters of degree – recognizing, for example, that in large democratic states the sheer existence of parliaments limits consultation and state agents sometimes commit injustices. Even breadth and equality, after all, have their limits; when Paul Peterson proposes "that all citizens, even our youngest, should cast votes or have their votes cast for them by their parents or guardians," even he must concede that the infants his proposal would enfranchise generally lack the reasoned political self-interest his argument requires; hence the extra votes his scheme entrusts to parents and guardians.[11] The definition, in short, simply allows us to designate polities as democratic *in so far* as they embody broad, equal citizenship which gives its beneficiaries binding consultation and protection from arbitrary state action.

Figure 15.1 represents the basic idea. The four criteria – equality, breadth, consultation, and protection – form continua from none (0) to complete (1). All real polities lie somewhere between. For conceptual clarification, nevertheless, we can conveniently split each of the four dimensions into Yes (1) and No (0). That step allows us to diagram competing forms of political organization in the same terms, as in Figure 15.2. There, patrimonialism appears as 0000: narrow, unequal citizenship with little or no consultation and protection. Oligarchy (0010) likewise entails narrow, unequal citizen-

Figure 15.1 Components of Democracy

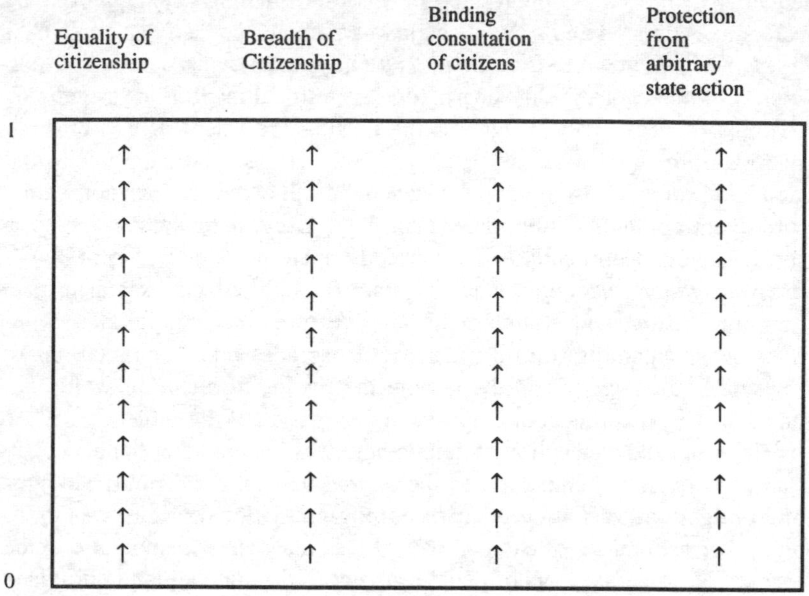

	Equality of citizenship	Breadth of Citizenship	Binding consultation of citizens	Protection from arbitrary state action
1	↑	↑	↑	↑
	↑	↑	↑	↑
	↑	↑	↑	↑
	↑	↑	↑	↑
	↑	↑	↑	↑
	↑	↑	↑	↑
	↑	↑	↑	↑
	↑	↑	↑	↑
	↑	↑	↑	↑
	↑	↑	↑	↑
	↑	↑	↑	↑
0	↑	↑	↑	↑

ship and little protection of citizens from arbitrary state action, but involves binding consultation of the small number who possess citizenship.

Dictatorship (1100) looks much different: equal, broad citizenship but little or no consultation and protection. Democracy comes out, then, as 1111, high on all four criteria. Aristotle's idea concerning the devolution of genuine political forms into perverted forms reads, in his terms, as:

Kingship → Tyranny: 0001→ 0000

Aristocracy → Oligarchy: 0011→ 0010

Polity → Democracy: 1111→ 1110

My representation of the transition polity → democracy displays the limits of a dichotomous formulation, since Aristotle actually argued that something like 0.25, 0.25, 1, 1 (many substantial citizens ruling collectively in rough equality on behalf of the entire population – i.e., polity) ran the risk of degenerating into rule by the poor in their own interest (Aristotle's conception of democracy), which might then read 0.75, 1.0, 1.0, 0. In each case, nevertheless, Aristotle sees a danger in any faction's, including a faction of

Figure 15.2 Contrasting political arrangements

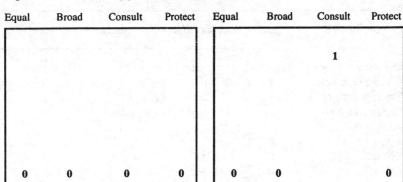

Patrimonialism

Oligarchy

Dictatorship

Democracy

the poor, mistaking its own interest for the population's general interest. Mass society theorists have gone a step beyond Aristotle in fearing that:

$$1111 \rightarrow 1110 \rightarrow 1100 \rightarrow 0000$$

Here extensive democracy degenerates into a corrupt form without protections, which devolves into a dictatorship over equally powerless citizens, a move that eventually eradicates citizenship itself in favor of subjection to a tyrant.

Table 15.1. Pure types of polity

Configuration	Equality	Breadth	Consult	Protect
Democracy	1	1	1	1
Corrupt democracy	1	1	1	0
Tutelary democracy	1	1	0	1
Dictatorship	1	1	0	0
Patriciate	1	0	1	1
Corporatism	0	1	1	1
Oligarchy	0	0	1	0
Paternalism	0	0	0	1
Patrimonialism	0	0	0	0

Table 15.1 generalizes the conceptualization by identifying a number of other types among the sixteen possible permutations of the four elements. (With values intermediate between 0 and 1 or with fluctuations in values between 0 and 1, we could produce still more types to our hearts' content.) A *patriciate* (1011), for example, looks a lot like a democracy, except that it adopts a narrow definition of citizenship. A *tutelary democracy* (1101) combines broad, relatively equal citizenship with substantial protections but has little binding consultation of citizens; state agents proceed quite autonomously. One might dispute my labels, but the main point remains: even in a simple dichotomous form, the four variables do a fairly effective job of distinguishing major types of polities, and of placing democracy among them.

Missing patterns also deserve notice. So far as I can tell, combinations 1001, 1010, 1000, 0110, 0101, 0100, and 0011 are either evanescent or nonexistent. Contrary to mass society theorists and many conservatives, the pattern suggests that 10XX (narrow but equal) and 01XX (broad but unequal) have inherent instabilities. If so, the explanation is probably simple: inequality and narrow citizenship reinforce each other through a process of coalition and exclusion. The movement of the Venetian Republic from a partial democracy of merchants to an oligarchy (1011 → 0010) through the narrowing of its already unequal citizenship and the reduction of protections for lesser citizens against arbitrary state action illustrates the transformation.

Despite the apparent existence of unstable types and empty cells, the wide variety of types that *have* existed raises doubts about any proposition that democracy appears and disappears as an interdependent package. Protection for citizens from arbitrary state action, for example, is compatible with broad and narrow definitions of citizenship, just as binding consultation of citizens combines with both equal and unequal definitions. Although it is conceivable that transitions among types follow some regular sequence (for example, that patriciates commonly precede full democracies, with the broadening of citizenship the last feature of democracy to arrive), each of the four elements very likely has a partly separate set of causes, sustaining conditions, and political consequences.

Let us distinguish tautologically necessary conditions for democracy from contingent conditions that may produce or sustain it. My proposed definition requires two interlocked conditions: a substantial state and citizenship relating people to that state. Citizenship has no substantial meaning in the absence of a relatively powerful and centralized state. It follows – likewise tautologically, but still usefully – that the forms of the state and of citizenship that have grown up in a given region or era prior to the formation of democratic institutions strongly affect the day-to-day operation of democracy. We can expect democratization and democracy to proceed differently as a function of variation in the prior trajectories of states and citizenship.

In European experience, at least, citizenship in the sense of rights and mutual obligations binding state agents and a category of persons defined by their legal attachment to the same state only became a widespread phenomenon during the nineteenth century. Before then, small units such as the city-states of the Low Countries, the Rhineland, and Italy had sometimes sustained patriciates of the rich and powerful; with respect to the state, these narrow segments of the total population had enjoyed relative equality, binding consultation, and protection from arbitrary action. But large states all ruled indirectly until the eighteenth or nineteenth century; they relied for troops, revenues, and compliance with state directives chiefly on regional powerholders who maintained substantial autonomy and dealt with populations having distinctive traditions, cultures, and rights.

In these circumstances, neither citizenship nor democracy existed at a national scale in any strong sense of the words. At most, nobles and priests constituted a semi-citizenry in countries such as England (but not Great Britain or, even less, the British Isles) where a skeletal administrative structure and a unitary state church intertwined. The greatest exception appeared in Sweden, where the articulation of a domestically recruited army, a state church, and direct peasant representation *vis-à-vis* the crown produced quasi-citizenship as early as the seventeenth century.[12] Given its great inequality and its limits to binding consultation, however, Sweden's polity remained far from democracy until the twentieth century. Extensive democracy awaited strong pressure from organized workers allied with fragments of the bourgeoisie and the popular movements that proliferated during the nineteenth century.[13]

For centuries, to be sure, many Europeans had exercised something like citizenship and even democracy in smaller units such as villages and municipalities. There, heads of propertied households commonly governed collectively or at least shared power with priests and nobles; they frequently led burgher militias as well. In very small states, the government of the capital city thereby established a narrow quasi-citizenship at a national scale. With its cantonal structure, Switzerland federated a set of partial democracies in this style beginning with the sixteenth century.[14] In such countries as the Dutch Republic, eighteenth-century revolutionary movements commonly took that municipal experience as a model for political transformation.[15]

After the middle of the eighteenth century, and especially during the nineteenth, the abandonment of intermittent mercenary armies in favor of large standing armies drawn from, and supported by, national populations engaged rulers in vast struggles with their reluctant subjects. The settlements of those struggles, in their turn, created the rudiments of citizenship. In large states, the French Revolution and the wars of 1792–1815 marked the crucial break. The revolutionary and conquering French provided both a model of citizenship, a stimulus to military mobilization, and – in their areas of conquest – a compulsion to reorganize on the French model. Thus citizenship went from being rare and chiefly local in Europe to being a predominant model of political organization.

With citizenship, limited democracy did not by any means become a necessity; plenty of European states developed political arrangements more closely approximating oligarchy or paternalism with some trappings of representation. Democracy did, however, become an option and a persistent program for reformers and revolutionaries. All over Europe, they began to demand equal, broad citizenship with binding consultation and protection for citizens from arbitrary state action. They began to demand democracy. Some even had their way.

European experience suggests strong hypotheses concerning the social bases of democracy's components:

(1) *Protection from arbitrary state action* depends on (a) subordination of the military to civilian control, (b) class coalitions in which old powerholders ally with relatively powerless but large segments of the population (for example, bourgeois and workers), thus extending old privileges and protections.

(2) *Binding consultation* depends on (a) subordination of the military to civilian control, (b) extensive domestic taxation (as opposed, for example, to state revenues drawn directly from exports), (c) representation with respect to the assessment and collection of taxes.

(3) *Equal citizenship* depends on (a) broad class coalitions including powerholders, (b) creation and expansion of electoral systems.

(4) *Broad citizenship* depends on (a) extensive domestic taxation, (b) broad class coalitions, (c) direct recruitment of large military services from the domestic population.

We might reasonably hypothesize that the relative strength of these factors prior to democratization also affects the kind of democracy that emerges, for example that systems growing up chiefly through subordination of the military via defeat in war, military occupation, or some other cause will emphasize protection and breadth more than equality or binding consultation, while domestic taxation alone will promote binding consultation and breadth of citizenship while leaving equality and protection more uncertain. As Hanspeter Kriesi has pointed out, democracy operates quite differently in Switzerland and the Netherlands as a result of the contrast between Switzerland's federal coalescence and the transformation of the Dutch state under French conquest in the 1790s. The Dutch creation of a centralized bureaucracy and a subordinated military promoted a greater emphasis on breadth and equality of citizenship, which in turn led to the incorporation of the population's competing segments by means of "pillarization" in parallel organizations rather than the creation of multiple local niches for different kinds of politics. The Swiss system operates quite differently, tolerating considerable inequality among geographically segregated niches.[16]

DEMOCRACY AND CITIZENSHIP IN GREAT BRITAIN

The unlikely case of Great Britain illustrates the ties among democratization, citizenship, and changes in the state. The British case seems unlikely because analysts have so regularly pigeonholed Britain as an example of political transformation in the absence of a strong state. John Brewer has demolished that conception of British political history during the eighteenth century, but his stopping around 1780 has left unclear how much the war-led growth he describes accelerated during the great wars with France after 1792.[17] In fact, the creation of large military forces, their supply with men, goods, and services, the repression of domestic dissidence, and expansion of the fiscal system wrought great changes in British government between 1790 and 1815: not only a large net increase in military forces and government expenditures despite the demobilization of 1815–1816 and a remarkable tightening of the central bureaucracy, but also a dramatic shift of political power from the king, his clients, and other great patrons toward parliament.[18] Under Pitt the Younger, Grenville, Portland, Perceval, and Liverpool, the state swelled in importance, and parliament grew within it like a goiter.

This process of expansion had enormous importance for citizenship. Remember that by "citizenship" we still mean rights and mutual obligations binding state agents and a category of persons defined exclusively by their legal attachment to the same state. Between 1750 and 1815 such rights and obligations multiplied as a result of the state's pursuit of war. War had its most visible effects in the realms of taxation and military service. Total taxes collected rose from about £17 million in 1790 to almost £80 million in 1815, a 371 percent increase during a period when the cost of living was rising by about 45 percent; war-driven taxes reached an extraordinary height: about 35 percent of Britain's total commodity output.[19]

Military service, including civil defense, likewise expanded enormously in scope. As Linda Colley sums up:

> In Great Britain, as in other major European powers, it was training in arms under the auspices of the state that was the most common collective working-class experience in the late eighteenth and nineteenth centuries, not labour in a factory, or membership of a radical political organization or an illegal trade union.[20]

Through the increasingly visible presence of the tax collector, the recruiting sergeant, the militia commander, and the member of parliament, ordinary British people acquired much more extensive direct contact with the state than they had experienced since the revolutionary period of 1640–1660. This time it lasted.

From multiplied encounters with agents of the state, Britons acquired a growing sense of Britishness, which did not keep many of them from attacking press gangs, evading tax collectors, or joining radical movements; on the contrary, the nationalization of daily life and consciousness nationalized British struggles and resistance to authorities as well. In the process, direct obligations between subjects and state gained enough scope and intensity to merit the name citizenship. As a revolution and a vast military mobilization were creating French citizens across the Channel, reaction to them were creating British citizens in England, Scotland, and Wales.

What of democracy? As of 1750, we can plausibly describe Great Britain as a 0001, a paternalistic polity involving narrow, unequal citizenship and only partial binding consultation of those aristocrats and gentry who enjoyed something like citizens' privileges, but substantial protections from arbitrary state action for them. The narrowness of citizenship did not reside so much in the small parliamentary electorate as in the mediation of most Britons' relations with the state through local and regional notables such as the Justices of the Peace, who enjoyed great autonomy in their exercise of state-authorized positions.

By 1835, Great Britain had moved closer to 1001 or even 1011, as a broader but arguably more unequal citizenry enjoyed extensive rights to assemble, associate, and communicate their grievances directly to the state, although the exclusion of the population's vast majority from the suffrage made binding consultation questionable. The Reform Act of 1832 had not greatly expanded the electorate, despite shifting the basis of representation from chartered privilege to population and wealth. But contention of the previous 75 years had significantly enlarged citizenship by establishing numerous channels, including mass associations, election campaigns, and public assemblies, through which even non-voters exercised strong collective claims to be heard directly by agents of the state. The working-class Chartist program of 1838–1848 demanded an extension of democracy by means of equalization: universal suffrage, secret ballot, annual elections, salaried members of parliament, no property qualification for members, and equal electoral districts – a call for 1111 (with the unstated presumption that British subjects already enjoyed a measure of protection from arbitrary state action). The movement collapsed in 1848, but its program gradually passed into law through the acts of 1867–1868, 1885, 1918, and auxiliary legislation. Through struggle from inside and outside the polity, the breadth and equality of citizenship increased as popular consultation – chiefly in the form of periodic elections – became more binding and protections extended as well.

Military mobilizations continued to inflate the state and extend the range of citizenship during the twentieth century.[21] By the enactment of female suffrage in 1918, Great Britain edged into the category of 1111 (in a more differentiated scale, perhaps 0.75, 0.80, 0.60, 0.75), by no means a "full" democracy, but nonetheless unusually democratic among the states of its time.[22] Thereafter, the chief alterations in citizenship consisted of openings to residents of former colonies and extensions of the state services or payments to which citizens had a right. If we included Ireland or British overseas colonies in the evaluation of democracy, to be sure, Britain's democracy scores would all plummet. Still that makes the point: even in the days of the British Empire and the United Kingdom of Great Britain and Ireland (roughly 1800–1945), the polity commanding Wales,

Scotland, and England remained somewhat distinct from the rest, and within its own confines significantly more democratic than them.

In a telling simplification, T.H. Marshall described the whole process of democratization as a movement from civic to political to social rights.[23] Marshall's formulation misleads us in two important ways: by substituting a neat succession for a tangled intertwining of civic, political, and social rights, and by erasing many curtailments of rights, for example the massive repression of 1795–1799 and the defeat of Chartism in the 1840s. Nevertheless, Marshall's scheme rightly calls attention to the alternation among relative emphases on the breadth of citizenship, its equality, its protections against arbitrary state action, and control of citizens over state personnel and policy. British history of the last two centuries illustrates the truism that changes in the character of the state and of citizenship entail alterations in the extent and character of democracy.

Once we recognize the importance of military activity to the British state's transformation, British history takes on a delightful irony. In the world as a whole, autonomous militaries generally inhibit democracy, even when they seize power in the name of democratic programs. They regularly inhibit democracy by diminishing the protections of citizens against arbitrary state action, and often by blocking the definitiveness of popular consultation – annulling or falsifying elections, bypassing or intimidating parliaments, evading public surveillance of their activities. Yet in Britain militarization of the state indirectly fostered democratization. It did so through the struggle and bargaining it generated, which fortified citizenship and subordinated military activity to parliamentary control.

The process began in the sixteenth century with Tudor checking of great lords' private armies and fortified castles. It ended, for practical purposes, in the nineteenth century with the elimination of press gangs. An aristocratically led military continued to draw a major share of the state budget, retained great freedom of action in Ireland and the colonies, and enjoyed great prestige at home, yet as such never wielded autonomous power in domestic politics after 1660. The reliance of the British military on parliament for finance and supply – still an acute issue in the struggles that led up to the revolution of 1640 – eventually subordinated the army and navy to civilian, parliamentary control. In retrospect, we can see the crucial importance of that subordination to the later creation of British democracy.

Parallel processes produced military subordination, and thereby promoted democracy, elsewhere in Europe. Where they had less force, as in Iberia and the Balkans, autonomous militaries posed barriers against democracy into the twentieth century. In Iberia, the weakening of the monarchy through Napoleon's conquest and the subsequent resurgence of military leaders in the peninsula's reconquest facilitated military intervention throughout the nineteenth century, while in the Balkans both the casting off of Ottoman control and the promotion of local military resistance to the Ottomans by neighboring powers such as the Russian empire similarly fortified the long-term involvement of militaries in politics. *Per contra*, Iberian and Balkan experiences underline the crucial importance of military subordination to democracy.

DEMOCRACY RESEMBLES A LAKE

The exploration of tautologically necessary conditions for democracy – states and citizens – clears the way for thinking about contingent causes and concomitants of democracy. No one has so far succeeded in separating common correlates of democratic arrangements from non-tautologically necessary, sufficient, or contingently causal conditions. The task is difficult for three main reasons: *first* because the crucial relationships are almost certainly multiple and complex; *second* because democracy-promoting and democracy-sustaining conditions have most likely varied and changed from one historical setting to another; *third* because the presence of compelling historical models such as Great Britain or Switzerland makes it so tempting to pack the whole of British or Swiss history, culture, and social organization into our theories of democracy, on the true but misleading ground that history, culture, and social organization all mark the ways those democratic systems work.

The problem resists solution because democracy does not resemble an oilfield or a garden, but a lake. A lake – a large inland body of water – can come into being because a mountain stream feeds into a naturally existing basin, because someone or something dams up the outlet of a large river, because a glacier melts, because an earthquake isolates a segment of the ocean from the main body of water, because people deliberately dig an enormous hole and channel nearby watersheds into it, or for a number of other reasons. Once it exists, nevertheless, a lake nurtures characteristic ecosystems and maintains characteristic relations with its surroundings, so much so that limnologists have built a scientific specialty around the study of those regularities. Democracy behaves like a lake: although it has distinguishing properties and a logic of its own, it forms in a variety of ways, each of which retains traces of its singular history in the details of its current operation.

Quick! Let's abandon the simile before it drowns us! Here is the point: we have absolutely no a priori reason to believe that only one set of circumstances produces and sustains democracy, even if during the last few hundred years' experience particular circumstances have often nurtured democracy. The most we can reasonably hope to get from scrutinizing historical cases of democratization is a map of alternative paths by which the process has occurred, an indication of sufficient – not necessary – conditions for that transformation, and a specification of general mechanisms that play a part in producing or sustaining democratic institutions when they form.

From their outstanding comparative study of democratization within four sets of states (Western and Central Europe, British settler states, mainland Latin America and Central America/Caribbean), Rueschemeyer, Stephens, and Stephens draw important conclusions. They confirm Barrington Moore's assertion that the political power of labor-controlling landlords inhibited democratization while denying Moore's association of democratization with a politically strong bourgeoisie. Instead, they show, workers allied with others (who were often bourgeois) and pushed much more reliably for democracy, sometimes over the resistance of bourgeois who preferred more limited forms of political participation.

Rueschemeyer *et al.* conclude that in general capitalism does, as often alleged, promote democracy, but not because capitalists prefer democratic government; all other things equal and enemies such as landlords absent, capitalists prefer something like oligarchies of wealth: 0010, not 1111. Such oligarchies allow them to use state power to control workers. But capitalism generates both working classes and the conditions under which they are likely to mobilize; working classes then press for enlargements of citizens' rights and full inclusion of workers among citizens. Given powerful allies, they often succeed. Rueschemeyer and colleagues do not quite recognize their argument's implication: not capitalism itself, but proletarianization constitutes the crucial conditions for democratization. To the extent that proletarianization occurs by non-capitalist means, all other things equal, it still promotes democratization. The relatively non-capitalist proletarianization that occurred in Russia with and after the abolition of serfdom (1861), for example, created strong pressures toward democratic enlargements of rights between then and 1917.[24]

Rueschemeyer *et al.* also understate the importance of their most powerful finding: armed men who exercise autonomous state power inhibit democracy. The finding connects closely with the inhibitory power of landed classes. For so long as great landlords command large numbers of peasants and serfs, they provide an alternative source of military manpower. Where landlords supply and command military units directly, they retain great political power. As my précis of British history suggests, one of the more surprising and crucial effects of expanding capitalism was that it allowed prosperous states to buy off their militaries, supplying and paying them well but subordinating them to tax-authorizing parliaments and civilian bureaucracies. Stirred by fears of armed workers, those states also disarmed the civilian population and created demilitarized police forces specializing in control of civilians. The result was to reduce the chances for any armed group to wrest power, locally or nationally, from civilian hands. Even in poor agrarian states such as Costa Rica, reduction of the autonomous power of military men has facilitated democratization.

More so than the other factors to which they draw attention, military power and autonomy depend on the polity's transnational connections: whether it includes powerful agrarian actors depending on labor-repressive export agriculture, whether foreign powers arm the state, whether foreign capital forwards the repression of workers. (This set of observations links to the contemporary propensity for militarization of states receiving protection from great powers and/or exporting valuable commodities, notably oil, whose revenues state agents control.)[25] Yet the domestic history of military activity likewise matters; in the age of mass military service, victorious wars strengthened ruling coalitions, while lost wars shook the grip of rulers. Lost wars therefore created openings to democracy in authoritarian systems, openings to authoritarianism in democratic systems.

As my tale of Great Britain suggests, Rueschemeyer *et al.* find that mass military mobilization empowers the classes supplying the bulk of military manpower, both in Europe and elsewhere:

> In the United States, soldiers' demands for suffrage rights at the time of the wars against Britain accelerated the broadening of suffrage. Over one hundred years later, the presence of black soldiers in the armed forces during World War II and afterward contributed to the movement which eventually resulted in the extension of suffrage to southern blacks. In Canada, the mass mobilization for World War I was critically implicated in the institution of universal suffrage there. In nineteenth century Latin America, on the other hand, repeated involvement in wars led to a build-up of the military and increased the political weight of the military.[26]

The formula does not run, then: war, hence democracy. If it did, every state in bellicose Europe would have democratized by the sixteenth or seventeenth century. Instead, the path runs something like this:

mass mobilization under the state's direct auspices
↓   ↓
civilian bureaucracy   bargaining with supplying populations
↓   ↓
containment of military   concession of rights & citizenship
↓   ↓
openings for democracy

The existence of openings does not guarantee passage through them. As Rueschemeyer *et al.* argue, in the absence of favorable class configurations such as an effective worker–bourgeois coalition, the path of mass militarization easily leads to authoritarian repression of the populace.

In any case, the militaristic itinerary constitutes only one road to democracy. Others pass through the federation of small-scale democracies, the defeat or self-destruction of authoritarian regimes, and the imposition of constitutions by outside powers. These alternatives define distinct processes that have, in their times and places, encouraged the formation of polities that afforded binding consultation and protection from arbitrary state action to relatively broad and equal citizenries. Each historic journey left its mark on the travelers: Swiss, Canadian, and Japanese democracies operate in quite different ways. In most of them, contrary to recent theorizing, bottom-up action, unintended consequences, and long-term transformations play a fundamental part. But in all of them, social construction matters greatly.

How, then, does social construction matter? It matters through its impact on shared understandings, as often tacit as publicly acknowledged. It matters because all four components of democracy – equality, breadth, consultation, and protection – concern the past and present less than the future. They concern expectations: that agents of the state will in the future honor the relatively equal rights of a broad citizenry, that they will yield to citizens' collective decisions, that they will protect citizens from arbitrary state action. Of course past and present performance in these regards provides much of the evidence from which citizens project these futures. But the secret of democracy lies in the expectation that one's day will come, that today's loss is only a temporary setback, that everyone eventually gets a chance.

Even in a smoothly operating democracy, a lost war, a deep depression, the formation of an authoritarian mass movement, economic dependency on an outside power, or the acquisition of autonomy by military forces sometimes undermines that expectation rapidly, as the experiences of Italy and Germany after the First World War illustrate vividly. Expectations, however much based on realistic observation, depend heavily on social construction, and remain subject to social deconstruction. That is why democracy, once formed, does not stay in place forever. That is why sites of democracy always display the sign 'UNDER CONSTRUCTION.'

NOTES

1. An earlier version of this chapter circulated as "Of Oilfields, Lakes, and Democracy," Working Paper 152, Center for Studies of Social Change, New School for Social Research, November 1992. I am grateful to Viviane Brachet, Marshall Johnson, Ariel Salzmann, Kumru Toktamis, Pavel Tychtl, and Viviana Zelizer for criticism and encouragement, and to the National Science Foundation for support of the research concerning Great Britain on which the chapter draws.

2. Barrington Moore, Jr., *Social Origins of Dictatorship and Democracy* (Boston, 1966).

3. Terry Lynn Karl, "Dilemmas of Democratization in Latin America," *Comparative Politics*, 23 (1990): 1–21.

4. Eva Etzioni-Halevy, "Democratic-Elite Theory. Stabilization versus Breakdown of Democracy," *Archives européennes de sociologie*, 31 (1990): 317–50.

5. Adam Przeworski, "Some Problems in the Study of the Transition to Democracy," in Guillermo O'Donnell, Philippe C. Schmitter and Laurence Whitehead, eds., *Transitions from Authoritarian Rule. Comparative Perspectives* (Baltimore, 1986), 63.

6. Dietrich Rueschemeyer, Evelyne Huber Stephens, and John D. Stephens, *Capitalist Development and Democracy* (Chicago, 1992).

7. Giuseppe Di Palma, *To Craft Democracies. An Essay on Democratic Transitions* (Berkeley, 1990).

8. Przeworski, "Some Problems"; Robert A. Dahl, *Polyarchy. Participation and Opposition* (New Haven, 1971), and *Democracy and its Critics* (New Haven, 1989).

9. Dahl, *Democracy and its Critics*, 1.

10. Rueschemeyer, Stephens, and Stephens, *Capitalist Development and Democracy*, 43.

11. Paul E. Peterson, "An Immodest Proposal," *Daedalus*, 121, no. 4 (1992): 151–74.

12. See Gunnar Artéus, Ulf Olsson and Kerstin Stromberg-Back, "The Influence of the Armed Forces on the Transformation of Society in Sweden, 1600–1945," *Kungl. Krigsvetenskaps akademius Bihafte – Militarhistorisk Tidskrift* (1981): 133–44; Klaus-Richard Böhme, "Schwedische Finanzbürokratie und Kriegsführung 1611 bis 1721," in Goran Rystad, ed., *Europe and Scandinavia: Aspects of the Process of Integration in the 17th Century* (Lund, 1983); Jan Lindegren, "The Swedish "Military State",

1560–1720," *Scandinavian Journal of History*, 10 (1985): 305–36; Sven A. Nilsson, "Imperial Sweden: Nation-Building, War and Social Change," in Sven A. Nilsson *et al.*, *The Age of New Sweden* (Stockholm, 1988).

13. Matti Alestalo and Stein Kuhnle, "The Scandinavian Route. Economic, Social and Political Developments in Denmark, Finland, Norway, and Sweden," Research Report no. 31, Research Group for Comparative Sociology, University of Helsinki, 1984; Helga Hernes, "Scandinavian Citizenship," *Acta Sociologica*, 31 (1988): 199–215; Sven Lundqvist, *Folkrörelserna i det svenska samhället, 1850–1920* (Stockholm, 1977); Bo Öhngren, *Folk i rörelse. Samhällsutveckling, flyttningsmonster och folkrörelser i Eskilstuna 1870–1900* (Uppsala, 1974. Studia Historica Upsaliensia, 55).

14. Thomas A. Brady, *Turning Swiss. Cities and Empire, 1450–1550*. Cambridge, 1985).

15. Maarten Prak, "Citizen Radicalism and Democracy in the Dutch Republic: The Patriot Movement of the 1780s," *Theory and Society*, 20 (1991): 73–102; Wayne Te Brake, *Regents and Rebels: The Revolutionary World of the 18th Century Dutch City* (Oxford, 1989), and "How Much in How Little? Dutch Revolution in Comparative Perspective," *Tijdschrift voor Sociale Geschiedenis*, 16 (1990): 349–63.

16. Hanspeter Kriesi, "Federalism and Pillarization: the Netherlands and Switzerland Compared," *Acta Politica*, 25 (1990): 433–50.

17. John Brewer, *The Sinews of Power. War, Money and the English State, 1688–1783* (New York, 1989).

18. Norman Chester, *The English Administrative System, 1780–1870* (Oxford, 1981); Eric J. Evans, *The Forging of the Modern State. Early Industrial Britain, 1783–1870* (London, 1983); Michael Mann, *States, War and Capitalism* (Oxford, 1988); Peter Mathias and Patrick O'Brien, "Taxation in Britain and France, 1715–1810. A Comparison of the Social and Economic Incidence of Taxes Collected for the Central Governments," *Journal of European Economic History*, 5 (1976): 601–50; Patrick K. O'Brien, "Power With Profit: The State and the Economy, 1688–1815," inaugural lecture, University of London, 1991.

19. Mathias and O'Brien, "Taxation in Britain and France"; Patrick K. O'Brien, "The Political Economy of British Taxation, 1660–1815," *Economic History Review* 41 (1988): 1–32, and "The Impact of the Revolutionary and Napoleonic Wars, 1793–1815, on the Long-run Growth of the British Economy," *Review*, 12 (1989): 335–95; Peter H. Lindert and Jeffrey G. Williamson, "English Workers' Living Standards during the Industrial Revolution: A New Look," *Economic History Review*, 2nd series, 36 (1983): 1–25.

20. Linda Colley, *Britons. Forging the Nation 1707–1837* (New Haven, 1992).

21. James E. Cronin, *The Politics of State Expansion. War, State and Society in Twentieth-Century Britain* (London, 1991).

22. James E. Cronin, "Politics, Class Structure, and the Enduring Weakness of British Social Democracy," *Journal of Social History*, 16 (1983): 123–42.

23. T.H. Marshall, *Citizenship and Social Class* (Cambridge, 1950).

24. Theodor Shanin, *The Roots of Otherness: Russia's Turn of Century*, 2 vols. (New Haven, 1986).
25. Charles Tilly, "War and the Power of Warmakers in Western Europe and Elsewhere", in Peter Wallensteen, Johan Galtung, and Carlos Portales, eds., *Global Militarization* (Boulder, Colo., 1985); "War and State Power," *Middle East Report* 21, no. 171 (July/August 1991), 38–40.
26. Rueschemeyer, Stephens and Stephens, *Capitalist Development and Democracy*, 279.

Index